W9-CFZ-146

THE DEGRADATION OF AMERICAN HISTORY

THE

Degradation

OF American

History

DAVID HARLAN

THE UNIVERSITY OF CHICAGO PRESS
Chicago and London

David Harlan teaches in the history department at California State University, San Luis Obispo.

The University of Chicago Press, Chicago 60637
The University of Chicago Press, Ltd., London
© 1997 by The University of Chicago
All rights reserved. Published 1997
Printed in the United States of America

06 05 04 03 02 01 00 99 98 97   1 2 3 4 5

ISBN: 0-226-31616-5 (cloth)
ISBN: 0-226-31617-3 (paper)

Library of Congress Cataloging-in-Publication Data

Harlan, David (David Craig)
    The degradation of American history / David Harlan
        p.   cm.
    Includes bibliographical references (p.   ) and index.
    ISBN 0-226-31616-5 (cloth : alk. paper). — ISBN 0-226-31617-3 (pbk. : alk. paper)
    1. United States—Historiography—Moral and ethical aspects. 2. United States—
History—Methodology. I. Title.
E175.H37   1997
973′.07′2—dc21   97-164
                                                                                          CIP

♾ The paper used in this publication meets the minimum requirements of the American National Standard for Information Sciences—Permanence of Paper for Printed Library Materials, ANSI Z39.48-1984.

For Sallie

History belongs above all to the man . . . who needs models, teachers, comforters and cannot find them among his contemporaries.

—Friedrich Nietzsche, *The Uses and Abuses of History*

Our teachers used to be able to pose the possibility of a national culture—a line connecting Thomas Jefferson, the slave owner, to Malcolm X. Our teachers used to be able to tell us why all of us speak Black English. Or how the Mexican farmworkers in Delano were related to the Yiddish-speaking grandmothers who worked the sweat-shops of the Lower East Side.

—Richard Rodriguez, "The Birth Pangs of a New L.A."

You will hardly know who I am or what I mean
But I shall be good health to you nevertheless,
And filter and fibre your blood.

Failing to fetch me at first keep encouraged,
Missing me one place search another,
I stop somewhere waiting for you.

—Walt Whitman, "Song of Myself"

CONTENTS

Part Two
THE RENEWAL OF AMERICAN HISTORICAL WRITING

ACKNOWLEDGMENTS

For the past ten years I have had the good fortune to be a member of the History Department, California State University at San Luis Obispo. I thank my colleagues for their warm collegiality and the former and current chairmen, Max Riedlsperger and Bob Burton, for encouraging me to teach the courses out of which this book emerged. Thanks also to the students in my historiography class, particularly Steve Tootle, Greg Robinson, and Rob Smith for forcing me to clarify my thoughts. I am grateful to Janice Stone, Zoe Brazil, and the staff of the university's Interlibrary Loan Department for supplying me with a host of otherwise unavailable books and articles.

Thanks to Alice Bennett of the University of Chicago Press for working over the manuscript so carefully and making so many helpful suggestions. I am particularly grateful to Douglas Mitchell, my editor at Chicago, for seeing some merit in an unsolicited manuscript and for his encouragement and sage advice. And to Hans Kellner for his valuable thoughts and comments. Thanks also to David Thelen for taking the time to read the entire manuscript so carefully and to write such an insightful and helpful critique.

John Patrick Diggins has been a teacher, mentor, friend, and inspiration for over twenty years. It was the moral seriousness of his teaching that first drew me to American intellectual history and the imaginative power of his books that forced me to write my own book. I know that he disagrees with many of the answers I develop here, but all of the questions are his. My friend George Cotkin is no more convinced by my arguments now than he was the first time he heard them, nearly ten years ago. But it is a measure of his generosity and openness of mind that he has continually prodded me to strengthen and refine them—and to finish this book. My understanding of American intellectual history owes much to his work on William James, on American modernism, and more recently on American existentialism. I have been living out of Leonard Wilcox's intellectual pockets ever since graduate school, running up debts I can never repay. But truth be known, I look forward to seeing my account sink even further into the red. I have admired and in various ways drawn upon Marta Peluso's photographs, especially her "Scar" series, with their celebration of selves seasoned to a hickory-like toughness.

I have learned much from my mother and father, who came of age during the Great Depression and the Second World War, know everything there is to know about sorrow and loss, and nevertheless gave their children a world of love and compassion. By the power of his own example, Roberto Lint-Sagarena has made me rethink my all-too-easy relinquishment of faith. I am every day more grateful for his affirmations, for his intellectual companionship, and for the way he has redrawn the emotional geography of our lives. Most of all I have been continually delighted and enlivened by my daughter Anna's love of American literature. She is the most thoughtful, resourceful, and reflective reader I know and continues to deepen and complicate my understanding not only of nineteenth-century American thinkers like Hawthorne and Melville but also of Joan Didion, Toni Morrison, and other contemporary writers. My son David has given me more than he knows. His instinctive cheerfulness, his refusal of despair, his eagerness in the face of life's unfolding possibilities are a constant source of inspiration, vitality, and hope. Finally, this book is for Sallie, who is her own pure poem and the luminous center of my life.

THE DEGRADATION OF AMERICAN HISTORY

Hans Holbein the Younger, *The Body of the Dead Christ in the Tomb* (1521). Kunstmu-seum, Basel, Switzerland. Giraudon/Art Resource, New York.

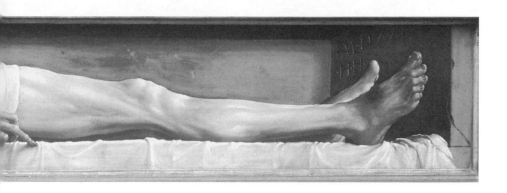

"It Hath No Relish of Salvation in It"
American Historical Writing at the End of the Twentieth Century

I

Once, not very long ago, history was one of our primary forms of moral reflection. American literary and intellectual historians wrote broad-gauged, morally instructive histories—histories that taught us how to speak in the first-person plural, histories that reminded us of what we, as a people, have always wished to become. By holding up a mirror to our common past, historians like Perry Miller, Richard Hofstadter, Alfred Kazin, and others encouraged us to say, "This is what we value and want, and don't yet have. This is how we mean to live and do not yet live."[1]

American historians no longer write that kind of history, of course. It has come to seem moralistic and elitist—and worst of all, grossly insensitive to the racial and ethnic diversity of the American past. Martin Luther King once said reading history made him feel "eternally in the red." But that was thirty years ago. Contemporary historians write history not to deepen our indebtedness to the past but to liberate us from the past. Though they write at the very end of the American century, they feel no need to say what is good in American history, what they identify with completely, what is worth insisting on and saving. Over seventy years have passed since William Carlos Williams pounded his fist on the table and demanded that American historians remember what America had promised: "I speak of fiercely contested things, practical in the extreme, that tortured the souls of the founders. . . . I say, unless a people conserve this yeast, it will not raise much bread."[2]

Williams was trying to yeast American sensibilities from within; that is why he wrote in the American grain.[3] But today's academic historians are not trying to yeast American sensibilities from within; they are not trying to remind us of those "fiercely contested things" that "tortured the souls of the founders." They do not write from within the main currents of American thought, and they do not speak in the first-person plural.[4]

We have lost our earlier understanding that the books and ideas we inherit from the past give us our best warrant for criticizing the present. We forget that Williams wrote his poet's vision of American history to demonstrate how American minds get beaten thin by waste, to explain why the pure products of America go crazy. We forget that Alfred Kazin wrote his histories of American literature to describe the terrible dialectic of national promise and self-betrayal that transformed Jimmy Gatz into Jay Gatsby and Clyde Griffiths into a murderer. Williams wrote in the American grain and Kazin wrote on native grounds because they both knew that American ideals provide the best authority for American criticism.

Moreover, both writers knew that if they wanted to reach their fellow citizens they had to write out of a practiced relation with the culture they criticized. They had to start from the views of justice and goodness and human worth they shared with their fellow Americans. For how else could they have a say? They criticized their society just as they criticized their friends: on the assumption that they shared a common set of moral references. Rather than celebrating their marginality, they wrote as "connected critics," as critics who fit in, if only as misfits. They thought the job of American writers and literary historians was to gather the strands of American history and weave them into a fabric of possibilities.[5]

If you went to college in the 1950s and early 1960s you first encountered academic history in the almost universally required freshman-level "History of Western Civilization," which served as a general introduction to the values and institutions of the Western democracies. The wonderful thing about "Western Civ" was that it taught you to think of history as a great conversation—an extended debate about human nature and the meaning of life, carried on across the centuries by the intellectual giants of Western thought: Plato and Aristotle, Luther and Erasmus, Darwin, Marx, Freud, all the way up to the present. It was pretty much the same thing in American history: you started with John Winthrop, Jonathan Edwards, and Benjamin Franklin, moved on to the great debate between Jefferson and Hamilton, then to Madison and *The Federalist Papers,* to Melville's quarrel with God and Lincoln's struggle with his own deeply melancholic mind—which, as he himself once admitted, "will some times wear the sweetest idea threadbare and turn it to the bitterness of death." To study American history in the fifties was to be inducted into this extraordinary centuries-long, transgenerational conversation. You didn't just *read* Edwards and Lincoln and the others; you tried to enter into their minds, to acquire their habits of attention, their ways of seeing, their arts of expression. You tried to think with their thoughts, to develop your own beliefs by working your way through their beliefs.

In the 1960s this whole way of thinking about the past came under withering criticism from two directions. First, historians on the left charged that the idea of history as a great conversation was inherently elitist, that it emphasized abstract ideas at the expense of political power, that it focused our attention on great white men at the expense of women and minorities, that it ignored the racial and ethnic diversity of national life, that it obscured the reality of class conflict in American history, and so on.All of which is a good part of the reason why, in the early 1970s, many younger historians began to explore the everyday lives of ordinary people—the inhabitants of seventeenth-century Dedham, Massachusetts, for example, who may or may not have pondered the perplexities of Puritan theology but who did tend their farms, work their shops, raise their kids, and squabble with their neighbors. Impatient with theology and political theory and the thoughts of privileged elites, the new social historians wanted to know what America looked like, how it worked. By the mid-1970s the earlier idea of American history as a great conversation had all but disappeared, replaced by tightly focused and rigorously contextualized minihistories—fine-grained, richly detailed accounts of religious experience in eighteenth-century Vermont, or Reconstruction politics on the Sea Islands of Georgia, or family life among the shoemakers of nineteenth-century Lynn, Massachusetts. If young historians still read the great white thinkers, they did so only to unmask them, to expose their complicity (however unwitting) in the violence and brutality that now seemed to be the most important truth about American history. Rather than asking what "Song of Myself" could tell us about the promise of American life, historians tried to explain the "ideological labor" it performed—how it rationalized slavery, excused racism, encouraged imperialism, and so on.

To see what all this has cost us, all you have to do is reread the first volume of Perry Miller's great work *The New England Mind*

(1939). Miller was one of the giants of American historical writing
in the 1940s and 1950s. He opened *The New England Mind* by jux-
taposing a passage from Saint Augustine with a passage Thomas
Hooker wrote nearly twelve hundred years later. Miller wanted us
to see that Hooker was describing the same interior emptiness, the
same spiritual hunger, the same longing for fulfillment that Augustine had described over a millennium before—and that Miller
himself, writing fifteen hundred years after Augustine and three
hundred years after Hooker, had come to know with all the intensity
of his own lived experience. Miller thought the historian's job was
not to describe the mundane routines of everyday life in seventeenth-
century Massachusetts, nor to expose the ideological complicity of
early American thinkers, but to show twentieth-century Americans
that Puritan books can dramatize the needs of the soul "exactly as
does some great poem or work of art." What Miller found in the
Puritans was the means to define his own interior experience—just
as the Puritans had found in Augustine a means to define *their* own
interior experience. The Puritans taught him how to see himself as
he needed to see himself: all naked, stripped of every pretense and
posture. They taught him how to talk to himself, how to admit himself into the polar privacy of his own mind. Moreover, by making
the Puritans illuminate his own doubts, his own vacant and barren
spaces, Miller revitalized all of American history. Though he wrote
mainly about seventeenth- and eighteenth-century New England, his
real achievement, the lasting accomplishment of his own errand into
the past, lay not in what he discovered about colonial America but
in what he demonstrated about American history. For by showing
us how to think with our predecessors' thoughts—and how to think
within a particular *progression* of thoughts—he taught us how to
place ourselves in time, how to see ourselves as part of an ongoing
tradition, the latest in a long historical sequence. For traditional historians, *The New England Mind* stands as a powerful reminder that
at its best American history is a conversation with the dead about
what we should value and how we should live.

Miller died in 1963. Since then the kind of history he wrote has
been shoved to the margins of American historical thought. Which
is not to say that it has altogether disappeared: some of our greatest
historians continue to write history in what might be called the
Grand Tradition. Eugene Genovese, for example, in *The Southern
Tradition* (1994), explains why "the genuinely tragic dimension" of
southern history allows it to speak "to all people in all times, warning
of the corrupt and cruel tendencies inherent in our common human-

ity, and the ease with which the social relations and institutions we sustain may encourage the most destructive aspects of our nature."[6] For traditionalists like Miller and Genovese, there is a distinctive set of moral and political values hidden away at the base of American history, a characteristic vocabulary of deliberation and obligation that defines us as a people. Arthur Schlesinger Jr. has put this as clearly as anyone: "Our values are not matters of whim and happenstance. History has given them to us. They are anchored in our national experience, in our great national documents, in our national heroes, in our folk ways, traditions, and standards. People with a different history will have differing values. But we believe that our own are better for us. They work for us; and, for that reason, we live and die by them."[7]

Schlesinger thinks American historians should set themselves to explaining the origins and continuing relevance of these distinctive American values. Historians on the left dismiss the whole bundle, of course, as an ideologically masked expression of power and privilege. Like all ideologies, it simply conceals the exercise of class rule. They think the values that traditional historians pretend to find in the American past, and the claims they make for those values, constitute the legitimating rhetoric that has sustained a regime of unparalleled greed and exploitation. It is all part of the apparatus of oppression. What we need, according to the Left, is a history that *demythologizes* the past, that strips away conventional pieties and ideological pretensions in order to reveal the social, economic, and ideological forces that have driven American history and shaped American culture. Instead of history as moral reflection, we get history as cultural unmasking.[8]

In the early 1970s historical writing came under attack from a second quarter: postmodern theory. Postmodernism first appeared in the visual arts, where it made a big splash and quickly moved on. It came to social theory more slowly, but the consequences have been much more profound, especially in historical studies. Conservative historians took one look at postmodernism and immediately saw the new face of an old enemy: philosophical nihilism, fitted out with a barbaric new vocabulary. Postmodern theory seemed little more than a moral vacancy, a round and empty cipher, a world of naught. It would destroy the possibility of truth, set our feet on the slippery slope of moral relativism, undermine the reliability of historical accounts, and on and on. One prominent conservative historian even charged that postmodernism was "an invitation to intellectual and moral suicide."[9] But it was not only conservatives: historians on the left also balked at the apparent dead-end skepticism of postmodern theory, especially its attack on historical objectivity. After all, their whole project depended on their ability to rip away ideological rationalizations in order to expose underlying structures of power. Though historians on the left may be cultural relativists, they have little patience with epistemological skepticism.[10] Nevertheless, by the end of the 1980s most historians—even most working historians—had all but given up on the possibility of acquiring reliable, objective knowledge about the past.[11]

Now, as we approach the end of the millennium, some conservative historians have talked themselves into believing that the Reign of Theory is finally over, that the revolution has spent itself, that we can all go back to the archives. They seem to think postmodernism is nothing more than a fashionable buzzword, a metaphysical frenzy that is finally collapsing under the accumulated weight of its own clichés and contradictions. In *Looking into the Abyss* (1994), Gertrude Himmelfarb, a well-known historian of nineteenth-century British history and perhaps the most outspoken of the conservatives, tried to reassure her colleagues: "If we have survived the 'death of God' and the 'death of man,' we will surely survive the 'death of history'— and of truth, reason, morality, society, reality, and all the other verities we used to take for granted and that have now been 'problematized' and 'deconstructed.' We will even survive the death of postmodernism."[12] Perhaps she is right; perhaps the postmodern moment has indeed come and gone.[13] But on its way out the door it pulled down one of the most important assumptions of American historical writing. As one observer put it, "Objectivity, that dull-witted monarch who despotically ruled the discipline of history since the late nineteenth-century, lies dethroned."[14]

Postmodernism is essentially an extension and elaboration of the old idea that we have no way of seeing or thinking or desiring that we have not acquired from the surrounding culture. We can experience or reflect on the world—or on ourselves, for that matter—only through one or another culturally derived *form* of experiencing or reflecting. It is simply not possible to step outside every interpretive framework and experience life "as it really is." The world and all its beauty come to us secondhand—a twice-told tale, as it were, a double-storied mystery. There is nothing new about this observation, of course. You can find it in Luther, Calvin, Hume, Jonathan Edwards, Edmund Burke, and any number of other writers. You can even find a version of it in the Book of Genesis. What postmodernism has added is simply the recognition that those of us in the rich demo-

cratic West now live in a media-saturated world in which the number
of available interpretive forms seems to be multiplying exponen-
tially. A popular culture of increasingly global dimensions confronts
us with an enormous and rapidly expanding kaleidoscopic array of
disconnected and unrelated ways to make sense of the world—and
ourselves. Movies and television especially invite us to identify with
so many different characters, on such intimate terms, so easily and
quickly—they encourage us to play such a huge variety of roles, to
experiment with so many different ways of "being ourselves"—that
the very idea of a single authentic self, with a stable and clearly
defined cluster of character traits, has come to seem hopelessly anachronistic. Edmund Burke's socially embedded self has given way to
Donald Barthelme's socially saturated self—a saturated self roam-
ing the electronic emporium of styles like some burned-out Natty
Bumppo wandering the frontier. F. Scott Fitzgerald once said "there
are no second acts in American lives." But he never met Madonna.
Or saw Cindy Sherman's photographs. Or heard the president of the
United States explain that "character is a journey, not a destination."
And was it not Fitzgerald himself who gave us the Great Gatsby,
that original protean man who once proclaimed that identity is nothing more than "an unbroken series of successful gestures"? As Fitzgerald knew all too well, we have been set adrift in a pasteboard world
of circulating images and fleeting epiphanies. How are we possibly
to find ourselves, to make sense of ourselves, in this empyrean of
multiplying and self-canceling possibilities?

Theory does not come easily to historians; they like to keep their
noses close to the ground, like hunting dogs. But even historians
are finding it difficult to ignore the implications of a worldwide,
consumer-driven economic system and the parallel development of
a universal mass culture characterized by the ceaseless appropriation,
recombination, and global dissemination of local styles and forms of
expression. No historian, even one who has made up his mind to
avoid reading Derrida and Foucault as a matter of intellectual hy-
giene, can fail to be alarmed at the astonishing overproduction of
information about the past—not just the flood of new historical accounts themselves, but the seemingly ungovernable proliferation of
new historical subjects, new perspectives, new interpretations, new
theories and styles of presentation. Nor is it possible to imagine the
imminent arrival of some new master historian who will present us
with an interpretation of the past so powerful and compelling as to
bring order out of chaos and establish a new paradigm for writing
history—a new professional consensus that would provide some

structure to the truly massive and overwhelming flow of books and articles and dissertations that pour off the presses on every imaginable aspect of American history. For the iron rule of writing in the age of information surplus applies to history as relentlessly as it applies to every other form of writing: the more powerful and authoritative the interpretation, the more counterinterpretations it generates.[15] Instead of clarifying the past, stilling debate and directing new research, a powerful interpretation merely provokes a whole new round of discussion and debate—more conferences and symposia, more books and articles, more interpretations to rival the previous interpretation. Thus the alarming, cancerlike thickening of the literature. Every subfield within the discipline—the French Revolution, for example, or the American Revolution—has been covered with a crust of interpretations so thick as to be virtually impenetrable. And they keep coming, almost daily. Not only do we have no dominant organizing interpretations and generally recognized exemplars (though we have plenty of academic superstars), we have no established procedures for evaluating all these new interpretations.

What now becomes of the "historical fact," once so firmly embedded in its proper historical context—firmly embedded, rightly perceived, and correctly interpreted from a single immediately obvious and obviously appropriate perspective? The overwhelming abundance of possible contexts and perspectives, the ease with which we can skip from one to another, and the lack of any overarching meta-perspective from which to evaluate the entire coagulated but wildly proliferating population of perspectives—all this means that the historical fact, once the historian's basic atomic unit, has jumped its orbit and can now be interpreted in any number of contexts, from a virtually unlimited range of perspectives. And if the historical fact no longer comes embedded in the natural order of things—if it is no longer bred in the bone, so to speak—then what happens to the historian's hope of acquiring stable, reliable, objective interpretations of the past? Is it really possible—as conservatives like Himmelfarb would have us believe—that the postmodern condition will simply disappear, that it will evaporate like the morning dew, and that we will go back to business as usual? If not, will the courage of our conventions be enough to see us through, as the pragmatists keep insisting?

In the mid-1970s a group of younger historians, repelled by the predictability and ideological coarseness of their colleagues on the left—and alarmed, like the conservatives, by the rise of postmodernism but realizing that a stiff upper lip was not going to be enough—

turned to the social sciences for guidance. What the social sciences promised, of course, was just what they have always promised: redemption through methodology; the holy grail of objective knowledge vouchsafed through the institution of established procedure. Of course historians would have to give up whatever remained of the personal, the private, the peculiar or idiosyncratic in their habits of reading and thinking. After all, social scientists like to imagine themselves a community of inquirers held together not only by a common grievance over parking but by a common set of research procedures. What historians had to give up, however, seemed as nothing compared with what they hoped to gain: release from yet another turn on the postmodern wheel of interpretation. What they hoped to attain, in other words, was nothing less than truth itself—or at least "warranted assertibility."

This pragmatic, methodologically obsessed professionalism is now the dominant tendency among academic historians—the most powerful and broadly influential attempt yet to cope with history's declining status. Historians drawn to this sort of thing—they tend to call themselves "neopragmatists"—think the guarantee of established procedures will save history not only from the outworn certainties of traditional historical writing and the ideological rigidities of left-wing history, but also from the debilitating nihilism of postmodern theory. But can the pragmatists really formulate a set of procedural rules that will prove acceptable to the majority of their colleagues? One can only wonder, especially given the continuing sociological diversification of the university and, as a direct consequence, the continuing proliferation of new historical subjects, new theories, new interpretations, and so on. But even if they manage to pull it off— even if they somehow bring their fellow historians together around a common set of research procedures—what then? Would common procedures really lead to common evaluations? Would agreement on methodological issues necessarily produce agreement on substantive issues—which almost always turn out to involve deeply held moral beliefs? In other words, is methodology enough? Can the humanities survive if they abandon their traditional responsibility of helping us think about what we should value and how we should live? Will historians have anything left to teach if they no longer insist on the redemptive power of the past—on the importance of learning how to think with our predecessors' thoughts, how to create our own vocabulary of moral deliberation by fiddling around with theirs? Or does this whole attempt to save us from the pit of postmodern theory miss something important?

I I

We burn with desire to find solid ground and an ultimate sure foundation
whereon to build a tower reaching to the infinite. But our groundwork
cracks and the earth opens to abysses.
—Blaise Pascal, *The Two Infinities*

The Body of the Dead Christ in the Tomb (1521), by Hans Holbein
the Younger, hangs at the Kunstmuseum in Basel, Switzerland. It
depicts the emaciated, mutilated, already stiffening body of Jesus
Christ stretched out on a mortuary slab. This is the body of a man
who had suffered horribly, who had been beaten and tortured for
six hours, nailed to a tree, beaten again. The face is smashed and
swollen, partially covered with dried blood, the glassy whites of the
eyes stare emptily, the mouth hangs open. *The Body of the Dead
Christ* horrifies us because it suggests not the promise of Resurrection
but the reality of abandonment, not the assurances of the Johannine
Gospel but the final, hopeless words that Christ speaks in the Gospels
of Matthew and Mark: "My God, my God, why hast thou forsaken
me?" Holbein's dead Christ is said to have shaken the Russian novelist Fyodor Dostoyevsky to his very bones. Friends report that he returned to the Kunst Museum over and over, staring at the painting
for hours on end. In *The Idiot* he has Prince Myshkin exclaim, "Why,
some people may lose their faith by looking at that picture!"[16]

There is a certain sensibility that has always been drawn to Holbein's dead Christ. It is the same sensibility that finds the Book of
Genesis the truest of books, with its terrible tale of human expulsion,
and Matthew and Mark the truest of the Gospels. It appeals to those
brooding souls who still find wisdom in the writings of John Cotton,
the seventeenth-century New England Puritan minister who once
asked his listeners: If God did forsake his only begotten son as he
hung on the cross, if he turned his face away in anger and shame
and refused to hear his anguished pleas, what makes you think he
will hear yours? All the liberal theology in the world will never convince these winter-bred minds that the wound of Genesis can actually
be closed, that we on this earth will ever experience a universe "humanly continuous and radiant with presence." Nor will all the arguments of all the realist philosophers who ever lived convince them
that they can know the truth of their own lives, much less the truth
of other lives. Melville writes to Hawthorne in the winter of 1851:
"This is a long letter, but you are not at all bound to answer it.
Possibly, if you do answer it, and direct it to Herman Melville, you
will missend it—for the very fingers that now guide this pen are

not precisely the same that just took it up and put in on this paper. Lord, when shall we be done changing? Ah! it's a long stage, and no inn in sight, and night coming, and the body cold."[17] Melville already knew what Holbein knew and what Nietzsche would soon discover: that we will always be unfinished persons, as mysterious and inaccessible to ourselves as we are to others.

Jacques Derrida, the literary critic and avatar of deconstruction, is often accused of tempting the young with a silly, playful-sounding nihilism, as if he were some sort of intellectual pied piper, leading his followers down his own secret path to nothingness. But Derrida writes out of the same sensibility that drove Holbein to his canvas and Nietzsche to his wanderings. Like Holbein and Nietzsche, Derrida speaks to those brooding minds that yearn for presence but refuse every suggestion of metaphysical comfort. Derrida's literary criticism is theology carried on by other means. In Derrida's attack on "the metaphysics of presence" it is not difficult to see a frontal assault on the Christian belief that the Word has been made flesh, that we do indeed live in a world "humanly continuous and radiant with presence"—and on the Protestant conviction that the Scriptures contain "the living Word of God," the revealed intentions of the Original Author. (Not for nothing does he sometimes sign his essays "Reb Derrisa, the laughing Rabbi.")[18] Catholics are not the only ones to affirm the principle of transubstantiation, for do Protestants themselves not insist that the New Testament contains a direct and unmediated presence, that it is not merely the type of truth but truth itself, the mystery of presence in a world abandoned? Is this not why they have always been known as "the people of the book"? And is this not the reason no one thought it unusual when the historian David Hollinger offered his confession of faith in the putatively secular pages of the *American Historical Review*? "I believe that authors remain present enough in texts to justify our listening for their voices. I do not understand the mystery of knowing, but I believe this mystery has survived."[19] Like Luther reading his Bible, Hollinger believes historical texts contain precisely the fixed and final meanings their authors intended; like the Scriptures themselves, they are deeply lit and ultimately knowable, all the vagaries of interpretation notwithstanding.

Hollinger's is just the sort of belief Derrida must have had in mind when he criticized "the theological certainty of seeing every page bind itself into the unique text of truth."[20] In *Of Grammatology* he asks us to abandon this redemptive theology and accept a world that contains neither truth nor foundations:

There has never been anything but writing; there has never been anything but supplements, substitutive significations which could only come forth in a chain of differential references, the "real" supervening, and being added only while taking on meaning from a trace and from an invocation of the supplement. And thus to infinity, for the absolute present, Nature, that which words like "real mother" name, have always already escaped, have never existed; what opens meaning and language is writing as the disappearance of natural presence.[21]

There is a deep and welling sadness in Derrida's writing, a pervasive melancholy that reminds us of Pascal. It is as if his writing had been shaped by some primal ruin, some dispossession so appalling that he finds himself helplessly reenacting it over and over again. As he says at one place, "We are dispossessed of the longed-for presence in the very gesture of language by which we attempt to seize it."[22] The New England Puritans would have recognized this sensibility immediately. In "A True Sight of Sin," the seventeenth-century minister Thomas Hooker described the self-convicted sinner who finds himself "afraid to approach the presence of the Lord to bewail his sins, and to crave pardon, lest he should be confounded for them, while he is but confessing of them."[23] Derrida can be startlingly, even painfully blunt about the implications of this dilemma. At one point he asks, "Does not the metaphoric origin of language lead us necessarily to a situation of threat, distress and dereliction, to an archaic solitude, to the anguish of dispersion?"[24] The answer, of course, is yes—which is why in the end "no one is there for anyone, not even for himself."[25]

There is a deep affinity between Derrida, raised in the rabbinic interpretive tradition, and the Augustinian strain of piety that runs through Calvin, Pascal, Edwards, Melville, Adams, Faulkner, and others—an affinity all the more remarkable for having been generally ignored. In *Institutes of the Christian Religion* (1536) Calvin warned his readers not to inquire too closely into the meaning of divine texts, for that way lies madness. "Let them remember," he warned, that "the careless and confident intruder will obtain no satisfaction to his curiosity, but will rather enter a labyrinth from which he will find no way to depart. For it is unreasonable that man should scrutinize with impunity those things which the lord has determined to be hidden in himself."

Four and a half centuries later Derrida warns his readers about the very same danger. In *Of Grammatology* he describes the historian who, trying to get at "the real meaning" of her text, finds herself drawn ever downward, hopelessly entangled in a living, writhing labyrinth of her own: "If a text always gives itself a certain representation of its own roots, those roots live only by that representation, by never touching the soul, so to speak. . . . One always interweaves roots endlessly, bending them to send down roots among the roots, to pass through the same points again, to redouble old adherences, to circulate among their differences, to coil around themselves or to be enveloped one in the other" (101–2).

Or to put it differently: we can no more find Richard Wright in *Native Son* than Ahab could find God in the white whale; we can no more discover what Milan Kundera intended when he wrote *The Book of Laughter and Forgetting* than we can discover what God intended when He wrote the book of nature.

Henry Adams and Michel Foucault knew this immediately and intuitively. Both historians—the older Adams and the younger Foucault—looked into the past and saw nothing but a discontinuous series of sudden, unexpected, inexplicable and inexplicably violent ruptures. Thus Henry Adams found himself "lying in the Gallery of Machines at the Great Exposition of 1900, his historical neck broken by the sudden irruption of forces totally new." Or again, twenty years later, standing on the steps of the Roman Forum, he arrived at the realization that

> Rome could not be fitted into an orderly, middle-class, Bostonian, systematic scheme of evolution. Not even time sequences—the last refuge of helpless historians—had value for it. The Forum no more led to the Vatican than the Vatican to the Forum. Rienzi, Garibaldi, Tiberius Gracchus, Aurelian might be mixed up in any relation of time, along with a thousand more, and never lead to a sequence. The great word Evolution had not yet, in 1860, made a new religion of history, but the old religion had preached the same doctrine for a thousand years without finding in the entire history of Rome anything but flat contradiction.[26]

In his autobiography Adams describes an accelerating spiral of doubt and despair as the seemingly solid ground of historical truth collapses into a multiplying multitude of purely personal perspectives. "One sought no absolute truth," he finally concludes; "One sought only a spool on which to wind the thread of history without breaking it. Among indefinite possible orbits, one sought the orbit which would satisfy the observed movement of the runaway star Groombridge, 1838, commonly called Henry Adams."[27]

In *The Sound and the Fury*, and then again in *Absalom, Absalom!*

William Faulkner described a history bereft of sense and sequence. For Faulkner, as for Adams before him and Foucault beyond him, the past was a fantastic, kaleidoscopic, outrageous, and utterly incomprehensible spectacle. Thus in *Absalom, Absalom!* we watch poor Quentin Compson grope and flounder around in his ramshackle and altogether incoherent past. Wedged between his father's cracker-barrel skepticism and his mother's irrelevant reverence, lacking any stable system of perception and belief, he can neither make sense of his past nor transcend it; dispossessed, he can neither ignore his dispossession nor come to terms with it. In the end he is simply destroyed by it.

Some historians will find all this competely irrelevant, of course. Adams and Faulkner may have written beautiful literature, they will say, but what does that have to do with history? What did they know about modern research methods, about footnotes and bibliographies, refereed journals and annual conventions, networking and schmoozing and how to write a successful research proposal? Masters of a merely literary art, they have nothing important to tell us about the possibilities of historical knowledge in the 1990s. Thus the historian Gordon Wood, steady as a rock, continues to insist that history is "an accumulative science, gradually gathering truth through the steady and plodding efforts of countless practitioners turning out countless monographs."[28] There may be something of the anthill in Wood's description, but "historians who cut loose from this faith do so at the peril of their discipline."[29] In *Telling the Truth about History* three well-known and widely respected historians—Joyce Appleby, Lynn Hunt, and Margaret Jacob—offer the same sort of counsel. Though we cannot capture "the fullness of past experience," we *can* undertake "modest inquiries about what actually happened [in the past] and what it meant to those who experienced it."[30]

This is the sort of intellectual modesty that John Locke popularized in the seventeenth century. A moderate and reasonable outlook, it reminds us of our limitations and advises us to be content with them, to live lives dedicated to the relative and the practical. Such a life may lack moral intensity, it may crimp the heart and cage the soul, it may fall hopelessly silent when the demons of the inner life heave into view at three o'clock in the morning, but it does keep us tuned to the grainy reality of life. As Locke explained in a famous metaphor, our sounding rope may not be long enough to "fathom the depths of the ocean," but it is long enough to warn us off the rocks: "Men may find sufficient to busy their heads, and employ their minds with variety, delight and satisfaction, if they will not boldly quarrel with their own constitution, and throw away the blessings their hands are filled with, because they are not big enough to grasp everything."

Like Locke, the authors of *Telling the Truth about History* think that weeping in our beards because we cannot have Real Knowledge about the past ignores the practical, down-to-earth knowledge we *can* have. They think it is precisely this yearning for the absolute, this incessant longing for what we can never attain, that always betrays us, and that turns our faces away from what we *can* have: the reality of *this document*, the garden of *this world*, the love of *this woman*. Thus the historian Gertude Himmelfarb: "If the historian can learn to dispense with absolute truth, to pursue not 'woman in herself' but a real woman, not the chimera of the 'Eternal Objective' but the reality of something only partially knowable, he can love the past and live happily with her—quite as if she were a beloved wife instead of an adored mistress."[31]

If this is the wisdom of John Locke, it is also the wisdom of Melville's Starbuck. A staid and steadfast man, sober and conscientious, right minded and honest hearted, Starbuck goes to sea "for duty and profit." But Starbuck's knowledge of things is radically incomplete, as we learn one mist-shrouded morning when he and Ahab are standing alone on the quarterdeck of the *Pequod*. Ahab beckons to Starbuck: "Come closer, Starbuck; thou requirest a little lower layer."[32] Virtuous and humane to a fault, Starbuck does not know and cannot see what Ahab and Ishmael have known from the beginning: that some men are driven to the sea by that very hunger for the absolute, that desperate need to grasp "the ungraspable phantom of life" that Himmelfarb, Appleby, Hunt, Jacob, and others continually warn us against. But Ahab knows all about cautions like these: "Ah, ye admonitions and warnings! Why stay ye not when ye come? But rather are ye predictions than warnings, ye shadows! Yet not so much predictions from without, as verifications of the foregoing things within. For with little external to constrain us, the innermost necessities in our being, these still drive us on."[33]

The God-haunted Ahab is not the only one driven to "strike through the mask." Visit the "insular city of the Manhattoes some dreamy Sabbath afternoon," Ishmael suggests.

What do you see? Posted like silent sentinels all around the town, stand thousands upon thousands of mortal men fixed in ocean reveries. Some leaning against the piles; some seated upon the pier-heads; some looking over the bulwarks of ships from China; some high aloft in the rigging, as if striving to get a still better seaward peep. But these are all landsmen; of week days pent up in lath and plaster—tied to counters, nailed to benches, clinched to desks. How then is this? Are the green fields gone. What do they here? But look! here come more crowds, pacing straight for the water, and seemingly bound for a dive. Strange! Nothing will content them but the extremest limit of the land; loitering under the shady lee of yonder ware-houses will not suffice. No. They must get just as nigh the water as they possibly can without falling in. And there they stand— miles of them—leagues. Inlanders all, they come from lanes and alleys, streets and avenues—north, east, south, and west. Yet here they all unite. Tell me, does the magnetic virtue of the needles of the compasses of all those ships attract them thither? Why is almost every robust healthy boy with a robust healthy soul in him, at some time or other crazy to go to sea? Why upon your first voyage as a passenger, did you yourself feel such a mystical vibration, when first told that you and your ship were now out of sight of land? Why did the Persians hold the sea holy? Why did the Greeks give it a separate deity, and own brother of Jove? Surely all this is not without meaning. (12-13)

Kierkegaard thought this yearning for the absolute—and the fear and trembling that inevitably accompany it—was life itself. So did Wittgenstein:

My whole tendency and I believe the tendency of all men who ever tried to write or talk Ethics or Religion was to run up against the boundaries of language. This running against the walls of our cage is perfectly, absolutely hopeless. Ethics so far as it springs from the desire to say something about the ultimate meaning of life, the absolute good, the absolute valuable, can be no science. What is says does not add to our knowledge in any sense. But it is a document of a tendency in the human mind which I personally cannot help respecting deeply and I would not for my life ridicule it.[34]

Himmelfarb and her fellow historians have missed something con-servatives usually see with striking clarity: the obstinate and utterly intractable nature of spiritual hunger. They have forgotten what Lio-nel Trilling never forgot: that this sort of yearning "is no more to be quarreled with, or reasoned with, than love itself."[35] To imagine that we can lay aside our longing for the absolute, our hope that we might somehow find some redeeming presence in this postmodern world of neon signs and revolving deceptions—to imagine that we can somehow escape the longing for presence that seeps from the very marrow of our bones—is to imagine that we can somehow escape our own humanity. Which is perhaps what Derrida was getting at when he described man as that being who, throughout the history of metaphysics or of ontotheology—in other words, throughout his entire history—has dreamed of full presence, the reassuring foundation, the origin and end of all play.[36] Pragmatists pretend to be shocked and dismayed by Derrida. But Derrida is only trying to tell us what the naturalist and historian Wilhelm von Humboldt tried to tell us over a century and a half earlier: "Man lives with things mainly, even, exclusively—since sentiment and action in him depend upon his mental representations—as they are conveyed to him by language. Through the same act by which he spins language out of himself he weaves himself into it, and every language draws a circle around the people to which it belongs, a circle that can only be transcended insofar as one at the same time enters another one."[37]

We historians must somehow get ourselves to the point where we no longer feel that if we cannot refute contemporary skepticism— or if, in some moment of inexcusable weakness, we allow ourselves to be seduced by the likes of Henry Adams or William Faulkner (not to mention the white-haired archfiend himself, holed up somewhere in Paris, writing yet another treatise on death and deconstruction)— then all is lost, history will slide into fiction, Holocaust deniers will rise up everywhere, and we will have to fight the Second World War all over again.

The Polish philosopher Leszak Kolakowski recently pointed out the obvious in a way that may help us here: none of the great metaphysical questions have ever been resolved. It is as intellectually respectable to be a nominalist—or an antinominalist, or a realist, or an idealist—at the end of the twentieth century as it was at the end of the twelfth century.[38] So it is with the question of historical objectivity, which is why we should simply drop the whole shopworn subject. It has not gotten us anywhere in our long, twisted past, and it is not going to get us anywhere in the crooked future that looms ahead of us. God knows we have wasted a lot of time and bored a lot of students with all our dreary polemics on this dreary subject. Blind Lemon Jefferson was right:

> God don't like it, you know.
> God don't like it, I know,
> it's a scandal and a shame.[39]

But what would historical writing look like, and what good could it possibly do us, if we abandoned our by now threadbare pretense to objectivity and truth telling? Not much, according to the authors of *Telling the Truth about History*. More interested in explanation than event, in context than text, they think historians should spend their time formulating objective descriptions of "the larger social universe" in which, say, John Winthop wrote "A Modell of Christian Charity," or Lincoln wrote his second inaugural address, or Emily Dickinson wrote "He fumbles at your soul like players at the keys." They want to know what we would do with all these letters and diaries and books and poems we have inherited from the past, these remarkable records of remorse and regret, these silent souvenirs of spiritual yearning and fleshy desire and the downward curve of self-betrayal. What would we do with all these writings if we were not going to use them to reconstruct the world in which their authors lived and wrote and wept and bewildered their children and confounded themselves and in the end gave up their souls to weariness and resignation? What good is a text, they wonder, if not to reconstruct its context?

III

During the last thirty years history as ethical judgment has been driven into exile by history as contextual reconstruction. Contemporary historians are more interested in what *The Souls of Black Folk* said to Americans living at the beginning of the twentieth century than in what it says to Americans living at the end of the century, more interested in what it tells us about W. E. B. Du Bois's contemporaries than in what it can tell us about ourselves. There is no sense of urgency in American historical writing, no sense that we must use the books and ideas we have inherited from the past to put our own lives to the test—for if we let them, they will surely force us to ponder what might lie behind our own best wishes and good intentions.[40] E. P. Thompson, the great historian of the English working class, used to say that our primary responsibility is to the people of the past, for they lived through those times and we did not. We can *not* possibly fulfill that responsibility by insisting that the books they wrote be returned forthwith to their "proper historical contexts," as if they were no better than apprehended fugitives. Nor can we fulfill it by trying to expose the ideological freight they supposedly carried. The only way we, as historians, can fulfill our responsibility to the dead is by making sure their works do not get lost in the past—in other words, by raising them up from the graveyard of dead contexts and helping them take up new lives among the living. The best way to respect the dead is to help them speak to the living.[41]

But if we wish to establish a connection with the dead we will have to forge it ourselves—each one of us. The novelist Wallace Stegner knew this as well as anyone: "In the old days, in blizzardly weather, we used to tie a string of lariats from house to barn so as to make it from shelter to responsibility and back again. With personal, family, and cultural chores to do, I think we'd better rig up such a line between past and present."[42]

No one pretends this is easy work. What makes it so difficult, of course, is that there is no single past, shrouded in snow like Stegner's barn, barely visible at the far end of the field. Moreover, it is *people* we wish to know, not barns. Just as we each have to rig up our own line to the past, so we each have to populate that past with our own heroes, our own moral and intellectual exemplars—people we admire, people we wish to emulate, people who can help us say: "This is how we mean to live, but do not yet live." The best way to think through our own values is to think through our predecessors' values—and to think of ourselves as the latest in a long tradition of such thinkers. History is a line we ourselves must rig up, to a past we ourselves must populate.

This is what it has traditionally meant to "have a sense of the past," and this is what it will no doubt continue to mean. Neither the hubris of the social sciences nor the challenge of postmodernism is going to change that. Nor is the fact that graduate schools of history have regularly ignored it for the last quarter of a century. Instead of trying to figure out what such rigging and populating might involve, and how we would go about it, we have spent our time trying to defend history's claims to objective truth. But the border that separates history from fiction is not going to disappear, all the horror stories about postmodern subversion notwithstanding. And indeed, this reactionary obsession with the validity of history's truth claims seems to have finally exhausted itself. As Emerson once said of a certain "western road," it "opened stately enough, with planted trees on either side, to tempt the traveler, but soon became narrow and narrower, and ended in a squirrel-track and ran up a tree."[45] Perhaps we can now turn our attention to the problems of rigging and populating.

PART ONE

The Legacy of the Sixties

CHAPTER ONE

Deeper into the Wilderness

History Takes the Linguistic Turn

> Once you start down the anti-formalist road,
> there is no place to stop.
> —Stanley Fish, *Doing What Comes Naturally*

I

There was a time when historians thought they had escaped the "merely literary," when they thought they had established historical studies on the solid foundation of objective method and rational argument. But during the 1960s developments in literary criticism and the philosophy of language began to undermine that confidence. After a hundred-year absence, literature returned to history, unfurling her circus silks of metaphor and allegory, misprision and aporia, trace and sign, demanding that historians accept her mocking presence right at the heart of what they had once insisted was their own autonomous and truly scientific discipline.[1]

The return of literature plunged historical studies into an extended epistemological crisis. It questioned our belief in a fixed and determinable past, compromised the possibility of historical representation, and undermined our ability to locate ourselves in time. The result of this upheaval was to reduce historical knowledge to a tissue of remnants and fabrications concealing, it was said, an essential absence. This chapter describes literature's return to history, examines the way some leading historians responded, and suggests where we might go from here.

An earlier version of this chapter appeared in *American Historical Review* 94 (June 1989): 581–609.

I I

During the late 1960s and early 1970s anthropologists and intellectual historians became increasingly interested in the cognitive and ideological significance of narrative forms and rhetorical strategies. For historians this led to a gradual shift of disciplinary focus, from the "history of ideas" to what eventually came to be known as "the history of discourse." Historians became less interested in ideas themselves and more interested in the discursive contexts in which they had originally been conceived. This was an immensely important transformation. It put historians in touch with some of the most interesting debates taking place in the humanities; it encouraged them to think of language as a constituting force, a dynamic structuring of perception and association rather than a passive and essentially invisible medium of expression; and it led them to examine the rhetorical and discursive traditions that had invested otherwise mundane terms with powerfully concentrated meanings ("Indian," "black," "white," "America," for example). But this was also a revolution that devoured its own subjects, for "the history of discourse" ended up reducing earlier thinkers to little more than place markers in a profusion of proliferating discourses.

Michel Foucault usually gets the credit for transforming intellectual history into a history of discourse. But in Anglo- American historical studies that transformation had already been set in motion by Quentin Skinner and J. G. A. Pocock. It was their indictment of intellectual history, and their vision of how it ought to be written, more than any other single influence, that determined the direction in which the discipline evolved during the 1970s and 1980s.

Quentin Skinner had written several important studies of early modern political thought and a series of methodological pieces. These writings had been so widely influential, his critics so generally ineffectual, and his attempts to reform intellectual history so apparently successful that many historians granted him his claim to have established "a new orthodoxy" among historians of ideas.[2] That new orthodoxy was erected on two pillars. The first was Skinner's recognition that recent developments in the philosophy of language and the philosophy of science—especially the work of Willard Quine, Thomas Kuhn, Paul Feyerabend, and others—had undermined the possibility of building a structure of empirical knowledge on any basis purporting to be independent of or prior to interpretation. The result was a wholesale retreat from empiricism—a retreat that occurred in virtually every one of the human sciences.[3]

The second pillar was an essentially romantic hermeneutics.[4] From

its origins in Greek mythology through its refinement in nineteenth-
century biblical scholarship to its emergence as an academic specialty,
the guiding objective of romantic hermeneutics remained constant:
the recovery of authorial intention. Skinner's appropriation of hermeneutics led him to insist that the historian's primary responsibility
is to recover the author's "primary intentions," wherein she would
find the text's real meaning.[5]

To recover the author's intention the historian had to reconstruct
the mental world in which the author wrote her book—the entire
set of linguistic principles, symbolic conventions, and ideological assumptions by which she lived and thought. Only by fixing the
author's text in this elaborately reconstructed context could the historian hope to recover "all that can have been intended." In "Hermeneutics and the Role of History" Skinner condensed his prescriptions
into a single syllogism:

> 1. "We need to recover an author's intentions in writing in or-
> der to understand the meaning of what he writes."
> 2. "In order to recover such intentions, it is . . . essential to
> surround the given text with an appropriate context of assump-
> tions and conventions from which the author's exact intended
> meaning can then be decoded."
> 3. "This yields the crucial conclusion that a knowledge of these
> assumptions and conventions must be essential to understand-
> ing the meaning of the text."[6]

Skinner's prescriptions may have become the "new orthodoxy"
among intellectual historians, but as every churchman knows, orthodoxies quickly generate heretics. In this case the apostates turned out
to be "the Yale formalists and their various philosophical allies," by
whom Skinner meant the poststructuralists. And they soon gained
adherents among Skinner's former allies, "a number of recent hermeneutic theorists" openly exhibiting "a curious tendency" to adopt "the
formalists' assumptions."[7] In "Hermeneutics and the Role of History"
Skinner attacked the poststructuralists' "crude analysis," and dismissed them as "confused."

What Skinner did not like about the poststructuralists, of course,
was their theory of language. For Jacques Derrida, Michel Foucault,
Paul de Man, and others, language is an autonomous system that
constitutes rather than reflects; it is a continual play of unintended
self-transformations and unrestrained self-advertisements rather
than a set of stable meanings and external references.[8] And it is intertextual rather than intersubjective, writing its own accumulated
meanings over the author's desires and intentions. The paradigm of

language for the poststructuralists is therefore not speaking but writing, with its absent authors, its unknown audiences, and its unruly texts spewing out their manifold significations, connotations, and implications.

This understanding of language had at least two immediate implications for historical studies. First, it suggested that the desiring, thinking, intending subject of that discipline—the author of the classic texts in, say, political theory—had been dissolved, her biography reduced to no more than another text, the authority for which lay in still another text, the authority for that text lying in yet another one, and so on, ad infinitum. Hence "the death of the author."[9] Second, if the author had disappeared, so had her text; as a discrete, autonomous entity with a determinate and discernible meaning, it too had been dissolved by the demon of intertextuality. For the poststructuralist, texts remain significant precisely because they eclipse and transcend their authors' intentions.[10]

But Skinner thought he could he can escape this difficulty by thinking of language as speech rather than writing—that is, by employing speech act theory.[11] Speech act theory asserts, first, that speech is the paradigm for all language use; second, that speech acts are intersubjective rather than intertextual; third, that speech acts are social acts, that is, that they occur in concrete social situations from which they derive their meaning; fourth, that in speech acts speakers purposefully manipulate language in order to perform certain actions—they command, they assert, they promise, and so on. In other words, speech acts are intentional human actions that occur in specific social situations.

If speech act theory could have been applied to intellectual history, as Skinner believed, it just might have provided the conceptual ground from which our traditional understanding of history could have been defended against the onslaught of poststructuralist criticism. Speech act theory might have defended intellectual history in four distinct but mutually reinforcing ways. First, the importance speech act theory attaches to the context in which utterances are made meant that texts and their meanings would have been anchored in the bedrock of specific historical situations; this would have put an end to free-floating signifiers and all the uncertainty they brought with them. Second, language would have resumed its formerly transparent nature and once again made itself available for the historian to gaze through. Just as we were accustomed to doing before the poststructuralists arrived, we could have read a historical text and peered through its language as if staring through a window, discovering all sort of things about the author and the world in which she lived, almost as if we had become one of God's spies. Third, because speech act theory focuses on the intentional subject doing something (speaking or writing)—because it is intersubjective rather than intertextual—it promised to rescue the author from the oblivion to which poststructuralism had consigned her. Fourth, and stemming directly from this, if speech act theory could have been applied to intellectual history it would have reinstalled authorial intention as the historian's primary concern. But would it have worked?

The short answer is no. The most basic reason is simply that speech act theory is about speaking rather than writing. Speech acts are events situated at specific points in time and in concrete sociocultural contexts. Speaker and hearer are immediately present to each other and share a common reality to which signifiers can be instantly referred and embedded. For these reasons, reference in speech acts is thought to be unproblematic.[12]

Skinner assumed that the same is true of writing: that writing is analogous to speaking, that writing merely transcribes speech into script, or that writing *is* speech, a sort of frozen speech, speech fixed in script. But this is clearly not the case: script is not the same as speech, writers are not the same as speakers, and readers are not the same as listeners; the writer's reader is not analogous to the speaker's hearer. And there is no dialogue between writer and reader: the reader does not interrogate the writer, and the writer does not respond to the reader. As Paul Ricoeur explained in *Hermeneutics and the Human Sciences* (1981), "The reader is absent from the act of writing; the writer is absent from the act of reading. The text thus produces a double eclipse of reader and writer."[13]

Moreover, if the common reality shared by speaker and hearer cannot be transferred to writer and reader, and signifiers therefore cannot be grounded by the act of pointing (as they are thought to be in speech acts), then reference and representation become highly problematic. And once the text has been liberated from authorial *reference* it has also been liberated from authorial *intention.* So the author vanishes, her intentions disappear, and the text begins suggesting possibilities its author may never have imagined.

As we have seen, Skinner's was a basically nineteenth-century romantic hermeneutics designed for and sharpened to a single point: the recovery of authorial intention. It required that the historian approach the text with her mind as open and free from prejudice as possible, and that she try to understand the text on *its* terms rather than in the terms peculiar to her own situation. In other words, it required that the historian transpose herself into the culture and into the mind of the author.

There is a humorous but stinging critique of this whole presumptuous project in one of Jorge Borges's most delightful and intriguing stories, "Pierre Menard, Author of *Don Quixote*."[14] Borges's character Pierre Menard was a poet and critic, the author of several eccentric monographs and journal articles on various technical subjects written in the first and second decades of the twentieth century. His real interest for us, however, lies in the fact that he also wrote the ninth and thirty-eighth chapters of part 1 of *Don Quixote*. These were not simply transcriptions of the corresponding chapters of Cervantes' *Don Quixote*; Menard did not merely copy Cervantes' *Don Quixote*; he wrote it himself. Menard's chapters are original works in their own right. That Menard's twentieth-century *Don Quixote* is word for word and line for line identical to Cervantes' seventeenth-century version only adds to the richness and depth of Menard's achievement. His feat of historical reconstruction is, in the narrator's estimation, "possibly the most significant of our time."

Menard's determination to write *Don Quixote* was apparently inspired by the idea that literary and intellectual historians should attempt nothing less than "a total identification" with the author they are studying. Menard knew, of course, that he would never actually achieve such total identification; but he felt that it was the historian's obligation to come as close as he could. As the narrator explains, "The initial method he conceived was relatively simple": "to know Spanish well, to re-embrace the Catholic faith, to fight against the Moors and Turks, to forget European history between 1602 and 1918, and to be Miguel de Cervantes."[15]

Having thus projected himself into seventeenth-century Spain—indeed, having projected himself into the mind of Miguel de Cervantes—Menard would compose not simply another *Don Quixote*, but *the Don Quixote*. After studying this procedure, however, Menard decided it was too easy and so rejected it: "To be, in the twentieth century, a popular novelist of the seventeenth seemed to him a diminution. To be, in some way Cervantes and to arrive at *Don Quixote* seemed to him less arduous—and consequently less interesting—than to continue being Pierre Menard and to arrive at *Don Quixote* through the experiences of Pierre Menard."[16]

The initial method would have been easier because, having "felt himself into" seventeenth-century Spain, his work of historical reconstruction would have been swept along by the emotional rhythms and linguistic conventions of the early modern Spanish culture that he had mentally imbibed. But to reconstruct *Don Quixote* while remaining in the twentieth century made the job infinitely more difficult—and therefore infinitely more challenging. After all, as Menard himself noted, "It is not in vain that three hundred years have passed."[17]

Taking up this challenge, Menard eventually produced two chapters of *Don Quixote*. And it is at this point, when we examine the chapters themselves, that we come to understand the wisdom of his decision to attempt the more arduous method of *historical reconstruction*. For though Menard's *Don Quixote* is literally identical to Cervantes', it nevertheless possesses a richness of texture that is altogether absent from the earlier version. The narrator tells us that historians and literary critics have offered a variety of competing explanations for the verbal resonance of Menard's version, some attributing it a Nietzschean influence, others seeing in it a reflection of Menard's lifelong fascination with William James. But whatever its source, the fact that Menard's *Don Quixote* differs from the original in this subtle and elusive way can hardly be surprising. After all, for Menard to have written the exact text of *Don Quixote* is remarkable enough; for him also to have produced its seventeenth-century tone and style would have been extraordinary indeed.

Borges's point should be obvious: parodying the historian's claim that he can somehow transport himself into a culture of the past, that he can project himself into the mind of a long dead author, and that once there he can relive the creative act and so come to know what Quentin Skinner called the author's "primary intentions"[18]—Jorge Borges makes us see that there is something wildly preposterous about the whole idea. When Menard rejected the method because it was "too easy," Borges had his narrator add, "Rather because it was impossible, the reader will say! I agree, but the undertaking was impossible from the start."[19]

In *Truth and Method* (1975) the German philosopher of history Hans-Georg Gadamer offered a similar critique of Skinner's hermeneutics. Gadamer contends, first, that the historian cannot strip herself of her inherited prejudices and preconceptions in order to project herself into the mind of her author because those prejudices and preconceptions are what make understanding possible in the first place. They are not merely obstacles to be overcome or discarded; they constitute the preconditions for understanding, even though they simultaneously limit its potential achievement. The historian is embedded in her own historical tradition; her understanding of a particular document is made possible by (and circumscribed by) her position in that tradition. "History does not belong to us," Gadamer writes; "we belong to it." "The self-awareness of the individual is only a flickering in the closed circuits of historical life. That is why the prejudices of the individual . . . constitute the historical reality of his being."[20] We approach the past, then, not in a state of historical virginity, but with all the presuppositions, assumptions, and prejudices that both make us concrete persons situated within a particular historical tradition and permit us to imaginatively approach some other moment in time.[21]

Gadamer's second point is that the text to be interpreted is also embedded in a particular historical tradition—not the tradition in which it was written (we can never recover that), but the tradition of interpretation that has grown up around the text *since* it was written.[22] Skinner, by contrast, thought we could strip the text of its accumulated meanings, reconstruct the historical situation in which it was initially written, reinsert the text in its reconstructed context, and there discern its indigenous, prenatal meaning. He wanted to "repristinate" the text. But Gadamer's analysis shows this to be quite impossible; the text can never be severed from the interpretations through which it has been passed down to us—interpretations that now "constitute the historical reality of its being." Understanding a text means understanding its effective history. To pretend otherwise is to transform the text, which "has grown historically and has been transmitted historically," into "an object of physics."[23] Gadamer can be quite scathing about this:

> the reconstruction of the original circumstances, like all such restoration, is a pointless undertaking in view of the historicity of our being. What is reconstructed, a life brought back from the lost past, is not the original. In its continuance in an estranged state it acquires only a secondary, cultural existence. . . . Even the painting taken from the museum and replaced in the church, or the building restored to its original condition are not what they once were—they become simply tourist attractions. Similarly, a hermeneutics that regarded understanding as the reconstruction of the original would be no more than the recovery of a dead meaning.[24]

Gadamer's critique has been the spearhead of what Skinner eventually acknowledged as a "growing refusal . . . to treat the recovery of an intended meaning as any part of the interpreter's task."[25] In the middle of the 1980s Skinner found himself called on to defend a position that only ten years earlier he had triumphantly called "the emerging orthodoxy." By the end of the decade his declarations had acquired a stridently defensive tone; he sounded increasingly besieged, as if he had barricaded himself in his office, writing from behind upended filing cabinets. He charged that the "proliferating philosophical doubts" and "moral objections that have been raised of recent years" had been planted by "all-purpose subversives" who were "seeking to demolish the claims of theory and method to organize the materials of experience." And he warned that these "threats to the foundations of the human sciences" confronted us with nothing less than "the spectre of epistemological relativism."[26]

III

The critical situation in which intellectual history found itself by the end of the 1980s was even more apparent in the theoretical writing of J. G. A. Pocock. Like Skinner, Pocock made major contributions to both the theory and the practice of history.[27] And also like Skinner, he began his career as part of the Cambridge University group that included Peter Laslett, John Dunn, and others. In a series of brilliant books and articles that started appearing in the early 1960s, the Cambridge group argued that historians should pay more attention to "the changing function, context and application of conceptual languages . . . found in particular societies at particular times."[28] Once the conceptual languages of a particular society had been recovered and described, historians would then have access to the menu of meanings those languages made available (or denied) to writers and readers living in that culture.

This was an enormously powerful idea that allowed the Cambridge historians to rewrite huge sections of the history of British political thought. By analyzing the conceptual language of seventeenth-century Britain, for example, they were able to show that the contemporary English landowning class could not possibly have seen the revolutionary implications that later generations read into Locke's *Second Treatise*. In other words, by studying the conceptual language of a particular culture we could learn what it was or was not possible for people in that culture to have thought. For as Pocock has put it, "Men cannot do what they have no means of saying they have done; and what they do must in part be what they can say and conceive that it is."[29] The historian should "point out conventions and regularities that indicate what could and could not be spoken in the language, and in what ways the language qua paradigm encouraged, obliged, or forbade its users to speak and think."[30] From which he could infer what writers living in a particular culture could (and could not) have intended by the words they wrote and what readers (e.g., Locke's readers) could or could not have *understood* by their words.

Skinner wanted to turn historians toward the study of language as a means of recovering authorial intention, but Pocock hoped to interest them in language itself, especially in the question of how

particular language systems have evolved over long periods. In this
he has been enormously successful. As early as 1971 he was able to
describe and celebrate "the emergence of a truly autonomous
method, one which offers a means of treating the phenomena of
political thought strictly as historical phenomena."[31] And indeed, on
both sides of the Atlantic intellectual historians now occupy themselves, as Pocock hoped they would, with "the investigation of entire
political languages, including the asking of how they interact with
and gain predominance over one another."[32]

Like Fernand Braudel, François Furet, Emmanuel Le Roy Ladu-
rie, and other members of the *Annales* school, Pocock emphasized *la
longue durée*, the enduring continuities of thought and perception
through long, sweeping movements of time. In *The Machiavellian
Moment,* for example, he described how the language of civic humanism had evolved over a period of five hundred years, from fifteenth-
century Italy to nineteenth-century America. But here we come to
the central problem of Pocock's approach: the focus on languages or
discourses as they evolve, expand, contract, and displace one another
over long stretches of time tends to obscure the contributions of individual thinkers. This was certainly not the intention of the Cambridge historians. But even in their own field of the history of British
political thought, their work sent Hobbes, Locke, and the other intellectual giants of the British past into what the historian Joyce
Appleby called "conceptual limbo."[33] Viewed from the perspective of
linguistic systems gradually evolving over hundreds of years, individuals—be they French peasants or British writers—simply disappear
in the passage of time.

No one knows this better than Michel Foucault, the acknowledged
master of the history of discourses until his death in 1984. Read
twenty medical texts written between 1770 and 1780, Foucault suggests; then read another twenty written between 1820 and 1830. "In
the space of forty or fifty years everything has changed: what one
talked about, the way one talked about it; not just remedies, of course,
not just the maladies and their classifications, but the outlook itself.
Who was responsible for that? Who was the author of it?" An entire
conceptual world has disappeared, its place taken by a new "discourse," a new *grille* with its own exclusions and erasures, "a new
play with its own rules, decisions and limitations, with its own inner
logic, its own parameters and blind alleys."[34] In other words, the rules
governing the formation and transformation of any discourse are invoked beneath the writer's awareness. Hence Foucault's decision, announced in the early pages of *The Archaeology of Knowledge*, to
"abandon any attempt to see discourse as a phenomenon of expres-

sion." "Discourse is not the majestically unfolding manifestation of a thinking, knowing, speaking subject, but, on the contrary, a totality, in which the dispersion of the subject, and his discontinuity with himself may be determined."[35] By its very subject matter, by its inevitable preoccupation with the abrupt transformations and sudden disruptions that mark the life of discourses, and by its focus on *la longue durée*, the history of discourses disperses the historical agent, "the knowing subject."[36] This is why Foucault speaks so derisively of "what you might call the creativity of individuals"; indeed, this is why such individuals have been virtually obliterated from his histories. The transformation of intellectual history into a history of discourse implies a loss that some historians may not want to accept.

Pocock being one of them. In *Virtue, Commerce, and History: Essays on Political Thought and History, Chiefly in the Eighteenth Century* (1985), his latest work, he draws a distinction between the "history of political thought" and the "history of political discourse" and acknowledges that the professional current is flowing from the first to the second. But Pocock sets himself solidly against that current. And he does so for a crucial and revealing reason: because he is, as he says, committed to writing history that is "ideologically liberal,"[37] by which he means history that preserves the integrity of the subject. Unlike the "history of political discourse," the "history of political thought" must remain the history of "men and women thinking."[38]

In *Virtue, Commerce, and History* Pocock asks us to think of the subject—the writer of political theory in seventeenth-century England, say—as a creative agent self-consciously manipulating a "polyvalent" language system. By "polyvalent" he means that the individual words of such a system "denote *and are known to denote* different things at the same time."[39] Viewed this way, every language system is a mélange of "sublanguages, idioms, rhetorics and modes of speech, each of which varies in its degree of autonomy and stability."[40] The writer stands *outside of and before* this linguistic jungle; she confronts it as a set of verbal possibilities that she can manipulate and exploit in order to realize her intentions—intentions she has *brought to* the scene of writing. "The author may move among these patterns of polyvalence, employing and recombining them according to the measure of his capacity."[41] The text she produces is not a linguistic heterocosm but the product of "a single powerful mind" and so possesses all "the rhetorical, logical, or methodical unity its author imposed on it."[42] It is "an articulation of the author's consciousness."[43] When the historian reads it she therefore enters into "a communication with the author's Self."[44]

But it is precisely this longing for the author's presence—a presence that seems to shimmer just beneath the surface of the text but a presence that is in fact always deferred, always elsewhere, always already absent—it is this yearning for communion with the author's self that poststructualism brought so powerfully into question.[45] Roland Barthes, Jacques Derrida, Michel Foucault, and others made us painfully aware of the desires we bring to our texts—our desire to find in them some compensating sense of connection and completeness, some reassurance of fullness and amplitude. It is difficult, after Barthes, Derrida, and Foucault, to approach texts as objects that *should* be transparent, as signs of something else, as masks concealing something held in reserve, something that will in the end be revealed as whole and primary and essential, a perfect presence.

Melville tried to tell us this over a hundred years ago. Is this not the meaning of Ahab's terrible quest for the white whale? Was Ahab not trying to read the whale as we read our texts, trying to pierce its empty whiteness, to penetrate its maddening blankness in order to reveal some original presence? Is this not what Ahab tried to explain to Starbuck as they stood on the quarterdeck of the *Pequod?*

> Hark ye yet again—the little lower layer. All visible objects, man, are but as pasteboard masks. But in each event—in the living act, the undoubted deed—there, some unknown but still reasoning thing puts forth the mouldings of its features from behind the unreasoning mask. If man will strike, through the mask! How can the prisoner reach outside except by thrusting through the wall? To me, the white whale is that wall, shoved near to me. . . . that inscrutable thing is chiefly what I hate; and be the white whale agent, or be the white whale principal, I will wreak that hate upon him.[46]

Pocock is well aware of all this, of course, as he is of recent developments in literary criticism and the philosophy of language. He knows, as he himself admits, that languages allow "the definition of political problems and values in certain ways and not in others."[47] He has acknowledged that intentions cannot exist outside language, that "the modes of speech available to [a writer] give him the intentions he can have."[48] And he knows that the image of a writer standing outside her own universe of discourse, anterior to it, as it were, manipulating and exploiting it in order to express intentions she has somehow *brought to it,* will seem highly improbable to literary critics and philosophers of language, if not to historians. He knows that we can no more hope to encounter "the author's Self"[49] hiding behind her text than Ahab could hope to confront God behind "the unreasoning mask" of the white whale. But Ahab did hope, and so does Pocock.[50]

J. G. A. Pocock is the most theoretically sophisticated of practicing historians. By his refusal to abandon the dream of authorial presence, by his insistence that intellectual history is and can only be a quest to recover "men and women thinking," he shows us, more clearly than anyone else, the impasse to which the discipline has been brought.

IV

The new discourse-oriented historians who now dominate the writing of American intellectual history seem happily oblivious of the danger that worries Pocock—that a history of discourses will dissolve the traditional subject of intellectual history, the thinking, creating author of past time, that it will reduce him, in Pocock's words, "to the mere mouthpiece of his own language."[51] They simply assume, without much discussion, that they can submerge the subject in a history of discourses yet somehow retain him as an intending agent.[52]

But if Pocock and the discourse historians differ about the dangers facing the subject, they are as one when it comes to the dangers of "presentism," which they all regard as the scourge of professional historiography. By "presentism" they mean, in John Dunn's words, "the weird tendency of much writing, in the history of political thought especially, to be made up of what propositions in what great books remind the author of what propositions in what other great books."[53] This is an old and familiar charge. Herbert Butterfield used to criticize his colleagues for what he called "the pathetic fallacy," by which he meant "abstracting things from their historical context and judging them apart from their context—estimating them and organizing the historical study by a system of direct references to the present."[54]

As Butterfield suggests, the flip side of "presentism" is "contextualism," the insistence that a particular text can be understood only by placing it in the "historically and socially specific *con*text of public discussion" in which it was written[55] In other words, in a particular "network of intellectual discourse."[56] The history of discourses— "radical contextualism," as some of its leading proponents now call it—has become the most prevalent and influential tendency among American intellectual historians—the dominant and now conventional orthodoxy.[57]

But contextualism faces real problems, problems that are becoming increasingly evident. The most obvious and pressing is the difficulty of defining the relevant "network of intellectual discourse" with any precision.[58] Some contextualist-minded historians have insisted that every text must be placed within "the immediate context of lesser people, institutions, and issues in which [its author] actually lived and worked."[59] But other contextualists contend that the relevant context may turn out to be less immediate; indeed, that it may be distressingly remote. In "Historians and the Discourse of Intellectuals," David Hollinger—one of the leading advocates of contextualism—concedes that the relevant context may have to be defined to include all "the theoretical knowledge, literary and religious traditions, and other cultural resources that historians know to have been accessible to most well-informed members of a given society at a given historical moment."[60] And in *Victorian Anthropology* George Stocking, a historian of anthropology who has played a prominent role in the debates over contextualism,[61] has developed an approach he calls "multiple contextualization." As one reviewer noted, "So 'multiple' are Stocking's approaches that even to list them would require more words than a review like this one can use. . . . He is sensitive also to the social, economic and political pressures that help shape ideas."[62] Similarly, the historian Dominick LaCapra has identified at least six kinds of networks in which texts would have to be placed for contextual analysis, each of which "must be understood to encompass not only other contemporaneous writers and readers but also the traditions tapped and even the partly repressed impulses that do not conform to the prevailing conventions of any community."[63] In other words, the relevant community of discourse may include all of Western civilization. And more.

Second, before the historian can place her text in its putative context she must (re)constitute that context—itself a poetic act—and then interpret it, just as if it were itself a text.[64] Which is to say, we can know no "context" that has not already been textualized.[65] This is hardly a novel observation. As William James explained nearly three-quarters of a century ago, a context somehow anterior to textualization—a "reality 'independent' of human thinking"—is "a thing very hard to find."

It reduces to the notion of . . . some aboriginal presence in experience, before any belief about the presence had arisen, before any human conception had been applied. It is what is absolutely dumb and evanescent. . . . We may glimpse it, but we never grasp it; what we grasp is always some substitute for it which previous human thinking has peptonized and cooked for our consumption. . . . We might say that wherever we find it, it has been already *faked*.[66]

The basic distinction between text and context may not have collapsed everywhere, but even among epistemological conservatives it seems to have become a problem.[67]

Finally, contextualism suffers from its often complained of tendency to reduce complex works to the status of documents.[68] When the discourse-oriented historian looks at a particular text, she wants to know how it functioned within a specific discourse, what (if anything) it contributed to that discourse, how it influenced or changed the discourse, and so on.[69] Her primary interest lies in the context rather than the text. Her interest in the text is purely instrumental: she wants to know what it can tell her about the discourse of which it is to her but a manifestation, a token, a document.[70] LaCapra has dubbed this "intellectual history as retrospective symbolic or cultural anthropology," a discipline in which "complex texts" are systematically diminished by being used as evidence in the reconstruction of one or another historical discourse—in other words, an activity in which texts are once again approached as something other than themselves.[71]

"Radical contextualism"—whether in the shape of Skinner and Pocock's history of political thought or in the guise of a history of discourse—is one of the most important and influential attempts yet made to halt the decline of intellectual history. It has acknowledged and has tried to incorporate some of the recent developments in literary criticism, the philosophy of language, and the philosophy of science, and it was once (not long ago) widely regarded as the blueprint for what Pocock called a "truly historical method." But it has not given us an effective response to the criticisms, doubts, and suspicions that poststructuralism has raised about intellectual history: the belief that language is an autonomous play of unintended transformations rather than a stable set of established references, a wayward economy of oppositions and differences that constitutes rather than reflects; the consequent doubts about language's referential and representational capacities; the growing suspicion that narrative may be incapable of conveying fixed, determinate, accessible meaning; and finally, the eclipse of the author as an autonomous, intending subject. For all its interest in language and discourse, radical contextualism has given us neither the means to rebut these claims and doubts nor any suggestions for how we might build upon them.

V

Suppose for a moment that the charges made against intellectual history are true, or at least warranted. Suppose that intellectual history does indeed stand naked before its critics, its canon exposed as a pretentious imposition on the past, its hope of recovering authorial intention seen to be little more than a metaphysical yearning, its traditional texts sacrificed to the insatiable maw of intertextuality. Northrop Frye's description of the New Criticism would fit intellectual history even better: "a mystery religion without a gospel."[72] Hence the obvious question: Where do we go from here?

We can begin with the problem of texts: with which texts should the intellectual historian concern herself? Any attempt to privilege a particular set of texts is bound to seem problematic these days, given the claims of intertextuality, which tends to dissolve the autonomous identity of individual works. The poststructuralist wants us to think of individual texts as the products and outgrowth of other texts written before them. Any particular text, we are told, is merely a "recoded" or "transcoded" version of other texts, whose antecedents are to be found in still earlier texts. Behind the individual text there are only other texts that refer (when they are not merely self-referential) to still others, and so on in an apparently infinite regress. Reference becomes intertextual, origin dissolves, and the individual text is dispersed. And along with it goes any meaningful distinction between "great books" and comic books.[73]

In fact, no one, not even the poststructuralists, has any trouble telling the "great books" from the comic books[74]—not even Roland Barthes, who first popularized the notion of "intertextuality." For Barth takes great pains to distinguish "readerly" *(lisible)* texts from "writerly" *(scriptible)* texts. By "readerly" texts he means texts that comply with accepted conventions of reading and interpreting. Because we "know how" to read them, we read them passively, finding in them exactly the meaning our conventions identify for us. "Writerly" texts, on the other hand, challenge those very conventions, that is, the conventions that isolate and identify meaning in the "readerly" text. To find meaning in the "writerly" text, the reader has to enter the text herself, has to actively participate in the fabrication of whatever meaning she ends up carrying away. "Writerly" texts thereby force the reader to compose an alternative or "virtual" text in her mind while she reads the physical text in her hands. In this way "writerly" texts "initiate performances of meaning rather than actually formulating meanings themselves."[75] They arouse, cultivate, and guide the reader's creation of her own meaning. They invite the reader to rewrite them and so seduce her into becoming a writer. This is what Barthes meant when he said "the text you write must prove to me *that it desires me.*"[76]

Dominick LaCapra probably had something like this in mind when he offered his own distinction between "complex works" and "documents." LaCapra argues that "complex works," like Barthes's "writerly" texts, are distinguished by their tendency to subvert the established protocols and conventions of reading. They carry out "the contestatory function of questioning [received understandings] in a manner that has broader implications for the leading of life."[77]

Barthes's notion of the "writerly" text is also analogous to Frank Kermode's definition of the "canonical" work.[78] Kermode thinks canonical works are texts that have gradually revealed themselves to be multidimensional and omnisignificant, works that have produced a plenitude of meanings and interpretations, only a small percentage of which make themselves available to any single reading. Canonical texts have "qualities not to be detected save at an appropriate moment in the future."[79] They generate new ways of seeing old things and offer new things we have never seen before. No matter how subtly or radically we change our approach to them, they always respond with something new; no matter how many times we reinterpret them, they always have something freshly illuminating to tell us. Their very indeterminacy means they can never be exhausted. As Wolfgang Iser put it, the canonical text "refuses to be sucked dry and thrown on the rubbish heap."[80] So canonical works are multidimensional, omnisignificant, inexhaustible, perpetually new, and for all these reasons, "permanently valuable." It is, then, possible to distinguish the "great books" from the comic books, intertextuality notwithstanding. By drawing on Barthes, LaCapra, and Kermode we can patch together a provisional working criterion for identifying the books with which intellectual history might concern itself.[81]

But now another problem arises: Is this list of canonical works, arranged in neat chronological order, the product of a genuine historical process? Does it actually represent the embodied voices of a great conversation that has been carried on across the ages by the intellectual giants of Western history? Have the great thinkers of every age really been talking to one another in an extended historical conversation, the great books being the textualized remains of that elevated dialogue?

These questions were raised at least as early as the 1930s, when they were directed against Arthur Lovejoy's "History of Ideas" project. And they were raised again, more aggressively, by the new social historians in the 1960s and in the early methodological pieces by

Pocock and Skinner.[82] What this questioning eventually revealed, of course, was that this "great dialogue" was a fiction; it had not taken place at all. Rather than a marvelous conversation carried on by successive generations of great thinkers, it was exposed as an intellectual construct that contemporary historians had devised in order to link together the various books they had come to think of as canonical. There were, as it turned out, virtually no real historical relations between the books themselves. As John Gunnell explained in 1979, "Over the years, by academic convention, a basic repertoire of works had been selected, arranged chronologically, represented as an actual historical [phenomenon], infused with evolutionary meaning, laden with significance derived from various symbolic themes and motifs, and offered up as the intellectual antecedents of contemporary . . . [patterns of] thought."[83]

It was at this point that Skinner and Pocock, faced with questions that threatened to expose their discipline as a trick, tried to rescue intellectual history by providing its canonical works with what everyone could now see they lacked: a genuine historical context. But the problems their attempt has encountered, combined with the onslaught from poststructuralism, have left intellectual history with a canon but no historical explanation for its existence. Intellectual historians are left to rummage through a pile of bones that had once been the connected skeleton of their own discipline.

Some historians think that if intellectual history is to be reconstructed this mound of bones will have to be given some form or shape, an overarching framework of one sort of another. They think we need something to take the place of our earlier belief that the great books were the products of an actual transgenerational dialogue of great thinkers; they want to give the canon a historically conditioned identity.

Some of them think they can find what they need in the argument over biblical interpretation that emerged during the Protestant Reformation. Central to the Reformation, of course, was Luther's conviction that every man was not only his own priest but his own interpreter. Behind this conviction lay two even more basic beliefs. The first was that the Scriptures were self-sufficient and self-interpreting, that is, that they possessed a clear, fixed, and determinable meaning that rose directly out of the text itself, without any assistance from the complicated interpretive apparatus that the church had gradually developed and now required. And second, that the Scriptures were meant to be taken literally rather than allegorically, as the church also insisted. "Origen's allegories are not worth so much dirt," as Luther put it; they are "the scum of Scripture."[84] For Reformation

Protestantism, the church's insistence on interpretive procedures and allegorical meaning stood between the Christian and her Bible, barring her from immediate access to the Word.

From this perspective Skinner and Pocock's proposal for reforming intellectual history begins to look like an essentially Protestant proposal. Like Luther, Skinner and Pocock think that historical texts convey fixed meanings and that those meanings are accessible and ultimately determinable, if the critic or historian will simply cut through the layers of interpretation that stand between the naked text and her inquiring mind. Like Luther, they look on these layers of accumulated interpretation as an impediment, an obstruction, an obstacle barring the historian from the "primary intentions" of the author. The wealth of interpretive material that surrounds a historical work they regard as so much scalelike incrustation that the historian must smash to pieces with her "truly historical method" in order to get at the pearl of authentic meaning—what the author "really meant," what the text "really says."

The problems this Protestant hermeneutics has encountered has suggested to some historians that we need an interpretive tradition erected not on the longing for authorial presence and invariable meaning, not on the illusion of the text as a "congealed intentionality waiting to be reexperienced," but on the recognition that every text, at the very moment of its inception, has already been cast upon the waters, that no text can ever hope to rejoin its father, that it is the fate of every text to take up the wanderings of a prodigal son who does not return. Interestingly enough, we can find some of what we need in the Catholic interpretive tradition, and even more in the rabbinic tradition.

Brevard Childs is professor of Old Testament theology at Yale. He is most widely known for his massive *Introduction to the Old Testament as Scripture* (1979). This is Childs's response to reformed orthodoxy's insistence on recovering the Scriptures' aboriginal meaning. As Childs explains, "Modern canonical exegesis must be post-critical in nature. It does not seek to repristinate first century Christian interpretation" but "to understand the massive interpretative construal by means of which the sacred traditions" have been transmitted across so many generations.[85]

By "massive interpretative construal" Childs means that in the course of transmission from one generation to another the sacred texts have been steadily reshaped, first by being gradually weaned from their original historical references and then by being drawn into larger textual complexes. In the course of this "traditioning process" the texts' primary meaning comes to be grounded in (1) their reference to other texts in the larger textual complexes into which they have been drawn; (2) their place within the larger interpretive apparatus that surrounds these textual complexes; and (3) the new historical references they acquire from a combination of 1 and 2 together. It is through this "traditioning process" that sacred texts acquire their multidimensional character, their plenitude of meaning—the very qualities that identify them as canonical.

Gadamer made a similar point in his critique of traditional hermeneutics. Just as the would-be interpreter's historically conditioned "prejudices" are not merely a series of obstacles to understanding but are in fact what makes understanding possible, so the interpretations that have gradually accumulated around a particular text—or around the canon as a whole—provide the only way we can approach that text or collection of texts. As Gadamer puts it, "Understanding is never subjective behavior toward a given 'object,' but towards its effective history—the history of its influence."[86] In other words, interpretation forms the medium in which the text lives—the only medium in which it can live. Without the sustaining amniotic fluid of interpretation the text would never have been born into our hands. Perhaps this is what T. S. Eliot was talking about in his famous 1919 article on tradition and the sense of history when he wrote that "the historical sense involves a perception, not only of the pastness of the past, but of its presence; the historical sense compels a man to write not merely with his own generation in his bones, but with a feeling that the whole of the literature of . . . his culture has a simultaneous existence and composes a simultaneous order."[87]

Childs's Catholic-inspired hermeneutics is clearly an improvement over the textual fundamentalism of Quentin Skinner and J. G. A. Pocock. First and foremost, it abandons Skinner and Pocock's attempt to find some immediate relation to the text, their determination to make the text yield up a stable and determinate meaning, once and for all. For no matter how desperately we may search our ancestors' texts for some round and final truth, the melancholy fact should be obvious by now: we can never escape the terminal estrangements of time and somehow reenter the house of origins. The humanly continuous universe that Skinner and Pocock promise—a universe radiant with authorial presence and textual meaning—simply lies beyond our earthly grasp. For us the past will always be just what it always has been: an unstable aggregation of unruly texts. How could it possibly be otherwise? How could Skinner and Pocock have missed what Augustine and so many others have always seen? Second, Childs's hermeneutics has the inestimable virtue of insisting that meaning is always intertextual, that it always emerges from a text's mingled relations with other texts in a larger economy of texts.

These advantages notwithstanding, however, Childs's hermeneutics contains two problems that are probably irresolvable. The first is simply this: If the fundamental instability of human language—its epistemological uncertainty and inherent undecidability; its propensity for slippage; the fact, as Pocock puts it, that meaning is always "in a state of perpetual flux"—cuts us off from direct access to the author's "primary intentions," and if narrative form has indeed proven itself an unreliable vehicle for conveying fixed and determinable truth, then how can we hope to establish, as Childs suggests, a true representation of "the massive interpretative construal" by which the "sacred traditions"—or *any* traditions, for that matter—have been handed down to us?[88] If we cannot recover the early modern discursive systems that interest Skinner and Pocock, how can we recover the early modern textual complexes that interest Brevard Childs? The answer, of course, is that we cannot.[89]

Here is the second problem with Childs's hermeneutics: it attempts to tie meanings down, to fix them in historical time, rather than inciting them to multiply themselves in the present. Childs wants to recover the meanings a text produced as successive generations of interpreters placed it in one textual complex after another. He has no interest in helping it generate new meanings in the present—that is, in helping us discover what a historical text might say to *us* when we place it in a textual complex of *our* devising. Childs's way of reading has nothing to teach us about how we should read the "writerly" texts (or "complex works") that constitute the greatest part of the canon.

These difficulties bring us to an obvious question: Do we really need to provide the canon with a historically conditioned identity—something akin to our earlier belief that the books we teach are the products of a marvelous transgenerational dialogue of great thinkers? More to the point, is such an identity even possible now? Is it still plausible to imagine that all the books in the (expanding) canon can somehow be integrated into a single (and truly historical) narrative? The Dutch historian F. R. Ankersmit was probably right when he declared that "autumn has come to Western historiography":

In the first place, there is of course the postmodernist notion of our own time. Our anti-essentialism, or, as it is popularly called these days, "anti-foundationalism," has lessened our [faith in] science and traditional historiography. The changed position of Europe in the world since 1945 is a second important indication. The history of this appendage to the Eurasian continent is no longer world history. What we would like to see as the trunk of the tree of Western history has become part of a whole forest. The *meta-récits* we would like to tell ourselves about our history, the triump of Reason, the glorious struggle for emancipation of the nineteenth-century workers' proletariat, are only of local importance and for that reason can no longer be suitable metanarratives. The chilly wind which rose around 1900 simultaneously in both the West and the East, finally blew the leaves off our historical tree as well in the second half of this century. What remains now for Western historiography is to gather the leaves that have been blown away and to study them independently of their origins. . . . What is important is no longer the place they had on the tree, but the pattern we can form from them now, the way in which this pattern can be adapted to other forms of civilization existing now.[90]

There is nothing new about all this; rabbinic commentators have been practicing just such a hermeneutics for centuries. Rabbinic interpretion begins not with the Word as the immaculate expression of God's will, the Word radiant with original meaning before every act of interpretation—as the Protestant interpretative tradition does—but rather with Torah as the promise of *multiple* meaning, an invitation to continual interpretation and reinterpretation. It is not incarnation—the Word made flesh—but interpretation—the Word made populous with meaning—that is the central divine act of rabbinic Judaism. In every word there shines "an infinite multitude of lights."[91] As Emmanuel Levinas once explained, "It is precisely a *discourse, not* embodied in God, that assures us of a living God among us. . . . The spiritual does not present itself as a tenable substance but, rather, through its absence; God is made real, not through incarnation but, rather, through the Law"—that is to say, through the text.[92]

This is what Gershom Scholem once called "pre-existent givenness," that is, the idea that the Torah implicitly contains every interpretation that later commentators would eventually discover. "So should it be that you would forsake Me, but would keep My Torah." As Rabbi Joshua ben Levi, a third-century Palestinian teacher, put it, "Torah, Mishnah, Talmud, and Aggadah—indeed even the comments some bright student will one day make to his teacher—were already given to Moses on Mount Sinai." And as

Scholem adds, "even the *questions* that such a bright student will some day ask his teacher!"[93] Finally, there is the wonderful story of Rabbi Eliezer's quarrel with the Sages about the oven of Aknai. When God cried out, "Why do ye dispute with R. Eliezer, seeing that in all matters the *halachah* agrees with him!" Rabbi Jeremiah replied, "The Torah has already been given at Mount Sinai; we pay no attention to a Heavenly Voice." At which point God "laughed with joy" and conceded: "My sons have defeated Me, My sons have defeated Me."[94]

From Barthes, LaCapra, and Kermode we can construct a workable set of criteria for identifying the books with which intellectual history should concern itself; and by drawing on the rabbinic interpretive tradition we can get ourselves out from under the obligation to provide a historically grounded and historically conditioned identity for those books. But what should the historian do with these materials? What are her particular responsibilities?

VI

It has been said that the historian bears a primary responsibility to the past, to the writers and thinkers she reads and studies, if for no other reason than because they lived through those times and we did not.[95] The historian is said to carry out this obligation by listening to the people of the past, by trying to understand them in their own terms, and by telling us "what they really said."[96] There is no gainsaying the importance of making this effort. But from all that has gone before it will be obvious that we should not expect to actually encounter now-dead authors in the body of their texts. The liberation of the text from "the glare of the Father's eye," the process of cultural transmission, and the continual decontextualizing and recontextualizing that cultural transmission entails all conspire to frustrate our hope that the text will be radiant with the presence of the past.[97] Though we grant the text a privileged *moral* status, we cannot grant it a privileged *epistemological* status; the text—every text—will always be epistemologically inadequate.[98]

Granted that the historian bears a responsibility to those who lived in the past, her *primary* responsibility must be to those of us who live in the present. For as Frank Kermode has explained, "We are necessarily more involved with the living than with the dead, with what learning cherishes and interpretation refreshes rather than with mere remains."[99] It is for this reason that the historian must set out not merely to *understand* the writers of the past but to *reeducate* them, anachronistically imposing "enough of our problems and vocabulary on the dead to make them conversational partners."[100] P. F. Strawson's *The Bounds of Sense: An Essay on Kant's "Critique of Pure Reason"* (1966) provides a good example. In *Bounds of Sense* Strawson rips Kant out of his historical context, strips his thought of everything Strawson thinks should not be there, and shows us that for our purposes, living in our present, this refurbished Kantianism works better than the original. As Rorty says, "Strawson's conversation with Kant is the sort one has with somebody who is brilliantly and originally right about something dear to one's heart, but who exasperatingly mixes up this topic with a lot of outdated foolishness."[101]

Historians do not generally condemn this sort of thing outright; they just do not think it is "history."[102] They regard placing historical actors in their "proper" contexts as "the first task of the historian," the historian's "first order of business," "a matter of conceptual propriety," and so on.[103] For intellectual historians, this means reconstructing the *mentalité* of a particular epoch, its central ideas and values, its modes of perception, its systems of discourse, its formal structures of thought, the ways in which it produced and disseminated meaning, the procedures it used for translating meaning from one discourse to another, and so on. Most historians regard this sort of historical reconstruction as their primary responsibility. They think it is epistemologically impossible to understand the dead in *our* terms unless we first understand them in theirs.[104]

It is time to rethink our commitment to historical contextualism. We need an approach centered not on the quest for textual origins— an obsession that has sent us groping our way backward toward some unreachable genesis—but on the resituating of historical texts. As Richard Rorty once said, history should be "therapeutic rather than reconstructive, edifying rather than systematic."[105] Intellectual history as "quick'ning power."[106] Here is Frank Kermode's description of the fin-de-siècle historian Aby Warburg, whose scholarly research enshrined Botticelli among the pantheon of Renaissance painters: "Like most ambitious thinkers, [Warburg] used other men's thoughts and systems of ideas as stimulants rather than as schemes he might or might not adopt; he was not looking for something ready-made, but for hints, for the stimulus that might give rise to a brainwave of his own."[107] For Warburg, meaning unfolds *in front of* the text rather than behind it. Texts do not point backward, to the historical context or putative intentions of their now-dead authors; they point forward, to the hidden opportunities of the present.[108]

Noam Chomsky's recovery and redeployment of Cartesian linguistics provides a good example. Until 1966, when Chomsky brought out

Cartesian Linguistics: A Chapter in the History of Rationalist Thought,
seventeenth-century philosophical grammar was "all but unknown."[109] Now, of course, thirty years later, we know a great deal
about that tradition; but it was Chomsky who pointed out its contemporary significance. What I want to emphasize here is the present-
minded, even anticontextualist nature of Chomsky's approach.[110]
Cartesian Linguistics, as Chomsky describes it, is "a projection back-
wards of certain ideas of contemporary interest rather than a systematic presentation of the framework within which these ideas arose
and found their place."[111] As such it makes "no attempt to characterize Cartesian linguistics as it saw itself but rather . . . concentrate[s]
on the development of ideas that have reemerged, quite independently, in current work."[112] In other words, Chomsky turned to the
past to find particular insights and discoveries that were "analogous"
to contemporary developments—precisely the "weird tendency" that
the contextualist historian John Dunn complained of so bitterly.
Chomsky is quite clear about the difference between his own presentism and Dunn's contextualism:

> I'm looking at history not as an antiquarian, who is interested
> in finding out and giving a precisely accurate account of what
> the thinking of the seventeenth century was—I don't mean to
> demean that activity, it's just not mine—but rather from the
> point of view of, let's say, an art lover, who wants to look at
> the seventeenth century to find in it things that are of particular
> value, and that obtain part of their value in part because of the
> perspective with which he approaches them.[113]

In *Cartesian Linguistics* Chomsky returned to the early modern
Port-Royal grammarians, evaluated their work in terms of its "contemporary significance," and showed us how it could be resituated,
recontextualized, and put to new and important uses.[114] He did something very similar two years later in *Language and Mind,* which, in
his own words, "illustrates how the [seventeenth-century] tradition
of philosophical grammar can be reconstituted and turned to new
and challenging problems."[115] In each case Chomsky set out to rescue
an idea or an insight from the historical context into which it was
about to disappear, resituated it in the context of contemporary research interests, and made us see that, thus resituated, it has the
power to inform us about certain possibilities of the present—possibilities we had not seen before.

Michael Walzer's *Exodus and Revolution* (1985) provides another
example of the sort of history I have in mind. *Exodus and Revolution*
is a history of the Book of Exodus as a paradigm of revolutionary

politics—indeed, as the engendering paradigm of virtually every revolutionary movement in the West, from the Peasants' Revolt in sixteenth-century Germany to the Puritan revolution in seventeenth-century England to the Boer revolt in South Africa to the Civil Rights movement in the American South to the liberation movements in contemporary Latin America. In other words, *Exodus and Revolution* is traditional intellectual history—an account of one particular idea as that idea has appeared in the thoughts of one thinker after another.

But it is more than that. As rabbinical commentators like to say of the Torah, "Turn it and turn it again, for everything is in it." One thing that is in *Exodus and Revolution* is an explicit attack on contextualist historiography. As one of the early reviewers noted, Walzer "is utterly uninterested in the findings of contemporary Biblical scholarship, which undermine the stated meanings of the text in order to locate it in its ancient Israelite context."[116] Walzer described such efforts in his Introduction, then dismissed them as outright failures.[117] His own approach to the past was governed by a quite different set of assumptions: "In returning to the original text, I make no claims about the substantive intentions of its authors and editors, and I commit myself to no specific view of the actual history. What really happened? We don't know. We have only this story, written down centuries after the events it describes. But the story is more important than the events."[118]

As this passage suggests, Walzer was less interested in the genealogy of the text than in the history of its meanings. But his project had little to do with the currently fashionable idea that intellectual history should explain the conditions that govern the production and transmission of meaning; it was not an attempt to explain "why certain meanings arise, persist, and collapse at particular times and in specific sociocultural situations."[119] It was rather an effort "to grasp the meaning of the text through a critique of interpretations," an attempt, in other words, "to discover its meaning in what it has meant."[120] *Exodus and Revolution* is a history of meaning rather than a history of the production and transmission of meaning.

But if *Exodus and Revolution* is a history of what the Book of Exodus has meant to certain people living in the past, it is also an explanation of what it can mean to us, living in the present. For *Exodus and Revolution* shows us how a text from the past can illuminate and instruct the present, even as the present rewrites the past. When Walzer said he was interested in "the radical potential of the Exodus story," he meant that he was interested in Exodus as a story that induced its readers to create their own stories, stories based on

the original story but stories that are nevertheless "new and empowering," stories that "engender human activity for a radical challenge
to social justice." Exodus has provided and continues to provide a
narrative framework within which people can think about slavery
and freedom, flight and deliverance, oppression and liberation. This
may be, as Walzer admitted, a "deliberately anachronistic" approach
to the past; but as he also says, "Every reading [of the past] is also
a construction, a reinvention of the past *for the sake of the present.*"[121]

John P. Diggins's book *The Bard of Savagery: Thorstein Veblen
and Modern Social Theory* (1978) offers a final example. Diggins is
an intellectual historian with an interest in comparative social theory.
In *The Bard of Savagery* he explained how Veblen's analysis of the
historical development of capitalism, particularly his explanation of
how unearned wealth is legitimated in capitalist society, differed
from the analyses offered by Marx and Weber. He did this by purposefully lifting all three thinkers out of their particular historical
contexts and strapping them onto a single intellectual *grille*, reading
each thinker in terms of the other, asking them questions they had
not thought to ask themselves. In this way he was able to reveal
certain limitations and exclusions, certain thoughts that remained
unthought in each thinker's work. Diggins developed this interroga-
tory, contestatory dialogue with the past—he called it "an exercise
in theoretical confrontations"—not in order to criticize Marx and
Weber for missing what Veblen grasped, but rather because, like
Chomsky, he wanted to rescue Veblen's thought from the historical
oblivion into which it seemed to be slipping. He wanted to return
to it, rewrite it, resituate it, and make us see that, placed in a new
and perhaps unexpected context, it has something interesting and
valuable to show us—in this case something about the historical
development and contemporary staying power of modern capitalism
that both Marx and Weber overlooked.

Notice that in doing so Diggins set out not only to recontextualize
Veblen but to rewrite him. He filtered out certain aspects of Veblen's
work that seemed irrelevant to Diggins's own concerns and under-
lined other elements to make them address those same concerns more
sharply. Like Strawson rewriting Kant, Diggins wanted to help Veblen make himself presentable for a new audience. But note, too,
that Diggins reeducated Veblen in order that Veblen might reeducate
us, that he might show us something we had previously overlooked
within our own present. Notice, finally, that this was a game in which
the stakes were particularly high: Diggins knew the risks he took by
flying in the face of professional convention, but he also knew that

if he could recontextualize Veblen's insights he might be able to effect a reevaluation not merely of Veblen's own work, but of contemporary social theory itself.[122]

But the American historical establishment would have none of it. Thomas Haskell, writing in *Reviews in American History*, rebuked Diggins for failing to "fix" Veblen "firmly in his times" and for the "arbitrariness" of his comparisons with Marx and Weber. Diggins had placed Veblen "in an artificial context populated by a handful of major figures" who had been selected "on the basis of their importance to us, not Veblen."[123] Though "a contextualist account of Veblen might have been more pedestrian . . . it would have permitted a finer understanding of what Veblen actually said and meant."[124] Dorothy Ross, writing in the *American Historical Review*, also complained that "the theorists examined and the questions asked of the material are generated not by history but by the author's theoretical concerns." Worst of all, Diggins seemed to feel that he was somehow "exempt" from the historian's primary obligation: "to place Veblen in historical context."[125]

VII

What are we to make of all this? Two observations seem in order. First, context-oriented historians should stop chastising their colleagues for "presentism" and acknowledge the value—if not the necessity—of letting the present interrogate the past. To paraphrase Bacon, we must put history to the rack, we must compel it to answer our questions.[126] *Our* questions, derived from *our* needs, couched in *our* terms.[127] Rorty once likened historians to anthropologists in a way that might be helpful here:

> The anthropologist is not doing his job if he merely offers to teach us how to bicker with his favorite tribe, how to be initiated into their rituals, etc. What we want to be told is whether that tribe has anything interesting to tell us—interesting by *our* lights, answering to *our* concerns, informative about what *we* know to exist. Any anthropologist who rejected this assignment on the grounds that filtering and paraphrase would distort and betray the integrity of the tribe's culture would no longer be an anthropologist, but a sort of cultist. He is, after all, working for *us*, not for *them*. Similarly, the historian of X, where X is something we know to be real and important, is working for those of us who share that knowledge, not for our unfortunate ancestors who did not.[128]

Second, if recent developments in literary criticism and the philosophy of language have indeed undermined our belief in a stable and determinable past, denied the possibility of recovering authorial intention, and challenged the plausibility of historical representation, then contextualist-minded historians should stop insisting that every historian's "first order of business" must be to do what now seems undoable.[129] Historians should simply drop the question of what counts as legitimate history and accept the fact that, like every other discipline in the humanities, they do not have, and are not likely to have, a formalized, widely accepted set of research procedures. And that nothing helpful or interesting is likely to come from attempts to define one.[130] If we ask, What is historical writing? the answer can only be, There is this kind of historical writing, and that kind, and then again that kind. If such an understanding could win even grudging acceptance from the historical profession, then a space might be cleared within which another sort of intellectual history could be written: a history concerned not with dead authors but with living books, not with returning earlier writers to their historical contexts but with reading historical works in new and unexpected contexts, not with reconstructing the past but with providing the critical medium in which valuable works from the past might *survive* their past—might survive their past in order to tell us about our present. For only through such telling can we hope to see ourselves and our history anew.

CHAPTER TWO

A People Blinded from Birth
American History according to the Left

I

For Perry Miller, American Puritanism was a demanding and un-compromising theology. A severe and sometimes terrifying religion, it offered to the eyes of the faithful a dark and searing vision of the fault that lies within. It was a kind of grim poetry, a somber and elegant meditation on the power of blackness. But it was also a redemptive discipline, a way of thinking against ourselves, even of transcending ourselves. And it was an indispensable guide for sojourners in the wilderness, counseling, as it did, perpetual doubt and the good that may come of a broken heart. If it demanded harsh and unrelenting self-interrogation, it also knew the dangerous deceptions of self-reliance; if it reminded us that we are all "strangers and pilgrims on the earth," it also made us see those around us as fellow sufferers.[1] It provided a necessary corrective to the pleasing pretensions of American culture, and it gave us our best ideas about what we should value and how we should live.

Historical fashions come and go, of course. In our more optimistic moments we think of this coming and going as natural growth, a form of intellectual renewal. We forget that, like everything else of value, a particular way of thinking may fall under the wheel of time and be lost forever, that even the most richly imaginative forms of historical reflection can wither and die. Some part of Miller's vision

An earlier version of this chapter appeared as "A People Blinded from Birth: American History according to Sacvan Bercovitch," *Journal of American History* 78, no. 3 (December 1991): 949–71.

may still survive, but it has been driven into exile. It has become the wandering outcast of professional historiography, its wounding power departed, its redemptive possibilities forgotten, its vision of the past reduced to a patchwork of motley remnants and irrelevant fragments. We no longer think about history the way Miller taught us. A practiced and developed way of thinking about the American past has been emptied of power, drained of meaning, and finally abandoned.[2] What William Carlos Williams once said of American culture might now be said of Miller's history: "It is only in isolate flecks that / something / is given off."[3]

Now we have new interpretations of Puritanism: Puritanism as mean spirited and hegemonic; Puritanism as self-flattering and pleasing to the heart; Puritanism as an insignificant and inconsequential episode in the history of colonial British America. What all these interpretations lack is a sense of gratitude; their authors do not believe that American Puritanism has anything special or compelling to tell us.[4] They do not think Puritan sermons can engage our minds or open our hearts; they do not think Puritan writers are morally instructive; and they do not think Puritan books contain anything necessary for us to know.[5] For them the Puritan tradition is little more than a graveyard of the mind. A mean and pinched theology, hollow and dry, it is nevertheless the origin of our many afflictions. As contemporary historians read them, Puritan texts no longer illuminate the dark corners of life, or help us resist the blind cravings of the ego, or to encourage us challenge the myths of self-realization and material progress that have come to dominate American culture.[6]

Sacvan Bercovitch is the most prominent and influential of these new historians, Perry Miller's apparent successor and now the leading authority on American Puritanism. Bercovitch's interpretation of the Puritan legacy is everywhere read as an extension of Miller's original vision, a filling-in of his interpretive structure. As Edmund Morgan put it, "What Bercovitch has done is to stretch our minds a bit further in the direction that Miller bent them."[7]

In fact, Bercovitch has come not to honor Miller but to bury him; his interpretation of American Puritanism is not an extension and completion of Miller's work but its denial and negation.[8] In his preface to *The American Jeremiad* Bercovitch condemned "the patricidal totem feast" that followed Miller's death.[9] But *The American Jeremiad* is itself a lance hurled straight into the heart of Miller's corpus. Like Milton's defiant protagonist, Bercovitch rebels against being spoken to by the dead.[10] He recovers only to transform. His work is a living dramatization of Whitman's precept, "He most honors my style who learns under it to destroy the teacher." And indeed it is

Sacvan Bercovitch who now sits in Perry Miller's place at Harvard University.

In the course of this struggle to defeat and displace his intellectual progenitor, Sacvan Bercovitch is rewriting the entire chronicle of American history—its underlying structure, its essential content, its fundamental meaning. He is reconstructing the American past, recasting who we have been and redefining who we should become— all under the sign of extending Miller's original vision. In the pages that follow I describe his reinterpretation of American history, compare it with the giant cryptogram of America that Perry Miller gave us, and ask whether Bercovitch's history is the kind of history we need.[11]

II

Like many literary historians, Bercovitch wants to study the history of American writing in order to grasp the imaginative structure and symbolic pattern of American thought. His earliest publications—a series of articles on Puritan aesthetics that appeared in the late 1960s and early 1970s—were close textual readings of classic Puritan texts. Like the New Critics before him, Bercovitch focused on allegorical structures, symbolic patterns, rhetorical forms, and so on.[12] But unlike the New Critics, he employed this formalist apparatus to examine something quite outside the texts themselves: what used to be called "the American mind" but what Bercovitch now calls "the American ideology." You can see this plainly in the most important and influential of his early essays, "Typology in Puritan New England: The Williams-Cotton Controversy Reassessed."[13]

Until Bercovitch's article appeared in 1967, debate about the Williams-Cotton controversy had revolved around Roger Williams's place in the history of American liberalism. Progressives associated Williams with the principles of religious toleration, separation of church and state, and so forth.[14] Conservatives replied that Williams was no liberal, that he was an utterly traditional man, even a medieval man, and that if he insisted on religious toleration and the separation of church and state it was not to protect the state from religious enthusiasm but to protect the church from secular authority.[15] What made Bercovitch's article so interesting and important was that he shifted the discussion from politics to rhetoric, that is to say, from manifest content to underlying structure.

Rhetoric for Bercovitch is more than verbal ornamentation; it is a set of aesthetic devices that constitutes a particular structure of perception, a particular pattern of thought and mode of expression.

It is highly figural, working through type and trope, allegory and symbol.[16] Rhetoric constitutes the basic arrangement of, and directs the basic operation of, the myth-making mind. Under Bercovitch's influence we have come to see rhetoric as the primary force that drove and shaped the Puritan imagination.[17]

Typology is a particular form of rhetoric. In Bercovitch's words, it is "the historiographic-theological method of relating the Old Testament to the life of Christ (as 'anti-type') and, through him, to the doctrines and progress of the Christian Church"[18]—and more particularly, to the doctrines and progress of that vanguard of the Reformation, that New World Israel, the Massachusetts Bay colony. For Bercovitch contends that typology was the rhetorical strategy by which the Puritans envisioned the meaning of their errand into the wilderness, the allegorical reading by which New England found its redemptive future figured forth in the types and tropes of the Old Testament. It was the imaginative energy of typology, its willed inferences, that enabled the Puritans to invest "America" with both a sacred history and an eschatological future, to fuse past, present, and future, to make New England both ancient Israel's long-awaited anti-type and the symbol of the New Jerusalem.

Perry Miller thought the Puritans had condemned typology. And he thought that John Cotton, in his dispute with Williams, had defended the Puritans' orthodox interpretive procedures against Williams's heretical use of typology.[19] But Bercovitch contends that the Puritans did not condemn typology per se; they condemned only Williams's particular brand of typology, his "allegorical" typology. Where Williams insisted that the Old Testament types be applied allegorically, the orthodox Puritans—in the person and writings of John Cotton—insisted they be applied literally and historically. So what we have in the Williams-Cotton dispute, according to Bercovitch, is not an argument about the validity of typological interpretation (as Miller had thought) but a dispute over two varieties of typology, "an opposition between two different typological approaches."[20] Far from having condemned typology, the Puritans were steeped in it.[21] Typology was not only pervasive but central and essential, the elementary adhesive that bound every facet New England culture into a comprehensive structure of perception, association, and expression, a single theocratic prophecy of "Theopolis Americana."[22]

Two things are important in this debate. First, Bercovitch thinks he has found the fundamental substructure that underlay, informed, and shaped the Puritan imagination—and, by extension, the *American* imagination. The typological imperative he discovered in the literature of seventeenth-century New England "pervaded all branches of early American writing, secular as well as religious."[23] And this holds true not only in the seventeenth century but throughout the eighteenth, nineteenth, and twentieth centuries as well, from the New England Puritans to present-day Americans.[24] In other words, in the typological imperative Bercovitch thinks he has discovered the critical and defining element of what he will later call "the American ideology."[25]

Second, in Bercovitch's hands this intuitive ideological consensus—almost a subliminal cultural mythology—takes on a hegemonic domination "unmatched in any other modern culture."[26] It becomes a sort of ur-Americanism that not only underlies all differences but collapses all oppositions and reconciles all contradictions, transforming every condemnation into an implicit assent.[27] This notion will become central to Bercovitch's later, more comprehensive treatment of American thought and writing, but it can be glimpsed as early as 1967. In that year Bercovitch concluded "Typology in Puritan New England" with a two-pronged suggestion that, however briefly stated and imperfectly developed at this point, foreshadowed the direction his later work would take. "The furthest implications of John Cotton's answer to Roger Williams," he suggested, are, first, that "it enlists the heretic's exegetical method as support for the theocracy" and, second, that it "binds all aspects of the New England venture—physical and theological, individual and communal—into a [single] comprehensive vision."[28]

All this was made much more explicit—and was greatly extended—in Bercovitch's first and finest book, *The Puritan Origins of the American Self* (1975). In his earlier work Bercovitch had described what he thought was the central rhetorical element of the Puritan imagination; now, in *Puritan Origins*, he described how the Puritans used this rhetoric—this "distinctive symbolic mode"—to create both individual selfhood and national identity, how they fused nation and self in the representative idea of "America." And he explains how this "central aspect of our Puritan legacy," this redemptive concept of "America," this millennial fusion of nation and self, was transformed into "one of the most powerful unifying elements of the culture."[29]

Like his earlier work, *Puritan Origins* is based on a close textual reading of a single canonical work—indeed, of a single chapter of a single work: Cotton Mather's "Life of John Winthrop," which originally appeared in the second volume of *Magnalia Christi Americana.*[30] Bercovitch thinks he can show that this nineteen-page capsule biography contains all "the complexity, the intricacy, the coherence, and the abiding significance of the American Puritan vision."[31] In other words, he believes it constitutes a miniaturized edition of our civil theology, a compressed version of the national dream, and that through it Cotton Mather continues even now, 250 years after his death, to "shape the distinctive American approach to virtually every major area of concern."[32]

Bercovitch finds the key to his reading of Mather in Mather's conjunction of "Nehemias" and "Americanus" in his title, "*Nehemias Americanus:* The Life of John Winthrop. . . . " Nehemiah, of course, was the old Testament prophet who led his people from Babylonian captivity to freedom in Judea. He was their first governor, the articulation of their hopes and the architect of their success. He managed their migration, he inspired their reformations, and he "directed the reconstruction of Jerusalem from a wasteland into a city on a hill."[33] As this last phrase suggests, Mather's conjunction of "Nehemias" and "Americanus" not only transforms Winthrop into Nehemiah, it also transforms the Atlantic migration into the Babylonian flight, the American Puritans into the ancient Israelites, and "America" into the Promised Land—not a *metaphor* for the promised land but the Promised Land itself. Secular America as sacred text; American history as scriptural prophecy.

And John Winthrop as the promise of fulfillment. For as we have seen, Mather identified Winthrop not only with Nehemiah but also with "Americanus." Self and nation fused together in John Winthrop as representative American. Mather's life of Winthrop is "auto-American-biography," that is, "the celebration of the representative self as America, and of the American self as the embodiment of a prophetic universal design."[34] To the extent that American selfhood is conceived as identity continually unfolding, identity perpetually in progress, "advancing from prophecies performed towards paradise to be regained," it is for Bercovitch a creation of Cotton Mather and the New England Puritans.[35]

In the final chapter of *Puritan Origins* Bercovitch argues that the Puritan allegory of history, the intertwining of personal selfhood, national identity, and prophetic history in the rhetorical form of the *Magnalia*, sustained American culture through the eighteenth and early nineteenth centuries, from the Great Awakening through the American Renaissance.[36] The visionary force, the imaginative patterns, and the sacred teleology that Mather presented in *Magnalia Americana* found their fullest expression in what Bercovitch refers to as "the transcendental vistas, the democratic *Magnalia Americana*" of Ralph Waldo Emerson.[37] And not only in Emerson: Bercovitch thinks every major American writer, "including the most belligerently anti-nationalistic among them," has, however unwittingly, celebrated "the American self as the embodiment of a prophetic universal design." For Bercovitch, classic American writing is without exception a figuration of the national dream in terms of the Puritan vision. The "inner substance," the "essential content," and the "obsessive concern" of *all* American writing, from Mather to Melville, is "America."[38] Whether America as redeemer nation or America as New World inferno, the compelling identification is always "America"; personal and national identity inextricably joined in "the bipolar unity of auto-American-biography."[39]

Three years later Bercovitch published his second book, *The American Jeremiad* (1978). Like *Puritan Origins, The American Jeremiad* describes a particular Puritan literary mode—in this case the jeremiad—and explains how it shaped and controlled American thought and writing from the early seventeenth century through the mid-nineteenth. Also like *Puritan Origins*, it argues that the Puritan imagination—as an integrated structure of thought, perception, and desire—persisted far longer than anyone had previously imagined.

Some reviewers thought *The American Jeremiad* was little more than a rewritten version of *Puritan Origins.*[40] It is true that it broke no new conceptual ground, but it did clarify and extend Bercovitch's general argument. It is also more theoretically sophisticated than *Puritan Origins*, drawing on the work of Antonio Gramsci, Raymond Williams, Clifford Geertz, and others. And it is far more ambitious: *The American Jeremiad* sets out to explain the influence of Puritanism on "the entire spectrum of [American] social thought" from the early seventeenth century through the middle of the nineteenth.[41] It is also more emphatic and revealing than *Puritan Origins*. Several issues that were only alluded to in the earlier work—and some that could only be inferred from it—are now fully developed and aggressively argued. The most important of these concern Bercovitch's insistence that Puritanism constituted "a comprehensive, officially endorsed cultural myth."[42] Bercovitch now contends that Puritan rhetorical strategies imposed on the American imagination an "ideological hegemony that reached to virtually all levels of thought and behavior."[43] Puritanism was the progenitor of "the free-enterprise system," an effective instrument of social control, and a prisonhouse of the mind.[44] Bercovitch thus drains American literature of its subversive energies and flattens American culture to a single dimension. Some of this was implied in *Puritan Origins*, but it was not made explicit until *The American Jeremiad*. Finally, *The American Jeremiad* presents a major reassessment of Perry Miller's classic essay "Errand into the Wilderness"—and, by extension, of Miller's work generally, since, as Bercovitch points out, "Errand into the Wilderness" was Miller's seminal statement concerning the historical significance of "the New England mind."[45] In all these ways *The American Jeremiad* is a cogent and revealing statement of the argument Bercovitch had been developing about American culture generally and American Puritanism in particular.

The jeremiad was a particular type of Puritan sermon that emerged in the 1650s. Miller taught us to see the jeremiad as a wail of lamentation sent up by the second generation, a ritual incantation in which the sons admitted they had forsaken their fathers' covenant and failed their trust, that the burning coal of faith their fathers had carried to the New World had shriveled to a cinder. The example of their fathers' faith had become the sign of their own inadequacy; try as they might, they simply could not draw near to God. As Miller read the jeremiads, they expressed the sons' "deep disquietude": they were "troubled utterances, worried, fearful."[46] But when Bercovitch read the jeremiads he saw the unfolding of possibility, the poise and energy of an out-bound culture. To his ears they spoke not anguish and remorse but a "litany of hope"; he read in them not exclamations of grief but expressions of confidence, not prophecies of ruin but promises of abundance.[47]

Actually, Miller had also seen this side of the jeremiads. He knew that their compendium of sins could, ironically, have a liberating effect, that the huge catalog of transgressions, by the very intensity of anguish it generated, could put paid to the sons' moral indenture, thereby fulfilling their obligation to the fathers and launching them on that "process of Americanization" that Miller found so appalling. Indeed, Miller thought the very essence of the jeremiad lay in this crucial ambivalence, this ironic process of liberation through lamentation.[48]

Bercovitch attacks Miller's interpretation at four points. First, he denies that the jeremiad exhibited any ambivalence at all. For Bercovitch its dominant and pervasive tone is "affirmation and exultation." Second, he insists that the jeremiad infused a prophetic meaning into "America." Third, he contends that the jeremiad originated with the Great Migration rather than the second generation, thereby suggesting that it was an *inherent feature of Puritan rhetoric*, present from the very beginning. Finally, he argues that the jeremiad persisted "throughout the eighteenth- and nineteenth-centuries, in all forms of the literature, including the literature of westward expansion."[49]

But there is a more fundamental difference between Bercovitch and Miller. In 1961 Miller composed a new introduction for his monumental history of "the New England mind." Recalling his "stubborn decision" to write about the Puritans—he was then a young graduate student—Miller wrote, "All around me, in the 1920s, I was being shown by pundits and philosophers whom I respected, that 'Puritanism' was the source of everything that had proved wrong, frustrating, inhibiting, crippling in American culture."[50] Almost single-handedly, Miller transformed seventeenth-century Puritanism from a dull and barren period into one of the most vital and important episodes in the history of American thought, a source of rich insight into human nature and penetrating criticism of American culture.[51]

But now, twenty-five years after Miller's death, the tide has turned, for Sacvan Bercovitch has returned Puritanism to the role Randolph Bourne and the "lyrical left" had assigned it in those halcyon days before the First World War.[52] Puritanism has assumed its earlier guise as one of the "old tyrannies" that threatened to frustrate our desires, quash our personalities and make us conform. Once again Puritanism has become the root cause of everything wrong with American culture. In less than twenty years our interpretation of Puritanism has undergone a complete inversion: from the source of our finest values, it has become the progenitor of our worst afflictions.[53]

III

Perry Miller entered the University of Chicago as a freshman in 1922.[54] Like so many other Americans who came to intellectual maturity during the postwar years, he was deeply affected by the sense of exhaustion and despair that pervaded the West in those years. Feeling "betrayed, adrift, belonging nowhere," he dropped out of college and drifted—to Colorado, to Greenwich Village, to the Belgian Congo.[55] Henry Adams's *Education* had appeared only four years earlier; like T. S. Eliot, Joseph Conrad, and the other fin-de-siècle writers, Adams left a deep impression on this pensive young isolate.[56] The modernist sense of estrangement and existential angst never quite left Perry Miller. As late as 1956 he described himself as "a lone-wolf historian," a "combative dissenter," a solitary brooder for whom "nonconformity was an act of intellectual courage."[57] Miller would have immediately and intuitively understood Thomas Mann's remark, "To be reminded that one is not alone in the world is always unpleasant."[58]

Miller felt deeply alienated from the culture around him—from what he once described as "this expanding, capitalist, exploiting America." He continually criticized its "ruthless individualism," its "profiteering merchants," its "manufacturing and huckstering," its "cloud of patriotic obscurantism."[59] He despaired over "the reports of children burned to death in what newspapers euphemistically call 'tenements,'" "the holocausts on the roads during holiday weekends," "the criminal pollution of the very air we breathe," and "the massive indifference of the populace." He worried about "the republic's appalling power" and, later, about "a war conducted through the mysteries of nuclear physics." Most of all he pondered the seemingly inexorable spread of "mass society" and the precarious status of individual conscience. He agonized over "the methods of Madison Avenue," the "perfection of the assembly line" that threatened to "turn workers into digits in an organized operation," and the "dwindling in the universities of the ideal of the lonely scholar." This last especially appalled him, not only in itself—he thought it "a transformation of immense importance"—but also because it struck him as "a dramatic index to what has been steadily at work in our culture."[60]

It was to confront this "civilization of machines," to find both a perspective and a source of meaning from which he could defy his own culture, that Miller turned to the Puritans. Of course he found just what he was looking for: an earlier America fiercely committed to psychological realism, moral responsibility, and the sanctity of individual conscience. The Puritan universe "had significance, and a man in such a universe, by the very fact of his existence, had what I should like to call a moral responsibility. That was not something he might or might not take upon himself; it was inescapable, inherent. In this universe there was distress, anguish, loss of life, danger, torment, and in it every man had a job to do. But not for what he might get out of it—rather for what the job had to contribute to the pattern of the whole."[61]

Miller made seventeenth-century Puritanism stand as a rebuke to the technocratic managerialism and flabby liberalism of twentieth-century America;[62] he transformed American Puritanism into an alternative vision and a source of strength. It was a harsh doctrine, unpleasant and difficult, but within its forms "the more terrible moments of human life—the ravages of disease, the pains of childbirth, the tomahawk, and the foundering vessel—could be presented to ordinary men as belonging in the scheme of things, as having a reason for being."[63] Though a grim and rigorous creed, Puritanism "did not leave individuals unequipped, with no other resources but themselves, to meet the onslaught of war, of death, of tyrants."[64] Miller could never forgive his follow Americans for abandoning a tradition that had given them such endurance and fortitude—a tradition that, "were it with us today, might enable us to meet our problems head-on with the resolution that so distinguished both the Puritan saint and sailor."[65]

Miller was not a religious man; he thought the attempt to resuscitate religious belief an inadequate response to the looming nihilism of the twentieth century; it was little more than a "regression into the womb of irresponsibility."[66] What he sought instead was a secular substitute for Puritanism—a substitute for its realism, its gothic intensity, its recognition of human weakness and finitude, a substitute for its acceptance of anguish and doubt, a substitute for its determination to confront our isolation and solitude without giving in to despair and without erecting creeds and codes and systems of belief.

Nor did Miller think of history as a priceless legacy from the past, a repository of national wisdom, a place we might come to rest. He did not want to perpetuate the past; he wanted to employ it. History was for him an agonistic discipline. It was that critical dialogue with our ancestors that enables us to refute the claims of the present instead of stuttering, staggering, pulling back, falling into paralysis, indecision, and finally compliance. Michel Foucault once said that the responsibility of the humanities "is not to discover what we are, but to *refuse* what we are, . . . to imagine and to build up who we could be."[67] In Perry Miller's hands the past became an incentive to self-interrogation and an inducement to grow less sentimental about ourselves; and it became one of the means by which we reconceive ourselves, one of the practices whereby we formulate our possibilities. "We do have resources," he insisted, "not so much in ourselves as in our past, in Protestantism and above all in *our* Protestantism. If it is no longer enough merely to be free, but if we must say for *what* we intend to be free, then like the Puritans we shall devote ourselves to formulating anew the ends of existence."[68]

Perry Miller came of age in the 1920s, Sacvan Bercovitch in the 1960s. Where Miller's generation read Eliot, Joyce, and Hemingway, Bercovitch's generation read C. Wright Mills, Herbert Marcuse, and Thomas Pynchon. They were influenced not by the modernist drama of personal anguish and permanent estrangement but by the proliferation of administrative power and the elimination of cultural difference. What impressed the students of the 1960s was the ease with which alienation and resistance were absorbed and contained—"co-opted" was the preferred term—by the one-dimensional world of advertising and entertainment. It seemed as though every visual image, every verbal expression, was being integrated into a single master discourse, a composite and all-encompassing American identity. In *The Crying of Lot 49* Pynchon has his narrator ask, "How had it ever happened here, with the chances once so good for diversity?"[69] How had this polyglot America—this Melvillean collection of "mongrel renegades and castaways and cannibals"—ever been brought to accept such a uniform, narrow, and inappropriate conception of itself? How had this odd assortment of idiosyncratic, contentious, and wayward people been ushered into this kingdom of single-mindedness? This is the quintessentially sixties question. And it is precisely this question that drew young Sacvan Bercovitch to early American history:

> What first attracted me to the study of Puritanism was my astonishment, as a Canadian immigrant, at learning about the prophetic errand of America . . . a country that, despite its arbitrary territorial boundaries—despite its bewildering mixture of race and genealogy—could believe in something called America's mission, and could invest that patent fiction with all the emotional, spiritual, and intellectual appeal of a religious quest. I felt like Sancho Panza in a land of Don Quixotes.[70]

Bercovitch approached American Puritanism not as a source of insight but as a system of deception. He set out not to recover the founding texts of American criticism but to counter the empty glare of Puritan mythology—a mythology that, he was convinced, had left America blinded from birth. It was only a matter of time, then, before he came face-to-face with Perry Miller's very different interpretation of American Puritanism.

Bercovitch begins his revision of Miller not where Miller himself began, not with the Puritans' "Augustinian sense of human finitude," nor with the loss of identity and meaning wrought by their errand into the wilderness, nor with American Puritanism as provocation and necessary resource; he begins, as we have seen, with the underlying rhetorical structures and essential symbolic patterns that shaped the Puritan imagination and with the continuities those fundamental structures and patterns display as they unfold over long, rolling stretches of time.[71] As we have also seen, Bercovitch thinks these underlying structures and patterns (which to his mind are *the* legacy of American Puritanism) have created a hegemonic consensus that, from the seventeenth century through the twentieth, has strangled real understanding and legitimated national ideology. This is "consensus history" with a vengeance; it is "the American consensus," "the American ideology," "the American way" suddenly exposed as "the repressive force of the dominant culture."[72]

Some reviewers have pointed out that this description is highly reminiscent of Louis Hartz.[73] There is indeed a sense in which Ber-

covitch has rewritten Hartz's *Liberal Tradition in America*, transfer-
ring to American Puritanism all the intellectually stultifying traits
Hartz had attributed to American liberalism.[74] Hartz was horrified
by the iron-fisted grip of the Lockean creed; it struck him as "an
absolute and irrational attachment," a "deep and unwritten tyrannical compulsion," the "secret root from which have sprung many of
the most puzzling of American cultural phenomena."[75] He thought
the "compulsive power" of the Lockean consensus had "hamper[ed]
creative action abroad," "inspir[ed] hysteria at home," and inflicted
"death by atrophy" on the liberal tradition—just as Bercovitch
thinks the jeremiad, by shackling the American mind to its own perpetually recurring forms and patterns, has blighted our imagination
and precluded the very possibility of change.[76]

All this notwithstanding, Bercovitch's view of American history
is much darker than Hartz's. In *The Liberal Tradition in America*
Hartz asked, "Can a people 'born equal' ever understand peoples elsewhere that have to become so? Can it even understand itself?" Can
American liberalism ever transcend its own "deep and unwritten tyrannical compulsion"?[77] For Hartz the answer was, Perhaps. He
thought the liberal tradition might muster "the counter resources" it
needed from its commitment to an almost antinomian individualism.
"There is always," Hartz insisted, "a logical impulse within [the liberal consensus] to transcend the very conformitarian spirit it breeds in
a Lockean society."[78] But he thought an even more powerful force—
indeed, "the *most* powerful force working to shatter American absolutism"—lay not in the realm of personality and character but in
international relations, especially in the fact that America would
sooner or later have to confront the revolutionary aspirations of the
Third World.[79] "Throughout the twentieth century," he wrote, there
has been "an impulse to transcend the American perspective, evoked
by the very clash of cultures. . . . America must look to its contact
with other nations to provide that spark of philosophy, that grain of
relative insight that its own history has denied it."[80]

Hartz was not at all convinced that the United States would rise
to this challenge. Nevertheless, at the very end of *The Liberal Tradition in America* he held out "the hope of an inward enrichment of
culture and perspective, a coming of age . . . a new level of consciousness, a transcending of irrational Lockeanism, in which an understanding of self and an understanding of others go hand in hand."
It was, he thought, a hope "worth fighting for."[81]

Bercovitch sees no such redemptive potential in the American future; indeed, he sees no hope at all. American history possesses no
"counter resources," no "powerful forces" working to shatter the

theocratic teleology of seventeenth-century Puritanism; there is only the surrounding authority of the jeremiad, the all-encompassing, monolithic, and hegemonic Myth of America, circumscribing the bounds of imagination and desire, skewing and deforming the entire course of American history.

If this looks like a more determined version of "consensus history" than the one we are used to, more unequivocal and categorical, that is because Bercovitch has combined Louis Hartz with Antonio Gramsci.[82] To Hartz's idea that America was "born free" and may therefore lack the capacity to transcend itself, he has added the Gramscian notion of "cultural hegemony." This is now a consistent feature of Bercovitch's work. In one of his most recent essays, for example, he writes that Hawthorne's literary method "has behind it all the weight of a culture that had used interpretation as a chief mode of hegemony, from the Cambridge Platform and the Half-Way Covenant through the Constitutional debates in the era of Compromise."[83] This Gramscian admixture both flattens and stiffens Bercovitch's view of the past. In his hands American history has become more monolithic and rigidly determined than Hartz ever imagined; it is a history stripped of differences and drained of nuances, a history with little variation and no possibilities.[84] "No doubt there were genuine polarities," Bercovitch admits, "political and intellectual as well as aesthetic, but they were polarities within the same ideological spectrum, the East Egg and West Egg of American literary discourse—antagonisms designed as it were by cultural reflex to direct all forms of conflict toward the needs of the same open-market society."[85]

This is, as Bercovitch says, an "astonishing cultural hegemony."[86] Though he nowhere provides an extended discussion of "hegemony," he does tell us that he borrowed the concept from Gramsci and that he uses it to designate a "historically organic ideology, based on genuine cultural leadership and spontaneous consent, as distinct from ideologies imposed by state coercive power."[87] By "historically organic" Bercovitch means that the roots of this cultural dominance were contained in the rhetorical forms and symbolic structures the Puritans brought to America.[88] As the passage above suggests, its most significant characteristic has been its capacity to absorb differences and co-opt dissent, to contain criticism and domesticate opposition, redirecting both into socially acceptable channels. In Bercovitch's own words, "The American ideology undertakes, above all, as a condition of its nurture, to absorb the spirit of protest for social ends."[89] The literature of protest may *appear* to question the American way; in fact it merely "re-present[s] the strategies of a triumphant middle-class hegemony." Intending to subvert the status quo, it only "attests to the capacities of the dominant culture to co-opt alternative forms." The hegemony of the dominant ideology thus "redefines radicalism itself as an affirmation of cultural values."[90]

Bercovitch employs the notion of hegemony in order to grasp "the culture in its totality"; he wants to reveal "the *Gestalt*, the overall coherence" of American culture, its "basic integrity of design."[91] But this is an impoverished notion of hegemony that blights whatever it touches.[92] Bercovitch does not think of American culture or American texts as pluralistic, many-layered, multivocal conversations; nor he does think of them as overpopulated with a multiplicity of voices, past and present. It does not occur to him that in their hidden spaces and interstices he might find traces of other books, other speakers, other voices.[93] His readings of classic American texts are complex, intricate, well-informed and often insightful; but in those readings the texts are always made to demonstrate the same monotonous and desolate lesson: how a monolithic American culture has absorbed all challenges and repressed every possibility. What is revealed always turns out to be just what anyone familiar with Bercovitch's work will be expecting. For all the brilliance of his exegetical readings, Bercovitch is an antagonistic reader armed with a notion of hegemony that reduces classic works to historical documents, that makes complex texts univocal, single-layered, one-dimensional.

As we have seen, all this was implied in Bercovitch's very first article, "Typology in Puritan New England: The Williams-Cotton Controversy Reassessed" (1967). Few of us saw it then; what now seems explicit and unambiguous was then only implicit and undeveloped.[94] But even in this earliest essay we can catch a glimpse of his tendency to collapse substantive differences onto a bedrock of underlying agreement; here as elsewhere, Bercovitch set out to disarm the critics of American culture by focusing on assumptions they shared with their orthodox opponents—assumptions he believed were more fundamental than the ones on which they differed. Thus he concluded "Typology in Puritan New England" by insisting that the controversy between Williams the heretic and Cotton the orthodox "took place within a culture thoroughly familiar with typology," that it was "not a clash between a typologist and a Puritan but an opposition between two different typological approaches."[95] Both Williams's criticisms of Puritan orthodoxy and the responses of the orthodox themselves arose from and were shaped by an underlying consensus. No matter how powerful and penetrating the criticisms Williams packed into "The Bloody Tenent of Persecution" and "The Bloody Tenent Yet More Bloody," they merely reflected, refined, and extended the very rhetoric they were designed to attack. What appeared to have been a critical conflict, a decisive confrontation over fundamental values, turns out to have been a difference of opinion over minor details. In Bercovitch's hands all differences are "rooted in the rhetoric of American identity," all contradictions are but "variant forms of the same dominant culture," all ideas are "ideas in the service of power."[96]

Though Bercovitch alluded to this in his very first article, he has rendered it far more explicit in his later work, especially in *The American Jeremiad* and, more recently, his work on the American Renaissance. Bercovitch takes the cue for his readings of Emerson, Thoreau, and the other romantics from a comment Loren Baritz once made about Herman Melville. Melville's work, Baritz said, was "so purely American because of the depths of his rejection of America."[97] What makes American romantic literature "culturally representative" for Bercovitch is its inherent subversiveness; it is quintessentially American precisely because it shouts "No-in-thunder" to the dream of "America." American writing is never more American than when it rejects America.[98] The major writers of the American Renaissance may have been "outcasts and isolates, prophets crying in the wilderness," Bercovitch admits, but they were "*American* Prophets . . . simultaneously lamenting a declension and celebrating a national dream; hypersensitive to social failings, and yet offering in their most communitarian, idealistic works a mimesis of cultural beliefs."[99]

Bercovitch uses the term "anti-jeremiad" to refer to the most extravagant examples of disillusionment—Melville's *Confidence Man*, Adams's *Education*, and Twain's *Connecticut Yankee*, for example.[100] And in one of his more dazzling inversions, he claims that these seeming denunciations of America actually bespeak "the optative American mood"; that the antijeremiad is itself "the most striking testimony we have to the power and reach of the jeremiad."[101] The key to understanding this apparent contradiction is Emerson's exclamation, "Ah, my country! In thee is the reasonable hope of mankind not fulfilled!"[102] Emerson's lament expresses what Bercovitch says had by this time become "a cultural reflex, an ingrained habit of mind": the identification of "America" with mankind's age-old hopes for a new beginning, for a universal redemption in time. The danger of such an identification is that if "America" failed, one was left with nothing. "If America failed, then the cosmos itself—the laws of man, nature, and history, the very ground of heroism, insight, and hope—had failed as well."[103] Perhaps the best example is Adams's *Education*, which Bercovitch calls an "entropic inversion of the work of redemption."[104] In that work the "errand into the wilderness" has become an "errand into the abyss."[105] Like Emerson, Melville, and the other anti-Jeremiahs, Adams inflates this specifically American abyss to global import. And with its inflation Adams becomes a universal prophet, reading the fate of all mankind in the descending curve of American history. Thus the antijeremiad emerges as a "denunciation of all ideals, sacred and secular, on the grounds that America is a lie."[106] *Pierre, The Confidence Man, Connecticut Yankee,* and all the other antijeremiads have to be read not as repudiations of the national covenant but as proof of their authors' "refusal to *abandon* the national covenant"; not as expressions of dissent but as "strategies of accommodation."[107] Those classic texts that had always seemed so deeply unsettling and radically subversive turn out to be rhetorically conformist and culturally conservative. Even Melville "could not envision a different set of ideals . . . beyond that which his culture imposed."[108] Instead of challenging American culture, Melville, like every American writer from Roger Williams to Henry Adams, ends up confirming it. In Bercovitch's analysis, even the most antagonistic American literature becomes yet another expression of the American consensus.[109]

Bercovitch wants to know how this literature "functioned" in the American past. What were its "effects" and "implications"? The answer comes: it functioned "as a vehicle of socialization"; it served "to control discontent and harness anarchy itself to the social enterprise."[110] Bercovitch first broached this notion of rhetoric as a means of social control in *The Puritan Origins of the American Self* (1975). But at this stage in his thinking the idea was still new and undeveloped. Midway through the book he simply declared that the Puritans "had devised their rhetoric, after all, as a means of social control."[111] This was the first time he had described Puritanism as a form of "social control," and he said nothing else about it in that book. As Alan Trachtenberg remarked in his review of *Puritan Origins,* the idea was "dropped into the text like a stone without ripples."[112] But it plays a larger role in *The American Jeremiad,* which appeared three years later, and it is even more fully developed in his recent work.[113]

In *The American Jeremiad* Bercovitch claims that the Puritans deployed the covenant of grace as a means of social control; but now he works this idea through the entire course of American history. In the crisis of the American Revolution, for example, he argues that the "libertarian spirit that terrified moderate and propertied democrats everywhere" was eventually contained by rhetorical means, by using the jeremiad to define the Revolution:

As the Whig Jeremiahs explained it, independence was not the spoils of violence, but the harvest of Puritanism. It was not some sudden turbulent challenge to the system, but the consummation of a process that began aboard the *Mayflower* and *Arbella* and matured in the struggles of 1776. . . . [The Whigs] intensified the Puritan emphasis both on process and on control. In the ritual of revolution they instituted, radicalism itself was socialized into an affirmation of order.[114]

In the early national period a fragmented social order was "bound and tamed" by redefining the jeremiad in purely secular terms: "The rhetoric of the jeremiad permitted a transference of focus over time from the ideal spiritual life (horological, absolute time) to a real secular one (chronometrical, relative time). Through this transference, Puritan ideology, insofar as it was implicit in its tropes and figures, persisted as a controlling influence on American culture."[115]

Thus reformulated, the jeremiad "gave contract the sanctity of covenant, free enterprise the halo of grace, progress the assurance of the chiliad, and nationalism the grandeur of typology."[116] We have already seen how American romantic writers contributed to this renewal of cultural cohesiveness; the more explicitly political literature of the period worked to the same end, identifying industrialization, westward expansion, even feminism and the cult of domesticity, with the Puritan sense of American mission, thereby absorbing dissent and welding together what was in fact a fractious and quarrelsome people.[117]

Some commentators have recently suggested that Bercovitch has complicated his vision, that he now sees a more pluralistic and multifocal "America." His "Afterword" to *Ideology and Classic American Literature* (1986) is usually cited as evidence. Most of the contributors to that volume approached "America" as a field of fierce contestation rather than a monolithic consensus. In his "Afterword" Bercovitch acknowledged this development, going so far as to concede that many of the classic American texts do, in fact, carry negative as well as ideological charges, that while they seem to confirm the dominant ideology they also criticize it and in some cases subvert it. Bercovitch here wrote for the first time of "ideologies in conflict" and of "the multivalence of the symbol of 'America.'" Indeed, "America" now seemed less an overarching synthesis than a rhetorical battlefield, "a symbol that has been made to stand for alternative and sometimes mutually antagonistic outlooks." Moreover, he has admitted that whatever coherence the "American ideology" once possessed, it now seemed to be breaking down; the "American consensus" was being replaced by a variegated and internally fragmented "dis-sensus."[118]

But having made these concessions, he quickly returned to his earlier preoccupation with "the dominant culture's" capacity "to conceal, exclude, and repress." Once again he insisted that "to varying degrees, the strategy of fusion through fragmentation informs the entire course of American literary criticism." After acknowledging that some classic American literature may indeed contain utopian criticism of the status quo, Bercovitch nevertheless insisted that his readers "consider a different prospect": "I refer to the historical fact that characteristically, as a matter of course, the dominant culture adopts utopia for its own purposes. It does not simply endorse the trans-historical ideals of harmony and regeneration; it absorbs and redefines these in ways that support the social system. . . . It ritualizes the egalitarian energies of the liminal process in such a way as to control discontent and harness anarchy itself to the social enter-prise."[119] Thus "the very act of identifying malfunction becomes an appeal for cohesion." Desire is harnessed to the treadmill of ideological reproduction, the utopian temptation is strategically contained, and dissent is transformed into "a vehicle of socialization." As Berco-vitch says, "The method is as old as ideology itself."[120]

IV

I believe that we are lost in America,
but I believe that we shall be found.
—Thomas Wolfe

Bercovitch reminds us—if we ever needed reminding—of the crushing weight of the American consensus, of its capacity to choke every hope and blast every wish. But if he reveals the constrictions and limitations of American culture, its morally impoverished mythology and its cast-iron borders, he does nothing to reveal its openings and possibilities. His is a history of domination rather than freedom, a history of acquiescence and submission rather than opposition and resistance. He sees nothing worth saving in the American past. For him it is a blind and barren history, formed through speechless, un-mindful process, a history possessing no more redemptive power than a vacant lot heaped with rubbish. As Lincoln said of the Kansas-Nebraska Act, "It hath no relish of salvation in it."[121] For Bercovitch, there is nothing in the American past to respect or admire: no instances of understanding or compassion to invoke; no examplars of character or temperament to emulate. There is only the tyrannical rhetoric of the jeremiad, wielding its despotic authority over the en-

tire course of American history, straddling it like some blind begetter.
It is a history that exposes our limitations but does nothing to help
us transcend them; it reveals our depleted imagination but does nothing to nourish our potential; it exposes our lack of vision but does
not remind us of how our culture has traditionally conceived of human worth and moral excellence.

Just as Bercovitch sees no saving antagonisms in the American
past—just as his history of America is a history of a monolith—so
he sees nothing of intrinsic value or innate goodness in American
Puritanism. Puritan books seem to him little more than empty ciphers, incapable of exposing moral illusions or providing moral guidance. They suggest to him neither the joyous affirmation that Andrew Delbanco, Robert Daly, Charles Cohen, and others have found
in them, nor the baffled sorrow that Patricia Caldwell encountered
in them, nor the conscience of American liberalism that John P. Diggins saw in them, nor the psychological depth and redemptive potential that Perry Miller knew they contained.[122] What Bercovitch sees
in Puritan books is the cultural hegemony of American capitalism;
what he does not see is their capacity to instruct, their power "to
open the heart and educate the soul."[123]

It is just here that Bercovitch's understanding of American Puritanism swerves so sharply away from Perry Miller's. For Miller saw
something of deep and abiding value in the Puritan tradition: an
acceptance of melancholy and sadness as ways of seeing, almost as
signs of grace. Puritanism gave voice to what Miller knew, with all
the intensity of his own melancholic mind, to be the very truth of
lived experience; Puritanism "dramatized the needs of the soul exactly as does some great poem or work of art."[124] What Bercovitch
sees in American Puritanism is not the redemptive power of remorse
and regret but the spiritual origins of Pax Americana. The Puritan
tradition is no longer a source of strength, as it was for Miller, but
a crippling limitation; it suggests not the hard, fine press of winter-
bred minds but the tyranny of iron-brained theocrats; it is not a
power that might guide us through the coming darkness but a nightmare from which we will never awaken. It is a positive torment, an
oppressive and utterly depraved father who lies upon us full length
and threatens to crush our life from us.[125]

Bercovitch makes no attempt to grasp the moral content of Puritan
books.[126] Eager to demonstrate the persistence of Puritan rhetorical
forms through the entire course of American history, he does not ask
what we might learn from Thomas Hooker's determination "to look
sin in the face, and discern it to the full," or from Thomas Shepard's
attempt to pass through this life without "sensible tokens of mercy

or grace." He sees nothing of political worth in Winthrop's "Modell of Christian Charity," or anything of moral value in John Cotton's belief that each one of us must find "a calling tending to publique good," or anything true or important in Cotton's warning to Roger Williams that self-reliant solitude will bring us only "brokenness and emptiness."

Why should we tell our students to read the New England Puritans if we ourselves suspect that they had no moral vision worth passing on, if we think their sermons and books and poems have nothing of value to impart? Why should we teach them about American Puritanism if we think the Puritan tradition has no redemptive power, if "it hath no relish of salvation in it"? Flannery O'Connor once said, about the idea that God may be an impersonal force, swirling through the universe like some gaseous vapor: "If God is not a person, then to Hell with Him." Just so: if the God-haunted Puritans of colonial New England have nothing to teach us about how we should live or what we should value, then to hell with them.

But they have a great deal to tell us. The South African poet Breyten Breytenbach wrote, "You do take your language with you wherever you go—but it is rather like carrying the bones of your ancestors with you in a bag: they are white with silence, they do not talk back."[127] It is the historian's job to make those bleached bones talk back. It is her distinctive and defining responsibility to make ancient texts speak to the present—speak to *us,* to *our* problems, in *our* language. She must transform the dead into conversational partners, asking again and again how the record of their relentless pressing can help us see ourselves as we need to see ourselves, "all pretense shattered, stripped of our moral makeup, naked."[128] For only by seeing ourselves refracted through the prism of our ancestors' books can we hope to grow less sentimental about ourselves. And only thus can we learn how to think against ourselves, how to "turn our impoverishing certitudes into humanizing doubts."[129]

Sacvan Bercovitch is right: Puritan books cannot teach us how to free ourselves from our past. But they can teach us something about goodness and human worth—and thereby give us a sense of history that nourishes our possibilities. And they can teach us something even more important: how to accept our permanent vulnerability in the world—our exposure to hard-heartedness and betrayal, to suddenly awakened fears and abrupt catastrophes, to personal humiliation and permanent loss.[130] Finally, as Perry Miller knew, the Puritans can show us how to make those shrewd compromises by which we might come to accept the indifferent heart of the world with at least a semblance of grace.

CHAPTER THREE

Doubts and Dispossessions
Feminist History in the 1990s

> What one wants, I thought—and why does not some brilliant student at Newnham or Girton supply it?—is a mass of information: at what age did she marry; how many children had she as a rule; what was her house like; had she a room to herself; did she do the cooking; would she be likely to have a servant? All these facts lie somewhere, presumably, in parish registers and account books; the life of the average Elizabethan woman must be scattered about somewhere, could one collect it and make a book of it. It would be ambitious beyond my daring, I thought, looking about the shelves for books that were not there, to suggest to the students of those famous colleges that they should rewrite history, though I own that it often seems a little queer as it is, unreal, lop-sided; but why should they not add a supplement to history? calling it, of course, by some inconspicuous name so that women might figure there without impropriety?
> —Virginia Woolf, *A Room of One's Own*

> Instead of a singular "women's" history, we now have fixed categories of working-class or African-American or Islamic women, . . . of bourgeois women, peasant women, lesbian women, Jewish lesbian women, socialist women, Nazi women—the list goes on and on.
> —Joan Scott, *Feminism and History*

> No longer the identification of our faint individuality with the solid identities of the past, but our "unrealization" through the excessive choice of identities.
> —Michel Foucault, "Nietzsche, Genealogy, History"

I

By the end of the 1980s even conservative historians had come to realize that postmodernism is not, after all, a slippery slope to nothingness. What they had once regarded as a cultural menace frightening enough to stop the blood had been thoroughly domesticated.[1] In fact, what only a few years earlier had looked like another loathsome attempt to kick away our epistemological crutches had—at least in the minds of some historians—become our best chance to renew American historical writing. Even the archalarmist Gertrude Himmelfarb seemed to have mellowed: "Nietzsche's muse turns out to be unexpectedly modest, sensible, even domesticated—one that most historians may find more congenial than Oakeshott's."[2]

To claim that we cannot have objective knowledge about the past is not, as it turns out, to claim that the past has nothing to teach us. Or again, to say that the meaning of a text will always remain indeterminate is not to say that texts have no meaning at all. Though we can never know the past "as it really happened," though it will never become the luminous center of truth and moral certainty that our hearts desire, it nevertheless continues to open its stores of wisdom and practical knowledge, even under the sign of postmodernism. After all, as the literary historian George Steiner once put it, "What would be our deficit of spirit at the close of the day without these well-springs of recuperation and self-surpassing?"[3]

The discovery of formerly marginalized works by previously unknown writers has wonderfully enriched American literary history. But for the most part we keep coming back to the same old classics—the same "well-springs of recuperation and self-surpassing." And with good reason. For the fact that a text has achieved canonical status means that over the years it has demonstrated a certain ability to help us see ourselves as we need to see ourselves: Adrift on a river too dark to photograph, unable to touch bottom, bestraddled by spiritual yearning and fleshly desire and sins that will follow us to the grave. We read seventeenth-century sermons, or eighteenth-century political tracts, or nineteenth-century novels, because we like what they do for us—and because we like what *we* can do *with them*.[4]

The most interesting historians expand the limits of our imaginations by incessantly recontextualizing thoughts and ideas from the past: overreading as a matter of policy, playing one text against another, taking wing on Emerson's assurance that "relations reach everywhere."[5] If historians differ from other people in the humanities, it is because they think the best way to multiply our possibilities is to cobble together a new foundation of predecessors for ourselves—a new genealogy of examplars, a new inheritance, a new American procession. They think the best way to catch a fresh glimpse of ourselves is by rearranging earlier thinkers into new historical sequences—by creating a new tradition in which to place ourselves. This constant reworking of tradition is said to be one of the characteristic marks of the postmodern;[6] in fact, it is simply another way of describing what many historians have been doing all along.

But not every inheritance confers an advantage: some turn out to be vacant and fallow, others are choked with weeds, still others are filled with poisonous plants. That is why, sooner or later, most of us find ourselves wondering if we have adopted the wrong set of ancestors and so acquired the wrong inheritance, if perhaps we have grasped the wrong possibilities and so become the wrong kind of person—knowing all the while, of course, that we lack any workable criteria of "wrongness."[7] There is nothing new about this dilemma, of course; Immanuel Kant grasped the nub of it nearly two hundred years ago: "The way I conceive the historical process, apprehended as a process of transition from past to present, the form which I impose upon my perceptions of it, these provide the orientation by which I move into a future with greater hope, or with despair."[8]

If the past seems always under construction, that is because each generation has to decide for itself what it wants to remember and what it wants forget—and *who* it will remember. For the kinds of persons we become is largely a function of the kinds of persons we adopt as predecessors, and the beliefs and values and ways of thinking they embody. Moreover, these intellectual predecessors—arranged in historical sequence so they constitute a tradition of thought—impose certain obligations on us. Like most things, they invariably come to mean both more and less than we had initially supposed—sometimes more than we are willing or able to bear.

No historian has thought about these problems more deeply or carefully than Elaine Showalter, perhaps the best known and most influential feminist historian in the United States.[9] For more than twenty years Showalter has been trying to define a feminist literary tradition. In her earliest work—beginning with *A Literature of Their Own* (1977)—she saw this as a strictly empirical project: she was simply recovering a lost tradition of women's writing. Showalter thought that by reconstructing "the continuities in women's writing"—"the minor novelists, who were the links in the chain that bound one generation to the next"—she could help contemporary women writers understand themselves in historical perspective.[10] But she eventually came to realize that to define yourself historically you have to find your own predecessors and arrange them in chronological order, so you can see your own work as the latest in a long historical sequence, with all the evaluative standards and moral obligations inherent in that particular tradition. Hence the title of her most recent and most interesting book, *Sister's Choice: Tradition and Change in American Women's Writing* (1991). The implications—implications she recognized and brought herself to accept only reluctantly and with extreme ambivalence—are twofold: first, "the historian is not a truthteller but a storyteller"; second, femininist historians therefore "will have to give up the dream of a common language," that is, the dream of a single feminist literary tradition.[11]

It was Showalter's long agonistic reading of postmodern theory that brought her to this double renunciation. No historian has embraced postmodernism with a deeper ambivalence than Elaine Showalter. In the end she was forced to accept much of what she initially resisted, but not without a commingled sense of power and dispossession, an acknowledgment of new opportunities coiled around a recognition of permanent loss.[12] Like the historians discussed in part 2, Showalter writes histories that are at the same time theoretically sophisticated and strikingly traditional—which is precisely what makes her work so interesting and instructive. The pages that follow describe her intellectual journey from the confident empiricism of *A Literature of Their Own,* through her wanderings in the theoretical wilderness during the 1980s, to the self-conscisouly provisional arrangment of predecessors she describes in *Sister's Choice.*

II

In *The Subjection of Women* (1869) John Stuart Mill wrote that "if women lived in a different country from men, and had never read any of their writings, they would have a literature of their own."[13] In *A Literature of Their Own* Showalter explained that nineteenth-century British women writers had in fact lived in a different country from men—a distinct female subculture, grounded in "women's experience" and unified by "elaborate rituals and lore, by external codes of fashion and etiquette, and by intense feelings of female solidarity."[14] More important, she argued that these writers had created not only a *literature* of their own but a literary *tradition* of their own.[15] And she noted that that tradition had evolved through three distinct stages. In an early "feminine" phase, beginning about 1800, female writers merely imitated the literary forms and moral values of the dominant (male) culture. In a second "feminist" phase, beginning with the death of George Eliot in 1880, feminist writers not only created forms and values of their own but went on to denounce the dominant culture and to demand substantive social and political changes-all in the name of "wronged womanhood." (As Showalter describes it, this was nothing less than "an all-out war of the sexes" in which British women writers "advocated the sexual separatism of

Amazon utopias and suffragette sisterhoods.") And in a third, "female" phase, beginning in the first decade of the twentieth century and culminating with Virginia Woolf's novels of the 1930s and 1940s,[16] women writers increasingly turned inward, preoccupied with self-exploration and self-definition. During the interwar years these writers—Woolf in particular—created what Showalter calls "the female aesthetic." For Woolf and others "female sensibility took on a sacred quality, and its exercise became a holy, exhausting and ultimately self-destructive rite."[17] Showalter thinks this female aesthetic was "as deadly as it was disembodied, for the ultimate room of one's own is the grave."[18] In the final pages of *A Literature of Their Own* Showalter tentatively outlined a fourth phase, beginning in the 1960s and continuing through the present, in which British women writers began drawing on all three of the earlier phases simultaneously, combining "feminine realism, feminist protest, and female self-analysis . . . in the context of twentieth-century social and political concern."[19]

A Literature of Their Own was an immensely important and powerfully influential book, not only because it seemed to have recovered and described an entire tradition of women's writing but also because, with Patricia Meyer Spacks's *The Female Imagination* (1975) and Ellen Moers's *Literary Women* (1976), it launched the much more ambitious project of "gynocriticism," which shifted the focus of feminist criticism from woman as reader to woman as writer, that is to say, away from feminist readings of canonical (mostly male texts) to the study of texts written by women.[20] After the histories by Spacks, Moers, and Showalter, "feminist literary criticism" came to mean "the study of women's writing and female creativity."[21] Showalter insisted that feminist critics and historians must recover and explain the work of women writers who have been "muted" or "marginalized" by traditional literary history.[22] Thus *A Literature of Their Own* did for English women writers what E. P. Thompson had recently done for English working people—it rescued them from "the enormous condescension of posterity." As Showalter explained in her opening chapter, "I have looked beyond the famous novelists who have been found worthy, to the lives and works of many women who have long been excluded from literary history. I have tried to discover how they felt about themselves and their books, what choices and sacrifices they made, and how their relationship to their profession and their tradition evolved."[23] Showalter wanted to recover the work of England's forgotten women writers, but she also wanted to demonstrate that together they had created something larger and more inspiring than any one of them could possibly have imagined on her own—a women's literary *tradition*, "the lost continent of the female tradition [rising] like Atlantis from the sea of English literature."[24]

Showalter has consistently—from *A Literature of Their Own* in 1977 to *Sister's Choice* in 1991—declared her commitment to what she calls "oppositional history." So on the surface, at least, there is a certain continuity to her writing. But beneath the surface, everything has changed. It has changed because during the late 1970s and throughout the 1980s she literally immersed herself in critical theory. What makes her writing during this period so interesting is that between each of her major historical works she published two or three critical essays in which she rethought the assumptions underlying her previous book. In other words, she has been continually rethinking the very tradition in which she has been writing.

Beginning in the late 1970s, when she started reading theory seriously, Showalter gradually abandoned the principal assumptions that had previously guided her writing. Four of these are particularly important: first, her empiricist conviction that in writing *A Literature of Their Own* she had recovered a literary tradition that had actually existed; second, her contextualist conviction that that tradition had been grounded in, and grown out of, "the daily lives, the physical experiences, the personal strategies and conflicts of ordinary women"; third, her essentialist belief that there exists "a unifying voice in women's literature"; and finally, her rather Whiggish belief that the tradition of British women writers she had described was a progressive tradition that had evolved through a series of "phases" in each of which women writers became more fully present to themselves.[25] *A Literature of Their Own* was "a literary history of female mastery and growth," a stage in "the wider evolution of women's self-awareness"—what Hayden White would call a "romance."[26]

By the time Showalter wrote *Sister's Choice*, fourteen years after *A Literature of Their Own*, she had abandoned every one of these assumptions—not with some easy postmodern affirmation of a world without meaning, but with a sense of profound loss:

> Studying American women's writing has not been a comforting return to my native idiom or an easy reclamation of a literature of my own. In recent years, while new critical developments have unsettled feminist confidence in the meaning of "women," the consensus on the "Americanness" of American literature and the validity of literary history has also collapsed. . . . As William Spengemann states the case, "We have American things, and we have literary things, but we have nothing that can be called uniquely or characteristically American."[27]

The literary historian whose first major work had described how British women writers had created "a literature of their own" returned to American women's literature at the very moment when "American women's writing ceases to be 'a literature of their own.'"[28]

III

The critical event that set all this questioning in motion was Showalter's encounter with poststructuralism in the summer of 1978, right after she had finished *A Literature of Their Own.* Though poststructuralism had entered Anglo-American critical discourse ten years earlier, Showalter seems to have been unaware of it at the time. If she was reading theory in the mid-1970s, she did not let on, for *A Literature of Their Own* is the most conventional of literary histories.

She published her first theoretical paper—"Toward a Feminist Poetics"—in 1978. She later explained that she wrote the essay because feminist historiography was being attacked by male critics for "its apparent lack of theoretical coherence." Showalter worried that without an up-to-date theoretical apparatus feminist criticism would be relegated "to the symbolic ghettos of the special issue or the back of the book for their essays."[29] Even so, she could find nothing useful or interesting in contemporary theory. It all seemed so male; indeed, it was "as manly and aggressive as nuclear physics—not intuitive, expressive, and feminine, but strenuous, rigorous, impersonal, and virile."[30]

Some feminist historians were arguing that contemporary theory was "an intellectual instrument of patriarchy, a tyrannical methodolatry" that reflected "male perceptions, experiences, and options."[31] Though she did not explicitly endorse those charges, she did repudiate historians who tried to adapt contemporary theory to feminist ends—"thrifty feminine making-do," she called it. It was as if feminist historians had started walking around "in men's ill-fitting hand-me-downs," as if feminist criticism had been reduced to "the Annie Hall of English studies."[32] Showalter worried that if feminists simply adopted "male theory" they would be "coopted by academia."[33] Just as British women writers had developed "a literature of their own," so feminist critics and historians would have to "break away from dependency on male models" and forge "a criticism of our own."

Showalter's call for "a feminist poetics" had a strong, assertive ring, but the critical model she described was decidedly reactive. Indeed, it was based on the very assumptions that contemporary theory was even then moving away from. Her poetics was *empirical* in its conviction that the lost history of women's writing could be "rediscovered," *contextualist* in its determination to ground that newly rediscovered history in "the newly visible world of female culture," *Whiggish* in its commitment to describing the "patterns and phases in the evolution of a female tradition," and *essentialist* in its conviction that literary history should express "women's experience," that is, in its conviction that being biologically female is prior to and constitutive of any and all other experiences a woman may have:

> While scientific [structuralist and poststructuralist] criticism struggles to purge itself of the subjective, feminist criticism is willing to assert (in the title of a recent anthology) *The Authority of Experience.* The experience of women can easily disappear, become mute, invalid, and invisible, lost in the diagrams of the structuralist or the class conflict of the Marxists. . . . We must seek the repressed messages of women in history, in anthropology, in psychology, and in ourselves, before we can locate the feminine not-said. . . . The academic demand for theory can only be heard as a threat to the feminist need for authenticity.[34]

At this point in her thinking Showalter was simply too suspicious of theory to find anything useful in it; like some other feminist historians, she tended to dismiss it as "patriarchal methodolatry."[35] She worried that it would overpower the emerging feminist historiography, probing its fault lines, fingering its fissures, mocking its assumptions, and in the end dismissing it as theoretically unsophisticated. Rather than drawing on contemporary theory or bending it to their own ends, she thought feminist historians and critics should formulate an alternative to it—a truly *feminist* criticism.

But the most interesting and perhaps the most revealing thing about "Toward a Feminist Poetics" was a remark Showalter attached to the very end. It went virtually unnoticed at the time, though it contradicted everything she had written in the essay itself. Nevertheless, it pointed in precisely the direction her later thoughts would take her. The fact is, she wrote, feminist critics will never have a truly autonomous criticism of their own, for the simple reason that feminist historians and critics will always have to work in two critical traditions at once: the dominant male tradition and the newly emerging feminist tradition. In other words, feminists will always be writing from within a "divided consciousness."[36] This would prove to be an enormously fruitful idea, but at this point Showalter did not stop to develop it. Indeed, it is not at all clear that she understood the implications of what she had written. Like the pebble dropped in Trochtenberg's pond, it sank with barely a ripple.

She mentioned this idea again three years later, in a 1981 essay titled "Feminist Criticism in the Wilderness." At this point Showalter still believed that "women's writing has its own unique character."[37] Though she rejected the notion of a "biologically grounded" women's history, she continued to insist that feminist literary history should explain "women's experience," that is, "how *womanhood itself* has shaped women's creative expression."[38] And she still assumed that historical texts can be made to reveal their true meaning to a thoughtful and sensitive historian.[39] This is all depressingly familiar; what is new and important is Showalter's admission—in stark contrast to her earlier call for a distinctive and autonomous feminist critical and historical practice—that any feminist poetics or feminist historiography will necessarily be implicated in the male tradition it seeks to challenge.[40] Feminist historians are not "*inside* or *outside* the male tradition; they are inside two traditions simultaneously," which is why feminist historiography will always be "a double-voiced discourse."[41] And maybe *triple*-voiced. After all, "There are muted groups other than women; a dominant structure may determine many muted structures. A black American woman poet, for example, would have her literary identity formed by the dominant (white male) tradition, by a muted women's culture, and by a muted black culture."[42]

And if triple-voiced, why not quadruple-voiced? After all, the literary identity of a particular American poet may have been formed by a jostling and commingling of *several* cultural traditions—perhaps "the dominant (white male) tradition," a "muted women's culture," "a muted black culture," and, say, the overlapping cultures of El Salvador and East Los Angeles that Reuben Martinez described in *The Other Side*. We are increasingly coming to think of identity as something formed in the context of a *plurality* of overlapping cultural *fragments*. And in fact this is exactly the understanding Showalter is moving toward, though it will not be apparent until *Sister's Choice* appears in 1991. By then she will have come to see the writing of history as a "gathering up of all the fragments so that nothing be lost."[43] But to write history like that "one must first become accustomed to living and working with fragments"—which, for Showalter, meant giving up most of the interpretive categories she had used in her earlier writing: "women's lives," "women's experiance," "women's literature," and even that most basic of all categories, "women."[44] She would eventually do just that; but in 1981, when she wrote "Feminist Criticism in the Wilderness," that sort of understanding was still ten years down the road.

She took another step in that direction four years later, in "The

Feminist Critical Revolution" (1985).[45] Here for the first time Showalter questioned the notion of a female aesthetic. That idea had first emerged in the late 1960s, shortly after the Black Arts movement to promote the Black Aesthetic. The notion of a distinctive black or female aesthetic implied not only a distinctive black or female creative style, but also a distinctive psychology, a distinctive language, a distinctive literature, and so on. For most of the 1970s feminist scholars tended to identify the Female Aesthetic with lesbian art and literature, but in the mid-1980s they turned their attention to mother-daughter relationships. Just how far Showalter had moved can be seen not only in the ironic tone with which she described the rise of the Female Aesthetic but, more important, in the remarkable diversity and heterodoxy of the essays she brought together for her anthology *The New Feminist Criticism*. Four years later, in "A Criticism of Our Own" (1989), Showalter described the "striking parallels between" the Black Aesthetic and the Female Aesthetic, criticized both of them for their "blatant theoretical weaknesses," and warned that in its preoccupation with trying to formulate a separatist female aesthetic, feminist criticism and historiography risked "permanent ghettoization."[46]

But there was a limit to how far Showalter could move in this direction. For gathered on her right were a number of conservative women writers and historians who rejected not only the idea of a female aesthetic but gender itself. In *Toward a Recognition of Androgyny* (1973), for example, Carolyn Heilbrun had argued that "our future salvation lies in a movement away from sexual polarization and the prison of gender."[47] For these women gender, like race and class, was precisely what a true literary imagination managed to escape. Joyce Carol Oates was the most articulate and well-known critic of gender theory. In a widely discussed article published in 1986, she insisted that "subject-matter is culture-determined, not gender-determined. And the imagination, itself genderless, allows us all things."[48] Showalter may have been prepared to drop the Female Aesthetic, but gender itself? Not in 1989. In "A Criticism of Our Own" and again in "The Rise of Gender" (also 1989) Showalter reiterated her conviction that gender was fundamental, that "all writing, not just writing by women, is gendered. . . . The imagination cannot escape from the unconscious structures and strictures of gender identity."[49] In 1989 Showalter was still convinced that the future of feminist literary history lay in "analysis of the construction and representation of gender within literary discourse."[50]

But not for long. By the time she published "Feminism and Literature," just a year later, she had already started moving away from that conviction. She still insisted that "women writers are not free to renounce or transcend their gender entirely."[51] But the whole burden and thrust of "Feminism and Literature" lies in Showalter's claim that women's writing cannot be grounded in a common female experience—a separate sphere, a generic "women's culture." Rather, it grows out of, and participates in, a vast array of jostling and often incoherent cultural influences. Given this diversity, feminist historians should try to construct "a female literary tradition that does not depend on [common female] experience, that recognizes differences between women, and that makes use of contemporary methods of literary interpretation. . . . The idea of a common women's culture has to be re-examined."[52]

Now, for the first time, she argued that "the future of feminist criticism" lies not in the reconstruction of a distinctive female culture, nor in the recovery of a female aesthetic, nor even in a rejuvenated form of gender theory, but rather "in the interpenetration of different national traditions and *the multiplication of all differences.*"[53] The last five words are especially significant: not the discovery of a *common female experience,* but the multiplication of different female experiences. "Feminism and Literature" represents the most significant development in Showalter's thinking since she published "Toward a Feminist Poetics" in 1978. All her earlier hopes have collapsed, most obviously and significantly her hope that by recovering a generic "women's experience," and the female culture or aesthetic it was thought to have produced, feminist historians would finally arrive at the holy grail of feminist historiography: a universal, transhistorical female subjectivity—what the poet Adrienne Rich once called "the dream of a common language." But Showalter can now see, as she herself admits, that "the dream of a common language has always been a utopian fantasy."[54] To be sure, "Feminism and Literature" contains vestiges of that dream (she still uses phrases like "the wordless sensual world of their mothers," for example), but they appear with decreasing frequency. More important, they no longer play a significant role in her thinking; they are simply traces of an earlier form of thought that she has now abandoned.[55] What strikes the reader of "Feminism and Literature" most forcefully is not these residual remnants but Showalter's growing awareness of epistemological uncertainty. There is an undercurrent of loss in "Feminism and Literature," a growing recognition that feminist historiography will have to give up much that it had set out to recover. But there is also a willingness to accept these losses without erecting new creeds or codes or systems of belief. "Feminism and Literature" represents a decisive turning point in Showalter's thinking, a change of mind that altered the moral landscape of all her subsequent work.

This became strikingly clear just a year later in *Sister's Choice: Tradition and Change in American Women's Writing* (1991). Showalter begins *Sister's Choice* by describing the African American literary critic Houston Baker's intellectual odyssey. In the late 1960s Baker was teaching British Victorian literature at Yale. Awakened from his Arnoldian slumbers by the Black Arts movement, Baker abandoned the Victorians and turned homeward, as it were, taking up the blues, the Black Aesthetic, African American literature, and most recently, the poetics of African American women's writing. Showalter was also teaching British Victorian literature in the late 1960s. And like Baker, she too turned homeward, in her case to American women's writing. But Showalter was and is far more theoretically sophisticated than Baker and therefore more intensely aware that the conceptual foundations of American literary history were already trembling beneath their feet. While Baker was staging his own intellectual homecoming, Showalter was forcing herself to accept the fact that she could never go home again: "Studying American women's writing has not been a comforting return to my native idiom or an easy reclamation of a literature of my own. In recent years, while new critical developments have unsettled feminist confidence in the meaning of 'women,' the consensus on the 'Americanness' of American literature and the validity of literary history has also collapsed."[56] Moreover, "in the wake of poststructuralism" even the authority of historical narrative had collapsed; indeed, "to many feminist critics it is an embarrassing remnant of pre-postmodernist humanism."[57] And not only to feminist critics; Showalter cites, among others, the admission by literary historian Emory Elliott, shortly after he finished editing *The Columbia Literary History of the United States,* that "we are not so sure we know what American literature is, or what history is, or whether we have the authority to explain either."[58]

I V

What kind of history can one possibly write after acknowledging such crippling doubts and dispossessions? In other words, what would history written under the sign of postmodernity look like? The answer comes in *Sister's Choice:* it looks remarkably traditional. This is history whose primary purpose is no longer to reconstruct the social, cultural, or linguistic contexts in which women writers supposedly wrote, or to describe their intentions, or to expose their "ideological complicities." *Sister's Choice* tells us absolutely nothing about any of these things, for the simple reason that by 1991 Showalter no longer thought it possible to do so. What she did think possible, what she now thought of as feminist history's primary responsibility, was simply to make sure that the best of women's writing does not fall victim to the revenge of time. Historical writing was first and foremost "the art of gathering up all the fragments so that nothing be lost."[59] This is a deeply conservative notion of the historian's responsibility, one that might have pleased Matthew Arnold—the Matthew Arnold who insisted that literary historians should set themselves to discovering and preserving "the best that is known and thought." Like Arnold, Showalter thinks literary historians should spend their time rereading the great works, "reinhabiting them," helping them speak to a new audience in a new age.

Second, history written under the condition of postmodernity necessarily becomes a "piecing together of salvaged fragments to create a new pattern."[60] "Fragments" because Showalter had come to realize that historians are necessarily condemned to working with pieces and slivers of a world that has died. By 1991 Showalter no longer believed that she or anyone else could reconstruct that world. What she did believe, what she was now prepared to insist on, was that feminist historians must "create a new pattern" for the fragments they have collected, a pattern of their own devising. For we simply have no way of determining the pattern of influences that actually led from one major literary work to another.[61] In *A Literature of Their Own* Showalter had described a single coherent and continuous tradition of British women writers that began with Charlotte Brontë and ended with Doris Lessing. But she herself was the first to admit that none of these writers actually thought of themselves as working within that tradition. Indeed, each of them had created her *own* tradition, had found her *own* predecessors—had reread, reinhabited, and redefined them, had lined them up so they constituted her *own* historical sequence or literary tradition. What these writers shared, in fact, more than any other single characteristic, was precisely this act of assembling a foundation of predecessors. Moreover, Showalter now came to see that this is exactly what she herself had done, first in *A Literature of Their Own* and again in *Sister's Choice*—though only in the latter book was she able to acknowledge the fact. Historical traditions are invented by what she now called "back-formation."[62]

But Showalter is under no illusions about this; she knows perfectly well that defining an inheritance may turn out to be more difficult— even harrowing—than it first appears. Stanley Cavell, for example, describes his book *In Quest of the Ordinary* (1988) as "a kind of progress report" on his twenty-year struggle "to inherit Emerson."[63] Toward the end of this intellectual autobiography he asks "why it took me so long to get my bearings in Emerson." "Why did it take me from the time I first remember knowing of Emerson's yoking of day and night and of my sense of implication in his words, until just over a year ago, some two decades later, to begin to look actively at his work, to demand explicitly my inheritance of him?"[64]

Feminist historians have wonderfully enlarged our understanding of American history, especially American literary history. But Showalter's intellectual journey over the past twenty years suggests that perhaps feminist history's most important contribution lies not in rediscovering previously marginalized writers but in demonstrating once again that the best hope for renewing American historical writing resides in our own doubts and dispossessions—what John Dewey used to call our "intellectual disrobings."

V

Joan Scott is one of the most influential and theoretically sophisticated historians in the country. Over the past twenty years she has played a defining role in no fewer than three different historiographical revolutions. Her first book, *The Glassworkers of Carmaux* (1974), helped to establish what was then called "the new labor history." Her second book, *Women, Work, and Family,* which she wrote with Louise Tilly in 1978, was one of the earliest and finest examples of "the new feminist history." And *Gender and the Politics of History* (1988) provided feminist historians with what have proved to be some of their most powerful and important theoretical insights.

But by the mid-1990s the feminist dream of a common history— a dream that Scott had done as much as anyone to bring into being— had all but collapsed, crushed by the accumulated weight of hundreds and hundreds of historically specific and rigorously contextualized women's histories. This extravagant anarchy of overproduction, this stupendous outpouring of historical singularities, now threatens to obliterate much of feminist history by canceling and invalidating all the analogies, affinities, resemblances, and comparisons that feminist historians have drawn over the years—indeed, by rejecting the very idea of analogy, affinity, resemblance and comparison. Even the category of "women" has splintered under the pressure of this insistent and unrelenting historicism. As the poet, postmodernist, and feminist historian Denise Riley recently explained (not without some satisfaction), since " 'women' is historically, discursively constructed, and always relatively to other categories which themselves change . . . the apparent continuity of the subject of 'women' isn't to be relied on; 'women' is both synchronically and diachronically erratic as a collectivity, while for the individual, 'being a woman' is also inconstant, and can't provide an ontological foundation."[65]

As we approach the end of the 1990s this astonishing proliferation of historical particulars shows no sign of abating. But this should not surprise us; after all, every region of the past is being pounded to bits by the jackhammer of historicism. What is surprising—at first glance, anyway—is that Joan Scott's usual insightfulness has failed her (and us) at just this crucial point. Though she sees this continuing pulverization of the past, she seems unsure how to deal with it—other than to suggest that "difficult as it is," feminist historians simply have to live with it.[66] But the reasons for her reluctance are not hard to find; indeed, they lie at the very center of the historical vision she has been nurturing and developing for over a quarter of a century.

No one has influenced Scott's sense of history more profoundly than E. P. Thompson. She read *The Making of the English Working Class* in the spring of 1963, almost as soon as it came out. Twenty years later she could still remember the exhilaration she felt: "Much of its excitement [lay] in its avowedly political purpose. In 1963 it provided historians like myself with a model for writing socially relevant history. For us, *The Making of the English Working Class* embodied a scholarship that fit a New Left purpose: it exposed the workings of capitalist political economy and demonstrated the virtues of 'purposive historical commitment' and the possibilities for 'the redemption of man through political action.' "[67]

But even more important than Thompson's vision of history-writing-as-political-action was his determination to rescue ordinary people from "the enormous condescension of posterity."[68] This was more than "history from the bottom up"; it was history as lived experience. The best example is his insistence that class is a cultural experience rather than an economic category: "Class happens when some men, as a result of common experiences (inherited or shared), feel and articulate the identity of their interests as between themselves, and as against other men whose interests are different from (and usually opposed to) theirs."[69] Class was an "active process" for Thompson; it was defined "by men as they live their own history, and, in the end, that is its only definition."[70] Class was something people *experienced*, every day: in the emotional dynamics of their families, in the spiritual lives of their churches, in the participatory democracy of the trade union movement. As Thompson saw it—and as he taught an entire generation of labor historians to see it—class was the shaping reciprocity between subjective experience and the

changing demands of the productive system. What Thompson
wanted to know was how this cultural transaction actually worked:
What pressure did it exert on young minds and old ones? How did
it flesh out a moral landscape for men who dug coal under the
ground? What stores of remedial wisdom did it offer textile workers
in the face of weariness and resignation? How did it shape their capacity for wonder and desire?

These are Thompson's questions, and Scott's. They spring from
the conviction that historians should write from their subjects' point
of view. As Thompson put it in a famous sentence, "The Luddite
cropper, the 'obsolete' hand-loom weaver, the 'utopian' artisan and
even the deluded followers of Joanna Southcott . . . lived through
these times of acute social disturbance and we did not"; thus "their
aspirations were valid in terms of their own experience."

For Scott this means that historians should spend their time un-
earthing the conceptual categories that, say, the power-loom weavers
in eighteenth-century Birmingham used to explain themselves to
themselves. They should try to discover how these hierarchical structures of meaning and identity were constructed, how they were used
to maintain differences of power and privilege, and so on.[71] Scott's
later work differs from Thompson's in several important respects, as
we shall see; but she continues to insist that historical writing is a
form of political activism.[72]

Scott began moving away from Thompson in her second book,
Women, Work, and Family (1978), which she later described as the
"ultimate apology" for having ignored women in her first book.[73]
Five years later, in December 1983, she publicly broke with Thompson in a widely discussed paper that she delivered at the annual convention of the American Historical Association.[74] This was twenty
years after she had first read *The Making of the English Working
Class,* nine years after her own Thompson-inspired study of the glassworkers of Carmaux had won two awards, and just three years after
she had taken up a new position as director of the Pembroke Center
for Teaching and Research on Women at Brown University. That
appointment, as it turned out, proved decisive: "In the Pembroke
Center seminar I was forced to take post-structuralist theory seriously
and wrestle with its implications for a social historian. The process
was at once rewarding and difficult. It addressed many of the most
pressing philosophical questions I had confronted as a feminist trying
to write women's history, but, at the same time, it brought me to a
critique more fundamental than I had anticipated of the presuppositions of my discipline."[75]

It was her reading in poststructuralist theory—especially her reading of Derrida and Foucault—that enabled Scott to break with Thompson.[76] Scott charged that Thompson had been insensitive to differences within the working class, that the story he told in *The Making of the English Working Class* "is preeminently a story about men," that it slights the role of women in the growth of the union movement, and so on. But what marked the paper as a major turning point in Scott's thinking—and a major step in the development of feminist historical thought generally—was her recognition and demonstration that *The Making of the English Working Class* is "gendered history."[77] It is not just that women rarely appear in Thompson's narrative, or that when they do appear they are usually associated with domesticity, even when they are in fact full-time workers. It is that "the master codes that structure the narrative" employ masculine and feminine symbols to identify what Thompson thought of as positive and negative characteristics: production is masculine, domesticity is feminine; secular politics are rational, progressive, and (as such) masculine, but religiously inspired political movements are irrational, "overly expressive," and (as such) feminine.[78] And so on. Scott's point was that by employing these and other such rhetorical strategies Thompson had unconsciously transposed the gendered hierarchies of eighteenth-century workingmen into twentieth-century historical writing. Scott hoped that by demonstrating that these oppressive assumptions about gender could be found in even the most respected—and ostensibly progressive—historical accounts, she could make historians who did not think of themselves as feminists more aware of and sympathetic to "the enormity of the problem" their feminist colleagues faced in trying to work within the established procedures of the profession, procedures that, as she demonstrated, were codified in the profession's most respected texts.[79] After Scott's article appeared, the feminist charge that gender provides one of the axes along which historical knowledge is typically organized seemed, if not irrefutable, then certainly no longer beyond possibility.

Scott ended her critique by calling for "a radical reconceptualization of the terms of history itself."[80] Two years later, in "Gender: A Useful Category of Historical Analysis" (1985), she explained what she had in mind.[81] "Gender" has been an enormously influential article—"an instant classic," as William Sewell called it.[82] It circulated in mimeographed form for several months, was read at the AHA convention in December 1985 and published in the *American Historical Review* the following year, and has been repeatedly anthologized. Even now, over a decade later, it remains the most convincing argument we have for the importance of gender in feminist historical writing—and the best statement yet of Scott's historical vision, with all its strengths and weaknesses.

Scott takes "gender" to mean "the social organization of the relationship between the sexes"; it is "a socially agreed upon system of distinctions, rather than an objective description of inherent traits."[83] In other words, it is a discourse. As such, the meanings it makes possible are always relational, always a function of the place a particular term occupies in a structured economy of such terms. Thus "feminine" acquires meaning by virtue of its relation to "masculine," just as "rook" has meaning only in relation to the other pieces on the chessboard. Part of "white" means not being "black," part of "English" means not being "Indian," and part of "feminine" means not being "masculine."[84] Knowledge about gender is not simply true or false; it is relative.

But if Scott has read Saussure she has also read Foucault, so she knows that discursive formations like these are "really" forms of social power.[85] Knowledge is never innocent. Knowledge about gender in particular is produced in discursive forms that are "the means by which relationships of power—of domination and subordination—are constructed."[86] Like race and class, gender is "a primary way of signifying relationships of power."[87]

But if Scott has read Foucault she has also read Derrida, from whom she draws the conclusion that to describe the origins of a discourse is, ipso facto, to "denaturalize" and thereby "deconstruct" it: "Analysing the history by which those differences [of race, class, and gender] have been produced disrupts their fixity as enduring facts and recasts them (and the social hierarchies they organize) as the effects of contingent and contested processes of change."[88]

So "Gender" is first a plea for theoretical sophistication on the part of feminist historians, and more specifically a plea for poststructuralist theory. Feminist history "seems to me to require a radical epistemology. Precisely because it addresses questions of epistemology, relativizes the status of all knowledge, links knowledge and power, and theorizes these in terms of the operations of difference, I think poststructuralism (or at least some of the approaches generally associated with Michel Foucault and Jacques Derrida) can offer feminism a powerful analytic perspective."[89] Scott argues that if feminist historians really want to write "stories of the oppressed," if they want to understand "the meaning and nature of their oppression," they will have to pick up their old dog-eared copies of Derrida and Foucault, brush up on literary theory, and generally make themselves more sensitive to the subtle and elusive ways power and knowledge commingle, how power constructs itself on the richly symbolic body of "woman."[90]

Second, and following immediately from this, "Gender" argues that feminist historians must transform feminist history into a history of discursive formations. Where the history of consciousness was, there shall be the history of discourses: "The story is no longer about the things that have happened to women and men and how they have reacted to them; instead it is about how the subjective and collective meanings of women and men as categories of identity have been constructed. . . . The objects of study are epistemological phenomena."[91]

As Scott sees it, this would represent a third phase of feminist history. The first—simply adding women to the histories we already have—failed because although feminist historians could show that women did in fact participate in all the major upheavals of Western history, they could not show that their participation changed the outcome (of, say, the French Revolution) in any significant way.[92] In the second phase, sometimes called "her-story," feminist historians insisted that women have their own history, that their as yet nameless arrangements of knowledge and sorrow, their secret stores of sadness, their anonymous talents and unknown triumphs have virtually nothing in common with the aimless and arbitrary agitations that constitute the history of men. But such a claim immediately raised the fear of ghettoization—as in, "Fine, let them go off and write their own history and leave the rest of us alone."[93] "What seemed to be called for," Scott explained in 1988, was neither a separate history nor an addition to the existing histories, but new historical studies that would expose the gendered nature of society's most basic conceptual categories—"class, worker, citizen, even man and woman."[94]

Finally, "Gender" argued that these new studies had to be rigorous contextualized: "The point is to find ways to analyze specific 'texts' in terms of specific historical and contextual meanings. . . . The questions that must be answered in such an analysis are how, in what specific contexts, among which specific communities of people, and by what textual and social processes has meaning been acquired?"[95]

But it is just here that we come upon the central problem in Scott's program for renewing feminist history—a problem she seems vaguely aware of but unable to resolve. Her call for more empirical studies has been eminently successful—indeed, all too successful. For we have been inundated with a truly prodigious outpouring of tightly focused, closely detailed, and richly contextualized historical studies.

Scott is convinced that this overwhelming flood of monographic detail will eventually give us just what the French positivist Auguste Comte thought it would give us: knowledge of the general principles that govern social development. Here is Scott in 1988: "The questions are: How do meanings change? How have some meanings emerged as normative and others have been eclipsed or disappeared? What do these processes reveal about how power is constituted and operates?"[96] Or again: "What is the process by which race or class becomes salient for making social distinctions in certain periods and not in others? Does race take priority over class and class over gender, or are there inseparable connections among them? Under what conditions? In what circumstances?"[97]

As early as 1985 Scott acknowledged that "the proliferation of case studies in women's history seems to call for some synthesizing perspective."[98] But none was forthcoming, with good reason, for no one could possibly have synthesized the flood of historical monographs that kept pouring off the university presses in the 1980s and 1990s. In 1996 she was finally forced to admit that the dream of a common history had become much more remote than it had seemed only twelve years before: not only had the category of "women" splintered, the politics of group identity had quick-frozen the individual splinters: "Instead of a singular 'women's' history, we now have fixed categories of working-class or African-American or Islamic women, . . . of bourgeois women, peasant women, lesbian women, Jewish lesbian women, socialist women, Nazi women—the list goes on and on."

Nor was that all, for younger feminist historians, armed with a far more powerful strain of poststructuralist theory than Scott had imbibed at the Pembroke Seminars, had begun to attack the truth-telling claims of history itself. Scott was convinced by these new studies but not at all sure what to do with them. Here she is in 1991, commenting on the Indian historian Gayatri Chakravorty Spivak's essay "Feminism in Decolonization" (1991):

> We cannot know precisely or definitively what the *devadasi* [a female temple dancer] means, who she is or how she feels. We cannot know her as a unified, completely definable person (or member of a collectivity) with a codifiable, categorical consciousness that follows from her occupation or her "experience.". . . The *devadasi* simply cannot be pinned down. . . . She cannot be read literally as a reflection of some cultural and political reality "out there.". . . Neither can ethnographic reporting, nor social science investigation, . . . nor an account by

an economic and social historian. A turn to the history of temple dance adds to the complexity instead of resolving it, as does a consultation of ancient sources. Like a good historian, Gayatri Spivak piles up the evidence, only to show us that it will not be resolved or cumulated into a single characterization or explanatory statement.[99]

The implication seems obvious: if the evidence that Indian feminist historians have been gathering over the years cannot be "cumulated into a single characterization or explanatory statement," then what can be said of the evidence British and American feminists have been gathering? Scott ducked that question in her comments on Spivak's paper. In other places she has refused to abandon history's truth-telling claims while simultaneously refusing to defend them. Her response to the psychoanalyst Sally Alexander reflects the difficulty of the dilemma she now faces. Alexander had suggested that perhaps the study of history "offers no final resolution, only the constant reshaping, reorganizing of the symbolization of difference." Scott responded: "It may be my hopeless utopianism that gives me pause before this formulation, or it may be that I have not yet shed the episteme of what Foucault called the Classical Age."[100]

A strange admission for a self-described poststructuralist, one might think, but such are the ironies of trying to write feminist history in the 1990s.

CHAPTER FOUR

After Looking into the Abyss

The Promise of Professionalism

I

By 1980 the expanding reach of poststructuralist theory had begun to alarm even liberal historians. As graduate students in the 1960s many of them had challenged the traditional interpretations of American history, criticizing them for, among other things, their lack of objectivity and racial inclusiveness. But twenty years later, when poststructuralists attacked the idea of objectivity itself, these same historians found themselves manning the other side of the barricades. Determined to defend the profession and its claim to objective knowledge, they reached all the way back to the rhetoric of professionalism that had first been developed in the early decades of the twentieth century—developed, fact, to quell just such an uprising of skepticism. Within its forms the historian, who once thought of himself as a writer, now became a "practitioner," working in a community of similar practitioners, all engaged in a common quest to discover the laws that govern social development, and all employing a common battery of tested and accredited research procedures. By the middle of the 1990s it had become abundantly clear that the resurrection of professionalism had failed. But that failure, more than any other single event, created the space in which an older, more traditional kind of history—history as a form of moral reflection—now seems to be reemerging.

The present chapter tells the story of four highly accomplished and widely respected historians—David Hollinger, David Haskell, James Kloppenberg, and Joyce Appleby (together with Lynn Hunt and Margaret Jacob)—who spent over ten years trying to formulate a theory of historical objectivity. As it turned out, they had to invent four *different* theories, because as each one foundered and finally sank they had to come up a new one. The pages that follow describe these theories and explain why each of them failed. But in the end it mattered not a whit, since a full-fledged theory of objectivity is about as useful to a historian as antlers would be to a duck.

I I

Quentin Skinner and J. G. A. Pocock had thought they could travel only halfway down the historicist road; they had imagined they could transform the history of ideas into the history of discourses without giving up history's traditional claim to objective knowledge about the past, especially knowledge about historical contexts and authorial intentions. But they knew they had a problem, for if the perceptions and understandings of seventeenth-century British political writers were shaped (and limited) by the universe of discourse within which they wrote, would not the same be true of twentieth-century British historians—Skinner and Pocock themselves, for example? As we saw, they thought they could avoid this embarrassment by portraying past ideas as intellectual strategies. But as we also saw, that solution ran into all sorts of problems, most of them irresolvable.

In the early 1980s Skinner and Pocock's project was taken over by a group of younger historians who called themselves "moderate pragmatists." Like Skinner and Pocock, David Hollinger, Thomas Haskell, and James Kloppenberg had already made significant contributions to intellectual history.[1] Also like Skinner and Pocock, they hoped to find an epistemological middle ground, a space located somewhere between the claims of traditional objectivist historians and those of their Nietzsche-inspired critics. Finally—and again like Skinner and Pocock—Haskell, Hollinger, and Kloppenberg wanted to formulate an "ideologically liberal" vision of intellectual history— a "moderate, pragmatic historicism" that would incorporate and build on the insights of contemporary historicism while nevertheless claiming objective knowledge about the past. As Kloppenberg put it, "Dissatisfaction with objectivity need not culminate in relativism or in skepticism. There is an alternative."[2] Haskell, Hollinger, and Kloppenberg hoped to provide what Skinner and Pocock had clearly failed to provide: in Kloppenberg's words, "a safe haven for principles that our culture will continue to cherish even though we now realize the metaphysical ground has been pulled out from under us."[3]

Skinner and Pocock focused their efforts on the twin problems of discursive context and authorial intention; they wanted to transform intellectual history into a history of discourses, but they did not want to sacrifice the traditional subject of intellectual history: the thinking, intending author. Hollinger, Haskell, and Kloppenberg, on the other hand, decided to tackle the most important and intractable problem of all: the problem of objectivity. There was a good deal of risk in making such a choice, for the professional currents were all running in the opposite direction. As these writers saw it, they were confronting "the virtual demise of the ideal of objectivity in our own time." As Haskell put it, "the ideal of objectivity is all washed up."[4]

So this was essentially a rearguard action. Haskell, Hollinger, and Kloppenberg were willing to concede some ground, most obviously the historicist insistence that knowledge is both contingent and context specific; but they dug themselves in around history's traditional claim to objective knowledge about the past. This was also a high-stakes game, for if they could pull it off—if they could rescue objectivity from the jaws of radical historicism—they would have a way to face down the postmodern challenge without giving up a single one of intellectual history's traditional knowledge claims.[5]

Objectivity has always been central to those claims, of course—the polestar of private judgment and professional evaluation. As Peter Novick recently put it, the ideal of objectivity has stood "at the very center of the professional historical venture." "It was the rock on which the venture was constituted, its continuing raison d'être. It has been the quality which the profession has prized and praised above all others—whether in historians or in their works. It has been the key term in defining progress in historical scholarship: moving ever closer to the objective truth about the past."[6]

For historians, "objectivity" has always meant, first and most important of all, a belief in the prior reality of the past—in other words, belief that the past exists prior to and independent of our own minds; and second, in historical truth as correspondence to that past reality.[7] The belief that one can "be objective" implies that there are certain "facts" about the past, that these facts exist outside and independent of the historian's mind, that they can be grasped and understood "right side up," and that when they are so understood they will "speak for themselves," quite apart from whatever interpretative conventions, ideological commitments, or particular perspectives we may bring to them.

But Hollinger, Haskell, and Kloppenberg know that contemporary theory has called these assumptions into question, that objectivity has become a "fiercely contested concept." Moreover, they take history seriously: they know that we can never completely escape our own historicity, that we and all our claims to knowledge about the past are hopelessly embedded in the contingencies of our own time and place. They know, in other words, that the past can be represented only through a particular historically specific ordering of perception and association, a continually changing web of narrative forms, symbolic modes, rhetorical devices, and figural patterns that simultaneously enables and mocks our every effort to know the past. The facts will never "speak for themselves"; the past will not be redeemed for the present. What Peter Novick has written of David Hollinger could just as easily have been written of Haskell and Kloppenberg as well: "Like others who took it for granted that old postures were no longer tenable, he used ironic quotation marks when he wrote of historians 'discovering' the 'objective truth,' and praised [Thomas] Kuhn for 'breaking down . . . the old monolithic concept of objectivity.' "[8]

Like Skinner and Pocock, Hollinger, Haskell, and Kloppenberg are extremely sophisticated historians; they know the objections that have been raised against objectivity but they are determined to find a way around them, to somehow save an ideal that has been central to historical writing since at least the nineteenth century. They want to redefine objectivity in such a way that it can rise above these apparently crippling objections and once again provide the moral, aesthetic, and methodological standard by which practicing historians can evaluate one another's work. As Haskell recentlly remarked, "I do not believe that facts speak for themselves. . . . Yet I regard objectivity, properly understood, as a worthy goal for historians."[9]

Hollinger, Haskell, and Kloppenberg have made three major attempts to reclaim and restore the concept of objectivity: first by trying to ground it in professional research procedures; then, when that did not work, by likening it to certain traditions and conventions associated with the eighteenth-century Enlightenment; and when that also failed, by transforming it into a general moral and aesthetic imperative.

They based the first attempt on Thomas Kuhn's book *The Structure of Scientific Revolutions* (1963). In "T. S. Kuhn's Theory of Science and Its Implications for History" (1973), Hollinger tried to formulate "a functional equivalent for objectivity" by applying Kuhn's ideas about "disciplinary matrices" and "disciplinary consensus" to the historical profession as a whole.[10]

Pocock had also borrowed from Kuhn, but with a difference. In *Politics, Language, and Time* (1971) he had celebrated Kuhn's *Structure of Scientific Revolutions* as "the most valuable single contribution" to "the reconstruction [of intellectual history] which we are conducting."[11] As Pocock read him, Kuhn was asking historians "to think of the history of science as essentially a history of discourse and of language."[12] This was Pocock's own particular reading of Kuhn, of course, as Pocock was the first to admit: "In thus defining 'paradigm' in strictly linguistic terms, I have already begun to diverge somewhat from Kuhn's employment of a term so much his own."[13]

But where Pocock had interpreted Kuhn in "strictly linguistic terms," Hollinger set out to give him "a profoundly sociological orientation."[14] Thus, where Pocock focused on what Kuhn had said about *historical discourses,* Hollinger focused on what he had said about *professional evaluation;* and where Pocock read Kuhn as insisting that a discourse had to be understood "in terms of the intellectual functions it performs," Hollinger read him as insisting that evaluation had to be understood in terms of "the experience of a given social constituency."[15]

For Hollinger it was this idea of a "disciplinary matrix" rooted in the common activities of a particular community of inquiry that made Kuhn's work so powerfully suggestive. For what Hollinger had found was a means of governing the seemingly ungovernable proliferation of historical interpretations that poststructuralism had recently unleashed. As Hollinger read him, Kuhn was saying that "a truth-claim becomes valid when the most learned practitioners of a technically sophisticated field agree that the theory on which the claim is based explains the range of phenomena under common scrutiny more satisfactorily than does any other known theory."[16]

According to this reading, Kuhn offered a theory of validity that was thoroughly historicized and deeply contextual: validity rises directly out of the shared experiences of a particular community. It rests on neither a "correspondence" theory of truth, nor an "internal coherence" theory, nor a "justificationist" conception (according to which truth is distinguished by its adherence to certain putatively transcultural standards of reasoning and logic). Rather, truth (or "validity") rests on a professional community's own historical experience, as defined by its leading practitioners and codified in what Hollinger called its "operative tradition" (roughly what Kuhn meant by "paradigm"). It is the existence of this shared paradigm that enables "communities of the competent" to test and evaluate competing accounts.[17] As James Kloppenberg once put it, historians should simply have "the courage of their conventions."[18]

This is an explicitly culture-bound theory of truth—truth as contingent, contextualized, and in that sense at least, relativist. Nevertheless, Hollinger thought it provided a bulwark against "the more complete relativism of 'every man his own historian.'"[19] If historians could no longer claim that a particular account was "objective" because it corresponded to "the facts," or because it possessed a high degree of internal coherence, or because it adhered to some timeless principle of rationality, they could nevertheless judge it against the profession's historically conditioned and in that sense "objective" standards. By giving Kuhn a strongly sociological reading, Hollinger seemed to have invested historical scholarship, as Peter Novick put it, with "a sort of 'primal validity.'"[20]

Six years later, in 1979, Thomas Haskell modified Hollinger's argument. Like Pocock and Hollinger, Haskell thought Kuhn's *Structure of Scientific Revolutions* was "one of the two or three most important works in intellectual history of our time"; and also like Hollinger, he read Kuhn from a "profoundly sociological" perspective. But Haskell was much more critical of Kuhn than either of his predecessors had been.

This was especially true when it came to Kuhn's ideas about paradigms and paradigm change—when it came, for example, to his assertion that "mankind's most fundamental assumptions (the 'paradigmatic' ones) are normally immune to the experiential evidence that might modify or falsify them."[21] As Haskell read him, Kuhn appeared to be suggesting that all the "relative presuppositions" of a particular paradigm can ultimately be traced back to one "absolute presupposition," and that though this one, paradigm-founding assumption "is constitutive of the meaning of all questions asked under its auspices, there is no way in normal discourse meaningfully to ask whether it is true or false."[22] Moreover, Kuhn seemed to be suggesting that the reasons scholars jump from one constellation of presuppositions to another has nothing to do with logic or reason.[23] Most disturbing of all, Kuhn had found this sort of irrationalism among scientists—the very people we had imagined were virtually immune to it. "If even the scientist is normally prisoner of his most fundamental assumptions," Haskell wondered, "what of the rest of us?"[24] Again and again, Haskell warned his colleagues to be careful with *The Structure of Scientific Revolutions*, that it would end up reinforcing the "deterministic current" in contemporary intellectual history. Haskell thought that liberal historians—those who have "celebrated the autonomy of ideas and conceived of their discipline as a bastion against materialism and behaviorism"—should take their Kuhn with a grain of salt.[25]

It is a measure of Haskell's determination to find some solid grounding for professional evaluation that he set these doubts aside and embraced Kuhn's definition of "objectivity" as a justificatory procedure constructed and established—and in that sense justified—

by historically specific "communities of inquiry." Like Hollinger, he hoped this "moderate relativism" would provide a solid "bulwark against skepticism."[26] To the hard-core objectivists on his right, he insisted on "the social, consensual quality of all that passes for truth among human beings"; to the Nietzschean skeptics and thorough-going relativists on his left—"the radical wing of historicism"—he insisted that "that opinion which wins the broadest and deepest support in the existing community of inquirers" fully deserves the label "objective" opinion.[27] "If expert claims to lay deference possess any validity, it arises from the workings of these special communities."[28] In other words, Hollinger and Haskell hoped to salvage the traditional concept of "objectivity" by thinking of the historical profession as a "community of inquiry."

But this failed to work for several reasons. First, consider Haskell's notion of professional communities. As he describes them, "They are essentially networks of practitioners bound together by dense webs of technical communication, and by 'traditions,' 'paradigms,' or 'research programs' that define reality within the field and supply practitioners with the indispensable basis of their practice."[29] Haskell thinks we should accept "the outcome" of such a community's "striving" as "objective truth": "If a community of inquiry exists in a field that interests us, surely its *current best opinion* is, in practice, the closest approach to the truth we can possibly hope for. We live now and need to distinguish between true and false propositions. Taking our cue from [Charles S.] Peirce, sound opinion becomes that opinion which wins the broadest and deepest support in the existing community of inquirers."[30]

The problem with this argument should be obvious. Haskell's description of a "professional community"—borrowed from Peirce—may or may not have described the historical profession as it existed in the last decades of the nineteenth century, but it bears no relation at all to the profession as it exists in the 1990s. Like every other discipline in what used to be called the humanities, history has simply become too socially diverse—too crosscut by questions of class, race, ethnicity, and gender—for a stable, widely accepted set of "traditions, paradigms, or research programs" (whether substantive or methodological) to "define reality within the field."

Moreover, several historians have recently insisted that there is a direct relation between the social diversification of the historical profession and the decline of methodological consensus.[31] Joan Wallach Scott has argued that the first attacks on "objectivity," in the 1890s, came shortly after the profession had opened its ranks to "people of scholarly ability but plebian origin," people with "swarthy complexions" and "strange-sounding Celtic, Latin, or Semitic names."[32] Once established in the profession, these formerly excluded groups began to expand the range of subjects professional historians could legitimately write about. Even more important, they began multiplying the *subject positions* from *within* which history could be written. Moreover, what began as a question of subject matter— Which people, events, or ideas should professional historians write about?—quickly became a question of epistemology: How should the past be conceived and represented? What should count as "historical knowledge"? Which rules and conventions should govern the production, evaluation, and dissemination of such knowledge? Do those rules and conventions constitute impartial criteria or ideological constraints?[33] And so on. As Scott has explained, the social transformation of both the profession and the university, along with the subsequent rise of women's history, labor history, and various ethnic histories, "occasioned a crisis for orthodox history by multiplying not only stories but subjects, and by insisting that histories are written from fundamentally different—indeed irreconcilable—perspectives or standpoints, none of which is complete or completely 'true.' "[34]

Hollinger and Haskell made their pitch for professional consensus in the 1970s, just as a second wave of racial and ethnic diversification began to break over the profession. The reemergence of women's history and labor history, the creation of African American history and gay history, and the emergence of several other "new histories" reawakened earlier fears that the historical field was being dispersed, that "history" was being scattered into a multiplicity of discontinuous and unsynchronized "histories" that could never again be gathered together. As one prominent historian recently explained, "The appearance of women and African Americans in the profession, of postmodern theories of knowledge, and of a significant number of leftist historians have all undermined (at times unwittingly) the rule of objectivity."[35] Scott was hardly alone when she wondered aloud, "How many of these 'other' histories can be allowed to proliferate? Where will it all end?"[36]

It was this sense of cultural fragmentation and epistemological crisis that brought formerly progressive historians like Hollinger, Haskell, and Kloppenberg running to the defense of traditional standards. During the middle and late 1970s you could see "moderate pragmatists" looking like startled deer as they realized they had been quaffing too thirstly at the stream of postmodern theory. Scott perfectly captured the irony of this frantic search for foundations by yesterday's antifoundationalists, this sudden need for permanence and security on the part of Neo-pragmatists and would-be historicists:

"What is most striking these days is the determined embrace, the strident defense, of some reified, transcendent category of explanation [like 'objectivity'] by historians who have used insights drawn from the sociology of knowledge, structural linguistics, feminist theory, or cultural anthropology to develop sharp critiques of empiricism."[37]

But if the sociological transformation of both the university and the profession continues—as it undoubedly will—then new histories, these new subject positions, vocabularies, epistemologies, and methodologies will also continue to proliferate, perhaps more quickly than before. It is this continuing proliferation that makes Hollinger and Haskell's hopes for a renewed disciplinary consensus—whether substantive or methodological—seem so improbable. For as Allan Megill recently explained: "In such a situation, unity on the substantive level can only serve to exclude. Likewise, when disciplines become fragmented and when the cross-cuts between them begin to take on lives of their own, unity on the methodological level disappears."[38]

So it was that by the end of the 1980s Haskell had come to see what Hollinger had not: that social changes within the profession had left the old disciplinary consensus "in tatters." Never again would the profession share a widely agreed on definition of "objectivity" or "validity"—one that could underwrite standards of judgment acceptable to most historians.[39] Hollinger had wanted us to think of the profession as a protoscientific research organization held together by a more or less coherent set of substantive beliefs and methodological principles—a disciplinary paradigm. But Haskell could see, as Hollinger could not, that this was clearly an idea whose time had come and gone.[40]

Now that it is indeed gone, Richard Rorty has offered a metaphor that might help us in thinking about truth and objectivity and the role of professional organizations like the American Historical Association. Think of such an association, Rorty suggested, along the lines of a Kuwaiti rug bazaar, surrounded by a collection of more or less private clubs. The advantage of such a scheme is that the people who haggle and bargain in the bazaar every day need have almost nothing in common other than their eagerness to strike a deal. As Rorty says, "I picture many of the people in such a bazaar as preferring to die rather than share the beliefs of many of those with whom they are haggling, yet as haggling profitably away nevertheless." They smile a lot, they make the best deals they can, and in the evenings they retreat to the sanctuary of their private clubs, where they are "comforted by the companionship of [their] moral equals."[41]

In other words, it might make more sense to think of the historical profession not as a protoscientific research organization but as a collection of more or less distinct groups and individuals, most of whom would not be caught dead with the heroes, values, and beliefs held by lots and lots of other people who also call themselves historians. Nevertheless, most of these people take the time to show up at the annual convention every year. And once there they always manage to find—in the hotel bars and restaurants that serve as the functional equivalent of the private clubs ringing the Kuwaiti bazaar—a number of people whose beliefs and ideas are similar enough that they can talk, that is to say, that they can try out each other's ideas by weaving them into the fabric of their own.[42]

But Haskell was far too worried by the specter of epistemological subversion to play around with the metaphor of a Kuwaiti rug bazaar. He worried that the profession's suddenly weakened disciplinary authority would create an opportunity for the leaders of its "radical wing"—"contemporary relativists" like Jacques Derrida, for example, whom Haskell derisively labeled "the high priest of interpretive liberty and the arch-enemy of intellectual foundations of all sorts"—to push "historicist claims of a truly extravagant nature."[43]

Haskell worried because, more than any of the other "moderate pragmatists," he thought intellectual history had to teach absolute moral truths—fundamental lessons about right and wrong that Western civilization must never lose sight of. For example, he insisted that "our moral revulsion over the horrors of Nazi Germany is one of the principal anchors of the twentieth-century mind. However strong the currents of relativism may run, however tempting it may be to accommodate oneself to them, we know that we cannot permit that anchor to break loose."[44] In Haskell's eyes, the more radical forms of contemporary historicism threaten to rip that moral anchor from its moorings, exposing us all to the formidable terrors of the Nietzschean abyss: "As historicist criticism converts the world of so-called facts into an evanescent mirage and puts in doubt the very possibility of grounded argument, more apocalyptic possibilities inevitably heave into view. The primordial intellectual enterprise of interpretation, fed by an imagination that no longer meets resistance in any direction and thus has learned to scorn the very idea of objective reality, throbs and swells in hopes of filling the entire cosmos."[45]

Though he could sound frighteningly apocalyptic at times, Haskell had little in common with the Straussian hard-liners in the profession. He was prepared to concede, as the Straussians were not, that there is no fixed moral order at the center of the world, that we can no longer pretend to an "objectivity" somehow freed from the coagulations of history—an untextualized and uninterpreted "view from nowhere."[46]

Nevertheless, he continued to insist that we can somehow acquire "knowledge that is not merely personal and subjective but impersonal and objective," that we do indeed have a "historically defensible sense of objectivity"—an objectivity that, if not quite Platonic and universal, does have at least "a *provisional* immunity to incursions of time, place, and circumstance."[47] Haskell published an initial version of this argument in 1987 and a revised version in 1990.

Peter Novick described the 1987 version as "an eloquent and moving statement of Haskell's anguish at the 'fashionable' tide of radical historicism."[48] Actually, it reads more like a general alarm in the night. Haskell thinks he sees, especially in the new historicism of the 1980s, a darkly subversive and essentially Nietzschean menace. He tells us that the new historicism "harbors within itself radical possibilities deeply antagonistic not only to ideas of natural right, but also to all hopes of expanding the sway of reason and moral order in the world."[49] As Haskell sees it, the historicists are inviting Western civilization to partake of their own moral minimalism and soul-numbing nihilism; they are leading us down a secret path to nothingness, whence we will be drawn into swirling undercurrents of moral relativism and universal skepticism that will leave us with nothing but the blind cravings of our individual egos.[50]

It is worth noting, once again, that Haskell is no epistemological fundamentalist; he knows, as he himself has said more than once, that "reason is enslaved by (or at least confined within) the particular social and historical context in which it finds itself," that we can never return to the imaginary Platonic moral order celebrated by the Straussians.[51] Nevertheless he continues, even in this 1987 essay, to insist that we can find a "safe haven," a bedrock "located somewhere in the middle" somewhere between the eternal verities of the Straussians and the self-transforming discourses of the historicists.[52] "There is a stopping place," he assures us; the radical historicists shall not "pull us down into Nietzsche's world. We are not on a frictionless slope, but on level ground, free to decide where to stand."[53]

But where Haskell and Hollinger had earlier tried to locate that "stopping place" in the formalized procedures of protoscientific research organizations, Haskell now tries to locate it in the values and traditions of the larger society.[54] This is a familiar argument. Two hundred years ago Edmund Burke asserted that customs, habits, and local traditions are all we have, that we simply *are* what they are.[55] In similar fashion, Haskell argues that the natural rights tradition of the eighteenth century has survived because it has been "so amply supported by the prevailing form of life" in the United States—indeed, so amply supported that "our inability to formulate an entirely satisfying theoretical justification for [it] has no direct bearing on [its] staying power."[56] Like Burke, Haskell admits that traditions and conventions are historically conditioned and culturally sanctioned fictions.[57] They neither have nor need "foundations sunk deep into the heart of nature."[58] But neither are they merely personal preferences. For the fact that they have rooted themselves so deeply in our history gives them an extra-personal and inter-subjective character. The natural rights tradition, as Haskell sees it, is neither grounded in the nature of ultimate reality nor bobbing on the waves of contemporary fashion.

If Haskell had stopped at this point he might have succeeded. After all, lots of reputable thinkers have suggested that we simply have to accept the fact that what we once thought were rock-bottom truths are, in fact, historically conditioned inventions. I take William James to have been saying something like this in "Does Consciousness Exist?" (1904),[59] where he answers that consciousness does not in fact exist but goes on to argue that it therefore has to be posited. I take Jerome Bruner and Daniel Dennett to be saying essentially the same thing in their recent work.[60]

But this does not even begin to provide the level of assurance Haskell wants. Burke was content to think of traditions and conventions as the accidental products of a random and utterly haphazard historical process. But Haskell demands a real philosophical foundation; he wants "our values" grounded in something deeper and more solid than the mere accumulation of historical contingencies. As we shall see, it is this desire that eventually drives his argument off the rails and into the ditch.

Beginning with the Burkean contention that traditions represent more than personal whim because they are historically conditioned, Haskell takes the further but fatal step of insisting that they are therefore *more* than human inventions, more than the coagulated remains of a particular history, that their persistence over time proves they must be rooted in humanity itself—in what he calls "the nature of man"—and that they thus embody objective and therefore universally valid moral truths: "Rights need not be either eternal or universal, but if they are to do us any good, they must be *rooted deeply enough in the human condition* to win the loyalty of more than a few generations (and ideally, more than a few cultures). Conventions possess the requisite durability."[61]

Since the natural rights tradition has demonstrated "the requisite durability" across "more than a few generations" and "more than a few cultures," Haskell thinks it is therefore objectively and universally "true": the category of "natural rights" is one of those "nonmetaphysical categories that are so deeply rooted in the human condition that they do not vary significantly between cultures or across time."[62]

So it is that Thomas Haskell, "moderate pragmatist" and would-be historicist, ends up insisting that "some claims to objective moral judgment may be valid," that terms like the human condition and the human predicament have individual, discrete, and stable references, that they are self-evident and utterly beyond the need for interpretion, and that for all these reasons they can provide both the basis and the criteria for "objective" evaluation of competing moral claims: "Even when rights are admitted to be conventions, they retain a kind of objectivity: debates concerning them can be rational; there is a basis for discriminating between better and worse conventions."[63]

Haskell thus wants it both ways. On the one hand, he wants to accept the central claims of the new historicism: he agrees, in his own words, that "we do not have any rational basis for choosing between frames of reference," that we lack "a mental faculty capable of transcending time and place," that "there are no eternal values or universal standards," and so forth. On the other hand, he continues to insist that the moral claims embodied in the natural rights tradition are "objective" and "universally" valid. He wants a world in which the claims of historicism and the claims to objective knowledge can both be true: "By mapping more precisely the pale beyond which morality is irredeemably historical, we do concede some territory to the criterionless wilderness, and bring a regrettable measure of satisfaction to the radical wing of historicism. But we also demarcate a spacious domain within which rights and other claims to *objective moral knowledge* can enjoy something like '*universal*' sway."[64]

But in the end this attempt to define objectivity as an essential aspect of "the Western tradition," and therefore deeply embedded in "the nature of man," proved no more successful than the earlier attempt to ground objectivity in the established procedures of professional communities. The reason is not hard to find; think about the Chinese student rebellion in Tiananmen Square in the summer of 1989. It was, as one observer described it,

> a spontaneous, self-organizing event dependent on decentralizing technologies such as the fax, two-way radio, motorbike, TV and telephone. . . . Its style and content were quintessentially hybrid, mixing quotes from Mao with phrases taken from the

French and American Revolutions and their Bill of Rights. Indeed, its symbol, the Goddess of Democracy, was a mixture of French *Liberté* and the American Statue of Liberty. . . . The music during the long hours of waiting varied from Chinese singing to broadcasting, on makeshift loudspeakers, the "Ode to Joy" from Beethoven's *Ninth Symphony* with its message of global brotherhood. Whenever an international television crew swung its cameras over the crowds, up went the two-finger salute of Winston Churchill. Headbands had dual-language slogans: "Glasnost" above its Chinese translation (again, so TV could beam the instant message around China and the English-speaking world)."[65]

During the past twenty years ABC, CBS, and NBC have been supplemented by over five thousand cable systems. In Los Angeles the range of available choices threatens to overwhelm the viewer: four major networks, an all-local news channel, CNN, separate Spanish-, Korean-, and Japanese-language stations, several religious stations, the Home Shopping Club, two music video channels and two C-SPAN channels, at least five movie channels, PBS, a nature channel, an arts channel, two adult video channels, an exercise channel, a multitude of local educational channels, a channel that specializes in old sitcoms from the fifties, and so on, ad nauseum.

Nathanael West saw this coming over half a century ago and described much of it in *The Day of the Locust* (1939). But the emergence of a global information network capable of sending our barbaric yawps across the roofs of the world has given West's nightmarish vision a new relevance and a new immediacy. Haskell wants to identify discrete, internally coherent traditions—cultural inheritances that have been handed down over the generations; he talks about "our history," "the traditions imbedded in our public life," "our deeper understanding of ourselves and our aspirations."[66] But this is the rhetoric of an age that has itself become part of the past, an age, for example, before the Italian director Luchino Visconti showed us Anna Magnani watching *Red River* in a Roman slum and shouting excitedly as the cattle waded across the river: "Look! The cows are all getting wet! It's marvelous!"[67]

Life in the wealthy democratic West has become a matter of incessantly choosing—of necessity—from a kaleidoscope of values and beliefs, of trying to assemble a temporary take on the world from a truly bewildering array of rushing, endlessly mutating cultural fragments. It is possible to identify some of these provisional assemblages as "true"—or deeply rooted in "the nature of man," or "the human condition"—but not without a highly developed sense of irony. For cultural pluralism has become so all pervasive as to be the only true "ism" of our time.[68] What is at issue now, at the end of the twentieth century, is not so much the "truth" of any particular description of the past as the right to fool around with the past, to assemble its materials in whatever impromptu configuration seems to work at the moment. It is a right Haskell and others have stoutly resisted and will no doubt continue to resist.

Haskell made one more attempt to save the concept of objectivity, in the spring of 1990. In "Objectivity Is Not Neutrality" he tried to redefine "objectivity" not as part of a research community's disciplinary matrix, nor as one of the essential components of Western civilization, nor as a reflection of "the human condition," but rather as "that minimal respect for self-overcoming, for detachment, honesty, and fairness, that makes intellectual community possible."[69]

This is a common and widespread understanding of objectivity; indeed, it is one of the few ideas that historians find they can agree on. As the historian Alan Brinkley explained, objectivity defined in this way is a "mythic but useful" concept. It has won wide, even general acceptance, and not only among historians:

> I suspect that most scholars, if pressed to discuss the issue, would concede that true objectivity is impossible to achieve, that all scholarship is coloured to some degree by the social or political inclinations of the writer. But most would admit that if objectivity is a myth, it is a useful one—something worth aspiring to if only because the aspiration serves as a check on a scholar's subjective impulses. There may be no "true" history in the sense that the positivists of the turn-of-the-century liked to claim. But some histories come closer to the truth than others, and the idea of objectivity—ultimately unattainable though it may be—can help scholars measure the distance.[70]

Like Brinkley, Haskell is now convinced that "the very tap- roots" of objectivity as a scholarly ideal can be found just where common sense would lead us to expect them: in the ordinary efforts we all make, every day, to judge people and ideas fairly and impartially: "As I see it, the ideal is invoked . . . every time anyone opens a letter, picks up a newspaper, walks into a courtroom, or decides which of two squabbling children to believe."[71] Acts of fairness like these, no matter how small scale and seemingly mundane, require a certain level of detachment, of self-discipline, and at least a modest effort at self-transcendence.[72]

Haskell now thinks he can find a stable, impersonal, and intersubjective basis for "objective" assessment and "professional" evaluation in these unexceptional and altogether familiar acts—in what we might call "the aesthetic of the everyday."[73] And indeed, he is now willing to rest the credibility of the historians' enterprise not on the sophisticated procedures of professional researchers, nor on the natural rights tradition of the eighteenth century, but on just this "homely" domestic aesthetic:

> The very possibility of historical scholarship as an enterprise distinct from propoganda requires of its practitioners that vital minimum of ascetic self-discipline that enables a person to do such things as abandon wishful thinking, assimilate bad news, discard pleasing interpretations that cannot pass elementary tests of evidence and logic, and, most important of all, suspend or bracket one's own perceptions long enough to enter sympathetically into the alien and possibly repugnant perspectives of rival thinkers.[74]

Conversely, Haskell thinks the absence of this will to objectivity presages not only the end of professional history but the collapse of all ethical obligation—indeed, the disappearance of morality itself. This is so because in this Manichaean world only the will to objectivity can restrain Everyman's voracious will to power. Thus Haskell reads Carl Becker's classic essay "Everyman His Own Historian" as "the harbinger of a remissive cultural movement corrosive of all constraints upon the will, a movement which over the course of the twentieth century has in fact succeeded in putting on the defensive the very idea of obligation, whether moral ('You ethically *ought* to do x') or epistemological ('you rationally/logically *ought* to believe y')."[75]

A dark and fearful reading, perhaps, but one that springs directly out of the basic opposition between "moral" and "immoral," between the saving light and the swallowing darkness, that lies at the heart of Haskell's sensibility. The distinction between "historical scholarship" and "propoganda"—which Haskell employs over and over again—is simply another expression of this primary, Manichaean opposition. Thus he tells us that "when the members of the scholarly community become unwilling to put intellectual values" (by which he means the basic virtues of "fairness, honest, and detachment") ahead of their own political values, "they erase the only possible boundary between politically committed scholarship and propaganda."[76]

And just as Haskell thinks he can distinguish "history" from "propaganda," so he thinks he can distinguish "incomplete" historical accounts from "more complete" ones. Indeed, he thinks historical accounts can be objectively ranked, on God's own scale as it were, from "incomplete" through "more complete" to "the most complete."[77] By continually striving for more objectivity "we can achieve higher levels of completeness." Moreover, since "the *most* complete" account obviously outranks a merely "*more* complete" account (to say nothing of an "incomplete" account), Haskell thinks we have a moral obligation to prefer the former over the latter: "The more complete a conception is, the greater its claim upon us—opening the possibility that we are sometimes obliged to give up incomplete conceptions for more complete ones."[78]

Given all of this, it makes perfect sense—and requires only one small step—for Haskell to claim that he can distingish "between two conflicting interpretations with confidence that they are not simply different, but that one is *superior* to the other, superior as a representation of the way things are."[79] A "superior" account—by definition a "more complete" account—is therefore a more accurate account. Instead of a particular interpretation, it is a faithful reflection, "a representation of the way things are."[80]

The struggle to formulate a "more complete" and therefore objectively "superior" understanding thus becomes, for Haskell, the moral imperative that distinguishes professional history from propaganda. This means, among other things, that professional historians must commit themselves to transcending their merely local identities—identities based on class, race, gender, ethnicity, and so forth—and try to write from what he thinks of as "a superior, more *in*clusive, less self-centered alternative."[81] One cannot hope to achieve perfect objectivity, of course, but one must try, for "detachment both socializes and deparochializes the work of intellect. . . . Only insofar as the members of the community [the profession] are disposed to set aside the perspective that comes most spontaneously to them, and strive to see things in a detached light, is there any likelihood that they will engage with one another mentally and provoke one another through mutual criticism to the most complete, least idiosyncratic, view that humans are capable of."[82] The problem, Haskell explains, is that some "scholar-advocates," masquerading as professional historians, no longer even *pretend* to transcend their own "parochial" identities.[83] Thus he laments the fact that many African American and feminist historians are no longer willing, as he sees it, "to think of themselves merely as historians who happen to be black and/or female."[84]

But what really appalls Thomas Haskell is the charge that "objectivity" is merely "one more link in the chain of oppression."[85] Haskell

once likened "these assaults on universalistic values" to Joseph Mc-
Carthy's attacks on political liberalism in the 1950s.[86] And he has
echoed C. Van Woodward's warning that "political orthodoxies of
the left can have the same 'chilling effect' on scholarship as those
of the right." Ironically perhaps, Haskell concludes what began as
an argument for "pragmatic historicism" by endorsing the call for
"a powerful reaffirmation of universalistic values."[87]

What are we to make of all this? Has Haskell succeeded in saving
objectivity as a regulatory ideal and a means of evaluating competing
historical accounts? The answer is clearly no, for a number of reasons.
The most obvious is simply that Haskell allows his fear of "moral
relativism" to overrun his commitment to "moderate historicism."
Like Skinner, Pocock, Hollinger, and Kloppenberg before him, he
wants to find some middle ground between the "radical historicists"
on his left and the "belligerent antihistoricists" on his right.[88] But
he is so deathly afraid of the former that he throws himself into the
arms of the latter at the first sign of epistemological slippage. In the
opening pages of "Objectivity Is Not Neutrality," for example, he
tells us that he has accepted the historicists' principal contention. As
he puts it, "after three centuries of inquiry into the basis of moral
judgment it appears that no ultimate, metaphysical foundations are
to be found—in nature, divine will, or anywhere else."[89] But this is
a reluctant acceptance of inevitability rather than an enthusiastic
affirmation of possibility; instead of an opportunity, Haskell sees only
menace: "I may as well confess from the outset that beneath the
surface of my text the reader will find a darker current of ambivalence and anxiety."[90] In the end, this darker current of apprehension
and dread proves the more powerful, pulling him down and finally
destroying his hopes for a "moderate, pragmatic historicism."

Haskell's entire project has been shaped by this fear that radical
historicism will plunge us into a world without principle. It's a zero-
sum game for Haskell: either we find some way to save historical
objectivity or we are doomed to moral relativism. If we give in to
relativism we set ourselves on Nietzsche's slippery slope to nothingness. "And their feet shall slide in due time." Haskell is a moderate
historicist longing for moral certainty in an age of interpretation. He
thinks he can find a "safe haven," a "stopping place" just short of
the epistemological abyss—a set of ethical principles so firmly rooted
in "the human condition" that they can withstand even the most
savage onslaught of the radical historicists.

Again, Haskell does not contend that he has found a Platonic
moral order built into the very nature of things; he is perfectly will-

ing to admit that the values he defends constitute nothing more than a particular historical convention. But he is not willing to say they are simply the *chance* results of a *random* historical process, for he does not think the historical process is random at all. On the contrary, he thinks that as it unfolds it throws up certain values—like the natural rights tradition—that by their very persistence over time can be taken to express some deep truth about "the nature of man." In other words, history *reveals* meaning rather than having meaning imposed upon it. And that meaning is stable, plainly discernible, autonomous and a priori, not only of any particular social or political context, but of any particular rhetorical devices, narrative constructs, or interpretive strategies.

This may sound like an odd position for a self-described historicist to find himself in. But the fact that Quentin Skinner, J. G. A. Pocock, David Hollinger, James Kloppenberg, and now Thomas Haskell all ended up at the same epistemological dead-end illustrates something that should have been obvious from the beginning: there is no such thing as a "moderate" historicism, just as there is no such thing as a moderate ahistoricism. Though Hollinger, Haskell, and Kloppenberg had hoped to find a stopping place somewhere only partway down the historicist road—someplace well before its "radical" destination began to loom on the horizon—Stanley Fish is almost certainly right when he says that "once you start down the anti-formalist road, there is no place to stop."[91] This is one reason the historical profession no longer has—and probably never will have—a high-level, nonlocal, ideologically neutral theory of historical knowledge, that is, a set of stable, widely agreed on principles that it can use to evaluate competing historical accounts "objectively," prior to and free of any particular context or interpretation.

But there is another reason. As Kant explained over two hundred years ago, we will never have a set of objective principles for evaluating historical accounts because our every attempt to define who we *have been* is so densely and irretrievably interwoven with our hopelessly subjective attempts to define both who we *are* and who we wish to *become.* We choose who we are by choosing who we have been; we choose moral exemplars from the past in order to govern our behavior in the present and guide our movement into the future. To choose a past is thus to choose a future by describing how men and women ought to live and what they ought to value.[92]

For Hegel, too, the past was a tool we use to create new forms of cultural life. But we cannot see the past as a tool until it has actually become the past; we can see its usefulness only retrospectively. Richard Rorty puts it this way:

We cannot see Christianity or Newtonianism or the Romantic movement or political liberalism as a tool while we are still in the course of figuring out how to use it. For there are as yet no clearly formulatable ends to which it is a means. But once we figure out how to use the vocabularies of these movements, we can tell a story of progress, showing how the literalization of certain metaphors served the purpose of making possible all the good things that have recently happened. Further, we can now view all these good things as particular instances of some more general good, the overall end which the movement served. . . . I construe this to mean "finding a description of all the things characteristic of your time of which you most approve, with which you unflinchingly identify, a description which will serve as a description of the end toward which the historical developments which led up to your time were means."[93]

I take Kant, Hegel, and Rorty to be insisting that the reason we do not have, and probably never will have, a widely agreed on and generally reliable set of objective criteria for evaluating historical accounts is that written history is always and necessarily a search for the meaning of our present.[94] Without this necessarily present-oriented assignment of meaning the past remains an inert and essentially meaningless chronicle. What Emerson tried to tell us about "nature" in his famous essay "The American Scholar" is every bit as true of history: "In its original state," Emerson wrote, "It cannot fly, it cannot shine, it is a dull grub"; but let some historian impose meaning on it and "the selfsame thing unfurls beautiful wings, and becomes an angel of wisdom."[95] On this view of things history is not an attempt to discover objective truth; it is a way of thinking about ourselves and our experience. The experiences of other people living in other cultures are helpful to us because they suggest possibilities, qualifications, and counterexamples that can sometimes help us challenge entrenched ways of thinking about the present—ways of thinking that have often become so routinized as to be habitual and even chronic.[96]

I read R. G. Collingwood as saying something very much like this when he noted that the way we think about history and the kind of history we write are ultimately functions of the kind of people we are.[97] And I read White, Rorty, Kant, and Hegel as saying that the opposite is also true. From this perspective, Haskell's insistence that we must refer our choice between competing historical accounts to a set of objective criteria looks pretty much like what Sartre meant by "bad faith."[98]

The irony is not simply that after two hundred years of searching we have yet to come up with the hoped-for set of objective criteria; it is rather that we do not *need* them. The dream of possessing a formula, a procedure that would guarantee the objectivity, neutrality, and reliability of professional judgments is just the sort of thing that pragmatists like William James and John Dewey tried to talk us out of—largely because the result so often turns out to be what Rorty once called "a string of platitudes, hooked up to look like an algorithm."[99]

It makes more sense to read the search for an objective methodology as a stand-in for the older (and now fairly well discredited) idea that "truthful" accounts must pass the test of "correspondence to reality."[100] After all, historians have been trying to apply "the logic of the scientific method" to historical writing ever since they heard about the new science in the seventeenth century. So far they have not come up with much. In fact, their repeated failures make one wonder if we should waste still more time searching for this particular philosopher's stone. Perhaps we would be better off trying to develop a gut feeling for when to *forget* about theories and rely on our own intuitive sense of what is important and what is not.[101]

But Haskell is afraid that if we let every woman become her own historian we will forget the moral lessons of Western history and lose sight of the values that have made us who we are. This fear is a large part of what drove the reaction against theory during the 1980s. It was an ethical backlash that arose from both Left and Right.[102] Among those on the left it is a powerful movement away from the ambiguities and undecidabilities of textualism, toward the more straightforward, explicit issues of power and identity; on the right there is an equally powerful insistence that deconstruction and other agents of befuddlement have undermined our traditional interpretation of the classics as respositories of universal moral truth. As Haskell sees it, "Derrida and other contemporary relativists" have bred a dangerous indifference to liberal values—an indifference that has led us into the swamp of moral relativism.[103] Both the Left and the Right complain that contemporary literary theory has weakened the moral fiber of American intellectual life, leaving us ethically indifferent, if not morally enfeebled. By inducing a dangerous relativism, contemporary theory's insistence on the irreducibility and opaqueness of language constitutes a cultural menace that threatens all of Western civilization.

The response to this sort of thing is just what it has always been: that we continue to cherish our beliefs, continue to regulate our conduct by them—indeed, continue to profess our willingness to lay down our lives for them—even though we know they represent nothing more than the random products of a random historical process. Indeed, they are all the more precious because they *are* so historically contingent. Not long ago the communitarian political theorist (and acute critic of liberalism) Michael Sandel asked, "If one's convictions are only relatively valid, why stand for them unflinchingly?"[104] But the answer had already come, years earlier, from no less a critic of liberalism than Joseph Schumpeter: "To realize the relative validity of one's convictions and yet stand for them unflinchingly, is what distinguishes a civilized man from a barbarian."[105]

If Haskell wants history to provide moral lessons he should stop trying to formulate an abstract, high-level, pseudoscientific theory of historical interpretation and start ransacking the past for men and women whose thoughts and lives exemplify the moral values he considers important. Instead of trying to convince the rest of us that we need a general theory of "objectivity," he should simply draw up a list of his favorite heroes and villains from the American past— historical figures who could help us think more clearly about what we should value and how we should live. We do not need to formulate comprehensive theories and innovative methodologies in order to do these things; all we need to do is find some moral exemplars from the past—people whose lives embody the values we think important. Instead of striving for detachment and objectivity, for "the most complete, least idiosyncratic, view that humans are capable of," we should be trying to convince other people (our students, for example) that their take on the world would be richer, more interesting, and more ethically pertinent if they added some of our heroes to their own list of heroes.[106]

Haskell's standards for ensuring objectivity would offer precious little help in making choices like these, which are, after all, moral and aesthetic choices.[107] That is not to say they are whimsical or capricious, but it is to say that this is not so much a matter of "getting it right" as of an intentional and deliberate participation in one or another historically conditioned sensibility or constellation of values and beliefs. This is one of the reasons we eventually come to admire Nick Carraway: for all his apparent aloofness and snobbishness, he has intentionally and even self-consciously laid claim to a particular identity—a midwestern identity—and along with it a particular sensibility. In the final chapter Nick returns to Minneapolis for Christmas. Passing between the cars of the train, inhaling the bone-cold air, he realized,

That's my Middle West. . . . I am part of that, a little solemn
with the feel of those long winters, a little complacent from
growing up in the Carraway house in a city where dwellings
are still called through decades by a family's name. I see now
that this has been a story of the West, after all—Tom and
Gatsby, Daisy and Jordan and I, were all Westerners, and perhaps we possessed some deficiency in common which made us
subtly unadaptable to Eastern life.[108]

What we need from American historians is not a new defense of
objectivity but a little help in finding the predecessors we need.

III

We have lost our grip on historical truth.
—Appleby, Hunt, and Jacob, *Telling the Truth about History*

Joyce Appleby, Lynn Hunt, and Margaret Jacob, three well-known
and highly respected historians, have made the most recent, the most
ambitious, and certainly the most widely discussed effort to defend
the objectivity of historical knowledge. Like others who have em-
barked on this particular exercise in futility, they describe themselves
as liberal pragmatists. And also like the others, they are working
historians rather than philosophers of history, which means that
reading their account is something like watching a collection of geese
try to hatch a duck's egg—uneventful, as it turns out, but not altogether uninstructive.

In their introduction to *Telling the Truth about History* (1994)
Appleby, Hunt, and Jacob describe themselves as "among the barbarians" who stormed the gates of the historical profession in the 1960s:
"We have not only witnessed but also participated in the dethroning
of once sacred intellectual icons. Trained to be 'scientific' in our
methods, we have challenged the inherited, traditional interpretations of both American and European history." But that was thirty
years ago. The barbarians are no longer at the gates, of course; now
they are inside the castle. Indeed, they have taken over as the new
aristocracy: "Although they may not control the budget, they sit on
the most important university committees, teach many of the biggest
courses, and write some of the most influential books."[109] And, of
course, enjoy all the privileges and prerogatives Theopolis Academia
has to offer: endowed chairs at elite universities; access to grants and
fellowships; medals and awards too numerous to mention. *Telling
the Truth about History* is their book, the testimony of three former
rebels turned faithful defenders of exhausted dogmas.

Telling the Truth is a double-voiced discourse: a lamentation over lost certainties and a prophecy of revelations to come. The lamentation begins at the beginning, on page 1:

> Once there was a single narrative of national history that most Americans accepted as part of their heritage. Now there is an increasing emphasis on the diversity of ethnic, racial, and gender experience and a deep skepticism about whether the narrative of America's achievements comprises anything more than a self-congratulatory story masking the power of elites. History has been shaken right down to its scientific and cultural foundations at the very time that those foundations themselves are being contested. . . . By the time our generation of students matured and became college teachers themselves, confidence in previous certainties had all but disappeared. No longer did people believe that any form of knowledge, including history, could be modeled on the scientific method of inquiry, or that progress in science and technology was unquestionably desirable—the more the better. Where value-free science had once made sense and offered hope of sustained progress, now neither an uncontested, edifying truth about the American past nor benign scientific advance seems possible to thoughtful people.[110]

Appleby, Hunt, and Jacob may have gone to graduate school in the sixties, but they grew up in the fifties. They may have come to accept the increasing diversity of American history, and they may even condone a bit of what they call "healthy skepticism," but as their opening passage suggests, they also yearn for the certainties of the past, especially for that grand "single narrative of national history." Like so many of our generation, they are trapped between the America in which they grew up and the America in which they came of age, between Eisenhower's America and Nixon's (or Norman Rockwell's and Saul Steinberg's). In *Telling the Truth* they try to convince us that we can have it both ways: that the doubts and diversity of the sixties need not deny us real, objective knowledge about the past, or a new synthesis of American history, or the single all-encompassing American identity that such a history would presuppose and reinforce.[111] It is a measure of the depth of our own longing that so many of us have embraced the redemptive promises they hold forth in *Telling the Truth about History*.

Like Hollinger, Haskell, and Kloppenberg, Appleby and her coauthors worry that the poststructuralist attack on objectivity will plunge us into a netherworld of multiplying perspectives and fragmenting interpretations, a gray and empty space, devoid of permanent mean-

ing or enduring truth. They are not reactionaries; indeed, they readily
concede that "a certain amount of skepticism about truth claims has
been essential to the search for truth."[112] But the specter of *"complete
skepticism"* unnerves them: "Every time people go down the relativist road the path darkens and the light recedes from the tunnel."[113]
Not only has it led some weedy intellectuals to deny the reality of
the Holocaust, it has "generated a pervasive lack of confidence in
the ability to find the truth or even to establish that there is such
a thing as truth."[114] In *Telling the Truth* they offer a middle road,
a safe passage between the naive realism they were raised on and
the "fluid skepticism [that] now covers the intellectual landscape,
encroaching upon one body of thought after another."[115]

Appleby, Hunt, and Jacob call that middle road "practical realism"
and gratefully acknowledge their apparent to the Harvard philosopher Hilary Putnam, who coined the phrase in 1981.[116] But what they
mean by "practical realism" bears little relation to what he meant by
it.[117] Putnam was and is intensely critical of what he calls "scientism";
indeed, he reserves his deepest criticism for those who have allowed
themselves to be "overawed by science."[118] What really interests him
are the problems posed by religious thinkers and religious forms of
discourse. Indeed,the philosophers who have influenced him most
profoundly are all religious thinkers: Kierkegaard, James, and the
early Wittgenstein.[119]

The "practical realism" that Appleby, Hunt, and Jacob give us,
on the other hand, is pretty much what Putnam dismisses as "scientism." As they themselves describe it, it is "a new way of thinking
about objectivity, one that argues for the centrality of science to
Western culture and to the search for truth."[120] By using the term
practical realism they simply mean to gesture in the direction of the
now-fashionable truism that all knowledge is socially constructed.[121]
That this is in fact simply a gesture can be seen in their repeated
insistence that "science can be historically and socially framed and
still be true," that "some words and conventions, however socially
constructed, reach out to the world and give a reasonably true description of its contents."[122] Appleby, Hunt, and Jacob employ a prose style
that has the quality of pea soup—except when they turn to praising
the wonders of science. For example, after a description of the rise
and fall of various ideological delusions ("nation-building," "the laws
of human development," and so on) comes this: "Behind all these
absolutisms was the radiant concept of nature—not the lush and
untamable nature of the primitive world or the nature that pushed
Adam and Eve to sin, but the nature of science, of progressive im-

provement and spontaneous order that human inquirers now perceived beneath the flotsam and jetsam that floated to the surface of daily life."[123]

Just as they want us to think of science as revealing a "spontaneous order" beneath the flux of appearances, so they want us to "think of history as a body of knowledge revealing a pattern or having a meaning."[124] And just as the development of science constitutes a story of "progressive improvement," so the development of history: "We hope to show how historians have conceptualized their task in the past, particularly how that task has developed from telling a simple story to answering a complex array of questions about the human experience."[125]

Finally, and again like science, they think of writing history as a group activity, "a shared enterprise," something one does "in a scholarly community."[126] Indeed, the idea of individual creativity belongs to "the heroic age": "To lavish all one's attention on the possibility of personal inventiveness on the part of those reading a text, to the neglect of the probability of shared understanding of words is to distort reality. . . . Far from exercising individual idiosyncrasies in reading, a community of readers will build up a strong consensus on meaning."[127]

It is the institutional structure of academic life—the whole dreary system of review committees and annual conventions and international conferences—in a word, the proverbial old boy network, which, now as then, one cultivates through the art of schmooze—that is said to guarantee the objectivity of historical writing.[128] It does this, as Appleby, Hunt, and Jacob suggest above, by reducing the writer to a "practitioner" engaged in "a shared enterprise in which the community of practitioners acts as a check on the historian." Thus do "individual idiosyncrasies in reading" get nipped in the bud.[129]

One wonders what Henry Adams would have thought about all this. Or Perry Miller. In his distinctly idiosyncratic and nonpragmatic essay "The Plight of the Lone Wolf," Miller described "the dignified isolation" of individual faculty members at the University of Chicago in the 1920s. "A professor was a kingdom unto himself," Miller remembered, "its sole ruler and only citizen." "Suffice it to say, all of them worked as individuals, alone in their studies, at the head of their own excavations. They spoke for themselves, out of their own researches, their own notes, or their own violent prejudices. The point is, not one of them can be imagined as ever forming part of a 'team.'"[130] It was "this dwindling in the universities of the ideal of the lonely scholar" that most dismayed Miller when he thought about intellectual life in America. "I point to this phenomenon as the one that has most interested, not to say appalled, me. . . . It is a transformation of immense importance."[131]

Miller dreaded precisely what the neopragmatists have since embraced: the institutionalizing of the American mind. But then, institutional life is their natural element, as solitude was his. The tragedy is that Miller died before he could see the one development that could possibly stop this flattening of intellect: the sociological diversification of the universities. The irony is that the neopragmatists, who both saw and applauded that process, somehow failed to see that it would inevitably shatter the professional consensus on which they staked so much. The opening of the universities has endlessly multiplied and wonderfully enriched the interpretive possibilities confronting American historians. But it has also fractured forever that magisterial narrative of national identity, that spiritual biography of American nationhood, that sustained the culture for over three hundred years—and that sustained Appleby, Hunt, and Jacob (and how many others of us?) through their childhood and into their twenties. But now, as Emerson said in another context: "This original unit, this fountain of power, has been so distributed to multitudes, has been so minutely subdivided and peddled out, that it is spilled into drops, and cannot be gathered."[132]

But Appleby, Hunt, and Jacob think it can be gathered—indeed, that it *must* be gathered: "A comprehensive national history is not now an educational option for the country; it is a cultural imperative."[133] Not that they minimize the difficulties; they know as well as anyone else that a consensus on American national identity no longer exists, that "the multifarious communities within the nation rightfully contest the privilege of officialdom to establish the parameters of national identity."[134] Nevertheless, they continue to insist that historians set themselves to the task of "creating a new narrative framework," an all-inclusive, multicultural history of the United States that would incorporate "all the identities that Americans carry with them."[135]

There are times when they seem to grasp the sheer impossibility of such a thing. For example, in a chapter titled "Competing Histories of America," they describe the "avalanche" of new histories that have poured down on us since the 1960s—and continue to pour down, without any sign of letting up. And they admit that, even to them, "it seems as though the new scholarship about ordinary people has produced more history than the nation can digest."[136] They even quote John Donne: " 'Tis all in pieces, all coherence gone." But thus poised on the edge of a critical insight into the central, defining characteristic not only of historical writing in postmodern societies, but of intellectual life generally in such societies—that is, the stupendous, totally unmanageable, and utterly unassimilable overproduction of information—they simply drop the subject. Instead of trying to figure out what all this might mean for the traditional notion of a single, all-inclusive narrative of American history, they reassure themselves with the altogether inadequate observation that "history has thus found itself linked to a new set of public issues, those connected with the dawning appreciation of America's multifaceted past and its multicultural heritage." With this happily incongruous comment their discussion simply stops.[137]

As any number of historians have pointed out, it is the very success of professional history—its enormous and utterly overwhelming production of historical narratives, written from every conceivable subject position, every conceivable point of view, every conceivable theoretical perspective—that has destroyed forever the possibility of a single, unifying narrative of national identity.[138] Appleby, Hunt, and Jacob do seem to understand this, if only on occasion. They admit, for example, that this monstrous overproduction "raises very forcefully the disturbing possibility that the study of history does not strengthen an attachment to one's country. Indeed, the reverse might be true, i.e., that open-ended investigation of the nation's past could weaken the ties of citizenship."[139]

But this is an observation they are neither willing to accept nor prepared to challenge. In the end their longing for a single, comprehensive history of America—a history that would redefine our collective identity and reinforce our mutual obligations—simply overwhelms their concomitant recognition that, as Peter Novick has explained, by the mid-1980s "even by the most generous definition, history no longer constituted a coherent discipline; not just that the whole was less than the sum of its parts, but that there was no whole—only parts."[140]

Though their new multicultural history would be primarily a social history, it would also include discussion of the key political events in the nation's past, since if "these momentous events are muddied, then the nation's collective identity is put at risk."[141] Nor must it lose sight of the political *values* the country is thought to stand for—the recitation of which will sound eerily familiar to those of us who grew up in middle-class suburban America in the 1950s: "Then and today, America stands for a set of abstractions pointing to the superiority of individual freedom, restrained government, open opportunity, mutual tolerance, and diplomatic support for free nations."[142] Foremost among these distinctively American values is pragmatism itself, which is now seen to underlie our democratic creed and to offer us our best sense of who we are and what we stand for. Pragmatism not only runs through the entire course American history, it *defines* that history. Indeed, by the end of this remarkable book, pragmatism turns out to be nothing less than Americanism itself:

> Pragmatic initially without philosophers, Americans developed democratic practices which promoted experimentation, invention, and education. A century later a formal theory of pragmatism emerged which depended upon the rules and civility of an open republic and a commitment to the knowability of nature and hence to scientific truth. Today the nation's democratic creed as well as its pragmatic tradition rely upon a consensus of beliefs about reality and the possibility of arriving at common goals.[143]

This is a vision of historical writing in the service of consensus building and the celebration of traditional American values. It may seem like an odd position in which to find former rebels and would-be defenders of historical objectivity, but such are the ironies of pragmatism in the 1990s.

PART TWO

The Renewal of American Historical Writing

CHAPTER FIVE

The Return of the Moral Imagination

I

For over thirty years Hayden White has been trying to free histori-cal writing from the assumptions and limitations of nineteenth-century realism. In three major books and a long series of articles he has tried to make the rest of us see what now seems obvious to almost everyone: that a historical account is basically an act of the moral imagination, that is, a search for predecessors, an ordering of value, a conversation with the dead about what we should value and how we should live. The antinomian implications of this argument, though always apparent, did not become an issue until the early 1970s, when the rise of poststructuralism made White's defense of the moral imagination look like Nietzsche's celebration of the will to power. Partly to refute his critics and partly to work out the impli-cations of the structuralism he had picked up from Roland Barthes and others in the 1960s, White spent the next twenty years—from 1972 through 1992—developing an elaborate, highly formalist phi-losophy that he hoped would contain what critics condemned as the "rubbery relativism" of his original vision. He still thought of histori-cal accounts as acts of the moral imagination, but now he argued that the imagination itself is structured and governed by an underlying set of mental categories—categories that are both a priori and universal. This was the philosophy of history that White presented in *Metahis-tory* (1973), *Tropics of Discourse* (1978), and *The Content of the Form* (1987). What gave it life and made it so fascinating was the tension he maintained between his humanist insistence on the freedom of the imagination and his structuralist insistence that acts of the imagination are governed by "the deep structures" of human consciousness.

But in the past several years White has been quietly moving away from this by now rather antiquated structuralism. Indeed, by the mid-1990s it had virtually disappeared from his work. As Ralph Ellison might have put it, White has "changed the joke and slipped the yoke." This has been a long and gradual process, but he seems to have reached a turning point in 1992. In that year he published a subtle, elusive, and widely misunderstood essay titled "Historical Emplotment and the Problem of Truth."[1] That essay, more than any other, signals White's return from the discourse of structuralism (with its subsidiary problems of representation and correspondence) to the issues of ethics and agency that had originally engaged him in the 1960s. In "Historical Emplotment and the Problem of Truth" White took up, once again, his earlier conviction that historical writing is essentially a form of moral reflection, a way of coming to terms with ourselves. This is the Hayden White who once wrote that "the moral implications of the human sciences will never be perceived until the faculty of the will is reinstated in theory." It is the Hayden White who used to insist that stories about the past constitute the most basic unifying structures of the self, and that rethinking the past is a way of rethinking ourselves and reordering our values.[2] I begin part 2 with a discussion of White's intellectual odyssey because it is Hayden White, especially in his latest *ricorso*, who has contributed more than anyone else to the return of the moral imagination in American historical writing.

II

White published "The Burden of History" in 1966.[3] This was his first major theoretical statement, and it has turned out to be the polestar that has guided virtually everything he has written since then. What strikes one about "The Burden of History"—even now, over thirty years after it first appeared—is White's extraordinary sense not only of the *presence* of the past but of the *pressure* with which it bears down on the present. Like young Holgrave in Hawthorne's *House of the Seven Gables*, White felt as if the past were lying full length on top of the present, as if the living were pinned under the weight of a giant's dead body that threatens to crush the life out of them. And like Holgrave (and also like Marx, who wrote "We suffer not only from the living but from the dead. Le mort saisit le vif!"), White thought the historian's primary responsibility was not to reanimate the past but to get us out from under it—not to recover the past but to liberate us from it. "The problem," as he later remarked, "may not be how to get into history but how to get out of it."[4] This has been a consistent theme of his writing. Twenty years after "The Burden of History," in *The Content of the Form: Narrative Discourse and Historical Representation* (1987), he was still calling for a conception of the historical record as being not a window through which we might gaze upon the past, but a wall that we must tear down if the "terror of history" is to be directly confronted and the fear it induces dispelled.[5]

White's argument is too subtle and complicated to summarize easily, but the gist of it went like this. First, White described what he saw as a growing hostility toward historical studies, largely among novelists, literary critics, and social scientists. The novelists and critics despised history for its lack of imagination and sensibility, but especially for its debilitating sense of irony. Like Nietzsche in "The Uses and Abuses of History," they thought historical writing stripped men and women of illusion and robbed them of volition; it drained them of will and thereby reduced them to mere "shades and abstractions."[6] The social scientists, on the other hand, criticized history for its appalling lack of method and rigor, its failure to establish itself on the solid ground of empirical observation and rational argument.[7] Thus "the general consensus" in the liberal arts, according to White: history was neither "ennobling nor even illuminative of our humanity."[8] "It follows that *the burden of the historian* in our time is to reestablish the dignity of historical studies on a basis that will make them consonant with the aims and purposes of the intellectual community at large, that is, transform historical studies in such a way as to allow the historian to participate positively in the liberation of the present from *the burden of history*."[9]

Second, White argued that historians could escape the contempt of their colleagues by dropping the old-fashioned idea that history should explain what really happened. Historians should stop trying to reconstruct the past right side up and in true perspective. They should forget about trying to make their accounts correspond to (or provide causal explanations of) the facts and realize that, like every other discipline in the humananities, history does not have, and is not likely to have, a set of formal, objective, widely agreed on procedures for identifying what constitutes a fact, much less what constitutes a valid explanation of the facts.[10] And they should realize that nothing interesting or helpful is likely to come from attempts to formulate such procedures.[11]

White wanted to redefine history as an interpretive art rather than an explanatory science; he wanted historians to come up with new interpretive metaphors rather than new causal explanations. He argued that explanation presumes to tell us why what happened had to have happened—and why it had to have happened *just as it did.* It is the tyranny of historians' causal explanations that robs the present of its possibilities. Interpretation, on the other hand, asks historians to attribute *meanings* to past events. White wanted to substitute interpretation for explanation because, like William James, he wanted to think of the *present* as open, unfinished, incomplete, a "booming, blooming, buzzing confusion." He wanted a past that was teeming with as yet unavailable meanings, a source of imaginative possibilities rather than causal explanations, a warehouse to be ransacked rather than a burden to be acknowledged.[12]

You can see what he had in mind by looking at the examples he offered. The most important and illuminating of these was Jacob Burckhardt's classic *The Civilization of the Renaissance.* White appreciated Burckhardt's "impressionistic" style, but what he really admired was his commitment to interpretation over explanation:

> Like his contemporaries in art, Burckhardt cuts into the historical record at different points and suggests different perspectives on it, omitting, ignoring, or distorting as his artistic purpose requires. His intention was not to tell the *whole* truth about the Italian Renaissance but one truth about it, in precisely the same way that Cezanne abandoned any attempt to tell the whole truth about a landscape. He had abandoned the dream of telling the truth about the past by means of telling a story because he had long since abandoned the belief that history had any *inherent* meaning or significance.[13]

In White's earliest formulation, then, history was interpretive rather than explanatory and constructivist rather than empirical. White wanted historians to think of the past as a source of new perspectives and possible meanings, an invitation to interpretation and reinterpretation.[14]

Finally, White adopted an explicitly present-minded stance toward the past, urging us to read history from the present backward. He wanted us to think of history as "a way of providing perspectives on the present that contribute to the solution of problems peculiar to our own time."[15] Only three years earlier, in *The Making of the English Working Class* (1963), E. P. Thompson had argued that the historian's primary responsibility was to the people of the past, simply because they had lived through those times and we had not.[16] By contrast, White would rather have agreed with Frank Kermode that "we are necessarily more involved with the living than with the dead, with what learning cherishes and interpretation refreshes rather than with mere remains."[17] Rather than sending us backward toward the origins of our "looped and windowed raggedness," White wanted to point us forward, toward the hidden possibilities of the present.

White rounded out his basic argument in "What Is an Historical System?" a little-noticed but crucially important essay published in 1972. Here, for the first time, he made explicit a point he had only implied in "The Burden of History": that we have to choose our own precursors and predecessors—something White now called "retroactive ancestral substitution."[18] Now, instead of history as a burden to be escaped, we get history as a past to be chosen: "The historical past is plastic in a way that the genetic past is not. Men range over it and select from it models of comportment for structuring their movement into their future. They choose a set of *ideal ancestors* which they *treat as genetic progenitors.* This ideal ancestry may have no physical connection at all with the individuals doing the choosing. But their choice is made in such a way as to substitute this ideal ancestry for their actual."[19]

White illustrated this idea with a series of revealing examples: Lenin consolidated the Russian Revolution by "imposing a completely new set of ancestral models on Russian society"; Luther sparked the Protestant Reformation by "bestowing ancestry on a group which had lost it during the course of the Middle Ages"; the Roman Empire collapsed because "men ceased to regard themselves as descendents of their Roman forebears and began to treat themselves as descendents of their Judaeo-Christian predecessors."[20] In each case it was the creative reinterpretation of the past that broke the back of the present: it was "the constitution of a *fictional* cultural ancestry" that splintered the medieval church, destroyed the Roman Empire, and consolidated the Russian Revolution.[21]

So the past is no longer the given it seemed to be in "The Burden of History." Now we have to choose its various components and assemble them ourselves: "It has to be constructed, in the same way and in the same extent that we have to construct our socio-cultural present."[22] When we choose to emulate a particular set of exemplars we are, in fact, choosing to adopt a particular set of ancestors—and thereby constructing a particular past. By choosing who we wish to become, we choose who we have been; ancestry is conferred by descendants. As White put it, "Social fatherhood is only bestowed by the sons; it is bestowed by the choices men make of models of comportment offered by the socio-cultural system."[23] Conversely, to deny that we choose our own past is to deny that we choose our own future. For White, as for Jean-Paul Sartre, such a denial is the essence of bad faith: "By seeking retroactive justification for [the present] in our past, we silently strip ourselves of the freedom that has allowed us to become what we are."[24] Only human beings are truly free because "only human beings are asked to selectively choose their ancestry retrospectively."[25]

I I I

But in the early 1970s White began to worry that he had gone too far, that in trying to escape "the burden of history" he had unintentionally blurred the distinction between history and fiction. The turning point seems to have come in 1972. He wrote "What Is an Historical System?" that year, but he also wrote "Interpretation in History," which signaled a dramatic departure from everything he had written up to then. Where he had earlier talked about the possibilities of interpretation, he now talked about its dangers; where he had earlier celebrated the role of the moral imagination, he now tried to contain it, to hedge it round and hem it in, grounding its operations in the basic categories of the mind. By 1972 White had come to think that his earlier espousal of creative interpretation was encouraging the wrong kind of interpreters: free-wheeling, all-purpose "critics of historiography as a discipline" who "have taken more radical views on the matter of interpretation in history, going so far as to argue that historical accounts are *nothing but* interpretations."[26]

White was thinking of Claude Lévi-Strauss, among others.[27] In *The Savage Mind* (published in 1966—the same year White published "The Burden of History") Lévi-Strauss had argued that history was an interpretative discipline rather than an explanatory science, that its "facts" were made, not found, that they were constituted by the narratives ostensibly composed to explain them. White had said essentially the same thing in "The Burden of History," of course, but Lévi-Strauss went much further, charging that historical interpretation is inherently "mythical," that whatever coherence a historical account may achieve is no more than the coherence of "mythology."[28] As White read him, Lévi-Strauss seemed to be saying that historical narratives are "secured only by dint of fraudulent outlines" arbitrarily selected and imposed "on a body of materials which could be called 'data' only in the most extended sense of the term." If Lévi-Strauss was right, history "never completely escapes the nature of myth."[29]

White had already traveled partway down this road himself, of course, but until he read Lévi-Strauss he had not seen where it would take him. It was Lévi-Strauss who showed him. White had argued that historical accounts have to be judged not by their fidelity to the facts, but "solely in terms of the richness of the metaphors which govern their sequences of articulation."[30] Faced with an argument that was essentially an extension of his own but one that revealed the implications hidden away at its base, White began to rethink the whole project. He worried that the interpretive liberty he had celebrated in "The Burden of History" would reduce historical writing to little more than "coatwhirling artfulness,"[31] that historical accounts would become "nothing *but* interpretation," a pasteboard artifice of arbitrary assertions and dubious claims. Suddenly it seemed that historiography needed an underlying structure, something that could stabilize its rhetorical and explanatory forms, something that could order and regulate its interpretive processes.

White found part of what he needed in Northrop Frye's taxonomy of literary forms. In *The Anatomy of Criticism* (1957) Frye had argued that literary works are not the original creations of individual writers, created ex nihilo from their own fuming brains, but the working out of "embedded forms."[32] By applying this idea to the problem of historical interpretation, White was able to argue that historical accounts should be judged not by the richness of their metaphors—as he had suggested in "The Burden of History"—but by the degree to which they appeal and conform to one or another literary archetype, that is, to the "pregeneric plot-structures" and "archetypal story-forms" that Frye had described in *The Anatomy of Criticism*.[33] This gave White some of the interpretive controls he was looking for. It allowed him to contend that historical interpretation does not operate "capriciously, as Lévi-Strauss appeared to suggest": "It operates, rather, according to well-known, if frequently violated, literary conventions, conventions which the historian, like the poet, begins to assimilate from the first moment he is told a story as a child."[34]

But what exactly are these "literary conventions," "pregeneric plot-structures" and "archetypal story-forms"? According to White, they are the "informing patterns of meaning" that the larger culture has "explicitly provided" in its "literary art." The historian endows her narrative with determinable meaning by arranging its basic facts in the form required by one or another of these pregeneric plot structures. In other words, she gives meaning to a particular sequence of events—she makes it recognizable and understandable—by presenting it as "a story of a particular kind."[35] The historian still has to choose among the available plot structures, of course. But—and this is the crucial point for White—she chooses from a set of strictly limited, culturally sanctioned forms; she does not fabricate those forms de novo, from her own idiosyncratic imagination. Moreover, the account she writes will be judged on the wisdom of her choices and not, as White had earlier contended, on the richness of her governing metaphors. It was with almost palpable relief that White announced that "there are, then, 'rules' if not 'laws' of historical narration."[36]

To make sure he had quashed any chance of interpretive capriciousness, White next called on R. G. Collingwood's notion of the "constructive imagination."[37] On the face of it, Collingwood's idea bestowed obvious advantages: the constructive imagination is "both *a priori* (which meant that it could not act capriciously) and *structural* (which meant that it was governed by notions of formal coherency in its constitution of possible objects of thought)."[38] In other words, Collingwood's "constructive imagination" worked in much the way Kant's a priori imagination was thought to have worked: it shaped and formed the historian's most basic perceptions of the world; it "prefigured" the field for her. By adding Collingwood's idea of the constructive imagination to Frye's notion of "pregeneric plot-structures" and "archetypal story-forms," White was able to wring the last drop of "capriciousness" out of the historian's interpretive work. Historians could now be seen to approach their evidence "endowed with a sense of the possible plot-forms that any particular sequence of events can take"; the constructive imagination, and the limited number of pregeneric plot structures and archetypal story forms, served to "direct the historian's attention to the form that a given set of events *must* have in order to serve as a possible 'object of thought.' "[39] Thus it seemed that the specter raised by Lévi-Strauss been exorcised:

> If, as Lévi-Strauss correctly observes, one *can* tell a host of different stories about the single set of events conventionally designated as "the French Revolution," this does not mean that the *types* of stories that can be told about the set are infinite in number. The types of stories that can be told about the French Revolution are limited to the number of modes of emplotment which the myths of the Western literary tradition sanction as appropriate ways of endowing human processes with meanings.[40]

Nor was that all. In "The Burden of History" and other essays written during the middle and late 1960s, White had offered interpretation as an alternative to explanation. Instead of struggling with inappropriate explanatory forms borrowed from the sciences, he had wanted historians to experiment with interpretive forms borrowed from hermeneutics. But now, in the early 1970s, White returned to explanation. He found an acceptable model in Stephen Pepper's *World Hypotheses* (1966). What White liked about Pepper was that he seemed to do for explanation what Frye had done for plot: he provided Kantian explanations of their function, a useful inventory of their forms, and a strict limitation of their number. Just as historians come to their evidence "endowed with a sense of the possible plot-forms," so they "bring to their efforts to explain the past different paradigms of the form that a valid explanation may take."[41] And just as the plot forms were limited (there were only four: romance, comedy, tragedy, and satire), so the explanation forms were limited (again, there were only four (idiographic, organic, mechanistic, and contextualist). And just as before, the historian had to choose from this limited number the explanation form she thought most appropriate for her narrative.

But now the game grew more complicated because the choices the historian made on these two levels (plot form and explanation form) had to correspond: the appropriate choices on each level would naturally display an "elective affinity" for one another. Each form did not *have* to be used with its proper correspondent, of course; one could violate the natural correspondence of natural types. But "it is the felicitous combination of arguments with narrative representations which accounts for the appeal of a specifically 'historical' representation of reality."[42] Indeed, White argued that the correspondence of these "elective affinities" distinguishes classical from ordinary historical narratives.[43]

Plot form worked on one level, explanation form on another. The first gave historical *narratives* their recognizable form; the second gave historical *arguments* their particular mode of persuasion.[44] But there was a third level, "ideological implication," that gave historical accounts their ethical meaning. As on the other levels, here too the historian had to choose one among only four options: liberal, conservative, radical, and anarchist. And as before, her choice did or did not set up an "elective affinity" with its corresponding plot form and explanation form. So in the course of her interpretive labors the historian had to commit herself on three levels: the aesthetic (plot form), the epistemological (explanation form), and the ethical (ideological implication). The account she wrote could therefore be judged on the aptness of her decisions. In one sense her account simply *was* "the web of commitments" she had made on each level.[45]

After explaining all this, White raised what was for him the penultimate question: Are such commitments wholly arbitrary? The answer should come as no surprise: "The recurrence of the quaternary pattern in the various levels on which interpretation is possible [four plot forms, four explanation forms, four ideological implications] suggests that they are not."[46] How could they be? On every level the historian is forced to select from a fixed and limited set of forms. White had designed a machine that would go of itself. True, the historian still has certain decisions to make, but they are narrowly defined and purely aesthetic. She has clearly suffered an erosion of initiative and a loss of control. As we advance further and further into White's elaborate interpretive apparatus, we catch glimpses of her moving about its various levels, recording the movement of its "elective affinities." One might say that the historian's presence has been reduced to the status of a rumor, that, as White put it, she has been displaced by her own language: "It is obvious that in language itself, in its generative or prepoetic aspect, we might possibly have the basis for the generation of those types of explanation that inevitably arise in any field of study [such as history] not yet disciplinized."[47]

But there is more: a fourth and final level of interpretation, perhaps the most important of all. By language's "generative or prepoetic aspect" (in the passage above) White meant its capacity "to prefigure a particular field of perception in a particular modality of relationships."[48] He found an explanation for this generative capacity in the Renaissance idea of tropes. A trope is a figure of speech or a turn of phrase. The key word here is turn: tropes work by setting up unexpected associations, promiscuous comminglings that cause the discourse in which they are imbedded to "turn" or "swerve" in unforeseen directions. A trope thereby initiates a movement of thought from one mode of perception to another, and in that way it "prefigures" the historian's understanding of her field. Tropes are thus "the soul of discourse, the mechanism without which discourse cannot do its work or achieve its end."[49]

The historian has to choose her tropes, of course, but once again she is severely limited in her choice. From Kenneth Burke White learned that there are only four "master tropes": metaphor, metonymy, synecdoche, and irony. The first of these, metaphor, is a way of apprehending reality in terms of similarities and differences. This is the naive man's way of grappling with the world, a description of reality only one step removed from reality itself. It asserts that a similarity exists between two objects (or two persons, societies, processes, or historical moments) in the face of manifest differences between them. The comparison is meant to be taken only figuratively, of course, in such a way as to sustain the particularity of each element; one is not reduced to a function of the other.[50] In historiography the trope of metaphor is best exemplified by comparative studies.

The trope of metonymy, by contrast, organizes the historical field as a set of phenomena bearing cause and effect relationships to one another. This trope *does* reduce one set of phenomena to a function of another as, for example, in an agent-act relationship, or a cause-effect relationship.

Both metaphor and metonymy characterize the historical field in terms of extrinsic relations. Synecdoche, the third trope, organizes it in terms of the shared qualities that bind it together as a field. The historian construes the past as an integrated whole that is qualitatively different from the sum of the parts, and of which the parts are but microcosmic replications. In other words, synecdoche is the trope of microcosm-macrocosm relations. Here is an example: in the introduction to *The Uprooted*, Oscar Handlin's classic study of European immigrants in America, Handlin writes, "I hope to seize upon a single thread woven into the fabric of our past, to understand that strand in its numerous ties and linkages with the rest; and perhaps, by revealing the nature of this part, to throw light upon the essence of the whole."[51]

In contrast to metaphor, metonymy, and synecdoche, the fourth trope, irony, establishes no relations at all—indeed, it denies every relation. It is the trope of double visions and second thoughts. The troubling feature of irony—this was the heart of the novelists' criticism of history that White had described in "The Burden of History"—is that it drains one's will and exhausts one's purpose. Irony is the trope of despair. It represents that stage of historical consciousness in which the historian succumbs to the problematic nature of historical consciousness itself.

For White, the tropal structure underlying the text is precognitive, precritical, and utterly determinative. It exists in the historian's mind, consciously or no, *before* she sets to work. It determines the aesthetic structure (plot form), the epistemological structure (argument form), and the moral structure (ideological implication) of the account she writes. The historian's "interpretation" will therefore be little more than a translation and projection of determinations made on the precognitive level of the tropes. As White puts it, "Thought remains the captive of the linguistic mode in which it seeks to grasp the outline of objects inhabiting its field of perception."[52] The historian is the one who writes, but even as she writes the tropes are busy, commingling in the night, propagating ever newer versions of themselves, almost as if something obscene were at workin their bodies: "'Interpretation' in historical thought may very well consist of the projection, on the cognitive, aesthetic and moral levels of conceptualization, of the various tropes authorizing prefigurations of the phenomenal field."[53]

White made the generative and projective role of the tropes even more explicit in *Metahistory*, which appeared in 1973, one year after "Interpretation in History." More sure of his argument than ever before, he now insisted that the historian's choice of narrative strategy, explanatory paradigm, and ideological implication—even her constitution of the basic "facts"—is fixed by the determining dynamic of the tropes:

> The dominant trope will determine both the kinds of objects which are permitted to appear in [the historical] field as data and the possible relationships that are conceived to obtain among them. The theories that are subsequently elaborated to account for changes that occur in the field can claim authority as explanations of "what happened" only insofar as they are consonant with the linguistic mode in which the field was prefigured as a possible object of mental perception.[54]

The operation of the tropes, and the arrangement of their "elective affinities," suppresses the possibility of "arbitrary" interpretations, not merely by circumscribing the historian's interpretive decisions but by *displacing* them. White has been quite explicit about this: the tropes operate on a "more basic level of consciousness" than that on which historians make their intentional decisions; they perform on "a ground *prior to* that on which the emotive, cognitive and moral faculties can be presumed to function."[55] This "preconscious" domain—White calls it "the latent level" or the "deep structure" of the historical imagination—is structured and governed by its own internal dynamic. It is on this level that the historical field is constituted or "prefigured," that relations within the field are determined, that a particular narrative strategy is authorized, and that a particular explanation form and "ideological implication" are selected to match that strategy.

Moreover, White thinks the development of the mind—and from that the unfolding of history and of historical consciousness—follows a predetermined progression along the chain of the tropes. Thought is essentially metaphoric when it first emerges, then becomes metonymic, synechdochic, and finally ironic. Thus, for example, metaphor is "a primitive form of knowing" compared with irony. Movement along the tropal chain is therefore a movement through historical time—a predetermined and invariable progression that is not governed by any *consciousness* prior to itself. Tropal figuration of experience is "the *foundation* on which rational knowledge of the world is erected."[56] At one point White calls it a "prerational cognitive process"; at another point he likens it to a spontaneously activated "gestalt switch."[57]

Thus the tropes, and the operations of thought they authorize and direct, are rooted in the deepest layers of the human brain—not the mind, but the brain. In *Tropics of Discourse* White likens the movement of thought along the predetermined course of the tropes (from metaphor through metonymy and synecdoche to irony) to the stages through which Jean Piaget believed all human thought develops.[58] The tropes themselves, and the inexorable and invariable progression from one to another, possess an "ontogenetic basis"; they are "stages in the evolution of consciousness."[59] The "deep structure" of the historical imagination thus has its roots in "the psychogenetic endowment of the child."[60]

Moreover, White claimed that the intellectual and literary history of the West has been shaped and formed "in response to the imperatives of the tropes." Like the emergence of rational thought in the child, the development of ideas, beliefs, and values in the West has followed an "archetypical pattern." In mankind as in the child, thought begins in metaphor and terminates in irony.[61] Ontogeny recapitulates phylogeny.

The mind's struggle to know itself is therefore not a conscious effort of the will but an unconscious by-product of the tropes. Mind develops along the curve of the tropes, each trope representing "a phase or moment" in the history of the mind, "a stage in the evolution of consciousness."[62] The progress of thought, on every level, represents a "closed-cycle development," an inexorable movement down a one-way corridor, beginning in metaphor and ending in irony.[63]

This means that the progression of knowledge invariably ends in "an Ironic apprehension of the irreducible relativism of all knowledge." Irony, as White defines it, is "the moral equivalent of epistemological skepticism," where a round and final meaning is always deferred and finally absent. It is the realm of interpretive anarchy, the realm of the shifting, the elusive, the utterly provisional; once we enter the realm of irony we have entered the province of endless dissemination and universal doubt. The fall into irony, as White sees it, is a fall into moral relativism and nihilisitc despair. Irony points up the foolishness of all our attempts to characterize reality, the absurdity of all our beliefs. The point of it all, for the ironist, is that there is no point: no genuinely transforming moment, no redeeming epiphany, no ultimate reconciliation, no final transcendence. In the mode of irony, thought and language not only fold back on themselves, they burn right through themselves. Enlightenment produces—and White contends that the eighteenth-century Enlightenment did in fact produce—sophisticated skepticism, moral relativism, psychological pessimism, and a form of self-criticism so searing that it threatens self-annihilation. Irony may be the truth of lived experience, but it is a cracked and fractured truth. To adopt an ironic perspective on the past is to stare into a mirror that gives back no reflection.

The descent into irony begins as soon as the historian realizes that any particular event can appropriately appear in any number of conflicting and even mutually exclusive stories—and that it can play a different but still legitimate role in every one of them. *Metahistory* explains how the European historical imagination made its own descent into irony. That descent began when European historians first realized, at the end of the nineteenth century, that the aesthetics of realism had produced a swarm of *conflicting* "realisms," and that there were no empirically certain grounds for choosing between them. Indeed, the only grounds for choice were not objective or empirical at all, but moral and aesthetic.[64] For White, irony simply *is* the realization that no particular interpretive strategy can ever be authorized on purely empirical grounds.

We have now arrived at the primary meaning of Hayden White's early work, the inner substance and essential content of everything he wrote between "The Burden of History" in 1966 and "Figuring the Nature of the Times Deceased" in 1989—that is, White's determination to dismantle and destroy the specter of irony that haunts human life like a burying ground, that threatens to suck it dry and leave it gray and empty and drained of all human meaning. White's writing is driven by his yearning for some promise of deliverance, if not in the process of history itself then in what is, for White, mankind's defining characteristic: the capacity to infuse the otherwise meaningless and chaotic flow of events with *meaning*, to turn mere chronicle into human history. He knows irony to be corrosive and enervating. Expose the fabric of human belief to the burning acid of irony and we find ourselves "awash in a historical sea more threatening than that natural world which primitive savages confronted in their ignorance and debility at the dawn of human time."[65]

But White thinks the conditions that plunged the historical imagination into irony can also authorize its eventual redemption. Moreover, he is convinced that the means for transcending irony are to be found in irony itself:

If it can be shown that Irony is only one of a number of possible perspectives on history, each of which has its own good reasons for existence on a poetic and moral level of awareness, the Ironic attitude will have begun to be deprived of its status as the *necessary* perspective from which to view the historical process. Historians and philosophers of history will then be freed to conceptualize history, to perceive its contents, and to construct narrative accounts of its processes in whatever modality of consciousness is most consistent with their own moral and aesthetic aspirations. And historical consciousness will stand open to the reestablishment of its links with the great poetic, scientific, and philosophical concerns which inspired the classic practitioners and theorists of its golden age in the nineteenth-century. . . . We are free to conceive "history" as we please. . . . we have only to reject this ironic perspective and to will to view history from another, anti-Ironic perspective.[66]

White wants us to think of this as not naive romanticism but a form of existential defiance: historical consciousness imposing its own meaning on the blank of history, knowing all the while that its imposition is utterly futile. The one big truth White learned from his intellectual predecessors—especially Schopenhauer, Burckhardt, and Nietzsche—was the truth of existentialism: that the meanings we impose on experience will vanish as quickly as the morning dew.[67]

White thinks that once we have "seen through" irony we can "will to view history from another, anti-Ironic perspective." But this seems questionable, even within the terms of White's own Schopenhauer-inspired existentialism. Can the plunge into irony really be stopped by a simple exertion of the will? Can the threat of irony be broken by simply deciding to break it? White's assurance that it can is essentially the assurance of a Pelagian. Jonathan Edwards—or Pascal or Melville or Kierkegaard or Dostoyevsky or any number of other writers—might have suggested to White that the historian can no more will her way out of irony than the melancholic can will her way out of depression, or the young Luther could reason himself into belief, or even the most fervent and devout believers can call down an outpouring of grace on their upturned faces.[68] Moreover, whereas White—like Hegel and Nietzsche before him—thinks overcoming irony is "the central problem of a distinctively human thought," Pascal might have suggested to him that irony, like depression and melancholy, can sometimes be a way of seeing, an angle of vision so acute that it captures something fundamental and essential about human experience. Like metaphysical doubt or the loss of religious faith, irony may come as a sudden and complete withdrawal of love: "And their foot shall slide in due time." But it may nevertheless constitute a necessary stage in any meaningful encounter with life. Perhaps Edwards was right after all; perhaps men can truly know themselves only when they know themselves abandoned.

But if White's vision fails us when we look at it from within the terms of his own existentialism, it also fails us when we step outside those terms. White's philosophy is based on a set of ground-level oppositions—the opposition between "human" and "natural," for example, or "human meaning" and "natural chaos"—that he treats as privileged categories, even natural types. They perform the same work in his philosophy that the opposition between aesthetic idea and phenomenal reality performed in Kant's, or that the opposition between Apollonian rationality and Dionysian impulse performed in the early Nietzsche's philosophy. This apparently stable substratum of basic assumptions seems to stand outside the bounds of temporality, beyond the vagaries of rhetoric. But it can also be seen as simply another set of rhetorical constructs. And once seen that way, it becomes apparent that White has erected his interpretive structure on a floating foundation.

Moreover, he has already let the tropes undermine the very assertion of will that he later calls on to deliver us from the specter of irony. Indeed, the dynamism of the tropes has so hollowed out the intending subject that she appears as little more than a cipher. The epochal regime of rhetoric has reduced the historical imagination to incantation and ritual. Though White may refuse to admit it, Nietzsche's lament has finally become his own: "An evil eye has scorched our fields and our hearts. We have become dry."[69]

This is not at all what White intended, of course. He had originally turned to rhetoric to *shore up* the foundation of his Renaissance humanism, not to undermine it. The White who wrote "The Burden of History" had admired the early humanists because they used rhetoric to silence logic, to deny it dominion, to reduce it to a department of rhetoric.[70] Like them, White wanted to use rhetoric to break through the hardened crust of logic. In the early 1960s that meant challenging the dominance and prestige of logical positivism—and its corollary, Carl Hempel's "covering law" theory of historical explanation. White's attempt to turn historical studies from explanation to interpretation was essentially an attempt to substitute the play of rhetoric for the rule of logic. White thought rhetoric could subvert the dominion of logic by "swerving" its discourse, disturbing and diverting it, making it meander in unexpected ways, forcing it to produce unforeseen (and unwanted) meanings. As he himself put it, rhetoric could "deconstruct a conceptualization of a given area of experience which has become hardened into a hypostasis that blocks fresh perception or denies, in the interests of formalization, what our will or emotions tell us ought not be the case in a given department of life."[71] As White thought of it, rhetoric was always slipping through the grasp of logic, turning back on it, taunting it, challenging it, continually asking if it was really adequate to the demands of its subject matter.[72] If the tyranny of logical explanation had become the burden of history, then rhetoric would be White's deconstructive "antilogic," an anarchic force powerful enough to shatter logic and all its pretensions: "As antilogic, its aim would be to deconstruct a conceptualization of a given area of experience which has become hardened into a hypostasis that blocks fresh perception or denies, in the interests of formalization, what our will or emotions tell us ought not be the case in a given department of life."[73]

But rhetoric turned out to be governed by an underlying logic of its own—a logic that projected itself from deep within the "ontogenetic" structures of the human brain. Moreover, White insisted on this point for over a quarter of a century, even though he must have realized that it fatally compromised his simultaneous insistence that we can bend rhetoric to our own purposes, that we can use it to "will" ourselves out of irony. White continued to believe, as he put it in 1978, that "the moral implications of the human sciences will never be perceived until the faculty of the will is reinstated in theory."[74] And on the final page of *Metahistory* he insisted that "we are free to conceive 'history' as we please."[75] Like Nietzsche and Marx, White wanted to give man back his capacity for "heroic exertion." But he fatally weakened that possibility by continuing to argue that rhetoric is governed by a logic all its own, antecedent and fully autonomous.

So *Metahistory* ended in contradiction. White had hoped to liberate interpretation from the tyranny of explanation, thereby delivering us from "the burden of history" and the specter of irony. As he wrote at the end of *Metahistory*, "We are free to conceive 'history' as we please, just as we are free to make of it what we will."[76] But he had also wanted to guard historical writing against the danger of willful interpretations. Perhaps because he was so steeped in Renaissance humanism, White thought classical rhetoric could do both these jobs; that is, he thought it could break the logic of explanation and simultaneously ground the workings of the imagination (thereby warding off interpretive anarchy). But in the end, rhetoric simply imprisoned him in a logic of its own.[77]

Something similar (though not exactly the same) happened when

White turned his attention from rhetoric to narrative. He had always been interested in narrative, of course. After all, it was *Metahistory*, more than any other book, that signaled the historical profession's shift of interest from the logic of explanation to the dynamics of interpretation. But it was not until 1987, in *The Content of the Form: Narrative Discourse and Historical Representation*, that White addressed the issue of narrative itself (as opposed to rhetoric generally). Narrative is important to historians because memories are organized in the form of narratives; knowledge of the past is, ipso facto, narrative knowledge. But here as elsewhere, White's linguistic structuralism pulled against his Renaissance humanism and eventually overwhelmed it. White the structuralist wanted us to see narrative as a *structure:* an encoded expression of "the deep structures of consciousness" that "prefigure" our "experience of temporality"; but White the humanist wanted us to see narrative as a *process*, the historian's intentional imposition of moral value on the otherwise meaningless sequence of one thing after another.[78] On the one hand, he argued that narrative gives expression to "structures of meaning that are generally human rather than culture-specific. . . . Narrative is a metacode, a human universal, on the basis of which transcultural messages about the nature of a shared reality can be transmitted."[79] On the other hand, he insisted that "every historical narrative has as its latent or manifest purpose the desire to *moralize* the events of which it treats."[80]

The problem is that White tried to close the gap between these two by calling on a "will to narrativize" that he defined as precognitive and irreducible. There is "a *psychological impulse* behind the apparently universal need not only to narrate but to give to events an aspect of narrativity," that is, to impose moral value on the incoherent and indeed unintelligible passage of time.[81] But by finding the origins of the "moral imagination" in a "psychological impulse," White undermined his humanism and came perilously close to a Nietzschean celebration of the will to power.[82]

One can hardly fail to notice a remarkable hollowing out of agency in the progression from *Metahistory* (1973) to *Content of the Form*. The governing tropes that occupied center stage in *Metahistory* may have been a priori and universal, but at least the historian was thought to have chosen among them. But in *Content of the Form* there is literally nothing for the historian to do, at least not on a cognitive level. Moreover, to say that the real meaning of every narrative lies is its enactment of the experience of temporality is to say that every narrative conveys the same message. And if the writer has nothing to do, neither does the reader, for narrative form "calls up" and establishes in some part of her precognitive mind a specific subjectivity, an "experience of temporality" by virtue of which she knows the meaning of the book she is reading—that is, knows it to be "the manifestation in discourse of a specific kind of time-consciousness or structure of time." "The ideological element in art, literature, or historiography consists of the projection of *the kind of subjectivity that its viewers or readers must* take on in order to experience it as art, as literature, or as historiography."[83]

Most historians associate Hayden White with the epistemological relativism that has come to characterize so much of contemporary theory.[84] But the problem with White's work is not so much its relativism as its reductionism, its all too alluring suggestion that there exists some "deeper" level of analysis, some speechless, precognitive space, utterly beyond time and change, in which we will finally encounter the true and essential nature of our humanity. White thinks narratives exhibit a "deep structure" that operates independent of the historian's conscious intentions or personal awareness—indeed, independent of any human purposes or intentions whatever.[85] Like the structuralism on which it is modeled, this is a philosophy of history designed to satisfy all our Parmenidean yearnings. What we are dealing with here, in fact, as the literary critic Barbara Herrnstein Smith and others have pointed out, is an invocation of pure Platonic form. "Unembodied and unexpressed, unpictured, unwritten and untold," narrative's deep structure "occupies a highly privileged ontological realm of pure Being within which it unfolds immutably and eternally."[86]

White is a humanist, a moralist, and a deeply religious thinker. He conceives of history as a quest for ultimate reality and an act of personal transcendence. He is a theorist of redemption in a age of simulacra. He wants to save us from irony, from unbelief, from the fall into Nietzsche's pasteboard world of skepticism and artifice. Cast adrift in a postmodern world that has come to doubt the notion of reality itself, he longs to touch bottom, to find some absolute truth, some ultimate reality. And he thinks he has found it, for he has come to believe that "the experience of temporality" is the deepest and most universal of all human experiences, that narrative form "enacts" that experience, and that narrative can therefore bring us face-to-face with ourselves at the deepest level possible. This is a stunning claim—stunning alike in its spiritual hunger and its intellectual hubris. Augustine thought the passage of time was precisely what makes mankind a puzzle to himself, dimly lit and disembedded. But White thinks that narrative can rescue us from time, that by "enacting" "the experience of temporality," time can actually reveal us to ourselves and thereby save us from the unfulfilled yearning and brutalizing skepticism he associates with postmodernity. Indeed, once we grasp the nature and the power of narrative form, there is no "other"—not even Pascal's *Deus absconditus*—that can possibly escape our need to know. This is the significance of White's claim, following Paul Ricoeur, that "the notion of deep temporality . . . saves historical thinking from its most common temptation, that of irony."[87]

I V

But that was in 1982. Ten years later White published "Historical Emplotment and the Problem of Truth." People who have read it seem to think "Historical Emplotment" represents yet another retreat from the Emersonian constructivism of his earliest work (before *Metahistory*), but this is a hasty reading of what is in fact a remarkably subtle and elusive essay. "Historical Emplotment and the Problem of Truth" does not signal a *retreat from* but a *return to* and *reformulation of* his earlier Emersonianism. In "Historical Emplotment" White takes up Berel Lang's suggestion that historians of the Holocaust should employ the ancient Greek grammatical form of the "middle voice." Hans Kellner, White's most sympathetic and insightful critic, thinks White's adoption of this middle voice represents a further emptying out of the author-self, since it returns us to a time in history before the self as agent had fully emerged: " 'The middle voice,' once a relic from before the birth of the subject, is what may be spoken again after the death of the subject, the death of the author, and so forth, these 'deaths' being understood as the figural signs of an awareness of the historicity of discourse and the situated nature of any speech act."[88]

Kellner thinks White advocates the subjectless middle voice because he believes it will displace the author, canceling her presence, erasing her from her own text. The argument seems to be that White, thrown off balance by critics who charged him with giving aid and comfort to Holocaust deniers, has abandoned the last shred of his earlier volunteerism. Saul Friedlander, editor of *Probing the Limits of Representation: Nazism and the "Final Solution,"* in which "Historical Emplotment" first appeared, thinks it represents "a search for compromise, a way of escaping the most extreme corollaries or implications of his relativism."[89] The Holocaust historian Berel Lang thinks White has not only compromised and retreated but "regressed, honorably but mistakenly troubled by the phenomenon of the Holocaust in relation to his own earlier historiographical tour de force."[90] And

Martin Jay charges that White has gutted his own philosophy: "In his anxiety to avoid inclusion in the ranks of those who argue for a kind of relativistic anything goes, which might provide ammunition for revisionist skeptics about the existence of the Holocaust, he undercuts what is most powerful in his celebrated critique of naive historical realism."[91]

There is some plausibility to these charges. After all, White does ask whether there exist "any limits on the kind of story that can responsibly be told about these phenomena. . . . Can it be said that sets of real events are intrinsically tragic, comic, or epic. . . . Or does it all have to do with the perspective from which the events are viewed?"[92] And he does seem to suggest that

> in the case of the emplotment of the events of the Third Reich in a "comic" or "pastoral" mode, we would be eminently justified in appealing to "the facts" in order to dismiss it from the lists of "competing narratives" of the Third Reich. . . . It seems to be a matter of distinguishing between a specific body of factual "contents" and a specific "form" of narrative and of applying *the kind of rule which stipulates* that a serious theme—such as mass murder or genocide—demands a noble genre—such as epic or tragedy—for its proper representation.[93]

These are the passages on which White's critics have focused their attention and based their judgments. But immediately after this last passage White cites two examples, both of which demonstrate that there is in fact no such "rule," that German history during the Holocaust—and indeed, the Holocaust itself—can by represented using even the most incongruous of forms. For example, Art Spiegelman's *Maus: A Survivor's Tale* "assimilates the events of the Holocaust to the conventions of a comic book representation," yet "in this absurd mixture of a 'low' genre with events of the most momentous significance," *Maus* is "one of the most moving narrative accounts of it [the Holocaust] that I know."[94] White's second example points to the same conclusion. In *Zweierlei Untergang* (1986) Andreas Hillgruber "suggests that, even though the Third Reich lacked the nobility of purpose to permit its 'shattering' to be called a 'tragedy,' the defense of the eastern front by the Wehrmacht in 1944-45 could appropriately be emplotted—and without any violence to the facts—as a 'tragic' story."[95] Hillgruber's decision "to emplot the story of the Wehrmacht's defense of the eastern front as a tragedy indicates that he wants the story told about it to have a hero, to be heroic, and thereby to redeem at least a remnant of the Nazi epoch in the history of Germany."[96] The critics howled, of course, "yet Hillgruber's suggestion for emplotting the story of the defense of the eastern front did not violate any of the conventions governing the writing of professionally respectable narrative history."[97]

More important, White advocates "the middle voice" not as a means of self-erasure or self-cancellation but as a means of self-overcoming, of self-renovation. "In intransitive writing [in 'the middle voice'] an author does not write to provide access to something independent of both author and reader, but 'writes himself.'" Moreover, "For the writer who writes-himself, writing becomes itself the means of vision or comprehension, not a mirror of something independent, but an act and commitment—a doing or making rather than a reflection or description."[98]

Rather than gutting his philosophy, White renewed it. In "Historical Emplotment and the Problem of Truth" he reached all the way back to the Emersonianism that had fueled his earliest theoretical writing, especially "The Burden of History" and "What Is an Historical System?" Once again historical writing has become a form of moral reflection, a way of coming to terms with ourselves by coming to terms with our chosen predecessors—lest, as Melville feared, they come banging on our door some damp, drizzly November morning.

CHAPTER SIX

A Choice of Inheritance

I

Hayden White was one of the first historians to grasp the importance of linguistic theory for historical writing. In several books and dozens of articles he tried to make historians *look* at the language they use, rather than pretending to peer *through* it, at something presumed to lie beyond it. Moreover, in the 1960s and early 1970s, when historical realism and covering law theory were all the rage, White was urging historians to think of historical writing as an interpretive art. And at a time when Whiggish assumptions about history had been reduced to the status of curios and the individual had all but disappeared from historical explanations, Hayden White was insisting that human history has always been the story of human choice, that men and women have always chosen who they *are* by choosing who they *have been*, and that "no amount of 'objective' historical work pointing out the extent to which this *chosen* ancestry is *not* the *real* ancestry can prevail against the choosing power of the individuals in the system."[1] A liberal humanist in the finest sense of the word, White has spent nearly thirty years trying to convince his fellow historians that they can use contemporary philosophy of rhetoric to write good, liberal history—that is, history that not only strengthens our understanding but nourishes our possibilities.

But White was unprepared for the transition from structuralism to poststructuralism. Having bent structuralist theory to his own classically liberal ends, he was unable to do the same with poststructuralism. Steeped in the long, benevolent tradition of linguistic humanism, he hated poststructuralism's destabilizing strategies and its glacially cold antihumanism. Deconstruction in particular appalled him; he called it a "fascinating and at the same time cruelly mutilating activity" that seemed to tear at the very fabric of our humanity.[2] Finally, in the late 1980s, challenged by epistemological conservatives to account for the transparent horrors of the Holocaust, he seemed, even to his most sympathetic readers, to have retreated. Where he had earlier insisted that "there are no grounds to be found in the historical record itself for preferring one way of construing its meaning over another," he now seemed to argue that the Holocaust—and presumably such other moral abominations as the genocide of Native Americans, the enslavement of black Africans, the terrors of Soviet collectivization, the bombing of Hiroshima and Nagasaki, the French and American war against Vietnam, and so on—simply could not be emplotted as comedy.[3] But by appearing to make this crucial concession—that a series of historical events determines, *in and of itself,* the forms of emplotment that historians may use to interpret it—Hayden White seemed to cut the heart out of his own philosophy.

It is precisely at this point that Richard Rorty became important, especially for those historians who were intrigued by postmodernism and had lost all faith and confidence in history's increasingly dubious claims to objective knowledge (however defined), but who nevertheless thought of themselves as traditional, even culturally conservative historians. For these scholars Rorty seemed to pick up where White left off. Like White, he is a liberal humanist with a volunteerist and progressive vision of history. And for all his talk about antifoundationalism, his philosophy is firmly established on a foundation of traditional liberal assumptions: that human beings are inherently outgoing and creative; that they have the capacity to continually expand their range of emotional identifications; that they are capable of mastering their own history; that with a modicum of luck they just might create a more free and equitable society. And like White he continues to defend a classically liberal vision of individual autonomy and self-creation. Finally, and again like White, Rorty thinks philosophers and historians should give up their narrow and increasingly sterile professionalism and help the rest of us come to terms with "the blind impress that fate has stamped on our foreheads."[4] In other words, for Rorty as for White, history is a classically humanist discipline, deeply ethical and powerfully redemptive.

But Rorty has traveled much further down the postmodern road than White was willing to venture. As we saw in chapter 5, White harbored a strong metaphysical urge to touch bottom, to make contact with something real and authentic, something more ultimately satisfying than the rattle and hum of historical contingencies, something more permanent and enduring than the endless proliferation of new meanings and novel interpretations. White longs to escape what Derrida somewhere calls "the epochal regime of quotation marks." But for Rorty there is no escape, simply because there is no place to escape to, no natural order of things lying concealed behind the flux of daily appearances, no "intrinsic nature" or "real essence" waiting to be discovered just below the surface of life—not by the priest, not by the philosopher, and surely not by the historian.[5] Indeed, he thinks it is precisely this Parmenidean yearning for something deep down in the nature of things that keeps us imprisoned in antiquated and ineffectual habits of thought.[6] Thus when White seemed to retreat to the comforting assurance that the Holocaust can be described only in certain predetermined and sharply circumscribed ways, Rorty stuck to his grim conviction that "*anything* can be made to look good or bad by being redescribed."[7]

What makes Rorty's work so important for historians is that he tries to use this ethically empty insight to support a set of deeply ethical beliefs. He thinks he can use postmodern theory—that garret-spawned world of superreflecting surfaces and endlessly circulating images—to reinforce what is in fact a remarkably traditional humanism.

II

Rorty's humanist convictions were initially shaped by the sense of political betrayal and ideological disillusionment that his parents experienced in the interwar years. Both his mother and his father were well-known, politically active left-wing intellectuals in the 1920s and 1930s. Like so many other bright young men and women of their generation, they had been wildly excited by the promise of socialist theory but then deeply disenchanted by the reality of socialist politics. They were hardly alone, of course; this cycle of radicalization and disillusionment has become almost emblematic of their generation. Daniel Bell, Irving Howe, and a host of other prominent American writers made the same odyssey, groping their way from the socialist enthusiasms of the 1920s to the chastened liberalism of the 1950s. Moreover, as participants and historians have pointed out over and over again, this generational passage constituted a major turning point in American intellectual history—and the essential background for understanding the cultural climate in America during the postwar years.[8] As Bell later explained in a famous passage, the elder Rortys and their generation "were intense, horatory, naive, simplistic, and passionate but, after the Moscow trials and the Soviet-Nazi pact, disenchanted and reflective; and from them and their experiences we have inherited the key terms which dominate discourse today: irony, paradox, ambiguity and complexity. Ours is a twice-born generation; it finds its wisdom in pessimism, evil, tragedy, and despair. So we are both old and young before our time."[9]

Bell thinks that by the end of the 1930s this "twice-born generation" had ideologically exhausted itself. The passion with which its members had embraced socialism, and the intensity and severity of their later disenchantment, left them, after the war, with nothing but "the hardness of alienation, the sense of otherness." The claims of doubt rose so sharply and loomed so darkly that they completely overwhelmed the possibilities of faith.

That may be, but Rorty's own parents held on to a good deal of their faith. Though they broke with the Communist Party in 1932, they remained deeply committed to the humanist values and progressive hopes that had originally drawn them to the Party. Rorty remembers his mother and father's hiding fugitive Trotskyites in the attic of their home as late as the 1940s.[10] And just as his parents clung to their socialist beliefs and convictions, so their son describes himself—even now, in the second half of the 1990s—as "still faithful to everything that was good in the socialist movement."[11]

From his parents and their experiences Richard Rorty inherited his most fundamental, enduring, and informing beliefs: a profound distrust of ideological certainties; a determined commitment to the political and moral heritage of the Enlightenment; an abiding confidence in the progressive potential of Western history; and until recently, a lingering hope that a moderate, market-oriented socialism might somehow emerge midway between the unrestrained capitalism of the West and the monolithic communism of the East. Right up to the fall of the Berlin Wall in 1989 he "kept hoping that some country would figure out a way to keep socialism after getting rid of the *nomenklatura*."[12] But the events of that year, including the brutal repression of the Chinese students' rebellion, killed off whatever had survived of his parents' socialist beliefs. "People like me," he now says, "have given up on socialism in light of the history of nationalized enterprises and central planning in Central and Eastern Europe. We are willing to grant that welfare-state capitalism is the best we can hope for."[13]

Like so many of his parents' generation, Rorty is culturally conservative and politically liberal. He quotes William James on human nature—"The trail of the human serpent is over all"—but he also describes himself as a "typical left-wing democratic professor."[14] "My politics," he says, "are pretty much those of Hubert Humphrey." He thinks that with a certain amount of luck we in the United States *may* continue to do what he thinks we have been doing all along, however haltingly: using our democratic institutions to direct new technologies toward ever closer approximations of the original Enlightenment project of reducing suffering and increasing equality.[15] Though only too aware of how quickly and easily this country could slide into fascism, he insists that history could just as well go the other way, that we as a people *may* deepen our collective commitment to justice and equality—and perhaps even strengthen our capacity for human empathy and moral obligation. He is proud of America's past and "guardedly hopeful" about its future.[16]

But for all his cautious optimism about the chances for historical *change*, Rorty has inherited from his parents and their experiences a deep and abiding skepticism about the possibilities of historical *knowledge*. Like the early Richard Hofstadter, Rorty thinks history is simply not open to human understanding, except as paradox and irony. Whatever goodness and human worth we have been witness to have come not from enlightened reason or pragmatic adjustment but from what used to be called fate and now travels under the more fashionable name of contingency. American history has not been shaped and formed by the political genius of the Founding Fathers, the economic truths of capitalism, or the moral character of an agrarian people; it has been shaped and formed by the coincidental combination of unlikely circumstances and improbable events.

There is in Rorty an almost Augustinian sense of humility about the potential for human knowledge. It is as if, having come to intellectual maturity in the shadow of a deeply chastened generation, he feels some inherent or inherited need to reject every offer of epistemological certainty, the merest whiff of which he dismisses as "metaphysical comfort."[17] Just as Augustine insisted that Providence is never manifest, that we can never hope to know the reasons for our many afflictions, so Rorty insists that we must abandon every hope of learning the reasons for our tangled and clotted history. We will not be delivered from the seething coils of language, we will not be released from the gravitational pull of an infinite regress, we will never touch bottom. And we most certainly will not experience a manifestation of historical truth (the well-intentioned authors of *Telling the Truth about History* notwithstanding):

> The ambiguity of langauge is a matter of language moving into the vacancies left by the failure of all the various candidates for the position of "natural starting-points" of thought, starting-

points which are prior to and independent of the way some culture speaks or spoke. Candidates for such starting-points include clear and distinct ideas, sense-data, categories of the pure understanding, structures of prelinguistic consciousness, and the like. Peirce and Sellars and Wittgenstein are saying that the regress of interpretation cannot be cut off by the sort of "intuition" which Cartesian epistemology took for granted.[18]

If Rorty's sense of things differs from Augustine's in any substantial way, it is only in this: Rorty has had the advantage of reading Darwin and Freud. But what he takes from those two visionary brooders is just what Augustine would have taken from them: that the author of Genesis was right, that we have indeed been cast adrift on the ocean of time, that we will never make the landfall of certain knowledge, that our history will always be what it always has been— the unrecorded and unrecordable hum of discontinuous coincidence.

But unlike so much of what passes for "postmodernism," this is a theory of history driven by a deeply held ethical conviction. Its essential and unavoidable imperative is this: Give up the reassuring heaviness of "It must be!" and take up instead the almost unbearable lightness of "How easily it could all have been otherwise."[19] Melville would have understood this. He used to say that in landlessness alone resides whatever truth we might acquire; that is why he was constantly urging us to "crowd all sail off shore."[20] In just this same way, Rorty wants to drive us to the point where we see *everything*— our language, our conscience, our community—as a product of time and chance. To reach this point would be, in Freud's words, to "treat chance as worthy of determining our fate."[21]

So much for Rorty's intellectual background. But what has all this to do with us hobbit-like historians? What can we find here that might be use to *us?* Does Rorty really have anything important to tell us about the nature of written history in a postmodern world that no longer accepts the historian's claims to objective truth?

I I I

It was the rejection of certain knowledge and universal truths that attracted the elder Rortys and their friends to pragmatism in the late 1930s. Not that they had not known about pragmatism before. But having been seduced by the glittering promises of Marxist dialectics, they had little taste for the unpretentious, problem-solving character of Dewey's pragmatism. It lacked the moral intensity and intellectual force their superheated imaginations required; it seemed emotionally flat and conceptually crimped, a halfhearted and ethically shrunken philosophy, better suited to the quipping practicality of Babbitt's Main Street than to the visionary aspirations of young left-leaning intellectuals.

But having been exhausted by the ideological wars of the 1930s, pragmatism's intellectual parochialism came to look awfully attractive in the forties and fifties.[22] For what they now found in pragmatism was a warrant for abandoning the magisterial register of "ultimate truth," the search for some universally applicable metric that would catalog the permanent and universal features of human existence once and for all. By the end of the thirties the whole project had come to seem hopelessly utopian, as Sidney Hook explained in 1939: "Traditional metaphysics has always been a violent and logically impossible attempt to impose some parochial scheme of values upon the cosmos in order to justify or undermine a set of existing social institutions by a pretended deduction from the nature of Reality. . . . But once crack the shell of any metaphysical doctrine, what appears is not verifiable knowledge but a directing bias."[23]

In fact, it was not that the pragmatists had abandoned the search for truth; they had simply redefined it. To qualify as "true" for them, an idea no longer had to correspond to some external reality, nor did it have to cohere with existing ideas; it simply had to "work." In William James's famous formulation, a "true" idea was simply "any idea upon which we can ride, so to speak; any idea that will carry us prosperously from any one part of our experience to any other part. . . . Ideas become true just in so far as they help us to get into satisfactory relation with other parts of our experience."[24]

During the late 1930s John Dewey, Sidney Hook, and other pragmatists provided the disillusioned intellectuals of their own generation with just what they needed: an open-ended, liberal, and humanist alternative to the terrifying certainties of scientific Marxism.[25] Where the Left had formulated a comprehensive theory of history, a theory that purported to explain the underlying "economic forces" that were driving American society so recklessly forward, pragmatists said we would be better off drawing up makeshift diagrams—provisional sketches or local maps that we could redraw as the surrounding geography changed. It was not that they disagreed with the Left's theory of history; it was that they had come to fear the very *idea* of a theory of history—or a theory of justice, or truth, or goodness, or beauty, or anything else. It was the hankering for a complete and final understanding that frightened this twice-born generation, and those like Richard Rorty who had been bounced on their knees. For hadn't the thirties illustrated once again, this time with horrifying brilliance, how quickly and completely that old Platonic dream can mutate into the most hellish of nightmares?[26] We do not need a complete and final understanding of "how things really are," the pragmatists insisted; all we need are "curiosity, tolerance, patience, luck, and hard work."[27]

Moreover—and not incidentally—the pragmatists' insistence that moral philosophy was not a search for universal laws but the application of critical intelligence to immediate social problems had the inestimable advantage of offering disillusioned intellectuals a new social role.[28] As the younger Rorty has explained, "During the Depression, [when] Stalinism recruited whole battalions of highbrows, a small circle around Sidney Hook—Dewey's chief disciple—kept political morality alive among the intellectuals. . . . With the New Deal, the social scientist emerged as the representative of the academy to the public, embodying the Deweyan promise. . . . A whole generation grew up confident that America would show the world how to escape both Gradgrind capitalism and revolutionary bloodbath."[29]

But by the late 1950s the pendulum of intellectual fashion had completed yet another swing and the pragmatists' vision of an experimental and politically reformist philosophy had been pushed into the shadows of American intellectual life. Anglo-American philosophy was being transformed into an academic and highly professionalized subdiscipline, wrapped in its own specialized vocabulary and preoccupied with its own esoteric problems.[30] Once again graduate students in philosophy were being sent out to resolve the age-old Cartesian questions of correspondence, verification, justified inference, and so on—only this time they were marching under the banner of "analytical philosophy." Rorty recalls that by the early 1960s courses in moral philosophy had become "little more than elaborate epistemological sneers" at pragmatism's soft instrumental approach to questions of truth.[31]

But in Europe something very much like Dewey's vision of philosophy—philosophy as an essentially interpretive enterprise, ungrounded, discontinuous, and permanently provisional—was just then reemerging in the philosophy of difference associated with Nietzsche and Heidegger. Like the American pragmatists, the European disciples of Nietzsche and Heidegger were trying to dig their way out from under the whole theologically derived vocabulary of metaphysical absolutes—"God," "truth," "knowledge," "reason," "history," and so on—the vocabulary that had supported and guaranteed the Western intellectual tradition from its very inception. Like James and Dewey, they were less concerned with whether an idea was true than with whether it worked—less interested in where it came from than where it could take them.

Rorty's contribution was to read German "philosophers of being" like Nietzsche and Heidegger, French poststructuralists like Foucault and Derrida, and American antirepresentationalists like Wilfrid Sellars, W. V. O. Quine, and Donald Davidson as if they had all been talking to one another in a single unbroken conversation. In other words—and this is central to an understanding of what he has to offer us historians—Rorty simply arranged his favorite thinkers in such a way that they seemed to constitute a distinctive and continuous intellectual tradition. Moreover—though this is not nearly as important—he gave that tradition a new beginning in Dewey's pragmatism. Rorty now wants us to read Dewey, Hook, and the other pragmatists from the interwar years as if they had been waiting all along at the end of the road that Foucault, Derrida, Sellars, Quine, Davidson, and the other postmodernists are currently traveling.[32]

To put this differently: Rorty wants us to read James and Dewey through Nietzsche and Heidegger. He wants us to use the Germans to update the Americans, to help the latter prepare themselves for a new fin-de-siècle audience by fitting them out in postmodern rhetorical forms and contemporary modes of expression. All of which is to say: Rorty thinks he can use contemporary postmodernism to revitalize liberal pragmatism. Indeed, he has wagered his whole philosophical store on this one critical hunch: "If pragmatism (stripped of 'method') and Continental philosophy (stripped of 'depth') could come together, we might be in a better position to defend the liberalism that is exemplified by Hook's contributions to American political life."[33]

At first glance it is an extravagant and even audacious claim. For Nietzsche, Heidegger, Foucault, and Derrida are widely regarded as antihumanists of the first degree, philosophers of what Foucault used to call "the death of man." Historians especially tend to regard postmodern theory in general (and Foucault and Derrida in particular) not only as softheaded and silly but as ethically perverse—a trickster code of ruthless skepticism and soul-numbing nihilism. Yet Rorty thinks he can use this philosophy from the pit to support and even reinforce his own liberal humanism. He thinks he can turn postmodern theory from a cultural menace into a source of strength.

Those of us who wonder what history would look like if historians simply dropped their traditional claim to objective knowledge have a certain interest in this project. After all, many—if not most—historians think written history and postmodern theory are not only incompatible but mutually antagonistic. As they see it, the very idea of written history requires that the historian at least *try* to be objective; postmodern theory, on the other hand, denies the very *idea* of objectivity. But Rorty thinks we can junk the idea of objectivity and still write good history—history that is "ideologically liberal" (as Pocock had wished) and classically humanist (as White had wished).

I V

Rorty began with precisely the same insight as Skinner and Pocock. Like them, he was struck, at the very beginning of his career, by the apparent instability of discourses—the way they were continually proliferating and disintegrating, shifting their internal balances and redistributing themselves according to some unobserved and unobservable calculus: "Almost as soon as I began to study philosophy, I was impressed by the way in which philosophical problems appeared, disappeared, or changed shape, as a result of new assumptions or vocabularies."[34]

What Rorty took from this critical recognition was, first of all, an abiding conviction that "the great philosophical problems" of the Western tradition were not inherent and fundamental but transient and epiphenomenal; they were simply by-products of the shifting discourses in which they were embedded.[35] Second, he became convinced that if the "great philosophical problems" did not spring from some fundamental human necessity, if they were not permanent and essential in any discernible way, then he might just as well change them, or substitute others, or drop them altogether. And every bit as important, he realized that he could do any or all of these things simply by changing the vocabulary in which these problems had come down to him.

Skinner and Pocock's theoretical and methodological writings became so widely popular in the 1970s because they explained exactly how the conceptual languages prevailing in, say, seventeenth-century England had formed, shaped, and defined the problems that seventeenth-century English writers were and were not able to recognize, as well as the solutions they were and were not able to imagine.

But this is just where Rorty breaks with Skinner and Pocock. For the latter thought that with this insight they had finally come up with the master key that would open the way to what historians had always lacked: a method capable of guaranteeing that historical accounts were founded on objective understanding and accurate representation: "The historian's first problem is to identify the 'language' or 'vocabulary' with and within which the author operated, and to show how it functioned paradigmatically to prescribe what he might say and how he might say it. . . . If at this stage we are asked how we know the languages adumbrated really existed, or how we recognize them when we see them, *we should be able to reply empirically:* that the languages in question are simply there, that they form individually recognizable patterns and styles."[36]

In order to recover what they called an author's "primary intentions," Skinner and Pocock insisted that the historian project herself backward, into the conceptual languages—indeed, into the entire discursive universe—of, say, seventeenth-century England. For as Pocock explained, "Men cannot do what they have no means of saying they have done; and what they do must in part be what they can say and conceive that it is."[37] The historian had to reconstruct the entire mental and emotional world in which her subject had written his text—the complete set of linguistic principles, symbolic conventions, and ideological assumptions within which he had lived and worked.[38] Only by fixing the author's text in this elaborately reconstructed discursive context could the historian hope to accomplish what was now her primary responsibility: to recover what earlier writers had intended.

This particular conception of intellectual history and its defining responsibility became enormously influential in the 1960s and 1970s. As Joyce Appleby explained, "Quentin Skinner and J. G. A. Pocock saw in language an entry into a past conceptual universe. Self-conscious helmsmen, they steered an entire generation of scholars to their destination of recovering the meaning of historical texts through the reconstruction of authors' intentions."[39]

But the Skinner-Pocock project ran into two interrelated problems that together proved fatal, as we saw in chapter 1. The first arose from Skinner and Pocock's simultaneous commitment to the governing power of linguistic structure and the ideological primacy of authorial intention. Simply put, they wanted to have it both ways: they wanted to emphasize the importance and autonomy of a society's dominant conceptual languages while at the same time emphasizing the autonomy and creativity of the major thinkers who lived and wrote in that society. But the more they emphasized the first, the narrower and more precarious became the second, the realm of autonomous and relatively stable "thinking space" left for the writer. Throughout the 1960s and 1970s they described, in ever new and ever more fascinating detail, exactly how the operation of these conceptual languages prescribed "the definition of political problems and values in certain ways and not in others"—all the while insisting on the author's intellectual autonomy from those same prescriptions. On the one hand they explained, more clearly and convincingly than any historians had ever explained before, the ways language "always implicitly conveys more than we intend, that we commit ourselves, by the mere act of using the language, to these implications. . . . that to speak at all is to give some 'other' power over us."[40] That is why, they continued, "the paradigms with which the author operates take precedence over questions of his 'intention' or the 'illocutionary force' of his utterance." On the other hand, they also continued to insist, with what increasingly came to sound like ideological dogmatism, that "authors—individuals thinking and articulating—remain the actors in any story we have to tell."[41]

Pocock was eventually forced to defend himself against the charge that his discursive contextualism had reduced the author to "the mere mouthpiece of his own language."[42] In the end, the enormous interest in historical discourses that emerged in the 1970s and 1980s—an interest that Skinner and Pocock had themselves done so much to bring into being—overwhelmed their commitment to an "ideologically liberal" historiography, an intellectual history centered on "men and women thinking."

Like this first problem, the second arose from two simultaneous but contradictory commitments. On the one hand, Skinner and Pocock gradually came to see language as ever more powerful, shaping and limiting the way earlier writers had been able to see the problems and possibilities confronting their societies. On the other hand, they continued to insist that *we historians*, living in the present, can somehow escape the bonds of our own language in order to acquire real objective knowledge of theirs. And once we knew the language in which seventeenth-century English (or fifteenth-century Venetian or eighteenth-century American) writers wrote, it was only a hop, skip, and a jump to knowledge of their "primary intentions," which Skinner and Pocock insisted was "indispensable" for a truly historical account.[43]

During the 1970s and 1980s, as the linguistic turn deepened and sharpened, historians and others began attaching even more importance to language as an active shaping, regulating force. Skinner and Pocock were pleased, of course, but they could hardly have been unaware that the growing power of language was undermining their primary ideological beliefs: their belief in the autonomy and creativity of historical subjects and their belief in the possibility of objective knowledge. Although this inherent conflict between conceptual insight and ideological belief grew increasingly obvious and indeed critical during the late 1970s, neither Skinner nor Pocock ever addressed it. As a result, by the mid-1980s their "truly historical method"—their discursive contextualism—had come to seem increasingly inadequate; by the end of the decade it had simply become obsolete, relegated to the margins of academic discourse. Though their histories of intellectual life in the early modern West are still widely read and greatly admired, their theoretical work is generally ignored.

But if Rorty began at the same place Skinner and Pocock began— with the recognition that a society's conceptual languages shape and define the ways problems and solutions can be envisioned—he and they moved out from there in very different directions. For Skinner and Pocock, the linguistic turn was essentially a U-turn—it took them right back to (and reinforced) their basic Enlightenment beliefs in the unity and sovereignty of the intending subject—the Cartesian cogito—and in the possibility of real objective knowledge about the past. They insisted again and again that these two principles were fundamental and essential, the necessary foundation for any "ideologically liberal" history. Indeed, without them there could be no written history at all.

For Rorty, on the other hand, the linguistic turn was no turn at all; it was simply a straightforward extension of the chastened pragmatism he had acquired from his parents' generation. Deconstruction and poststructuralism merely gave him a novel way of expressing his already growing conviction that an ethically meaningful historiography requires neither a general theory of objectivity nor the presumption of a centered and unified self. Indeed, he was ready to abandon both concepts. Contemporary theory gave Rorty another way of formulating what he, from deep within his own Augustianian sense of piety, had already begun to call "Ungrounded Hope."[44] The pages that follow describe Rorty's critique of objectivity and his conception of the self, then explain how these two together have shaped his understanding of written history, its problems and possibilities.

V

The possibility—or rather the impossibility—of objective knowledge is the central subject not only of Rorty's best-known work, *Philosophy and the Mirror of Nature* (1980), but of virtually everything he has written since then; moreover, he has been developing what is essentially the same argument about objectivity in every one of his books, from first to last. That argument goes roughly like this: What we think of as "truth" is merely a function of the vocabulary we happen to be using at the time, rather than a fixed and permanent characteristic of the world itself. The world really is out there, but "truth"—that is, a particular *description* of the world—is simply a function of our language rather than a function of the world itself. Louis Althusser must have had something like this in mind when he said that "the knowledge of history is no more historical than the knowledge of sugar is sweet."[45]

This is a Nietzschean—that is to say, a deeply historicist—account of truth, one that Rorty has supplemented with ideas borrowed from Wittgenstein, Heidegger, Dewey, and others. Like Wittgenstein, Rorty regards any particular vocabulary (or language, or discourse) as the product of innumerable historical accidents—in contrast to romantics like, say, Emerson, who thought words were natural signs, as fixed in their meaning as the planets in their orbits. For Emerson it is their grounded and stable character that allows words to mediate between interior thoughts and exterior things. For Rorty, on the other hand, language is the orphaned child of time and chance, forever changing its course, transforming itself, shifting its internal relations and external references.

You would think historians might find a historicist account of language eminently acceptable, but they do not. Indeed, they back away from it horror-struck. And for the same reason Skinner and Pocock backed away: because it erases their assumption that *their* vocabulary—a highly specialized (not to say abstruse) vocabulary that can be acquired only through years and years of formal training—is a precision instrument that has been gradually and painstakingly calibrated to reflect not its own historicity but the true shape of a world that no longer is.

The problem, of course, is simply that we have no way to test this precision instrument. As William James once put it, "No bell in us tolls to let us know for certain when truth is in our grasp."[46] With a little practice we may become adept at stepping outside the vocabulary we happen to be using at a particular moment and comparing its findings with those available in some other vocabulary. But we do not have a *meta*vocabulary we could use to take account of the oddities of any *particular* vocabulary; we do not have a vocabulary for comparing our various descriptions of the world with the world "as it really is" (or accounts of the past with the past "as it really was").

Rather than thinking of any particular vocabulary—the vocabulary of professional historians, for example—as a precision instrument, carefully designed and adjusted to represent reality with the least possible distortion, Rorty wants us to think of vocabularies the way Darwin taught us to think of living organisms—coral reefs, for example, or the "tangled bank" he describes at the end of *On the Origin of Species*. He wants us to think of a vocabulary as "a collection of old metaphors that are constantly dying off into literalness, and then serving as a platform and foil for new metaphors." From this perspective the vocabulary of professional historians looks "as much a result of thousands of small mutations finding niches (and millions of others finding no niches), as are the orchids and the anthropoids."[47] Rorty thinks that if he can break down the idea that language copies nature, rather than merely *coping* with it, he will have exploded the very possibility of objectivity, and thereby all our hand-wringing about the creeping menace of moral relativism.

But of course nothing in the world is more common than the desire to achieve some larger, more "objective" point of view. Simply because we are thinking, reflexive creatures (for the most part), each one of us will sooner or later find ourselves thinking about our own thought processes—stepping back, as it were, trying to see beyond our own limited and limiting sense of things, reaching out for a more inclusive—or merely different—point of view.[48] Moreover, most historians are not conscious liars; very few of them doctor the documents, claiming, for example, that Mary Henderson said she was in El Pueblo de Los Angeles on the afternoon of 26 July 1742 when she said nothing of the kind.

If this is all that is meant by the quest for objectivity, who could object? And indeed, all but the most conservative historians have now conceded that anything more—real empirical knowledge about the past, for instance—is simply not available. If objectivity survives among academic historians, it survives as little more than a reminder that truth is plural, that we are saved only by our own humanizing doubts. The historian Alan Brinkley is surely right about this:

> Something like a consensus appears to have emerged within the historical profession. I suspect that most scholars, if pressed to discuss the issue, would concede that true objectivity is impossible to achieve, that all scholarship is coloured to some degree by the social or political inclinations of the writer. But most would admit that if objectivity is a myth, it is a useful one—something worth aspiring to if only because the aspiration serves as a check on a scholar's subjective impulses.[49]

But again, if this is all that "objectivity" means, who will object?

Moreover, the important decisions we historians make are almost always subjective rather than objective—and not just subjective but ethical. This is true on a formal, rhetorical level, for all the reasons Hayden White insisted on more than twenty years ago in *Metahistory* (see chapter 5). But it is also true on a more substantive level. Take only the most obvious example: we have no objective calculus that can tell the historian what she should write about; she simply has to use her own sense of what is important and what is not. Kant explained this nearly two hundred years ago: to write our own history is to define who we have been, and that project is hopelessly tangled up with our sense of who we are and who we wish to become—in other words, with what we should value and how we should live. I read Charles Beard as saying something like this in his 1933 presidential address to the American Historical Association: "Written History as an Act of Faith."[50]

Rorty's understanding of "self" flows directly from his rigorously historicist critique of objectivity. Like Foucault—but in direct opposition to White, Skinner, and Pocock—Rorty denies that individuals create their own vocabularies, at least with any conscious intention. As we have seen, he talks about vocabularies almost as if they were living organisms, following the dictates of some internal dynamic all their own: mutating, evolving, transforming themselves, promiscuously commingling with other vocabularies, interpenetrating one another, all to the frenzied rhythm of blind chance.

Rorty thinks selves are simply the by-products of this mindless process. Indeed, selves are created by vocabularies, rather than the other way around.[51] You can see this clearly by comparing the way Hayden White describes the relation between self and vocabulary (or "language," or "discourse") with Richard Rorty's description. Here is White, writing in 1972:

> What happened between the third and eighth centuries was that men ceased to regard themselves as descendents of their Roman forebears and began to treat themselves as descendents of their Judaeo-Christian predecessors. And it was the constitution of *this fictional cultural ancestry* which signalled the abandonment of the Roman socio-cultural system. When Western European men began to act *as if* they were descended from the Christian segment of the ancient world; when they began to structure their comportment *as if* they were *genetically* descended from their Christian predecessors; when, in short, they began to honor the Christian past as the desirable model for the creation of a future uniquely their own, and ceased to honor the Roman past as *their* past, the Roman socio-cultural system ceased to exist.[52]

Compare this with Rorty writing seventeen years later, in 1989:

> Europe did not *decide* to accept the idiom of Romantic poetry, or of socialist politics, or of Galilean mechanics. That sort of

shift was no more an act of will than it was a result of argument. Rather, Europe gradually lost the habit of using certain words and gradually acquired the habit of using others. . . . We should not look within ourselves for criteria of decision in such matters any more than we should look to the world.[53]

There simply is no "substratal self" for Rorty, no underlying human reality, nothing deep down inside each one of us that we could describe as "characteristically human."[54] And there certainly is no transhistorical "inner space" that can guarantee the sanctity of individual conscience or the uniqueness of particular persons.[55] For Rorty, "Socialization, and historical circumstance, go all the way down— there is nothing 'beneath' socialization or prior to history that is definatory of the human."[56]

This position is meant to stand in contrast, of course, to the "Cartesian cogito" that René Descartes gave us in the seventeenth century: "I noticed that, while I was trying to think that everything was false, it was necessary that I, who was thinking this, should be something. And observing that this: *I am thinking, therefore I exist* was so firm and secure that all the most extravagant suppositions of the skeptics were not capable of overthrowing it, I judged that I should not scruple to accept it as the first principle of the philosophy I was seeking."[57]

Instead of this firmly grounded Cartesian self, or even a solid Freudian core of instinctual drives, Rorty leaves us with a self that is nothing more than a centerless, ever mutating web of multiplying desires and fragmenting beliefs.[58] But note once again: despite the contemporary sound of all this, we can trace its roots back through postmodernism to modernism itself. Here, for example, is Van Wyck Brooks, writing over eighty years ago but sounding for all the world like Roland Barthes on "The Death of the Author": "As for originality, it seems to me that all true originality immediately reconciles itself with tradition, has in itself the elements of tradition, and is really the shadow of tradition thrown across the future."[59]

But Rorty looks on this psychic chaos with all the ambivalence, even dread, that we traditionally associate not with the postmodernists but with the modernists. Certainly there is none of the playful subversiveness that we associate with Gilles Lipovetsky, for example, or Roland Barthes. It is this deep ambivalence that makes Rorty's work so interesting and important. On the one hand, he urges us to embark on what he calls "the poet's quest." He wants us to reinvent ourselves, to overcome who we have already become, to refuse what we are. "Only he who loses his soul will save it."[60] Like all romantics,

Rorty is gripped by the fear that he might end his days in an inherited world, a world he has not made.[61] And even worse, he dreads the horror of discovering that he himself is only a copy—a mere replica of someone else.[62]

Hence his remarkable reading of Freud. Instead of Philip Rieff's Freud—Freud the Stoic, with his almost Christlike sadness, the man who explained all our sorrows to us—Rorty gives us a positively upbeat Freud. This is the Freud who "democratized genius by giving everyone a creative unconscious."[63] Rorty's Freud is less a scientist describing the fundamental structures of the human unconscious than a poet for whom every life represents "the working out of a sophisticated idiosyncratic fantasy."[64] Rorty's Freud gives us a new vocabulary, one he hopes we will use to identify "the fortuitous materials out of which we must construct ourselves."[65]

But Rorty is no romantic. He knows as well as Freud—or as well as Max Weber, brooding on the Protestant ethic and the spirit of capitalism, or Melville, holed up somewhere in New York, pondering the steady advance of the confidence man—why men and women are driven to reinvent themselves, always and continually, without resolution or consolation. In *Civilization and Its Discontents* (1929), his final and surely his darkest book, Freud insisted once again that anxiety—that "tormenting uneasiness"—lies sullen and menacing right at the heart of every human life: "Anxiety is always present somewhere or other behind every symptom; one time it takes noisy possession of the whole of consciousness, while at another it conceals itself so completely that we are obliged to speak of unconscious anxiety."[66]

For Rorty as for Freud, men and women are driven to doubt themselves, and thus to remake themselves, not by some deep-hungering desire for more life but rather by a permanent and deeply embedded sense of anxiety—an anxiety that constantly tears at their provisional and always precarious sense of who they are and why they matter. Here is Rorty's description of "the liberal ironist," whom he seems to embrace almost as an ideal character type: "The ironist spends her time worrying about the possibility that she has been initiated into the wrong tribe, taught to play the wrong language game. She worries that the process of socialization which turned her into a human being by giving her a language may have given her the wrong language, and so turned her into the wrong kind of human being. *But she cannot give a criterion of wrongness.*"[67]

Moreover, Rorty knows that no one can *really* give birth to himself, that no attempt at self-invention and personal autonomy can ever be more than "marginal and parasitic."[68] And he also knows that a solid sense of self is not something most people can afford to play around with. More important, he knows that every attempt to redescribe yourself necessarily involves redescribing other people— redescribing them in your terms rather than their own. This has become a central concern of much recent criticism.[69] The feminist critic Bell Hooks put it this way: "No need to hear your voice when I can talk about you better than you can speak about yourself. No need to hear your voice. Only tell me about our pain. I want to know your story. And then I will tell it back to you in a new way. Tell it back to you in such a way that it has become mine, my own. Rewriting you I write myself anew."[70]

In *Contingency, Irony, Solidarity* Rorty calls on George Orwell to remind us that the most effective way to humiliate and ultimately destroy another human being is to show him that his own vocabulary—on which he has constructed his sense of self—is not only inadequate but ultimately futile.[71] Like Orwell, Rorty knows that the drive for autonomy and independence necessarily draws others into the gravitational pull of one's own myth-making imagination; individuality and selfhood come only at the expense of other people. In the final third of *Contingency, Irony, Solidarity* Rorty argues that literature can help us "attend to the springs of cruelty in ourselves . . . not by warning us against social injustice but by warning us against the tendencies to cruelty inherent in searches for autonomy."[72]

The essential emptiness of the self; its ever-present sense of anxiety; its insatiable desire for autonomy and independence; and the inherently aggressive nature of that quest—this is the sensibility not of a contemporary postmodernist but of a classical modernist. Like the modernist masters he in fact admires, Rorty's understanding of the self grows directly out of his underlying and more fundamental awareness of a terrible vacancy at the center of the world. When the postmodernist Richard Rorty tells us that there is no intrinsic "self" for one to "realize," or that there is no extrinsic "reality" that we can possibly "know," he is telling us essentially what modernists like Thomas Wolfe told us decades ago. Here is Wolfe's description of young Oliver Gant, the protagonist of *Look Homeward, Angel:* "He understood that men were forever strangers to one another, that no one ever comes really to know any one, that imprisoned in the dark womb of our mother, we come to life without having seen her face."[73]

This sensibility is hardly original with Wolfe, of course, or even with the modernist writers generally. In fact, you can find it—or something very much like it—almost anywhere you look in the historical record. In the brooding Rainer Rilke, for example: "We can go this far, and this is ours, to touch one another this lightly; the gods can press down harder upon us. But that is the gods' affair."[74] Or in the sorrow-laden melancholy of Montaigne:

> There is no constant existence, neither of our being, nor of the objects. And we, and our judgement, and all mortall things else do unecessantly rowle, turne, and passe away. . . . We have no communication with being; for every humane nature is ever in the middle between being borne and dying; giving nothing of itself but an obscure apparence and shadow, and an uncertaine and weak opinion. And if perhaps you fix your thought to take its being; it would be even, as if one should go about to grasp the water.[75]

Instead of being provided at birth with a system of universal and humanly distinctive features (such as "reason" or "conscience"), we have only the local and singular—only the particular strategies of perception and structures of belief implanted by *this* culture, *this* community, *this* family.

There is something oddly reminiscent of the great eighteenth-century conservative Edmund Burke in Rorty's thought. When the French philosophes charged that traditions were "merely" artificial constructs, that they lacked any real foundation in nature itself, Burke immediately agreed. But he went on to explain that traditions are precious precisely *because* they are artificial, precisely *because* they lack any foundation in nature. If Edmund Burke and Richard Rorty would have agreed on nothing else they would have agreed on this: that beneath tradition lies only more tradition, that beneath one interpretation of the self lies only another interpretation, that there is no "real" self hidden away at the base of one's personality, that there are only habits of thinking and ways of being. Similarly and by extension, what we eventually come to think of as "human nature" merely marks the depth of our identity with certain of these inherited modes of thought and behavior. Moreover—and for precisely the same reason—both Burke and Rorty would have agreed that "the past" too is merely an interpretation, a figure of speech, an accustomed way of thinking.

VI

Historians do not usually think of Richard Rorty as one of their own. But this has more to do with academic convention than intellectual substance. After all, his most important work to date, *Philosophy and the Mirror of Nature,* is a history of the problem of representation in Western art and philosophy from the seventeenth century to the present. His second major book, *Consequences of Pragmatism,* is a collection of traditional intellectual biographies, arranged in chronological order, beginning with Wittgenstein and ending with Derrida et al. His larger, long-term, overarching project is an attempt to reconstruct the history of American pragmatism from John Dewey through Donald Davidson—just the sort of thing intellectual historians used to do. Rorty has also published several important essays in which he discusses the problems and possibilities of writing history under the sign of postmodernism. In *Contingency, Irony, Solidarity* he repeatedly describes himself as a "historicist."

There may be, then, some justification for reading Rorty as an intellectual historian. But the sort of history that interests him is an *older,* more *traditional* history. If we want to know what written history would look like once we dropped our current obsession with historical context and objective truth—and more important, if we want to know how history might reoccupy its former office as one of our primary forms of moral deliberation—we have only to look at the sort of history Richard Rorty has been writing these past several years.

When historians think of Richard Rorty they usually think of what he has done with John Dewey: whether he got Dewey right side up or upside down or missed him altogether. But this slides over something more obvious and important: Rorty did not just reinterpret Dewey, he *adopted* him. He transformed Dewey into a mentor, a predecessor, an intellectual ancestor. Indeed, he has come to think of his own work as essentially building on and extending Dewey's work. Rorty is continually saying things like "Dewey thought, as I now do, that such-and-such." After describing how he worked himself out of his youthful infatuation with Hegel, for example, Rorty wrote: "I had gotten back on good terms with Dewey."[76] And it is not just Dewey; Rorty has adopted—he also sees himself as continuing and extending the work of—Nietzsche, Wittgenstein, Heidegger, and several others. The remarkable thing about Rorty is not his *interpretations* but his *appropriations.* He seems to have an almost instinctive need to search out predecessors—writers and thinkers he can adopt as mentors and nestors.

There is nothing unusual about this, of course. Indeed, if Harold Bloom is right, most of our intellectual life proceeds in just this fashion, under the sign of the Freudian family romance. As Bloom sees it, writers truly create themselves only through a fierce Oedipal struggle with their literary forefathers, creatively misreading and revising them, trying to appropriate and consume them, burning them as fuel to power their own prophetic self-begetting: "Somewhere in the heart of each new poet there is hidden the dark wish that all the libraries be burned in some new Alexandrian conflagration, that the imagination might be liberated from the greatness and oppressive power of its own dead champions."[77] So it is that "the hungry generations go on treading one another down."[78]

All fathers are despotic and overbearing patriarchs in Bloom's eyes; they straddle their progeny, they cripple and disfigure them, they threaten to crush the very life out of them. How can I live, how can I draw my own writer's breath, pressed under the weight of my father's corpus?

But Bloom seems oblivious to those writers and artists who feel not that they must struggle against their fathers' oppressive presence but rather that they have been abandoned by their fathers. He would not have understood Martin Luther King Jr.'s insistence that he was permanently indebted to those who had gone before him. King used to describe himself as "eternally in the red."[79] Nor would he have understood Alice Walker. In "Looking for Zora" she describes how she found in Zora Neale Hurston's books the courage to breech-birth herself as a writer. And she describes her subsequent search, in the long hot summer of 1973, for Hurston's unmarked grave: how she eventually found it in the far corner of a weed-choked, snake-infested field in Fort Pierce, Florida; how she ordered a proper headstone and had it placed over Hurston's grave; how she cut the grass and planted Hurston's favorite flowers all around it—azaleas, gardenias, and lots of morning glories. "Though by that time I considered her a native genius, there was nothing grand or historic in my mind. It was, rather, a duty I accepted as naturally mine—because Zora was dead and I, for the time being, was alive."[80] That Walker bears no biological relation to Hurston matters not a whit: "As far as I'm concerned, she *is* my aunt."[81]

Though Rorty cites Bloom repeatedly, his own sensibility—and his own understanding of history—is closer to King's or Alice Walker's than it is to Bloom's. Like Walker, he spends his time searching for dead writers and thinkers he can add to his personal pantheon of heroes.[82] When he reads "the mighty dead" (as he reverently refers to them) he does not care about formulating what historians like to call "a full and complete understanding" of their lives or their work. He is looking for people he can "develop an attitude toward," writers who can inspire him, thinkers who can give him a new idea or concept, an image, a metaphor, bits and pieces of a new vocabulary—anything he can use to open up a new and, he hopes, more acute angle of vision.[83]

But Rorty's sense of history differs from Alice Walker's in one significant respect: Rorty is a textualist. For him it is books that count, not the people who are said to have written them. While Walker was tramping around Florida looking for Hurston's grave, Rorty was back home rereading *The Birth of Tragedy*. Rorty assumes—as Walker does not—that the past has "always already" been textualized, that it is accessible to us only in textual form. He simply does not expect to find the author in her books, any more than he excepts to find God in the book of nature. David Hollinger thinks authors actually inhabit their books, but for Rorty the author is just another character flitting through the text. When Rorty says he is trying to "work up an attitude" toward a particular writer, we should read him as saying that he is trying to work up an attitude toward the character of the author. For Rorty could not care less about the blood-and-bone author himself—the real personage named Friedrich Nietzsche, for example—or about his life and times. What he does care about is the character "Nietzsche" who seems to haunt all those books said to have been written by Friedrich Nietzsche. Alexander Nehamas recently described this attitude in *Nietzsche: Life as Literature*. When we read Nietzsche's books, he says,

> we are not engaging with the miserable little man who wrote them but with the philosopher who emerges through them, the magnificent character these texts constitute and manifest, the agent who, as the will to power holds, is nothing but his effects—that is, his writings. Always his own best reader as well as his own author, Nietzsche knew this, too: "The 'work,' whether of the artist or of the philosopher, invents the person who has created it, who is supposed to have created it."[84]

If you were to tell Rorty that the "real" John Dewey was not at all like the "John Dewey" that Rorty has extrapolated from Dewey's books, he would simply shrug his shoulders. As he explained in *Contingency, Irony, Solidarity*, "We treat the names of such people as the names of the heroes of their own books. We do not bother to distinguish Swift from *saeva indignatio*, Hegel from Geist, Nietzsche from Zarathustra, Marcel Proust from Marcel the narrator, or Trilling from *The Liberal Imagination*. We do not care whether these writers managed to live up to their own self-images. *What we want to know is whether to adopt those images.*"[85]

The other side of such textualism, of course, is a strong antipathy to the *con*textualism that has come to dominate academic history in the past twenty years. Everyone knows that you cannot really recreate the context in which a given text was written, though everyone thinks you ought to try. But Rorty suggests that the supposed context of a given text is no more important than its supposed author. It is the books that interest him. After all, it is the books that bring him new metaphors, new words, new metaphorical uses of old words, new ways of thinking and fresh ways of seeing. To help these rather elderly books put on a good performance for their new audiences, Rorty rips them out of their "proper" historical context, strips them of everything that, from his own vantage point in the present, looks like "outdated foolishness," and reads them anew.[86] He is not the only one doing this sort of decontextualizing, of course; it is precisely what P. F. Strawson did in his famous study of Kant, for example. And it is what Jacques Lacan did with Freud: he rethought what Freud might have thought had he—like Lacan—been trained in twentieth-century linguistics rather than nineteenth-century thermodynamics.

Historians do not think much of this sort of thing, of course; they like to swallow their heroes whole. Here is a recent example: Henry Louis Gates celebrates Frederick Douglass's commitment to the struggle against slavery but ignores some of the less attractive aspects of his thought. But the historian Andrew Delbanco objects: Gates cannot just pick and choose what he likes about Douglass, Delbanco says; he "must assent to other crippling assumptions imposed on him by the same culture that enslaved him."[87] Were such a rounded and final assessment even conceivable (let alone possible), one would still want to ask, Why should it be the only "historically valid" assessment? Why should it not be just as historically valid for the historian to describe Douglass's thoughts in such a way that they shine new light on issues and problems *we* think interesting or important? Indeed, how can Douglass continue to live otherwise? Could the selfless, disinterested account Delbanco wants ever amount to more than an assemblage of raw material for the powerful and pointed accounts that committed historians like Henry Louis Gates will continue to write?

Rorty is talking about lifting texts out of their "proper" historical context, rearranging their internal balances, then using these newly arranged texts to illuminate something that concerns him in the present. But he is also talking about recontextualizing texts—plopping them down in new and unexpected contexts. This is what Gates calls "productive juxtaposition"—laying one text alongside another hitherto unrelated text and discovering, in Rorty's words, that "they have interpenetrated and become warp and woof of a new, vividly poly-chrome fabric."[88] He thinks the writers he admires proceed in just this way: they recontextualize "whatever memory brings back," thereby extending their own possibilities.[89] Rorty does not really care about the social or intellectual context in which Dewey wrote *Liber-alism and Social Action*, any more than he cares about Dewey him-self; it is the possibility of using Dewey's texts to create a "new, vividly polychrome fabric" that interests him. And since he works as an intellectual historian, he prefers using the texts of long-dead authors to weave these "new, vividly polychome" fabrics. In other words, he has learned that the best way to push back the boundaries of his own imagination, and to expand the range of his intellectual and emotional identifications, is to incessantly recontextualize every book, every idea, every image or metaphor the past has to offer, tear-ing them out of their original contexts, reinserting them into contexts of his own devising, weaving them together with other books and ideas he has found in other parts of the past, thereby creating a new conceptual web for himself, a new "polychrome fabric."

This approach is a long way from the sort of thing they teach in university history departments, of course. Indeed, it will sound fop-pishly postmodern to most historians. But Rorty thinks it is precisely what makes intellectual history a vital and necessary form of moral reflection. Certainly there is nothing new about it; indeed, Rorty in-sists that it is as old as the hills, that our most interesting thinkers have always been our most extravagant recontextualizers: "Socrates recontextualized Homer; Augustine recontextualized the pagan vir-tues. . . Hegel recontextualized Socrates and Augustine . . . Proust recontextualized (over and over again) everybody he met; and Der-rida recontextualizes (over and over again) Hegel, Austin, Searle, and everybody else he reads."[90]

Rorty thinks that coming up with a brilliant correlation of for-merly disparate and incongruous texts (or images or ideas or meta-phors) is the very essence of intellectual achievement. In the second volume of *Philosophical Papers* he even argues that "the most an original figure can hope to do is recontextualize his or her predeces-sors"—and conversely, that no original thinker "can hope to avoid being fitted into contexts by his readers."[91]

There is something else about the way Rorty writes intellectual history that I have not yet mentioned: what he calls "rational recon-struction." By this I understand him to mean arranging his cast of adopted predecessors in such a way that they appear to constitute "a conversational sequence" or intellectual tradition.[92] He wants us to arrange our favorite thinkers so they constitute "a long conversational

interchange."[93] He knows he will have to organize and frame that
conversation himself, of course—but then every working historian
knows that. If we want intellectual traditions, we will have to gather
the texts and arrange them ourselves, just as—to pick a recent example—Casey Nelson Blake did in *Beloved Community: The Cultural
Criticism of Randolph Bourne, Van Wyck Brooks, Waldo Frank, and
Lewis Mumford* (1990). In his foreword to Blake's book Alan Trachtenberg wrote: "Behind the voices [Blake] orchestrates we can hear
his own, arguing that in the legacy of these four cultural critics we
can find elements for a heritage, a tradition of communitarian vision
based on 'cultural citizenship.'"[94]

Rorty describes his own work in just this way. In *Contingency,
Irony, Solidarity*, for example, he says he was trying to construct a
line of thought connecting certain ideas he found in Blumenberg,
Nietzsche, Freud, Davidson, and several others.[95] In the introduction
to *Philosophical Papers* he wrote that he wanted "to assign [Heideg-
ger and Derrida] places in a conversational sequence which runs from
Descartes through Kant and Hegel to Nietzsche and beyond."[96] In
Consequences of Pragmatism he explained his attempt to read Foucault and Derrida as if they were trying to extend some of the ideas
James and Dewey had formulated fifty years earlier.[97] In *Philosophy
and the Mirror of Nature* (1980) he said he was trying to "extend"
a bundle of ideas he had borrowed from Wilfrid Sellars and
W. V. O. Quine (who had borrowed those ideas from Wittgenstein,
Heidegger, and Dewey).[98] Eleven years later, in the introduction to
the first volume of his *Philosophical Papers* (1991), Rorty wrote that
he had "come to think of Donald Davidson's work as deepening and
extending the lines of thought traced by Sellars and Quine" and that
he himself was now trying "to extend [Davidson's ideas] into areas
which Davidson himself has not yet explored."[99]

Finally, notice what happens to the texts in this process: as soon
as Rorty inserts a text from the past into one of his "conversational
sequences," its meaning and significance become functions of the
sequence rather than the text itself (much less a function of something presumed to lie behind the text, such as the author's intentions). It is the newly contrived sequence, the improvised intellectual
tradition, that generates meaning (*real* meaning, not merely "significance," as E. D. Hirsch would have it, or "understanding," as
Quentin Skinner contends). Rorty thinks intellectual historians
should concern themselves less with explaining the meanings of individual books than with explaining what happens when you place a
book or an idea in the context of other books or ideas. After all, there
are as many possible meanings to a text as there are possible contexts:

"People often say, quite reasonably, that they only found out what they meant by listening to what they said later on—when they heard themselves reacting to the consequences of their original utterance. [In the same way,] it is perfectly reasonable to describe Locke as finding out what he really meant, what he was really getting at in the *Second Treatise*, only after conversations in heaven with, successively, Jefferson, Marx, Rawls."[100]

VII

Rorty's importance for historians rests on two central points: his critique of objectivity and, growing out of that, his belief that intellectual history is mainly a matter of finding intellectual predecessors and lining them up in chronological order. But what are we to make of all this?

Concerning Rorty's denial that historians can produce reliable, objective knowledge about the past, when all the arguments are laid on the table it finally comes down to this: historians who defend the possibility of objective knowledge are saying, "Look, we *can* hold the world steady in our gaze—or at least steady enough to count as steady." But to many of us, historians and others, the world just does not *seem* steady; indeed, the very ground seems to be quaking and trembling beneath our feet, even as we listen to all this healthy-minded, Vaseline-impregnated, responsible-sounding professional Methodism. And we suspect—especially if we have made the mistake of reading too much Adams and not enough Dewey—that things will get worse before they get better, that only skulls will be grinning at the final awards banquet. For many of us, William James hit it right on the head: "We stand on a mountain pass in the midst of whirling snow and blinding mist, through which we get glimpses now and then of paths which may be deceptive. If we stand still we shall be frozen to death. If we take the wrong road we shall be dashed to pieces. We do not certainly know whether there is any right one."[101]

But the pragmatic purveyors of "historical method" and other household gods rush in to reassure us, once again, that things are not as bad as they seem: "Here is the path, here in front of us. True, there is a precipice over there, but right here is solid ground. Trust me." But even the seemingly solid ground seems to be riddled with appalling enigmas:

Here is a story that is going around the desert tonight: over across the Nevada line, sheriff's deputies are diving in some underground pools, trying to retrieve a couple of bodies known to be down in the hole. The widow of one of the drowned boys is over there; she is eighteen, and pregnant, and is said not to leave the hole. The divers go down and come up, and she just stands there and stares into the water. They have been diving for ten days but have found no bottom to the caves, no bodies and no trace of them, only the black 90° water going down and down and down, and a single translucent fish, not classified. The story tonight is that one of the divers has been hauled up incoherent, out of his head, shouting—until they got him out of there so the widow could not hear—about water that got hotter instead of cooler as he went down, about light flickering through the water, about magma, about underground nuclear testing. . . . What does it mean? It means nothing manageable.[102]

What does it mean? What could it *possibly* mean? Maybe every event really does contain some certain significance, as Ishmael wanted to believe and as the authors of *Telling the Truth about History* continue to believe. But the rest of us can only wonder. For the truth is that God grinds us round his mill as he will, and all our professional procedures will no more save us than the Royal Navy's measured forms could save Billy Budd.

So Rorty gives up any pretense of discovering "what really happened" in the past. He does not want to explain the origins of Dewey's ideas; he wants to employ them—along with Hegel's and Nietzsche's and Freud's and Heidegger's and anybody else's he can use to fabricate a new angle of vision. He is not trying to explain how the past flowed into the present; he is trying to ransack the past for images, metaphors, ideas—anything that may cast new light on the present. Someone once called the past a foreign country; for Rorty it is more like a huge warehouse, stuffed to the rafters with political essays, philosophical treatises, religious tracts—uncountable attempts by various and sundry people to make sense of their lives; scribblings and musings written and hoarded out of fear or cunning or the need to establish a small fund of minor consolations—a fund that Rorty thinks we should pillage and plunder.

Historians do not like this sort of thing very much. The labor historian Daniel T. Rodgers probably spoke for most of his colleagues when he berated the "postmodernists" for portraying the past as "a vast attic of referents and motifs open to a multitude of ransackers, not just those pledged to historical rules of sequence and context."[103] And indeed, Rorty's way of doing history—especially his rejection of historical objectivity, and thus of objectively discernible "sequence and context"—may be just what Rodgers thinks it is: an attack on professional standards. But Rorty is probably right when he claims we can learn more than most of us have wanted to admit by giving up our claims to objective knowledge and embracing the perished past for what it obviously is: an anarchy of discontinuous images and thoughtless clamor, a theater of shattered ciphers, all glimmering and sparkling with an appalling brilliance.

Which brings us to the second issue: as we have seen, Rorty thinks history is largely a matter of adopting intellectual predecessors and lining them up in chronological order, so they seem to constitute an intellectual tradition. He thinks we should spend less time trying to reconstruct historical contexts and more time trying to assemble genealogies of predecessors. He is right, of course, for all the obvious reasons, but here we need mention only one: the seemingly simple act of adopting a particular predecessor is freighted with moral consequences, not all of which are immediately apparent. We historians do not talk about this very much, but it is just here, in this always complicated and often impenetrable business of arguing with our adopted ancestors, that history comes into its own as an essential and indispensable form of moral deliberation.

Literary critics tend to leave the room when anyone starts talking about ethical criticism. They think it is simplistic and dogmatic, that it deadens the reader to the purely literary qualities of the text, to its incessant play of images and signifiers, its hidden complexities and ironies.[104] They read literature because they like what it does for them, and what they can do with it, rather than for any normative function it may perform. Harold Bloom is a good example: if you asked him what he thinks about ethical criticism, he would probably say that literature teaches us how to talk to ourselves rather than how to deal with other people.[105] Literature opens the door to "that polar privacy / a soul admitted to itself."[106]

This is essentially what Rorty says about intellectual history. After all, to adopt a particular thinker as an intellectual predecessor is to adopt a particular patterning of thought and desire.[107] What Rorty values in intellectual history is pretty much what Bloom values in literature: they both teach us how to talk to ourselves.[108] The books we read, the characters we learn to care about, the thinkers we admire, the predecessors we adopt—they all color our perceptions and shape our desires.[109] They teach us what to want, what to value, who to admire. In a very real way, they define the kind of persons we are—and the kind of persons we hope to become.[110]

But getting to the point where we can seriously think of ourselves as working in a line of descent that begins with, say, Emerson may be more more difficult, more personally bedeviling, than Rorty has so far admitted (I will discuss these problems more fully in chapter 8). And as if that were not enough, it turns out we need a *multiplicity* of genealogies, a plurality of traditions. Nothing less will work in this polyglot America, composed, like Melville's *Pequod,* of "mongrel renegades and castaways and cannibals."[111] Arthur Schlesinger Jr. and some others insist that what they call "the American creed"—always and unambiguously singular—must become "the common possession of all Americans."[112] He wants us to transform our immigrant diversity into an American unity.[113] But as Henry Louis Gates has pointed out, this is "to dream of an America in cultural white face, and that just won't do."[114] Those who see merely a trendy multiculturalism in Gates's caution need only remind themselves that Gates is saying pretty much what Randolph Bourne said three- quarters of a century ago. In "Trans-national America" (1916) Bourne warned us, "We shall have to give up the search for our native 'American' culture. . . . There is no distinctively American culture; it is apparently our lot rather to be a federation of cultures."[115] Melville, of course, had suggested as much sixty years earlier.

The difference between Melville, Bourne, and Gates on the one side and Schlesinger on the other is this: Schlesinger thinks the various cultures and traditions of this compound America can be trimmed and shaved till they fit what he calls "a common American culture."[116] But Melville, Bourne, and Gates are thinking of *opposed and competing* traditions, traditions that are constantly jostling and clashing with one another, traditions we can use to confront and challenge other, more deeply held traditions. They think we should concentrate on learning to negotiate our way *between* and *among* these opposing traditions; that we should teach ourselves how to play them off against one another, how to use one tradition to see what cannot be seen—and ask what cannot be asked—with the others.

This is what the historian John Patrick Diggins seems to have done in the best of his many books, *The Lost Soul of American Politics* (1984). Like William Carlos Williams, Diggins wants a criticism deeply embedded in the American grain. And he thinks he has found the essential components in New England Calvinism and the American liberal tradition. Most of us tend to follow V. F. Parrington's lead when it comes to Calvinism and liberalism: they are ideological opposites—the two mutually repelling poles of American political thought. And so they are in many respects. But Diggins wants us to see that the Calvinist tradition can be made to serve as the conscience of American liberalism, giving it the psychological depth and moral content that it otherwise lacks.[117]

Moreover, he argues that the greatest thinkers of nineteenth-century America—Abraham Lincoln and Herman Melville—did just this. Thus Lincoln, apostle of Lockean individualism and defender of "the sacred rights of property," knew instinctively what Locke could never had known, even had he lived through the American 1860s: that it was God himself who unleashed the terrible horrors of the Civil War, and that he did so as just and fitting punishment for the sin of claiming other men as property:

> Woe unto the world because of offences! For it must needs be that offences come; but woe to that man by whom the offence cometh! If we shall suppose that American slavery is one of those offences which, in the providence of God, must needs come, but which, having continued through His appointed time, He now wills to remove, and that He gives to both North and South, this terrible war, as the woe due to those by whom the offence came, shall we discern therein any departure from those divine attributes which the believers in a living god always ascribe to him? Fondly do we hope—fervently do we pray—that this mighty scourge of war may speedily pass away. Yet, if God will that it continue until all the wealth piled by the bond-man's two hundred and fifty years of unrequited toil shall be sunk, and until every drop of blood drawn with the lash shall be paid by another drawn with the sword, as was said three thousand years ago, so still it must be said, "The judgments of the Lord are true and righteous altogether."[118]

VIII

Many historians continue to insist that history is "an accumulative science, that it gathers truth through the steady, if plodding efforts of countless practitioners turning out countless monographs."[119] What is at issue in American history, however, is not our ability to know the past but our ability to find the predecessors we need—to think with their thoughts, to work through our own beliefs by working through their beliefs. Only thus does history become a mode of moral reflection.

CHAPTER SEVEN

The Dream of a Common History

I

Does an African American literary critic schooled in the acrobatics of deconstruction have anything to offer historians who still admire Henry Adams and Perry Miller? The obvious answer would seem to be no. After all, Derrida and Foucault made short work of traditional historical writing. And historians, for the most part, tend to look on deconstruction as nothing short of a cultural menace. It seems to them a radical loosening, an undoing, a deliberate dismantling of their tested and accredited ways of knowing. If they read Derrida at all, they read him with the kind of weary despair more appropriately reserved for the waste products of the social sciences.

This is unfortunate, because Henry Louis Gates has much to offer traditional historians. Indeed, his work can help them make American history a powerful and compelling form of moral reflection. For Gates is trying to tell us the same thing Edmund Burke tried to tell us over two hundred years ago: that our most deeply valued traditions rest on nothing more than custom and habit, that beneath one layer of tradition lies only another. Moreover, for Gates as for Burke, the fact that our traditions are historically contingent is precisely what makes them so valuable. They may not reflect truth embedded in the nature of things, but they do reflect what we and our forebears have learned from living alongside and fighting with one another for over three and a half centuries.

Moreover, a careful reading of Gates's early work suggests a posture toward the past that even *conservative* historians would find familiar and congenial. Indeed, Gates's appraoch is not unlike T. S. Eliot's ("these fragments I have shored against my ruin")—or Henry Adams's. After all, it was Adams, conservative Christian anarchist and doubting historian, who explained why historical continuity had collapsed, why truth had been reduced to "the value of a relation."[1] As Adams saw it, history had become little more than "a tangled skein that one may take up at any point, and break when one has unraveled enough."[2] Like Eliot and Adams, Gates knows the terrible vacancy that lies at the center of things, but he also knows that American history does not leave us unequipped to face that vacancy. And what is more important for our purposes, he shows us how to construct histories from which we can confront our isolation and our solitude without giving in to despair and without imposing prophecy upon experience.

Gates probably would not call himself a conservative. He does not take his cues from Henry Adams or Perry Miller—much less T. S. Eliot or Edmund Burke—and he certainly should not be confused with neoconservatives like Thomas Sowell and Shelby Steele. Nevertheless, in three closely argued books and a long series of articles he has redrawn the contours of African American literary history along what can only be described as traditional and even conservative lines. And he has demonstrated that such a history can deepen and strengthen our capacity for historical reflection, nourish and quicken our moral imagination, and help us figure out what we should value and how we should live. Which is why Henry Louis Gates has become, as Wahneema Lubiano of Princeton recently described him, "one of the most read and misread" African American historians of the century.[3]

II

Gates's ideas have been shaped by the tension between two powerful but contradictory developments: the Black Arts movement of the 1960s and the rise of literary theory in the 1970s. The Black Arts movement had already collapsed when Gates came to intellectual maturity in the early 1970s. Nevertheless, it gave him his initial inspiration and, together with the literary theory of the 1970s, it continues to shape his deepest sense of American literary history.

The Black Arts movement first appeared in the early 1960s as a response to the use of "black" as a metaphor for "absence." For twenty-five hundred years or more, "black" has been used to signify empty space, nothingness, the void. To the extent that it suggested

a presence, it was the presence of absence; to the extent that it constituted a sign, it was the sign of zero—the terrible terror of a naught
at the center of creation.[4]

The Black Arts movement countered this racist aesthetic with
"the Black Aesthetic." Rather than an original absence, "Blackness"
signified a positive presence. It was the "inner life of the African-
American folk," the interior dynamism that shaped its expressive
forms. Black music, black art, black literature, all became expressions not merely of black culture but of "Blackness" itself—of
"Blackness" as a generic entity, a biological essence that lay at the
very core of African American culture, that which was its gist, its
marrow, its shaping center and vital spirit. White folks could no more
understand black culture than white boys could play the blues. LeRoi
Jones once described the difference between listening to a white boy
lost in the blues and listening to a black man play the blues as "the
difference between watching someone have an orgasm and someone
having an orgasm."[5]

The poetics of the Black Arts movement was largely shaped by
the politics of the Black Power movement. As Amiri Baraka, Larry
Neal, Stephen Henderson, and other Black Arts writers explained
over and over again, the Black Arts movement was "the aesthetic
and spiritual sister" of the Black Power movement, its "cultural
wing" and "ideological counterpart."[6] Not suprisingly, writers associated with the Black Arts movement adopted a poetics of racial essentialism and social realism. They celebrated the black vernacular as
"the poetry of the people," asserted the moral superiority of black
urban culture, and interpreted black art, black music, and black literature as "the expressive products of the black American masses."[7]

Though the Black Arts movement had exhausted itself by the mid-
1970s when Gates began teaching and writing, he was (and continues
to be) strongly influenced by its respect for the black vernacular and
its hopes for a genuine black Renaissance.[8] Indeed, his own work can
best be read as a modification and extension of the project first outlined by the Black Arts writers. Like them, he hopes to describe a
distinctive African American literary and cultural tradition; like
them, he wants to find an interpretive system within the black vernacular that he can use to discuss and evaluate that tradition; and
like them, he believes that by redescribing the African American
cultural tradition, together with its indigenous interpretive system,
he can force a critical reevaluation of the larger "American" literary
and cultural traditions.[9] But Gates's project differs from the Black
Arts project in one crucial respect: he has rejected its racial essentialism, its insistence on "Blackness" as biological entity and meta-

physical presence. That rejection came as a direct result of the literary formalism he absorbed at Yale University in the 1970s.

Gates spent seventeen years at Yale, from 1969 through 1985.[10] These were crucial years, every bit as important as the Black Arts movement in shaping the direction in which his thinking would evolve. Moreover, not only were they formative years for Gates's own development (he was nineteen when he arrived as a freshman and thirty-five when he left as an associate professor), they were also important years in the development of American literary criticism. For it was during the late 1960s and early 1970s that Jacques Derrida, Paul de Man, Harold Bloom, Geoffrey Hartman, J. Hillis Miller, and others in the Yale English Department formulated the deconstructive and poststructuralist theories that would dominate American literary criticism well into the 1980s.

Gates was the leading figure in what Elaine Showalter has called "a new wave of young black intellectuals trained in such deconstructionist centers as Cornell and Yale."[11] As Houston Baker later explained, "Their proclaimed mission was to reconstruct the pedagogy and study of African-American literature so that it would reflect the most advanced thinking of a contemporary universe of literary-theoretical discourse."[12] This was a decisive turning point in the history of African American criticism, one of those intensely creative moments when intellectual traditions are set on a new course, invested with new meaning and a new sense of purpose. Even now, in the 1990s, Gates remembers "the profound reorientation of energy and vision which took place among African-American thinkers, writers, performers, and their audiences during this period, centering on considerations of a nationalist, or *sui generis,* understanding of the 'black self.' "[13]

The Black Arts movement had countered the essentialist equation of Western civilization (black = absence) with an essentialist equation of its own (black = positive presence and original essence).[14] The younger black critics studying at Yale and other elite institutions in the late 1960s and early 1970s were inspired by the Black Arts movement's celebration of African American expressiveness but were dismayed by its racial essentialism. So they brought their newly acquired deconstructive skills to bear on the concept that stood right at the center of that essentialism: the concept of "Blackness" itself. Is "Blackness" biologically given or culturally constructed? Is it an essence or a sign? Is it analogous to "sex," or is it analogous to "gender"? Is a person *born* "black" or does she learn to be black? Is racial identity hereditary or contractual? Are race and ethnicity matters of *des*cent or *con*sent?[15]

These were exactly the right questions; indeed, everything depended on how one answered them. For if the Black Arts movement
was right, if "black" is not a sign but an essence, then black literature,
black music, black art could only be expressive and mimetic; they
could never be appreciated for what they are in themselves but would
always have to be read as expressing something presumed to lie outside, behind, or beneath them—something they were thought to express or represent, something they were supposed to be "about." And
that something was always the same: "Blackness." If "black" is not
a sign but a racial essence, a natural type, then African American
cultural products could be understood only as expressions of that racial essence. Moreover, they could be appreciated only in their
"proper" context. If "black" is biologically given rather than culturally constructed, then the only defensible poetics would be a poetics
of contextualism and social realism. If racial identification is hereditary rather than contractual, we would not see "Blackness" as arbitrarily constructed, "culture by culture, language by language, discourse by discourse."[16] We could approach "black" only as a naturally
given essence, never as a culturally assigned or freely chosen role.

For these reasons Gates and others insisted that "black" is not an
essence but a sign, that neither "black" nor "white" has any *intrinsic*
meaning whatever, that they possess meaning only as they stand in
relation to one another, that is, only by virtue of their assigned places
in a structured economy of meanings. Instead of naturalizing and
reifying the sign of "Blackness," as the Black Arts critics continued
to do, Gates and his young co-conspirators set out to reveal its arbitrary and artificial character. In other words, they set out to deconstruct it. As Gates explained in his first book, *Figures in Black,*

> The idea of a transcendent signified, a belief in an essence called
> "Blackness," is a presence our tradition has tried of late to will
> into being in order to negate two and a half millennia of its
> figuration as an absence. As healthy politically as such a gesture
> was, as revealing as it was in this country and abroad of the
> very arbitrariness of the received sign of blackness itself, we
> must criticize the idealism, the notion of essence, implicit in
> even this important political gesture. To think of oneself as free
> simply because one can claim—one can utter—the negation
> of an assertion is not to think deeply enough.[17]

The new black historians and literary critics that Gates hung out
with were no less committed to the recovery of African American
history and literature than their predecessors in the Black Arts movement. And they were no less committed to the formulation of a

"black aesthetic." But unlike Black Arts writers, they insisted that "black" is a socially constructed category rather than a natural type.

Moreover—and this will turn out to have been at least as important as their rejection of racial essentialism—they were impressed, in a way their Black Arts predecessors had never been, with the "literariness" of African American literature. If "black" had any meaning at all, they reasoned, that meaning must lie in the *formal* and *literary* qualities of African American texts—with the texts themselves rather than with what they were "about."

Gates's "Preface to Blackness: Text and Pretext" (1978) was the first comprehensive statement of this new black antiessentialism. As Gates later admitted, "Preface to Blackness" is largely a "polemic for formalism."[18] In it he traced the racial essentialism of the Black Arts movement back to the seventeenth century, explaining why it has always seemed so powerful and compelling. And he accurately predicted the direction in which African American criticism would develop in the 1980s. This was a very early article: Gates was only twenty-eight at the time, still working on his dissertation. Yet "Preface to Blackness" is one of the most interesting, revealing, and important articles he has ever written. It begins with a forthright attack on contextualism in African American literary history. Contextualism is the interpretive assumption that regardless of what a text *seems* to say, it is "really" about the circumstances in which it was written. In other words, the meaning of the text lies in its context, or in the presumed relation between text and context—which is what Gates meant by his subtitle, "Text and Pretext." For the contextualist, no cultural expression—be it book, poem, essay, or painting—can ever escape the limitations of its original occasion. All must be returned to what the historian John Patrick Diggins once called "the graveyard of dead contexts."[19] The trouble with this approach, as countless critics have explained over and over, is that it reduces literary works to the status of cultural artifacts or historical documents.[20] Contextualism systematically diminishes complex texts by treating them as fragments of evidence to be cobbled together in the reconstruction of one or another historical discourse. Its basic assumption is that texts are always "about" something other than themselves.

Contextualism has always belabored the social origins of literary works. This has been especially true of African American texts. In "Preface to Blackness" Gates demonstrates that from the publication of Briton Hammon's *Narrative of Uncommon Sufferings and Surprising Deliverance* in 1760 through the Black Arts movement of the 1960s and 1970s, African American texts have always been read contextually, as evidence of one or another special quality thought to characterize black people collectively (or "the black experience" generally). This is not a matter of white critics' belittling black literature, for black critics have reduced black literary works to the status of historical documents as eagerly as white critics have. Black or white, approvingly or no, critics of African American literature have invariably given priority to the testimonial or documentary status of black literature. As Gates demonstrates, the capacity to write has historically been regarded as evidence not only of innate mental equality but of humanity itself. In the seventeenth century it was the ability to write (and to a lesser extent the ability to read) that separated the African from the African American, the slave from the freedman, species of property from human beings.[21] Thus when Phillis Wheatley's *Poems on Various Subjects,* the first book of poems by a black person ever published in England, appeared in 1773 it was immediately taken up by British and American abolitionists as proof positive that Africans possessed the mental capacity of Englishmen, that they were indeed human beings. Though *Poems on Various Subjects* was reviewed by dozens of prominent figures, literary and political, on both sides of the Atlantic, not one of those reviewers discussed the book as poetry, so taken were they by it as evidence of the intellectual potential and essential humanity of African people.[22]

The slave narratives of the nineteenth century were read the same way. *Narrative of the Life of Frederick Douglass, an American Slave,* for example, was everywhere celebrated as "a specimen of the powers of the black race."[23] Similarly, when William Dean Howells reviewed Paul Laurence Dunbar's *Majors and Minors* in 1896 he concluded that "a race which has reached this effect in any of its members can no longer be held wholly uncivilized."[24]

But as Gates notes, Howells took this argument one crucial step further. Here is Howells:

> I have sometimes fancied that perhaps the negroes *thought* black, and *felt* black: that they were racially so utterly alien and distinct from ourselves that there never could be common intellectual and emotional ground between us, and that whatever eternity might do to reconcile us, the end of time would find us far asunder as ever. But this little book has given me pause in my speculation. Here in the artistic effect, at least, is white thinking and white feeling in a black man, and perhaps the human unity, and not the race unity, is the precious thing, the divine thing, after all. God hath made of one blood all nations of men: perhaps the proof of this saying is to appear in the arts, and our hostilities and prejudices are to vanish in them.[25]

As Gates points out, this double assumption—that blacks think and feel differently than whites do and therefore *are* different from whites, but also that this difference could be mediated through art and literature—is precisely the assumption that shaped W. E. B. Du Bois's early thought, that informed and guided the early African American magazine *Crisis,* and that animated the writers of the Harlem Renaissance during the 1920s and 1930s.[26] It is the prevalence and ubiquity of this assumption, Gates argues, that explains why black writers have preoccupied themselves with the essence of "Blackness."

And it was precisely this idea of "Blackness" as the essential content and animating force of *all* African American literature that the Black Arts movement adopted in the 1960s.[27] In his original Black Arts manifesto, *Understanding the New Black Poetry* (1972), Stephen Henderson insisted that African American literature could be understood only as "the communication of Blackness and fidelity to the observed or intuited truth of the Black Experience in the United States."[28] Similarly, in *Long Black Song* (1972) the literary historian Houston Baker argued that African American literature could be understood only against the background of "the black folk experience," which, in sharp contrast to the larger American culture, has always been "oral, collectivistic, and repudiative."[29] Or again, in *The Way of the New World* (1975) Addison Gayle contended that in order to understand African American literature "it is necessary that one live the black experience in a world where substance is more important than form, where the social takes precedence over the aesthetic, where each act, gesture, and movement is political, and where continual rebellion separates the insane from the sane, the robot from the revolutionary."[30]

The Black Arts movement asserted a fixed and determined relation between the physical fact of "Blackness" and a metaphysical essence it also called "Blackness." As we have seen, this approach was simply an extension of the essentialist and contextualist assumptions that have always driven critical discussion of African American literature. But as Gates points out, it also bears a striking resemblance to vulgar Marxist criticism: instead of "base and superstructure" we get "race and superstructure"; instead of consciousness determined by the forms of production, we get consciousness determined by "the experience of Blackness."[31]

Gates thinks this sort of criticism has been disastrous for African American writing. For it has meant that all the great works of the African American literary tradition have been portrayed as merely different expressions of this same unvarying "Blackness." Every African American text testifies to the mental and moral equality of black people, or to the degradation visited upon black people, or to the endurance and creativity of black culture, and so on.[32] Under the spell of this "race and superstructure criticism," African American language has been robbed of its metaphorical capacity and African American literature has been stripped of its allegorical power. The novel has been reduced to a tract, the poem to an essay.[33]

This is not to say that Gates thinks cultural productions bear no relation to their social context, or that literature is somehow autonomous, or that canonical works free-float in some ethereal realm of timeless values. He thinks none of these things.[34] But he does think that literary works are sign systems rather than symbol systems, that there can be no fixed or determined relation between a sign and its referent (or between a text and its meaning), and that texts therefore can be read (or "decoded") using a virtually endless (and endlessly multiplying) variety of methods or protocols. For all these reasons, Gates argued in "Preface to Blackness" that no single method of reading can possibly claim to be final, definitive, or even superior in any but the most sharply delimited and narrowly parochial sense.[35]

For Gates the trouble with the Black Arts movement was twofold. First, it thought African American literary works conveyed a fixed, determined, and determinable meaning—"the experience of Blackness." In other words, meaning was determined by color and culture. Second, it insisted that "Blackness" was an original, antecedent, and completely authentic entity. Stephen Henderson even called it a "commodity." For Henderson and others, "Blackness" (always with a capital *B*) was a natural type rather than a literary metaphor, an essential presence rather than a figure of speech. It existed prior to and outside of all discursive constructions. Indeed, discourse merely expressed its presence. "In the beginning was the deed," wrote Trotsky; for the Black Arts movement the deed was *black*.[36] "Blackness" determined consciousness, and consciousness determined meaning; conversely, the meaning of a literary work lay in "the experience of Blackness." The sense and significance of every black text lay in the portrayal of that single, unitary essence, "Blackness."

For Gates, however, "experience" and "Blackness" are merely signs. As such, they have meaning only by virtue of their place in a complex and intricately structured *system* of signs. Neither "experience" nor "Blackness" can be understood apart from such a system, since neither *exists* prior to or apart from such a system. This is what Gates had in mind when he wrote, in "Preface to Blackness," that " 'Blackness' is not a material object or an event but a metaphor; it does not have an 'essence' as such but is defined by a network of relations that form a particular aesthetic unity."[37] "Black" is a category constituted by its opposition to the category "white."

In "Preface to Blackness" Gates shifted the discussion of African American literature from context to text, from factors outside the text (color and culture, "Blackness" and "the experience of Blackness") to the text itself.[38] And following Derrida's precept that "there is nothing outside the text"—that we can know nothing that has not "always already" been "textualized"—Gates insisted that neither "Blackness" nor "the experience of Blackness" has any meaning outside the immense, discontinuous, and utterly contingent network of semiotic relations that is language. "It is *language,* the black language of black texts, which expresses the distinctive quality of our literary tradition."[39] "Blackness" and "the experience of Blackness" are not the starting points of analysis but that which analysis must explain.[40]

In these and other ways, "Preface to Blackness" signaled a decisive break with the past and charted a new direction for the future of African American literary history in the 1980s and beyond. In it Gates defined the key principles of the new formalism, then used those principles to explain why the historical contextualism and racial essentialism of the older generation no longer seemed credible or convincing, why the interpretive system of the Black Arts movement seemed so full of blind spots and self-deceptions, why younger African American historians and critics were coming to see it as both a fiction and a tyranny.[41]

If that was all Gates had accomplished in "Preface to Blackness" it would still have been an important and even a seminal article. What makes it even more interesting for our purposes is that toward the end of that article, in his discussion of and response to Stephen Henderson, Gates suggested the project that would occupy his own later work and that would eventually reach fruition in *The Signifying Monkey* (1988).

In *Understanding the New Black Poetry* (1972) Henderson had argued that "Black poetry is most distinctively Black whenever it derives its form from two basic sources, Black speech and Black music."[42] Gates, of course, criticized Henderson's assumption that black speech and black music are referential and mimetic, that they are "about" something other than themselves—that "something," of course, being "the experience of Blackness." As Gates pointed out, Henderson's argument amounted to little more than a tautology: "Poetry is 'Black' when it communicates 'Blackness.' "[43]

But Gates went on to describe something much more positive in Henderson's formulation, something he thought was both critically important and highly suggestive. Once we get past Henderson's essentialism and contextualism, Gates wrote, his formulation "seems exciting, since it implies a unique, almost intangible use of language peculiar to African-Americans."[44] Gates then suggested what Henderson might have done with this appreciation of African American language. And in this suggestion he previewed what he himself would accomplish in *The Signifying Monkey:*

> Had Henderson identified some criteria by which we could define an oral tradition in terms of the "grammar" it superimposes on non-literary discourse, then shown how this comes to bear on literary discourse, and further shown such "grammars" to be distinctly black, then his contribution to our understanding of language and literature would have been no mean thing indeed. . . . On this one could build, nay one must build, that elusive "Black Aesthetic" the race and super-structure critics have sought in vain.[45]

Up to this point Gates's work had been largely preparatory—clearing the ground, using the critical principles he had learned at Yale and Cambridge to challenge the prevailing assumptions of African American criticism.[46] But here, at the very end of "Preface to Blackness," Gates announces a more ambitious and potentially more significant project: to discover a "black aesthetic"—a truly indigenous interpretive system—within the black vernacular itself, and to employ that system to redraw the lines of African American cultural and literary history: "This is the challenge for the critic of African-American literature: not to shy away from literary theory, but rather to translate it into the black idiom, renaming principles of criticism where appropriate, but especially naming indigenous black principles of criticism and applying these to explicate our own texts."[47]

Gates was determined to center *his* version of the "Black Aesthetic"—his formulation of whatever it is that makes black literature "black"—on the *figurative* uses of black language, on *how* black language says rather than *what* it says.[48] He wanted to replace the racial organicism of the Black Arts movement with his own emerging sense that the black writer is "the point of consciousness of his *language*" rather than his race.[49] If African American literature really does contain a "black aesthetic," it will be found in the *language* of African American texts, in their formal, nonreferential, nonmimetic properties rather than in their putative *content;* in the power and diversity of their imaginative structures and symbolic patterns, the richness and variety of their rhetorical devices and expressive forms.

By 1978 Gates had broken with his predecessors in the Black Arts movement and formulated the basic assumptions that would guide his later work: that the African American literary tradition is not so much a collection of thoughts as a way of thinking; that it offers improvisational skills rather than timeless values; that it incites new performances instead of revealing universal truths. In other words, it is a heightening of energy rather than an arrangement of knowledge. "Meaning" in African American literature is figurative rather than mimetic, metaphorical rather than representational, allegorical rather than referential.

III

The only problem with this, as Gates quickly came to see, was there was nothing distinctively African American about it; it read like an early but otherwise typical poststructuralist prescription for any literary history. Indeed, it was not unlike the redescriptions of American literary history that Harold Bloom, Richard Poirier, and other white critics were working out during that same period. By the late 1970s Gates was beginning to wonder if perhaps the interpretive principles he had learned at Yale and Cambridge were actually a snare, a sophisticated strategy of intellectual containment, a shrewd technique for bleaching out the "power of blackness" in African American literature. Perhaps poststructuralist criticism was simply another form of domination and control, a new and more subtle expression of the monolithic and hegemonic power that "white male intellectualdom" had always exercised over black attempts at self-understanding.[50]

Some such possibility had clearly begun to haunt Gates by the early 1980s. In "Criticism in the Jungle," published two years after "Preface to Blackness," he declared that for black historians to indiscriminately utilize critical methods "borrowed whole from the Western tradition" amounted to a kind of "slavish imitation."[51] It was a "deadly trap" that threatened to ensnare and entangle African American historians, reducing them to little more than "Talking Androids."[52] Three years later, in an exchange with the black feminist critic Joyce Joyce, Gates wondered if "the use of theory to write about African American literature [is] merely another kind of intellectual indenture, a form of servitude of the mind as pernicious in its intellectual implications as any other form of enslavement."[53] And again in *Figures in Black*, published that same year, he worried that "the use of theory to write about African-American literature" was "merely another form of intellectual indenture."[54]

But having voiced these fears, Gates went on to argue that black critics and historians do not, in fact, "borrow mindlessly" from the "Western critical tradition." They may use that tradition, but they transform it in the using. Reading African American texts through Western critical theory, black critics and historians invariably transfigure both the theory *and* the text.[55] "We use Western critical theories to read black texts," Gates explained, but we "repeat, as it were, in order to produce a *difference*."[56] The African American critic and historian evades intellectual serfdom by working in and negotiating between two different traditions at once, reading the texts of the black tradition against those of the white, then reading the texts of the white tradition against those of the black, shuttling back and forth in a self-transforming play of differences and possibilities. Rather than "slavishly" reducing the canonical works of one tradition to the critical terms of the other, the African American historian transforms both of them. "The sign of the successful negotiation of this precipice of indenture, of slavish imitation, is that the black critical essay refers to two contexts, two traditions—the Western and the black. Each utterance, then, is double-voiced."[57]

In his justly famous essay "Tradition and the Individual Talent" T. S. Eliot explained that the historian writes "not merely with his own generation in his bones, but with a feeling that the whole of the literature of . . . his culture has a simultaneous existence and composes a simultaneous order."[58] In "Criticism in the Jungle" Gates argued that because the black historian works within and between two traditions at the same time, her work forces a major revision of Eliot's dictum, "a profound reformulation of the question of the relation the individual talent bears to tradition(s)."[59] Unlike Eliot's ideal historian, the African American historian carries dual citizenship: she works *between* traditions rather than *within* a single tradition; she learns to interpret one antithetical tradition against the grain of another; she hangs out at cultural intersections and intellectual border crossings; she becomes a specialist at altering internal balances by shifting external relations; she becomes a master of recontextualization, a literary electrician manipulating the changes of voltage produced by changes of context.[60] She pitches her tent at the margins of discourse, practicing a chiastic criticism, a criticism of repetitions, revisions, and ironic reversals. She does not merely repeat "white forms"; she consumes them in order to construct her own *black* forms, her own styles of language use "related to, but distinct from, Western literary traditions."[61] "The challenge of our endeavor is to bring together, in *a new fused form,* the concepts of critical theory and the idiom of the African-American and African literary traditions. . . . When this occurs, the results are original."[62] They can also be powerfully subversive. Here is Gates describing the work of literary historian Barbara Johnson: "Rather than (re)colonizing the black text through the imposition of Western theory, she deconstructs Western theory by re-reading it through the canonical black text. This gesture represents a major departure in contemporary black criticism, one potentially able to redefine the terms of the power relation that is thought to obtain between what Chinweizu calls 'the West and the rest of us.' "[63]

This is what Gates calls "the signifyin(g) black difference that makes black literature 'black.' "[64] Signifying is preeminently a matter of negotiating between traditions: "Preexisting aesthetic systems arise from a specific body of texts. When these texts—be they artistic, musical or discursive—emerge from *another* tradition, they often clash with the aesthetic systems that are being used to interpret them. It's what I call the signifying black difference in a painting, a musical composition or a work of fiction."[65]

With this notion of "signifying" we have arrived at the very center of Gates's work. "Signifying"—or "signifyin(g)," as he usually writes it—is the central metaphor that shapes Gates's interpretation of African American literary history and, indeed, his interpretation of black cultural expression generally. He first described his theory of signifying in "The Blackness of Blackness: A Critique of the Sign and the Signifying Monkey" (1983), which is essentially a synopsis of the argument he will later present in *Figures in Black* (1987) and again—with considerably more detail—in *The Signifying Monkey* (1988): "My theory of interpretation, arrived at from within the black cultural matrix, is a theory of formal revisionism, it is tropological, it is often characterized by pastiche, and, most crucially, it turns on repetition of formal structures and their differences."[66]

In this capsule statement Gates alludes to all the important elements that comprise his theory of signifying. Notice first that he presents signifying as a truly indigenous interpretive theory, a critical system that can be found within the "black cultural matrix" itself.[67] In "The Blackness of Blackness" he traces the history of signifying and its most visible signs, the trickster figures of Esu and the Signifying Monkey, from their origin in the Yoruba, Fon, and Dahomey mythological systems of West Africa through their "New World figurations" in Cuba, Haiti, and the American slave South, to the jazz compositions of John Coltrane and Charlie Parker and finally to the novels of Ralph Ellison and Ishmael Reed.[68] In Gates's own words, the history of signifying constitutes "an unbroken arc of metaphysical presupposition and patterns of figuration shared through space and time among black cultures in West Africa, South America, the Caribbean, and in the United States."[69] Gates is thus able to offer his theory of signifying as a true "black aesthetic."

In this sense Gates's work represents a coming to fullness of the project first initiated by the Black Arts movement in the 1960s.[70] Gates may have rejected the Black Arts movement's insistence that "Blackness" constitutes a biological and metaphysical presence, but he agrees that there is something distinctive about the cultural products of black expressiveness—something that sets black music, black art, and black literature apart not so much from "American" cultural products but from the cultural products of other racial and ethnic groups in America. For all his criticism of the Black Arts movement, then, Gates has defined, just as it had tried to define, that holy grail of African American cultural studies, the elusive "Blackness of Blackness."

Second, Gates contends that signifying is "a theory of *formal* revisionism." In other words, it is figural and revisionary rather than referential or representational; it is a practice, a technique, a way of revising rather than a method of representing, a way of saying rather than something said. As Gates puts it, "One does not signify something; one signifies in some way."[71] The African American literary tradition is unique, Gates contends, not because it reflects or refers to an antecedent, autonomous, and underlying reality—"Blackness" or "the experience of Blackness"—but because it is inherently figurative: "The African-American tradition has been figurative from its beginnings. How could it have survived otherwise [for] Black people have always been masters of the figurative: saying one thing to mean something quite other has been basic to black survival in oppressive Western cultures."[72]

The African American literary tradition is preeminently a tradition of revisionary interpretation. It does not describe what actually exists but rather celebrates the possibility of continual repeation, elaboration, and revision. It exalts "figural multiplicity" rather than referential correspondence; it provokes recasting, recontextualizing, and reconstituting.[73] It is not an expression of an underlying reality but an invitation to create new realities, an incitement to think up new metaphors.[74]

Gates finds his best examples in jazz and in the sermon tradition of the southern black church. Especially jazz. After all, variations through repetition and revision are so fundamental to jazz that they virtually define it as a musical form. What is a jazz performance but a continuous series of recapitulations and revisions, a successive run of internal improvisations on recurrent variations, an uninterrupted play of signifying riff on signifying riff? And what is Oscar Peterson's "Signify," or Count Basie's "Signifyin'," but a masterly riff on the whole history of jazz?

Gates finds the same embellishing and embroidering, the same repeating and revising, in the antiphonal structure of the classic African American church sermon. You can see this most strikingly in a passage he quotes from Ralph Ellison's story "And Hickman Arrives" (1960):

> And the two men [Daddy Hickman and Deacon Wilhite] standing side by side, the one large and dark, the other slim and light brown, the other reverends rowed behind them, their faces staring grim with engrossed attention to the reading of the Word, like judges in their carved, high-backed chairs. And the two voices beginning their call and countercall as Daddy Hickman began spelling out the text which Deacon Wilhite read, playing variations on the verses just as he did with his trombone when he really felt like signifying on a tune the choir was singing.[75]

Like jazz, and like the black sermon tradition, signifying is a figurative act, a metaphor for formal revision through an endless playing off of. It is a way of talking, a verb rather than a noun, the present participle rather than the simple substantive. In Gates's words, signifying is "a blackness of the tongue."[76]

Third, as Gates explained in his discussion of Barbara Johnson's work, the African American literary tradition is inherently subversive. This is most evident in the central place that tradition has always accorded the metaphor of the Signifying Monkey. "The Western imagination" has traditionally portrayed blacks as simian, baboonish, somehow related to the orangutan, and so on.[77] But as Gates explains in "The Blackness of Blackness," and again more fully in *The Signifying Monkey,* African Americans have consistently responded to this racist characterization by signifying upon it, that is, by repeating and revising it, making it work *for* them instead of against them, using it to celebrate themselves instead of allowing it to define and demean them. They have countered a racist metaphor with repetition and ironic reversal: the signifying monkey becomes the trickster figure, continually outsmarting her slower, more literal-minded oppressors by her quick-witted, street-smart, double-dealing talk. As Gates explains, "We have been deconstructing white people's languages—as 'a system of codes or as mere play'—since 1619. That's what signifying is all about."[78]

Fourth, notice once again that "Blackness" has become a metaphorical construct rather than an actual presence. Near the end of Ishmael Reed's novel *Mumbo Jumbo,* Papa La Bas orders his assistant T Malice to open the "text of blackness" (which in *Mumbo Jumbo* is called the "Sacred Book of Thoth"). Papa La Bas hopes the box's contents will finally resolve his long search for the essence of "Blackness":

> T Malice goes out to the car and returns with a huge gleaming box covered with snakes and scorpions shaped of sparkling gems. The ladies intake their breath at such a gorgeous display. On the top can be seen the Knights Templar seal: 2 Knights riding Beaseauh, the Templars' piebald horse. T Malice places the box down in the center of the floor and removes the 1st box, an iron box, and the 2nd box, which is bronze and shines so that they have to turn the ceiling lights down. And within this box is a sycamore box and under the sycamore, ebony, and under this ivory, then silver and finally Gold and then . . . empty!![79]

Reed's point, of course, is that "Blackness" does not exist. It is an empty concept, an uninhabited category. It has meaning only as it is *given* meaning in the act of interpretation. It is not a preexisting property that finds expression in particular texts; it is defined *by* particular texts. jazz and the blues do not *express* "the black experience," they *define* it.[80] So Gates contends, first, that the African American literary tradition is indeed a truly indigenous and uniquely black interpretive tradition; second, that it is figurative and revisionary rather than representational or referential; third, that it is inherently subversive; and fourth, that it constitutes the "reality" it pretends to merely reflect (the "Blackness of Blackness").

Finally, Gates thinks "signifying" is inherently autobiographical. It is a way of chiseling out one's personal selfhood, of creating one's identity by rewriting one's predecessors. "Autocritography," Gates calls it: self-fashioning with the pen.[81] "Black writers read and critique other black texts as acts of rhetorical self-definition."[82] Thus Zora Neale Hurston revised W. E. B. Du Bois, Ralph Ellison revised Richard Wright, Toni Morrison revised both Hurston and Ellison, and Ishmael Reed revises everyone he reads.[83] In "The Blackness of Blackness" Gates argues that the entire African American literary tradition has been constituted by these autobiographical acts of signifying: "Our literary tradition exists *because of* these precisely chartable formal literary relationships."[84]

Gates thinks this Nietzsche-like self-fashioning impulse constitutes the primary content and driving force of all African American imaginative literature. From Phillis Wheatley to Zora Neale Hurston to Alice Walker, the African American writer has signified on her own tradition in order to create her own identity, to fashion herself in written words, to bring ever new versions of her own subjectivity into being through the generative power of signifying.[85]

And through the generative power of African American history. The literary historian Françoise Lionnet has described how Zora Neale Hurston created her own cultural genealogy, and thereby her own identity as a black female writer, by simultaneously reiterating and revising—signifying on—the Southern black "folk" traditions she had discovered in the 1930s.[86] What Gates calls "autocritography" Lionnet calls "autoethnography." Either way, it is one more form of signifying, one more way of defining one's identity by repeating and revising one's inheritance.[87]

Gates thinks African American writers have traditionally taken up writing as a way of creating the self that slavery denied them. This is why formal autobiographies play such an important role in his account of the African American literary tradition.[88] Gates thinks autobiography's primary place in the African American literary tradition distinguishes that tradition from every other. For unlike the writers of other literary traditions, who usually write their autobiographies (if they write them at all) at the very end of their careers, black American authors typically write their autobiographies at the *beginning*, before they have published anything else. It is as if they need to discover who they are before they can figure out what they think. For Gates this autobiographical urgency has driven the whole tradition of African American literature. In the introduction to his most recent anthology of African American autobiographical essays Gates argues that the African American tradition, "more clearly and directly than most, traces its lineage—in the act of declaring the existence of a surviving, enduring ethnic self—to this impulse of autobiography."[89]

But Gates thinks African American autobiographies chronicle more than the creation of *individual* selves; he thinks—and this is crucial—that they also chronicle the emergence of African Americans as a people. Black autobiographies testify to "the existence of 'the negro,' rather than isolated Negroes"; they are "parts, in the arbitrariness of alphabetical order, amounting to an African-American whole."[90] Every African American autobiography chants the exemplary African American self; each one reenacts the rhetorical construction of *representative* African American selfhood. Personal and collective identity fuse in the bipolar unity of African American autobiography.[91]

So in Henry Louis Gates we have a prominent and sophisticated historian who has developed his own poststructuralist interpretive theory and is using it to redraw the map of African American literary

history—and, by extension, the map of *American* literary history—
along very traditional lines. Historians are not generally known for
their conceptual daring. They tend to worry about "the dangers of
theoretical innovation" and "the infinite complication of events."
Hume was right: historians are congenitally attracted to "the monk-
ish virtues." But here we have the historian and critic Henry Louis
Gates, constantly risking absurdity on the professional high wire of
contemporary theory. What are we to make of his interpretive theory
and more generally of the way he has used poststructuralist theory
to write a traditional account of African American literary history?

I V

The best place to start is with Gates's critics. He has lots of them,
right, left, and center.[92] Those on the African American left regard
Gates's adoption of "white Western aesthetics" as an act of racial
betrayal, a form of "complicity in hegemony." As Houston Baker
recently explained, "African-American scholars who are academic
theorists appear traitors to a nativist purity, humanism, and love."[93]
They think he has internalized the values of "the white power structure."[94] Here is Joyce Joyce: "The adoption of poststructuralist ideology by a Black critic necessitates that he/she both renounce the entire history of African-American literature and criticism and that he/
she 'defamiliarize' or estrange him/herself from the *political* implications of his/her *black* skin."[95]

To Baker, Joyce, and others, Gates's "New Black Formalism"
amounts to little more than a refurbished and recirculated version
of the old white formalism that dominated Anglo-American criticism
during the middle years of this century.[96] As far as they can see, it
is the work of the same old "white-male-dominated, scriptocentric
academy," only now it appears in blackface.[97]

Those on the African American left do not like Gates's formalism
because it refuses to recognize the social involvements and political
implications of the literary works it studies. It removes the text from
the circumstances and conditions that originally produced it and that
(according to them) continue to determine its meaning. In Joyce's
words, Gates "treats Black literature as if it were exclusively a system
of linguistic signs divorced from feelings, meaning, and social or political relevance."[98] From the perspective of the Left, Gates is trying
to effect a critical retreat; he is trying to withdraw African American
criticism from the real world of African American oppression and
take it into the self-enclosed, self-reflecting, language-bounded world
of the text.[99] They contend that by hermetically sealing off the text

from the world around it Gates's formalism will trivialize African American literature and disfigure African American culture.[100]

Moreover, they think his "literary-critical professionalism" has isolated him from the real cares and worries of the African American community. As they read it, his work betrays a conspicuous failure of compassion, a breakdown of empathy, a diseased response to the suffering of black people in America. They think he is more involved in the works of successful writers than in the lives of ordinary people, more interested in the major texts of the black American canon than in "the expressive products of the black American masses."[101] To put it baldly, they think he cares more about African American literature than about African American people. They feel that in Gates's work the river of African American sympathy has suddenly run dry.

The African American left wants a criticism of compassion but it also wants a criticism that will challenge "the white power structure"—not only white political and economic power but white aesthetic power. African American literature must become a record of what black people have suffered in this country, but it must also become a means of inspiring and empowering those same people. It must make men change and women grow; it must "destroy that white thing within us"; it must "rip up the roots of society, and create a new humanity!"[102]

There is a good deal of truth to these charges. Gates is a textualist, a literary formalist. As such, he tends to isolate the text from its social context and its apparent references. He approaches the text as a disparate collection of writings rather than an integrated system of representations; he concentrates on its internal relationships rather than its external references; and he tries to multiply its interpretive possibilities rather than figuring out what it "really says." Critics on the left, of course, contend that the text *does* carry a single, determinable meaning, if the critic will only look for it—and that the best way to look for it is simply to return the text to the context in which it was written.

But as we have seen, Gates has always felt uncomfortable with contextualism. To him it seems to combine the worst aspects of nineteenth-century historicism with the worst aspects of nineteenth-century social realism. It places the text in an interpretive straitjacket, constraining and constricting its meanings, limiting the range of its possible readings to those sanctioned by the circumstances in which it originated.[103] Even as an undergraduate Gates was convinced "that the most radical shift I could make as a critic of black literature would be to stress that which I have identified as the most repressed element of African-American criticism: the language of the text."[104]

At Yale he had the great good fortune to study under Charles T.
Davis, the distinguished African American literary historian. It was
Davis who taught him to think of "blackness" as a literary trope
rather than an empirical description. As Gates later remarked,

> Charles Davis trained a generation of critics and scholars of
> African-American literature whose central concerns are matters
> of language. He taught his graduate students to eschew the ex-
> pressive realism of literary theories which see the text essen-
> tially as a complex vehicle by which the critic arrives at some
> place *anterior* to the text, such as the author's ideology or espe-
> cially his or her sense of a supposedly transcendent "racial con-
> sciousness," a literary sense of the fact of blackness in Western
> culture.[105]

This argument is not without precedent, of course. In *White Man,
Listen!* (1964) Richard Wright had written, "Truly, you must now
know that the word Negro in America means something not racial
or biological, but something purely social, something made in the
United States."[106] But in the 1970s African American poststructuralists, many of them trained by Davis and virtually all of them inspired
by the deconstruction of binary oppositions like "black" and "white,"
began making the same argument in a more formal and analytically
rigorous manner. The philosopher Anthony Appiah, for example, deconstructed "blackness" and even "African." Like "blackness" and
"race," "African" is only a figure of speech. It does not *express* an
existing reality, it *defines* it—and by defining it, calls it into being.[107]

Joyce Joyce and other critics on the African American left will
have none of this, of course. For them it illustrates exactly what is
wrong with poststructuralism. As Joyce sees it, to deny the reality of
"blackness" and "race" is to deny the reality of "racism," and thus
to deny the reality of everything that oppresses black people: "Gates's
denial of blackness or race as an important element of literary analysis of Black literature . . . attest[s] to the prevalent, malevolent, uncon-
scionable, illusionary idea that race and (it goes unsaid) racism have
ceased to be the leading impediments that thwart the mental and
physical lives of Black people at all levels of human endeavor."[108]

Gates's hostility to the notion of "blackness" brings us to the very
heart of his differences with the African American left. Joyce Joyce
is probably typical when she claims that "my views of Black literary
criticism are inextricably and unembarrassingly tied to my identity
as a Black person." Gates's critical views, by way of contrast, "are,
by nature, inextricably related to an absence of identity. Thus, the
central issue here is identity."[109] She is right, of course: the central

issue *is* identity, both personal and collective. Instead of denying the reality of blackness, Joyce thinks African American historians should embrace it, devoting themselves to describing "the shared experiences of black people." Instead of borrowing literary theory from whites to formulate what Houston Baker once called "a mulatto aesthetics," black historians should come to terms with "the existence of a separate and distinct culture" in black America.[110] More important, they should work to create "an overall, orchestrated surge of energy—economic, political, social, personal, and intellectual—to counteract the abusive, binding, numbing effect of the historical oppression of Blacks around the world."[111]

But Gates could save those on the left the inconvenience (not to say embarrassment) of trying to demonstrate that there really is something universal and unchanging about "blackness," that it really is an essence, "an ahistorical natural kind with a permanent set of intrinsic features."[112] Every attempt to find the permanent and intrinsic features of "blackness," like every attempt to find the permanent and intrinsic features of "femaleness," has led us down a blind alley.[113] Gates is suggesting that African American literary critics simply drop the attempt to define what "blackness" really "is" or really "means" and spend their time demonstrating how African American literature can give us new *metaphors* for "blackness," new associations and connotations.

The same is true for African American historians: Yes, they should continue reminding us how black people suffered under slavery, how they endured Jim Crow, how they created a rich and sustaining culture, and so on. But they have to do more than simply remind us of what *happened* in the past; they also have to invent new ways of using the past to think about the present—especially new ways of thinking about "blackness." For only thus can African Americans invent new moral and civic identities for themselves.[114]

Yet this attempt to fashion a richer African American identity must be accompanied by an attempt to fashion a broader *American* identity, a more inclusive sense of "we." For as Robert Reich recently explained, and as everyone living in this country knows, wealthy Americans are seceding from the rest of us. They are withdrawing into their own gated and guarded enclaves, into their own parks and schools and universities and hospitals. More important, they are disconnecting themselves from the rest of us economically. Increasingly now, their work, their incomes, their savings and investments are located in the global rather than the national economy. And knowing that their own future is no longer tied to the future of the American economy, or even of American society, they no longer think in terms of a broadly inclusive American "we." They no longer feel the responsibilities of American citizenship, or even an American identity.[115]

Can the attachments and identifications that underlie the habits of citizenship still be nurtured in twenty-first-century America?[116] Not if the Left continues to promote ethnic and racial subcultures as *alternatives to* American culture rather than an *expression of* that culture.[117] And not if the rest of us continue to accept this sort of thing in the name of cultural diversity or ethnic pluralism. Richard Rorty is right: "we have become so open-minded that our brains have fallen out."[118]

Conservatives bewail the spread of identity politics, which they see as little more than tribal politics played out on a national stage. But this objection is pointless, for identity politics is as old as politics itself.[119] Moreover, identity politics can deepen and enrich our understanding and appreciation of American culture. But this presents the Left with a dual responsibility: it must continue to rummage through African American history and literature for new ways to be African American. Yet it must also insist that being African American is not an alternative to being American but simply another way of being American, just as being a Southern Baptist is merely another way of being Baptist.[120] Gates's attempt to rewrite the terms of African American literary history is one of the best ways we have to bring this double optic into sharp focus.

V

But it is the cultural conservatives associated with the Anglo-American humanist tradition who stand to gain the most from Gates's work. Conservatives have not paid much attention to Gates; when they have noticed him they have tended to see a spokesman for multiculturalism. Gates does have important things to say about multiculturalism, as we shall see, but he has even more important things to say about history as a discipline, a way of thinking. By using poststructuralist literary theory to reconstruct African American literary history, Gates has done more than anyone else to show us how history might become again what it once was: an essential form of moral reflection and our best warrant for cultural criticism.

Conservatives tend to see multiculturalism as a threat to the perceived unity of American culture.[121] In a recent speech to Yale's incoming freshman class, for example, Donald Kagan, dean of Yale College and a frequent contributor to conservative journals, argued that because America is the immigrant nation par excellence, Americans share neither a common ancestry nor "common blood." All we share, all that holds us together as a people, Kagan explained, are the cultural values we have inherited from Western civilization. Even uniquely American values have developed "within the context of Western civilization."[122] Like many conservatives, he sees multiculturalism as an attempt to discredit, dislodge, and displace that cultural bedrock. In Kagan's words, "Western civilization is under attack."[123]

Carl Degler makes the same point. America's enormous diversity means that "America" has always been more of an ideal than a reality. But contemporary multiculturalism "threatens to shunt aside . . . that cluster of ideas and shared experience that constitutes America." Like Kagan, Degler fears that "the national slogan of *E Pluribus Unum* [is] in danger of being transformed into 'Out of One, Many.'"[124]

Similarly Arthur Schlesinger Jr., perhaps the most prominent and distinguished of multiculturalism's critics. Like Kagan and Degler, Schlesinger is impressed with the enormous racial, ethnic, and cultural variety of America. And like them, he readily concedes the need for a more culturally diversified curriculum. He recently insisted, for example, that "our students should by all means be better acquainted with women's history, with the history of ethnic and racial minorities, with Latin American, Asian, and African history."[125]

But also like Kagan and Degler, Schlesinger is convinced that only "the American Creed" can bind the various peoples and cultures of America into a single coherent nationality.[126] "What has held the American people together in the absence of a common ethnic origin has been precisely a common adherence to ideals of democracy and human rights that, too often transgressed in practice, forever goad us to narrow the gap between practice and principle."[127]

Schlesinger worries that the "ethnic upsurge" that began in the 1960s as a gesture of protest against the Anglocentrism of American culture now "threatens to become a counter-revolution against the original theory of America as 'one people,' a common culture, a single nation."[128] Faced with the prospect of "a society fragmented into ethnic groups" and a culture in which the American creed will no longer be "the common possession of all Americans," Schlesinger wants the educational establishment "to continue to do what it has done so well in the past: to lead newcomers to an acceptance of the language, the institutions, and the political ideals that hold the nation together."[129]

For Schlesinger, as for Kagan, Degler, and other cultural conservatives, those institutions and ideals are exclusively European. In Schlesinger's words, Europe is "the source—the *unique* source—of those liberating ideas of individual liberty, political democracy, the rule of law, human rights, and cultural freedom that constitute our most precious legacy and to which most of the world today aspires."[130] Moreover, Schlesinger is convinced that these ideals provide both authority for social criticism and incitement to political activism. If we teach our students the values and ideals embodied in the Western tradition, Schlesinger contends, "they will move into social criticism on their own."[131]

Gates has a good deal in common with Kagan, Degler, Schlesinger, and other cultural conservatives. Like them, he wants to see a common American identity—a widely shared set of cultural values and social ideals, a common understanding of who we are, what we value, and how we mean to live. "The challenge facing America will be the shaping of a truly common public culture, one responsive to the long-silenced cultures of color. If we relinquish the ideal of America as a plural nation, we've abandoned the very experiment America represents. And that is too great a price to pay."[132]

But if Gates shares the dream of a common culture with conservatives like Kagan, Degler, and Schlesinger, the common culture he envisions is not the Eurocentric culture they imagine. Gates is emphatic about this: "To demand that Americans shuck their cultural heritages and homogenize themselves into a 'universal' WASP culture is to dream of an America in cultural white face, and that just won't do."[133]

Instead of American culture as the pure product of Western civilization, Gates wants us to think of it as "a conversation among different voices."[134] For Gates, a common American culture will emerge not from our gradual adaptations of a "uniquely European" heritage but from the jostling and shoving and negotiating that goes on *between* American traditions. This is the importance of signifying, for given the nature of black culture in white America, signifying necessarily takes place *between* traditions: "Preexisting aesthetic [or literary] systems arise from a specific body of texts. When these texts— be they artistic, musical or discursive—emerge from another tradition, they often clash with the aesthetic systems that are being used to interpret them. It's what I call the signifying black difference in a painting, a musical composition or a work of fiction."[135]

Gates has been particularly struck by the way American traditions weave themselves into one another—how the black vernacular has woven itself into the black literary tradition, or how black and white literary texts have spoken to, impinged on, and written themselves into one another over a period of three centuries. For example, in *Figures in Black* he explains the oscillating relation between slave narratives and the plantation novel, then explains how that peculiar polarity informed (and was informed by) the great gothic works of Hawthorne, Melville, and Poe.[136] Instead of pointing back to their putative origins in British or European civilization, Gates wants us to see that American texts are invariably "mulattoes," that every American text carries "a two-toned heritage." American *traditions* too are double-voiced discourses.[137] "There can be no doubt," he writes, "that white texts inform and influence black texts (and visa-versa), so that a thoroughly integrated canon of American literature is not only politically sound, it is *intellectually* sound as well."[138]

This means that African American literary works cannot simply be added to the existing canon of American literature, as conservatives imagine. Gates condemns the separatist call for an autonomous African American literature: "To say that black art is a thing apart, separate from the whole, is a racist fiction." But he also insists that to simply add African American texts to the established canon is like "trying to place works of black tradition on a bed of Procrustes, lopping off their arms and legs to make them fit a shape which is not really theirs."[139] What we need is "the production of new aesthetic systems that account for the full complexity of American art, music and literature—in all of their multicolored strains. . . . We have to conceive a new aesthetic status for American art in all of its facets—whether Hispanic, Native American, Asian American or white."[140] In other words, a truly "American" canon—and by extension a truly American culture—will only come out of the commingling and interbleeding of *particular* canons and traditions.

Gates thinks the present moment is particularly auspicious for the creation of a common culture because there now exists, for the first time in American history, a black professional class with the resources to act as patrons and critics for black artists and black writers.[141] Gates thinks that in the end this will give us a more complex and richly diversified culture. Thus, while he celebrates the emergence of a black patron class, he also insists that "we need to connect with wealthy white patrons, so that we have *a more integrated patronage class.*"[142] Gates shares the conservatives' desire for a common culture, but he laments their tendency "to see pluralism as forestalling the possibility of a communal 'American' identity," their conviction that "the study of our diverse cultures must lead to 'tribalism' and 'fragmentation.'"[143] Gates would like them to see that "it's only when we're free to explore the complexities of our hyphenated culture that we can discover what a genuinely common American culture might actually look like."[144]

Critics on both left and right contend that Gates emphasizes process at the expense of content, that his vision of a common American culture lacks any *specific* values, that it is ethically empty. Andrew Delbanco, for example, has pointed out that when Malcolm X "repudiated his Stepin Fetchit self and asserted the vigor of his blackness, . . . he came back to the sanctification of the individual and the colorblind vocabulary of human rights. Even these angriest of black writers came to doubt that Signifyin(g) on Mister Charlie is ultimately the best means toward real freedom. They have looked instead for a transcendent language into which race might disappear. Gates is caught, I think, in something like the same pincer."[145]

But as cogent and compelling as this criticism appears at first glance, it misses something that lies right at the heart of Gates's vision—at the heart of his theory of African American literary history and of his hopes for American culture. Gates's notion of signifying suggests that a culture's traditions are endlessly repeated and revised, endlessly produced and reproduced, endlessly made and re-made. It suggests a process of continual growth and extension of cultural forms, not unlike the conservative Diane Ravitch's suggestion that "American culture belongs to us, all of us; the U.S. is us, *and we remake it in every generation.*" As she says, this is a process of continually "extending or revising American culture."[146]

But Delbanco writes as if signifying were an act of cultural nihilism, the downward curve of self-betrayal. In actual fact, Henry Louis Gates is one of our great traditionalists; indeed, in his literary and historical criticism he sometimes reminds one of T. S. Eliot. He has a more pluralistic sense of tradition than Eliot, and he has none of Eliot's belief in the importance of religion and guilt, nor anything like Eliot's anguished sense of living at the end of an era, a time of spiritual exhaustion, cultural depletion, and universal collapse. Certainly Gates would not describe his own work as fragments shored up against the ruins of his culture.

Nevertheless, like Eliot, Gates thinks of literary tradition as a compilation of a culture's most enduring values.

For Gates, as for Eliot before him, the literary canon is a public compilation of our individual commonplace books: "The passages in my commonplace book formed my own canon, just as I imagine each of yours did for you. And a canon, as it has functioned in every literary tradition, has served as the commonplace book for our shared culture."[147] Personal selfhood and collective identity twine together for Gates, but only when planted in the soil of a living, continually contested tradition. For only a tradition that invites the incessant play of self-reflexive signifying, a tradition endlessly repeated, revised and renewed, can provide individuals with the wherewithal to fashion strong, resourceful, and imaginative selves. And in fact, African American literature provided just this sort of sustenance and direction for Gates himself during his formative years: "Finding James Baldwin and writing him down at an Episcopal church camp during the Watts riots in 1965 (I was fifteen) probably determined the direction of my intellectual life more than did any other single factor. I wrote and rewrote verbatim his elegantly framed paragraphs, full of sentences that were at once somehow Henry Jamesian and King Jamesian, yet clothed in the cadences and figures of the spirituals."[148]

Like Eliot, Gates feels himself deeply indebted to the cultural traditions in which he was raised. And also like Eliot, he feels a personal, almost organic connection to those traditions. He once described how he first learned about "black language rituals": not by reading about them at Yale but by hearing them from his father, who had mastered them "to a T," who could "analyze them all, tell you what he is doing, why, and how."[149] In a similar vein he recently admitted that "much of my scholarly and critical work has been an attempt to learn how to speak in the strong, compelling cadences of my mother's voice."[150] In other words, African American culture is for Gates a means of transmitting vital cultural values from one generation to the next. This is a classically conservative vision, of course. Gates always seems to be asking, just beneath the surface of his prose, the same question conservatives have always asked: What would be our deficit of spirit at the end of the day if we lacked such a cultural inheritance?[151] In fact, Gates has described his reconstruction of African American literary history as "an act of love of the tradition."[152]

Gates has little patience with those contemporary theorists who debunk the idea of "literature," who deny the importance of the "great books," who insist that the distinction between the "great books" and comic books is arbitrary and capricious, another example of racial domination and cultural power. Such critics are what George Steiner calls "wasters"—intellectual charlatans who squander "our limited receptive means, our tested and accredited assets of grace."[153]

Confronted with the downward curve of such a desolate and disabling hermeneutics, Gates defends both the canonical status of the "great works" and the literary traditions they comprise. He once told his fellow African American historians, "We are the keepers of the black literary tradition."[154] For Gates the African American literary historian has one primary responsibility: she must ensure that African American works of enduring value never get lost in the details of the past, that they never get buried in "the graveyard of dead contexts." As Gates insists, "this relation is one of trust."[155]

Gates's commitment to the "great works" of the African American literary tradition, and to the autobiographical impulse he believes drives that tradition, has also led him to defend subjectivity and the subject against attacks from the cultural left. Applied to African American literature, he says, this "paradigm of dismantlement" amounts to little more than a "critical version of the grandfather clause." "Consider the irony: precisely when we (and other third world peoples) obtain the complex wherewithal to define our black subjectivity in the republic of Western letters, our theoretical colleagues declare that there ain't no such thing as a subject, so why should we be bothered with that?"[156]

Gates is fully aware of what he calls "the dynamics of subjection and incorporation through which the subject is produced."[157] Nevertheless, he condemns the contemporary attack on subjectivity because it leaves black people "nowhere," because it renders them "invisible and voiceless in the republic of Western letters."[158] Aesthetically, he thinks the autobiographical impulse has been central to the whole tradition of African American literature; politically, he thinks subjectivity and self-identity are crucial conditions for political empowerment—for what he calls "collective agency."[159] He is probably right on both counts, especially the latter. After all, it is hard to imagine how a self dismantled by contemporary theory can inspire a movement for social change.

Conservatives have let their fear of multiculturalism blind them to the fact that Gates's interest in African American literature is part of a larger and more ambitious attempt to broaden and enrich America's common culture. What is even more surprising, they have failed to notice the deeply conservative nature of Gates's work: his rejection of black nationalist aesthetics and the materialist vulgarity of "race and superstructure" criticism; his defense of the self and its autobiographical impulse; his commitment to the very traditional idea of a literary canon; his Eliot-like appreciation of literature as a primary means of transmitting values from one generation to the next; and his condemnation of the contemporary attacks on subjectivity and personal identity.

By using contemporary theory to rewrite American literary history, Gates has expanded our catalog of American exemplars and given us a critical dialogue with predecessors we did not even know we had. This is the sort of densely populated, richly diversified, and morally instructive history that can rescue American historical writing from its ever-present temptation to feed on the street-level epiphanies offered up by the social sciences.

CHAPTER EIGHT

Love and Objectivity

I

Content is more important than context. Understanding what Lincoln's Second Inaugural Address says to us, living at the end of the twentieth century, is more important than understanding what it said to Americans living in the middle of the nineteenth century. Else why should we bother with it? Why should we read Abraham Lincoln if we think he has nothing important to tell us about what *we* should value, how *we* should live?

But this immediately raises the specter of relativism. If historians were no longer obligated to analyze historical documents in their proper historical context, would they not start reading their own biases into them? The answer is no, but not for the usual reasons. What stops us from turning historical documents into "ideological trampolines" is not our determination to be objective but our capacity to be moved—our ability to care about and find ourselves indebted to particular books we have inherited from the past.[1] Most of us have relationships with certain books that are as intimate, complex, and sustaining as any in our lives—after all, that is what drew us into this perpetually jobless field. Without the sustaining love of certain books, we might as well do social science. If academic history is to be delivered from the massive indifference into which it seems to be disappearing, we shall have to rethink the nature and significance of our relationships with the books we have come to care about.

I I

For all his interpretive brilliance, Richard Rorty, like Stanley Fish, has somehow convinced himself that texts are nothing more than empty vessels, that they have no inherent qualities or characteristics of their own. Certainly they have no powers of their own; they simply say whatever their readers—or the relevant "community of inter- preters"—decide they say. As Rorty puts it, "A text just has whatever coherence it happened to acquire during the last roll of the herme- neutic wheel, just as a lump of clay only has whatever coherence it happened to pick up at the last turn of the potter's wheel."[2]

But this cannot possibly be true. We all know, from our own expe- rience as readers, that certain texts resist certain readings. We have all had the experience of struggling for weeks on end—sometimes for months or even years—to understand a particular book. Some books simply force us to read them over and over. They seem to refuse us every time, to always be holding something back from us. Moreover, as a result of this continual resistance, some books force us to reread *ourselves*, to reconsider our own assumptions and inter- pretations. And if the truth be known, this is exactly why we value them. Like husbands or wives or grown-up children, we can always count on them to resist us. This does not happen with every book, of course. But like Dr. Johnson stubbing his toe on the proverbial rock, it happens often enough to let us know there is something out there—and that whatever it is, it is more than a lump of clay.

In other words, something happens when we read certain books. Admittedly, the books that make something happen to me may not be the books that make something happen to you, but that is another issue. Moreover, even if we were to somehow come up with exactly the same list of important books—the dream of a common canon— we would not be able to agree on why we think these particular books are more important than others. So we would not agree on why or how we should read them. But again, that is another issue. All that matters at this point is the simple and obvious fact that something happens when we read certain books.

What happens is that we are eventually made to care about, to take an interest in, the characters and ideas we encounter in those books—characters and ideas we had not cared about before. We are made to care, and in that way we are changed. For we are who we are, at least in part, by virtue of the people and ideas we care about. It is not just that by reading certain books we add new characters or ideas to the list of things we care about; nor is it simply that our sense of what we should care about is changed, or even that our understanding of what it means to care about someone or something is deepened and complicated, though all of these things are obviously important. But even more important is the fact that certain books have the power to change the way we see and think, to alter our ingrown patterns of perception and desire—what Jonathan Edwards called the "prevailing inclination of the soul."[3] Reading certain books may not change the world, but it does change our *understanding* of the world, of the problems and possibilities the world presents. Certain books make us think, imagine, and desire in ways we might never have thought, imagined, or desired before. It is not simply that we notice things we had not noticed before; it is rather that we notice in *ways* we had not noticed before. We become more richly attentive, more finely aware—of the limited range of our imaginations, of the constricted reach of our sympathies, of the secret springs and hidden shape of our own desires.[4]

This may sound more like new age therapy than intellectual history. In fact, it is simply another expression of that Augustinian strain of piety that runs through the entire history of Western thought and writing. You can find it in Augustine's *Confessions,* in John Duns Scotus's voluntarism, in Luther's response to Erasmus (and more generally in his response to the Thomist intellectualism of the sixteenth-century Catholic Church), in the Puritans' response to the Aristotelian Scholasticism of the seventeenth-century English church, in the New Lights' response to the doctrine of preparation in eighteenth-century New England, and so on. It is what the Scottish moralist Francis Hutcheson meant by "sentiment" and what Jonathan Edwards meant by "true virtue." In other words, it is a spontaneous and distinterested responsiveness—a heightened receptivity to what Edwards called "genuine beauty and amiableness."[5] To the rationalists who claimed that the basic problem was not the carnal will but "the darkness of the rational judgment," Edwards replied, "Our people don't need to have their heads stocked, they need to have their hearts touched."[6]

This Augustinian skepticism about Scholastic (and Thomist and Cartesian) claims for the autonomy of the will and the primacy of the intellect, this perennial suspicion that the will is blind and the intellect passive, has also played a major role in contemporary criticism—for example, in Derrida's well-known contention that language possesses an inherently destablizing power. Derrida thinks the words and phrases that constitute a text have their own individual histories—previous lives, as it were—in which each one of them has accumulated layer upon layer of meanings and associations. Placed side by side in a particular text, they turn the author's intended meaning in a multitude of unforeseen (and unforeseeable) directions. The relations between the signs and tropes that compose a text are thus constantly shifting around with changes of context. These unexpected shifts in meaning challenge the reader's ingrained associations and expectations. From a Derridean perspective, then, changes of meaning are not produced by the creative will of a conscious, intending author or by the reading habits of even the most alert and attentive reader; rather, they come upon the reader from without, as if with a power of their own. It is this constant slipping and shifting of signifiers that prevents even the most gifted reader from finding the author's intentions hidden away at the base of the text.

But we have not been left completely without resources. Though we may be denied immediate access to the author's intentions, we have been given something much more valuable: a vision of what the text *might* might be saying. And this is compensation enough, as Emerson might have said, for all the limitations and disabilities imposed on us as readers. For by resisting our various readings and interpretations, by frustrating our efforts to understand them directly, certain books help us get some distance on ourselves and thereby help us rethink ourselves. For only by allowing the text to arrange itself in altogether new and hitherto unimagined configurations can we see the limitations of our own assumptions; only thus can we force ourselves up against the cast-iron borders of our own imaginations. Note, however, that insight like this comes only when we muster the courage to throw away the crutch of context, to abandon the assumption of a privileged point of view that promises access to the author's intentions and, instead, follow the movements of the text, the hum and buzz of its shifting signifiers and inconclusive implications. As the New England Puritans used to say, "Hold up sail and wait for wind."[7]

In other words, read with an alert and willing mind. Not a blank or objective mind, a mind somehow cleansed of its personal prejudices and local assumptions, but an open mind, a mind receptive to the possibilities of the text, a mind alert to the appearance of something unexpected: an intrusion, an imposition, the arrival of an exteriority that knocks the reader off balance, that imposes itself, that quickens and provokes, engendering a yearning that will not be fulfilled. The philosopher Stanley Cavell recently described how John Austin's book *How to Do Things with Words* "hit me like a ton of bricks. It was as if a wall fell on me. I threw away a Ph.D. thesis that was pending and I talked to him for months."[8] Several years later Thoreau's *Walden* struck him with such force that it nearly crushed him: "I hadn't read it in twenty years, and when I read it again a wall fell. The entire edifice of everything I had been doing collapsed on top of me and I had to make my way out brick by brick."[9] This is precisely what made the young Richard Wright, growing up in black-belt Mississippi in the 1920s, hunger for books, for "new ways of looking and seeing": "It was not a matter of believing or disbelieving what I read, but of feeling something new, of being affected by something that made the look of the world different. . . . Reading grew into a passion. . . . The plots and stories in the novels [I read] did not interest me so much as the point of view revealed. . . . It was enough for me to see and feel something different."[10]

We may decide to read *Narrative of the Life of Frederick Douglass*, but we do not decide to care about what happens to the boy Frederick Bailey; we simply find that we *do* care, that reading Douglass's book has somehow engendered an active caring within us. Nor is that all: as soon as we realize this, we also realize that we have been made to feel an obligation, no matter how murky and obscure, how muddled and inarticulate. If we are teachers, for example, we find ourselves obligated not only to have our students read *Narrative,* but to present it "right side up," to "do it justice," though we know perfectly well that we have no criteria of "right-side-upness" or "doing it justice" to fall back on—no rule or established procedure for pinning down such things. Nor do we have any idea how this caring comes about; we have no direct access to the process itself, no reason or explanation. We cannot even say whether this interest in, this caring about, this obligation to, is inherent in the act of reading generally, or whether it arises from reading this particular narrative, or whether it springs from an all-too-human inclination to mistake the former for the latter.[11] All we know is that we have been made to care, that a sense of obligation and responsibility has been imposed on us, and that it is no more to be quarreled with than love itself. Indeed, like love and suffering, like remorse and regret, obligation simply lays hold of us: we find ourselves—if we find ourselves at all—in the service of something that somehow takes us beyond ourselves, "something that all along has been and will be greater than ourselves."[12] This is what people meant when they used to talk about "a sense of the past."[13]

Very little of this gets taught in graduate history programs, of course. Rather than teaching students how to use historical texts to imagine new arrangements of thought and desire, we teach them to search out the "discursive structures" and "textual practices" of the culture in which the text was written. In this we are—irony of ironies—not unlike the generation of the 1930s, which taught its students to look for the "social forces" the text was thought to reflect. In the end it all comes down to the same thing: instead of teaching our students to be alert, responsive, and resourceful readers, we teach them how to analyze documents. The result, of course, is that they read complex texts as if they were bills of lading. This may make a certain amount of sense for economic or social historians, but it makes no sense at all for intellectual or literary historians. The contextualist (or historicist) imperative that has dominated intellectual and literary history for the past thirty years has become an elaborate mechanism for reducing complex texts to the status of documents. It is essentially a restraining apparatus, a device designed to shackle the text, to restrict and repress its suggestive powers while the historian cuts it open to examine its historical origins. What we *should* be doing is teaching students how to become aware of and move with the suggestive powers of the text. For how can we hope to understand the text if we do not encourage it to do the work it is manifestly capable of doing? How can we make the ethical judgments required to teach Lincoln's Second Inaugural Address if we refuse to open ourselves to the power of Lincoln's words? We historians do not possess an ethics of reading, but if we did this would surely constitute its categorial imperative.

What needs to be explained is why historians have so completely forgotten this cardinal rule of reading. In fact, the reasons are not hard to find, for the experience of being seduced by the concentrated power of the words on the page is exactly what history had to deny in order to establish itself as an academic profession, an autonomous discipline with its own specialized vocabulary and elaborate methodology, its own programs, procedures, and prohibitions. Allowing oneself to be moved and enlarged—or diminished—by the suggestive power of the text blurs the distinction between history and the other humanities. That is why words like submission, responsiveness, and obligation, though they be the very soul of thoughtful, reflective, resourceful reading, have come to constitute history's repressed and excluded "other"—what the process of professionalization has forced it to deny about itself in order to take its place in the academy as a formal, rule-bound, truth-testing discipline. What John Stuart Mill once said about Jeremy Bentham's utilitarianism could just as well be said about academic history: "There is no need to expatiate on the deficiencies of a system of ethics which does not pretend to aid individuals in the formation of their own character; which recognizes no such wish as that of self-culture, we may even say, no such power, as existing in human nature."[14]

It should be clear by now that the act of reading is rarely a matter of a sovereign reader arbitrarily imposing her own values and preferences on a text that has no more integrity than a lump of clay. There is no reason to take up Dominick LaCapra's worry that younger historians, discovering that the interpretive constraints have suddenly fallen away, will simply read whatever they wish into their texts. The interpretive guidelines LaCapra and others want the historical profession to adopt in the face of these perceived threats would prove no more successful than did the interpretive procedures established by the Council of Trent in 1564. Nor need we worry about the "emotivism" that so horrifies Alastair MacIntyre. Conservatives spend too much time wringing their hands about this sort of thing. The readings that an alert, reflective, and resourceful historian comes up with may not be what the author intended, but neither will they be what the reader intended. We do not need a set of formal rules and established procedures—an algorithm for reading that would somehow guarantee the objectivity and reliability of historical accounts, reassuring everyone that the books we write really do convey the single, transparent meaning of the texts we discuss. What we need are historians who are alive and responsive to the unruly play of their primary materials, to the multiple possibilities and drifting implications that characterize the richest and most rewarding texts—especially when read in *our* present rather than theirs.

But this account makes the reader sound far too passive. By describing only what happens *to* us when we read certain books, it makes the act of reading sound like a religious experience: the reader is visited by some mysterious force that comes upon her from without and changes her forever. In fact, the reader must enter into conversation with the text; we ourselves must negotiate a rearrangement of our perceptions and desires. We do this in at least two ways. First, when we read certain books we naturally relate them to other books we have read, weaving them into one or another of the conceptual webs we think with. Second, we do this as part of a larger project of trying to place ourselves in time, trying to see ourselves as the last in a long sequence or tradition, with all the obligations and responsibilities that working within a tradition entails.

I will discuss both of these in detail. But first, note that, like the willingness to be challenged and changed by the books we read (and for precisely the same reasons), they have both been vigorously repressed, by the professionalization of historical study, but also by the insistence that texts can be properly understood only in their original, historical contexts. So strong has this imperative become in the past thirty years that most younger historians can imagine no other way of writing history. The idea of lifting books *out* of their original contexts, of making them speak directly to the present, has come to seem the very mark and insignia of amateurism: it is unprofessional; it reeks of "Whiggish presentism"; it is "the demon of anachronism"; and so on.[15] Younger historians are regularly taught to view the past "from the angle of those who lived it"; anything else, as James Kloppenberg insists, will "distort our understanding by imposing meanings different from those that ideas had historically."[16] Perhaps. But if we wish to renew and reinvigorate American history we will have to recapture and restore to full intellectual legitimacy precisely what the process of professionalization has delegitimated and repressed.

III

As we have seen, this means making ourselves available to the texts we read, reading them with an open mind, inviting them to do the work they were designed to do, hoping that their concentrated suggestive powers can crack the crust of our own hard-won assurances—that they can "turn our impoverishing certitudes into humanizing doubts."[17] That is part of it. The other part is that we have to make these books and ideas our own. That means figuring out what we find in them that we cannot find anywhere else—why we would know ourselves poorer without them, just as Perry Miller, for example, came to believe, in the early 1950s, that Roger Williams's understanding of freedom was "more pertinent to our necessity than many of the eighteenth- and nineteenth-century formulas that have tragically crumbled before our very eyes."[18]

We do this, first of all, by weaving a new book or a new idea into the web of ideas and beliefs we already have.[19] There are several ways to do this, of course, but they all amount to the same thing: reading one book or thinker through another, using one book to illuminate the hidden recesses of the other. It would be nice to think we could get what we need directly, that we could read ourselves right into the center of our texts, or back them into a corner and force them to explain themselves.[20] George Santayana, all his hard-won skepticism failing him on just this point, came to believe he could do exactly that.[21] But the rest of us have to work with reflected images and twice-told tales. Among American historians no one does this better than John Patrick Diggins. In *The Bard of Savagery: Thorstein Veblen and Modern Social Theory* (1978), for example, he used Veblen to ask questions about Marx and Weber that neither Marx nor Weber had thought to ask himself—indeed, questions that Diggins would not have thought to ask had he not read Veblen. Similarly, in *The Lost Soul of American Politics: Virtue, Self-Interest, and the Foundations of Liberalism* (1984) he explained how Lincoln and Melville, steeped in both the Calvinist and Lockean traditions, used the former to provide the latter with what everyone could see it lacked: a social conscience. And in *Max Weber: Politics and the Spirit of Tragedy* (1996) he read the "Hamiltonian Weber" against the "Emersonian Weber"—in other words, he used the tensions in Weber's thought to illuminate and explore the tensions in our own divided psyche. Diggins calls this approach "an exercise in theoretical confrontations," but it is pretty much what we all do when we come upon a new book that we suspect has something important to tell us.

Second, we use certain books and ideas to place ourselves in time, to stretch our understanding of ourselves backward and forward, to embrace both past time and future time.[22] In part this is simply a substratum of consciousness itself. The phenomenologists—Dilthey, Husserl, Heidegger, and Ricoeur in particular—have always insisted that the need to identify our lives with a continuous and progressive movement through time, beginning in the past, flowing through the present and into the future, is a fundamental and indispensable feature of human thought. Indeed, they argue that it constitutes a necessary condition for personal identity and, beyond that, for experience itself.[23] They do not mean that from our vantage point in the present we simply decide to envision a particular past and project a particular future, at least not at the level of immediate, prethematic experience. Rather, they mean that the present is unavailable to us—literally inconceivable—except as part of a continuous movement from past to future, just as we can grasp a single musical note only in relation to the notes (and moments of silence) that precede and succeed it. As Derrida might say, the present is constituted by—can be conceived only in terms of—an essential absence, that which absolutely is not; in this case, past and future.

But note: Augustine worked out most of this nearly fifteen hundred years ago.[24] Augustine thought in terms of extending the soul rather than weaving a web, of course, but it comes to the same thing—especially when we move from the problem of time to the problem of the self. Like the later phenomenologists, Augustine was convinced that we cannot conceive of ourselves outside a temporal dimension, that we can grasp ourselves only in time, only in a present that necessarily includes a past and a future, and that we do so through memory and narrative. It is Augustine rather than Aristotle who has shaped Western thinking on the subject of time. Indeed, you can trace his influence all the way up to and through contemporary literary criticism. Derrida, for example, would obviously object to Augustine's model of a unitary consciousness (what Augustine variously called "memory" or "the soul") functioning as the supposed originating source and foundation of time, and he would surely balk at the primacy Augustine accorded the present (past and future being, for Augustine, simply different versions of the present). Yet he begins just as Augustine began, by insisting that the illusion of presence is founded on an essential absence, that "the present" can be defined only by what it is not (the past and the future). More important, Derrida's insistence that we are "always already" narrativized finds its origin in Augustine's argument that consciousness is structured like a language, that our attempt to "grasp ourselves in time" can be enacted only in narrative.[25] Conversely, the *collapse* of this ability to grasp ourselves in time would mean the dissolution of consciousness, that is, a descent into madness. At the level of immediate, prethematic experience, then, placing ourselves in time is inseparable from consciousness itself; the unification of past, present, and future is not so much achieved as given.

But once we move beyond the level of immediate experience the unification of past, present, and future becomes problematic—rather than an inherent aspect of consciousness, it does become something that must be achieved. This is because the moment we set about constructing a life story for ourselves—a past that makes sense of the present—the present has vanished. So we are constantly having to rewrite our individual and collective autobiographies—on the run, as it were.[26] At this level (what the philosopher Leszek Kolakowski calls "mythopoeic activity") the specter of narrative chaos, that is, the collapse of history into mere chronicle, the degeneration of autobiography into mere sequence, threatens us not so much with the dissolution of the ego as with anomie, the feeling that our lives do not add up, that they lack coherent shape or intelligible meaning.[27] In Sam Shepard's play *Curse of the Starving Class* the character Weston, World War II veteran, failed farmer, sometime father, sits on a barstool and tries to piece together the disparate bits of his chaotic life: "The jumps," he says; "I couldn't figure out the jumps. From being born, to growing up, to droppin' bombs, to having kids, to hittin' bars, to this. . . . I kept looking for it out there somewhere."[28]

The importance of narrative meaning applies at least as forcefully to collective histories as it does to personal autobiographies. "We" exist as "a people" only to the extent that we imagine ourselves possessing a common past that explains our common present—and that projects us into a common future. But like our individual autobiographies, our collective histories are constantly in danger of lapsing into mere sequence—as anyone who has lived through the past thirty years can testify. Sam Shepard's plays speak to us so strongly because they voice an undercurrent of bewilderment that runs just beneath the surface of American life, a dimly lit, Lyotard-like recognition that the stories we have been telling ourselves all these years no longer add up, no longer connect our remembered past with our actual present, much less project us into a desirable future. Those large, sweeping, deeply resonating national histories we use to read and write have somehow lost their ability to describe "the jumps," to explain how we got where we are, how we became the people we are. Like Lupe and Lisa in Shepard's play *Action*, we cannot find our place in the book; like Todd Hackett in Nathanael West's *Day of the Locust*, we have been reduced to wandering the back lots of American history, poking around in the scattered debris of earlier narratives, trying to find something we can use to make sense of ourselves.[29]

I V

African American and Mexican American writers have been grappling with this problem for a long time. In *Notes of a Native Son* (1955) James Baldwin described the shock of discovering, in Paris in the late 1940s, that he, a black man from Harlem, had more in common with white Americans than he did with black Africans. It was in the unyielding eyes of his white countrymen, in their blank refusal to acknowledge his presence, that Baldwin found most vividly reflected his own past, his own present, and his own forebodings of the future. White Americans and black Americans had loved and hated and obsessed about and feared one another so long that they had become bone of the bone and flesh of the flesh. Deny each other as they would, they could never be divorced. Thus he found his life's work: he would forge an identity for himself by laying claim to the very culture that had denied him an identity. Like Shakespeare's Caliban, he would have some run of this isle. And like Caliban, he would have it by appropriating "their" culture: "their" writers, "their" musicians, "their" artists—indeed, "their" entire cultural history, just as if it had been offered to him as a birthright:

> I was a kind of bastard of the West; when I followed the line of my past I did not find myself in Europe but in Africa. And this meant that in some subtle way, in a really profound way, I brought to Shakespeare, Bach, Rembrandt, to the stones of Paris, to the cathedral of Chartres, and to the Empire State Building, a special attitude. These were not really my creations,

they did not contain my history; I might search in them in vain forever for any reflection of myself. I was an interloper; this was not my heritage. At the same time I had no other heritage which I could possibly hope to use—I had certainly been unfitted for the jungle or the tribe. *I would have to appropriate these white centuries, I would have to make them mine.*[30]

As Baldwin later explained, "I was trying to locate myself within a specific inheritance."[31] He knew he could do that only by *laying claim* to that inheritance, using its finest ideals to condemn its worst failures. He also knew that if he failed to lay his own agonistic claim to American culture, American culture would certainly lay claim to him.

Ralph Waldo Ellison was driven by the same determination. Like Baldwin, he knew that American culture had to be won, that he had to confront it like the raging bull it was. But he also knew that if he armed himself with his most brazen dreams—*American* dreams—he could bring it heaving to its knees.[32] In fact, he had been preparing for this battle all his life. He and his friends had "yearned to make any and everything of quality *Negro American;* to appropriate it, possess it, re-create it in our own group and individual images."[33] Ellison was far more eclectic than Baldwin. He spent his teenage years ransacking the whole of Western civilization, searching for the models, the ideas he needed. Here he is describing himself and his fellow obsessives growing up in Oklahoma during the Great Depression:

We were seeking examples, patterns to live by. . . . We fabricated our own heroes and ideals catch-as-catch can, and with an outrageous and irreverent sense of freedom. Yes, and in complete disregard for ideas of respectability or the surreal incongruity of some of our projections. Gamblers and scholars, jazz musicians and scientists, Negro cowboys and soldiers from the Spanish-American and First World Wars, movie stars and stunt men, figures from the Italian Renaissance and literature, both classical and popular, were combined with the special virtues of some local bootlegger, the eloquence of some Negro preacher, the strength and grace of some local athlete, the ruthlessness of some businessman-physician, the elegance in dress and manners of some headwaiter or hotel doorman. . . . Our imaginations processed natural man and traditional hero, literature and folklore, like maniacal editors turned loose in some frantic film-cutting room. Culturally, play is a preparation, and we felt that somehow the human ideal lay in the vague and constantly shifting figures—sometimes comic but always versatile, picaresque and self-effacingly heroic—which evolved from our wildly improvisionary projections—figures neither white nor black, Christian nor Jewish, but representative of certain desirable essences, of skills and powers physical, aesthetic, and moral.[34]

Baldwin tried to locate himself within what he thought of as an already established, well-defined, ongoing culture—the "great tradition" of Western literature. But Ellison was a rag picker, a *bricoleur*, rifling through the archives of American culture, cobbling together a tradition from whatever bits and pieces caught his eye. Ever since the Black Arts movement in the late 1960s, African American critics have berated Baldwin and Eillison for their apparent lack of interest in African American culture.[35] True as that may or may not be, the larger truth is that African American criticism continues, to this day, to oscillate between the poles Baldwin and Ellison established—between Baldwin's attempt to locate himself within an existing tradition (be it white or black) and Ellison's determination to assemble a tradition of his own, a "two-toned" tradition. Amiri Baraka, Larry Neal, Barbara Christian, Houston Baker, and others have all followed Baldwin in their insistence that African Americans must find themselves within an already established tradition: "the wholeness and continuity of African-American culture." On the other hand, Robert Stepto, Anthony Appiah, Henry Louis Gates, and others, inspired more by contemporary literary theory than by the Black Arts movement, have followed Ellison rather than Baldwin. They think of African American culture—like every other culture—as always under reconstruction and dissemination, at a variety of sites, by a multitude of cultural ragpickers who are endlessly weaving bits and pieces into new webs of identity and belief—webs that help them place themselves in time, locate themselves in one or another historical sequence.

Many Mexican American writers seem driven by the same uninhibited eclecticism. Quintessential borderlanders and crossbloods, they are constantly rearranging the scattered fragments of Mexican, American, Mexican American, and Latino culture into new and sometimes startling historical sequences. Sandra Cisneros in *Woman Hollering Creek*, for example. Or Richard Rodriguez in *Hunger of Memory*. Born in 1942, educated in the Catholic schools of Sacramento, California, Rodriguez learned from his teachers how to weave the strands of American history into powerfully new sequences, just as Ellison had learned in the Oklahoma Dust Bowl twenty years before:

Our teachers used to be able to pose the possibility of a national
culture—a line connecting Thomas Jefferson, the slave owner,
to Malcolm X. Our teachers used to be able to tell us why all
of us speak Black English. Or how the Mexican farmworkers
in Delano were related to the Yiddish-speaking grandmothers
who worked the sweatshops of the Lower East Side.[36]

Finding themselves at the confluence of conflicting cultures, African American and Mexican American writers have become skillful
bricoleurs, continually recontextualizing the figures of their multiple
pasts, linking them together in unexpected genealogies, rethinking
who they are by reconceptualizing who they have been.

Again, there is nothing new about this: it is pretty much what
men and women have always done—early medieval Europeans, for
example, as Hayden White explained in chapter 5:

What happened between the third and eighth centuries was
that men ceased to regard themselves as descendents of their
Roman forebears and began to treat themselves as descendents
of their Judaeo-Christian predecessors. It was the constitution
of this *fictional cultural ancestry* which signalled the abandonment of the Roman socio-cultural system. When Western European men began to act *as if* they were descended from the Christian segment of the ancient world; when they began to structure
their comportment *as if* they were genetically descended from
their Christian predecessors; when, in short, they began to
honor the Christian past as the desirable model for the creation
of a future uniquely their own, and ceased to honor the Roman
past as *their* past, the Roman socio-cultural system ceased to
exist.[37]

Abraham Lincoln thought recent immigrants to the United States
were doing the same thing with American history:

If they look back through our history to trace their connection
with those days [of the Founding Fathers] by blood, they find
that have none, they cannot carry themselves back into that
glorious epoch and make themselves feel that they are part of
us. But when they look through that old Declaration of Independence they find that those old men say that "We hold these
truths to be self-evident, that all men are created equal," and
then they feel that that moral sentiment taught in that day
evidences their relation to those men, that it is the father of
all moral principle in them, and that they have a right to claim

it as though they were blood of the blood, and flesh of the flesh of the men who wrote that Declaration. And so they are.[38]

As Margaret Mead put it nearly a hundred years later, "George Washington does not represent the past to which one belongs by birth, but the past to which one tries to belong by effort."[39] It was exactly this sense of choosing one's ancestors, and thereby one's past, that prompted the Polish immigrant and American writer Mary Antin to proclaim, "I desire that the mantle of the New England prophets should rest on the shoulders of our own children."[40] Nathan Glazer remembers that in New York City in the 1930s, when the Jews and the Italian Americans had finally come to dominate the city's public schools, Jewish and Italian American teachers taught their students "that the forefathers of the American commonwealth were *their* forefathers."[41]

Glazer thinks it is important that he and his fellow students embraced Washington and Lincoln rather than Herzl and Garibaldi. To us it is not important; what is important is the embrace, that they were taught that by adopting a particular set of predecessors they could deepen and enrich their sense of living in historical time, in an ongoing sequence of historical figures with whom they had become fully conversant. For as Gates put it in explaining why he worked so long and hard to define his relationship to W. E. B. DuBois, "without the unbroken animation of a chosen past, we become flat shadows."[42] The novelist and essayist Alice Walker says she became a writer by thinking of herself as working within and extending a literary tradition that she herself had made up, that she had cobbled together from the various writers who had challenged and provoked and enlarged and enriched her over the years. It is a rambunctious and barely containable tradition, one that begins with Virginia Woolf and somehow includes Zora Neale Hurston, Jean Toomer, Colette, Anaïs Nin, Tillie Olson, and of course, Flannery O'Connor.[43] But like the traditions that Ellison and Gates assembled for themselves, it has provided her with the predecessors and the sense of historical continuity she needed to confront the brutality and degradation of American life that saw bubbling up like blood all around her.

But there is more involved here than individual psychology. The fact of countless individuals adopting their own predecessors and shaping them into coherent traditions is the yeast that raises our common culture. That is what Henry Louis Gates was getting at when he wrote,

> The canon is, in no very grand sense, the commonplace book
> of our shared culture, in which we have written down the texts

and titles that we want to remember, that had some special meaning for us. How else did those of us who teach literature fall in love with our subject than through our own common-place books, in which we inscribed, secretly and privately, as we might do in a diary, those passages of books that named for us what we had for so long deeply felt, but could not say? . . . Finding James Baldwin and writing him down at an Episcopal church camp during the Watts riots in 1965 (I was fifteen) prob-ably determined the direction of my intellectual life more than did any other single factor. I wrote and rewrote verbatim his elegantly framed paragraphs, full of sentences that were at once somehow Henry Jamesian and King Jamesian, yet clothed in the cadences and figures of the spirituals.[44]

Harold Bloom thinks all this necessarily and always takes place under the sign of the Freudian family romance. To the extent that we create ourselves at all, he thinks we do so in the cauldron of what are essentially Oedipal struggles with our intellectual forebears, creatively misreading, recasting, and revising them, appropriating and consuming them, burning them up to power our own solipsistic self-begetting.[45] In *The Progressive Historians* (1969) Richard Hof-stadter offered his own intellectual biography—a narrative of "my own parricidal forays"—as an example:

> I started this book out of a personal engagement with the sub-ject, out of some of the incompleteness of my reckoning with my intellectual forebears. . . . At the point at which I began to have some identity as a historian, it was the work of these three men [Turner, Beard, and Parrington], particularly Beard and Parrington, that interested me as supplying the guiding ideas of the understanding of American history. . . . A good deal of what has gone into this book is, then, a reprise of that perennial battle we wage with our elders, particularly with our adopted intellectual fathers. If we are to have any new thoughts, if we are to make the effort to distinguish ourselves from those who preceded us, and perhaps pre-eminently from those to whom we once had the greatest indebtedness. Even if our quarrels are only marginal and minor (though I do not think that can be said of the differences discussed here), *we must make the most of them.*[46]

In other words, we can define and order our own values only by playing them off against other people's values. Charles Taylor describes this in slightly different terms, but it comes to the same thing: "We can only get clear how we think things are by drawing sharply the differences with how they have been misconceived. Clarification of our own views is inseparable from our fighting clear of the erroneous views which were handed down to us. Plato started this kind of thing, and we have never stopped. It is hard to see how we could stop, and escape altogether from this contrastive correction of our past."[47]

Perhaps the only thing that can stop it is the near-suicidal despair that William James ascribed to the "sick-souls" of this world—and that he discovered in himself when he chanced upon an epileptic huddled on the floor of a Paris hospital.[48] That experience forced James—just as it had forced John Bunyan's Christian before him and the young Martin Luther before him—to reach beyond himself, to grasp something more than himself, to perhaps transcend himself. Not that such reaching is always successful, of course. In December 1889 Vincent van Gogh wrote to his friend Emile Bernard: "I myself am suffering an absolute lack of models." Six months later he was dead, a silent suicide in Saint-Rémy, France.[49] "My God, my God, why hast thou forsaken me?"

To encounter a particular thinker is to encounter a particular patterning of perception and desire. Our sense of what we should desire, what we should value, how we should live is shaped by the thinkers we argue with and the traditions we devise for coming to terms with them.[50] And it is just here, in learning to do this thoughtfully and reflectively, that American history comes into its own as a form of moral deliberation.[51]

V

But claiming a particular inheritance is more difficult than it may first appear. Stanley Cavell describes *In Quest of the Ordinary* (1988) as "a kind of progress report" on his twenty-year struggle "to inherit Emerson."[52] Toward the end of this intellectual autobiography he asks "why it took me so long to get my bearings in Emerson." "Why did it take me from the time I first remember knowing of Emerson's yoking of day and night and of my sense of implication in his words, until just over a year ago, some two decades later, to begin to look actively at his work, to demand explicitly my inheritance of him?"[53]

Some thinkers simply require more of us than we are willing or able to give. The New England Puritans, for example, demanded a soul-searching more intense, more piercing and searing than most of us could possibly bear. You must "bring the soul upon the rack," Thomas Hooker insisted; you must "keep the Conscience under an arrest . . . so that the soul is held fast prisoner, and cannot make escape."[54] And the heart too must be "broken and humbled," for "all grace is in His gift, and He doles it only to the bruised and abased." Should this cup prove too bitter—and the Puritans knew it would prove bitter indeed—we must drink it nevertheless, for we are meant to "judge the dregs of God's vengeance by some little sips of it; and the torments of hell by some little beginning of it."[55] Even a good man could be led to "revenge himselfe upon himselfe," as Jonathan Edwards discovered when his uncle walked out of the Northampton church and slashed his throat with a pair of rusted sheep shears.[56] "Thou dost not think so now," Hooker warned, "but thou wilt find it so one day."[57] Moreover, sometimes a thinker we have struggled to understand—someone whose writings have inspired and provoked us, have brought us to some new insight or perspective—even a thinker like this can suddenly go dead for us, sometimes without the slightest warning, almost as if in response to her own perception that we have invested too much in her.[58] Not only that: sometimes we find that we have taken up with the *wrong* thinker, that we have consructed the wrong sort of past for ourselves and thus become the wrong kind of person—though, like Richard Rorty's liberal ironist, we know perfectly well that we lack even the most rudimentary criterion of wrongness. In the early 1970s Joyce Carol Oates reimagined and rewrote several of her favorite authors' stories and published them under the title *Marriages and Infidelities.* In an interview conducted shortly after the book appeared she called it "a testament of my love and extreme devotion to these other writers. I imagine a kind of spiritual 'marriage' between myself and them."[59] Oates thinks "marriages" like these are tremendously important, that we purchase our own salvation (or ruin) by the "marriages" we enter into, the predecessors we adopt. But she also knows that most of us—being just the sort of unfinished persons Freud thought we were—read the wrong books, adopt the wrong predecessors, construct the wrong traditions, and so end up confounding ourselves. Bobbie Ann Mason's 1984 story "Love Life" warns of just this danger: not only will we be ill served by many—perhaps most—of the thinkers we adopt, there may be something "morbid, self-deceptive, and even self-destructive in our efforts to reclaim them."[60] Choosing the wrong predecessors, we weave a past for ourselves that can no more guide us through the coming darkness than a spiderweb could stop a falling rock. The mind feeds on poisoned bread, pollutes its vision, locks its gates, withdraws into desert places, gives up trying to formulate its own living connection between past and present, and so begins its accelerating descent into solipsism and self-betrayal.

The literary historian Elaine Showalter thinks this is precisely what happened to the nineteenth-century American writer and feminist Margaret Fuller. Raised on the frigid and barren theology she found in her father's library, seduced by the man-making words of Emerson and Thoreau, her generous and susceptible imagination thickened and hardened, and nothing beautiful or joyous came out of it. Thus she went to her watery grave entombed in the ill-fitting ideas of her ill-chosen predecessors.[61] William Carlos Williams thought (though less convincingly) that the same thing had happened to Emily Dickinson: "starving in her father's garden, the very nearest—starving—never a woman: never a poet."[62]

It would be reassuring to think that the historical profession had devised a reliable methodology for helping us find the forebears we need, and so constructing the histories we need. But no such methodology exists, of course. Nor are we likely to acquire one in the near future. The sad truth is that the conventions and procedures we historians have pieced together over the years always stop at just this point. And beyond this point the roads have been washed out and all the bridges are down. We simply have to strike out on our own— which is precisely why, sooner or later, we all find ourselves in the dilemma Rorty ascribes to "the ironist," worried that she's read the wrong books, adopted the wrong moral advisers and so become the wrong kind of person, though she knows perfectly well that she has no criterion of wrongness.[63]

The turn-of-the-century modernists did not have to worry about this sort of thing, of course. T. S. Eliot could spend his time linking "the new (the really new)" literary works to "the existing monuments" of Western literary history, shaping and shoring up the whole against our common ruin. But it never occurred to him to question the inherent value of the existing monuments themselves.[64] Some contemporary conservatives—the British historian Michael Oakeshott, for example—have abandoned Eliot's assumption that a culture consists of its "Great Books," or that these canonical works "form an ideal order among themselves." For Oakeshott, a culture is rather an ongoing conversation among a variety of "voices"—"the voice of poetry," "the voice of science," "the voice of politics," and so on. One gains access to the culture—acquires the ability to participate in its "conversation"—by learning one or more of the its voices: "Education, properly speaking, is an initiation into the skill and partnership of this conversation in which we learn to recognize the voices, to distinguish the proper occasions of utterance, and in which we acquire the intellectual and moral habits appropriate to conversation. And it is this conversation which, in the end, gives place and character to every human activity and utterance."[65]

Oakeshott thinks each one of these voices is particular and unique, that each has its own distinctive idiom, that they are historically "authentic."[66] Their boundaries are not porous or permeable, they do not bleed into one another, they are not subject to penetration and population by other voices. In a word, they are not heteroglossic. The same is true of the larger "conversation": it is closed, stable, singular, coherent, evolving by its own internally governed dynamic. Though any one of us may, by virtue of a brilliant life's work, hope to alter its internal balances somewhat or even shift its ultimate trajectory a bit, we all begin by being initiated into a coherent, well-established, historically grounded, and ongoing conversation—one that has somehow escaped the sudden, inexplicable ruptures and discontinuities that the early Michel Foucault attributed to all discourses. "The conversation of mankind" is not like one of Foucault's disjointed archipelagoes, its deepest connections unknown and unknowable; it is more like a slow-moving, continuously visible river.

What makes Oakeshott's perspective attractive for our purposes is that it provides an alternative to the neopragmatist vision of history as another quasi-scientific form of inquiry—an established set of research procedures for "testing truth claims," as David Hollinger recently put it.[67] For if we think of history as a conversation with the dead about what we should value and how we should live, then Oakeshott is undoubtedly right: "There is no 'truth' to be discovered, no proposition to be proved, no conclusion sought."[68]

What makes it problematic is that American culture simply cannot be thought of as a single conversation carried on by a limited number of distinct and autonomous voices. It is not, as the champions of multiculturalism contend, that American culture has become too pluralistic and diversified to carry on such a conversation—as if we had become a collection of isolated, marginalized, and exotically distinct subcultures, each one speaking its own private language.[69] In fact, it is pretty much the opposite, for all those putatively distinct subcultures have actually been commingling in the night, combining and coalescing with an unrelenting ferocity:

> The U.S. Border Patrol works through the night to arrest the flow of illegal immigrants over the border, even as Americans stand patiently in line for La Bamba. While Americans vote to declare, once and for all, that English shall be the official language of the U.S., Madonna starts recording in Spanish. . . .

Expect bastard themes. Expect winking ironies, comic conclusions. For Hispanics live on this side of the border, where Kraft manufactures Mexican-style Velveeta, and where Jack in the Box serves Fajita Pita. Expect marriage. We will change America even as we will be changed. We will disappear with you into a new miscegenation. . . . For generations, Latin America has been the place, the bed, of a confluence of so many races and cultures that Protestant North America shuddered to imagine it. The time has come to imagine it.[70]

This is the point at which Eliot and even Oakeshott fail us. If we are to have the predecessors we need we must find them ourselves—find them and arrange them such that we can see ourselves as the latest in a long sequence or tradition of such thinkers. As always, our best hope lies in excess: more books, more predecessors, more competing traditions from which to argue with ourselves. And thereby more obligations by which to define ourselves. That we learn how to do all this with a measure of tact, insight, and thoughtfulness must become the characteristic and defining responsibility of American history in the twenty-first century.

Epilogue

Where do we find ourselves?
—Ralph Waldo Emerson, 1842

A sense of the past is a way of being in the present. At its best it is a way of arguing with ourselves, a means of rethinking who we might become by rethinking who we once were. As Tolstoy never tired of insisting, history and literature are essentially forms of moral reflection, tested and accredited means of pondering what we should value and how we should live. Since the early 1960s this traditional vision of history has been driven into exile, first by the professionalization of American historical writing, then by the expanding influence of the social sciences. But as early as 1966 Hayden White was warning his colleagues that these developments would eventually leave history isolated from the main currents of American intellectual life—currents that were even then transforming the rest of the humanities. "The most difficult task which the current generation of historians will be called upon to perform," White explained, "is to preside over the dissolution of history's claim to autonomy among the disciplines, and to aid in the assimilation of history to a higher kind of intellectual inquiry. . . . The burden of the historian in our time is to reestablish the dignity of historical studies on a basis that will make them consonant with the aims and purposes of the intellectual community at large.[1]

Nothing remotely like this happened, of course. And now, as the century's terminus looms ahead of us, the historians who dominate the profession—the men and women who occupy the endowed chairs, run the professional organizations, and preside over the distribution of academic patronage—are more fiercely committed to the professionalization of history and its reduction to a social science than their predecessors in the early 1960s. Thirty years after White wrote "The Burden of History," the discipline has become just what he feared it would: the great reactionary center of American intellectual life. At the end of the 1990s, as disciplinary boundaries blur and the disciplines start bleeding into one another, historians have risen up to insist on the autonomy and intellectual integrity of historical studies. At a time when disciplinary paradigms have become increasingly decentered and irrevocably plural, they reassure one another that we must have "the courage of our conventions"; just when anthropologists discover the virtues of cross-cultural comparison—of placing Balinese cockfighting, for example, or West African carving or New Guinea palm-leaf painting in interpretive tension with our own cultural practices, our own sense of how things stand in the world, so as to form a commentary on them—historians pound the table and insist that artifacts can be interpreted only in their proper historical contexts.[2] This last obsession has been especially crippling. For all their apparent willingness to follow cultural anthropologists like Clifford Geertz, historians stop dead in their tracks when Geertz talks about using the imaginative products of other cultures to deepen and enrich our own moral lives.[3] That the emergence of history as the reactionary center of the humanities has been presided over by historians who consider themselves liberal pragmatists will surprise only those who mistake the wan theology of John Dewey for the autobiography of God.

All but lost in the compression of ideas that inevitably accompanies the formation of such reactionary centers is a deeply ironic possibility that can now be glimpsed only from the margins of contemporary historical practice: the possibility that we could go all the way with contemporary theory and come out the other end with a reinvigorated but nevertheless traditional vision of history, that is, history as a form of moral reflection.

What would such a history look like? First and most important, it would *not* include a renewal of history's traditional claim to objective knowledge about the past, for all the reasons discussed in the preceding chapters (chapter 4 in particular). It is not so much that the arguments against historical objectivity seem convincing (though there is that); it is that we do not *need* a theory of historical objectivity—and that all our efforts to come up with one have only obscured issues far more pressing and important. Just as students of religious behavior have learned to bracket the ontological status of the religious experiences they study, so we historians must learn to bracket the ontological status of the historical narratives we read and write.

That does not mean we should treat them as fictions; it simply means we accept them as historical narratives without pressing too hard on the question of their ontological status. Peter Novick must have had something like this in mind when he wrote the following:

> Those who think as I do . . . want to offer what we hope will be fruitful—perhaps even edifying—new ways of looking at things in the past, without aspiring to any higher claims. Others are, in a sense that seems to me deluded but not pernicious, concerned with "moving toward the truth" or "getting it right." My friends and I can find the work of these historians suggestive and/or fruitful and/or edifying, while disregarding the far-reaching and, to us, irrelevant claims that are made for them. . . . Just as in matters of religion, nonbelievers feel that they can get along without a god, so we who are called historical relativists believe we can get along without objectivity. . . . To say of a work of history that it is or is not objective is to make an *empty* observation, to say something neither interesting nor useful. . . . Although the term "a-objectivist" is clumsy and difficult to pronounce, it would, I think, be more accurate, by analogy with "amoralists" and "agnostics" who aren't *against* morality or religion—they just don't think it very interesting, important, or relevant to their lives.[4]

All of which is simply to say, it is the stories that interest and sustain us, not the truth claims made on their behalf.

Second, it is the values we find in those stories that count for us, not the context in which they were written or the details of their authors' often wretched lives.[5] It is "Song of Myself" that moves us, that nurtures and nourishes our best hopes for democracy in America, not the personal life of the purportedly racist and bigoted little man who is reputed to have written that great poem. If we are told—as the historian David Reynolds recently told us—that "the real Walt Whitman" did not, in fact, live up to the vision of America he gave us in "Song of Myself," all we can do is shrug our shoulders and say, "Too bad for the real Walt Whitman."[6] The only Whitman that matters to us is the Whitman who emerges from his poems.

Contemporary theorists call this "the strong textualist position." In fact, it is an utterly traditional way of reading history, as the outspokenly conservative historian Gertrude Himmelfarb has (more than once) reminded her colleagues:

> The Victorians, even while relishing the scandals about their heroes, knew them to be scandals about their *lives*, not about

their *work*. Byron's poetry was not thought to be less great because his morals were less than admirable. Nor were George Eliot's novels tainted by her long-standing extramarital affair with George Lewes. Nor was John Stuart Mill's philosophy discredited by his relationship with his great and good friend Harriet for the twenty years while she was still Mrs. John Taylor. Nor was Carlyle's reputation as a moralist diminished by the revelations of his sexual "irregularities," as the Victorians delicately put it. Nor was Gladstone's political career jeopardized by his well-known habit of prowling the streets at night, seeking prostitutes and lecturing them on the evils of their ways, sometimes bringing them home, where his wife dutifully served them tea—or hot chocolate, according to some accounts.[7]

Third, it is in trying to make Whitman's hopes and Tocqueville's fears and Du Bois's tragic vision our own—trying to make them grow in our own minds, transforming them from something that merely existed in the past into something we have made ours—that history comes into its own as a mode of moral reflection, a way of curing up life into meaning. As Geertz puts it, "The passage is from the immediacies of one form of life to the metaphors of another."[8] But this act of appropriation, this attempt to use other people's cultural expressions to reflect on our own, to unsettle our moral lives, to "turn our impoverishing certitudes into humanizing doubts," is of course deeply problematic. For Whitman, Tocqueville, Du Bois—or any other thinker worth spending time with—will almost always resist our attempts to appropriate them. And if they come to us at all they come later rather than sooner, almost as if unbidden. Over the years you simply find that a thinker you have come to know— a way of grasping life that you have come to admire, a sensibility you think worth cultivating—not only has stayed with you but has become part of your own internal patterns of perception and reflection. Trying to figure out what all these chosen predecessors may or may not have in common, trying to perceive affinities and attractions between them, trying to arrange them in chronological order so you can think of yourself as the latest in a long line of such thinkers— this is pretty much what people used to mean when they talked about acquiring "a sense of the past."

That none of this gets taught in graduate school goes without saying. But that is beginning to change, if for no other reason than because the whole tired debate about the ontological status of historical narratives—a debate that has preoccupied us and bored our students for how many years now?—has finally exhausted itself. If the entire body of American historians ever gathered in one place—say, at the Whaleman's Chapel in New Bedford, Massachusetts, presided over, even unto this day by Father Mapple himself—one would hear a single anguished cry rise up from the assembled multitude: "Dear God, please spare us yet another wearisome treatise on pragmatism and objectivity." If God does judge it meet and right to grant that prayer, then perhaps this particular fin de siècle will be the moment when American history sets out to become what it once was: not one of the social sciences in historical costume, but one of our primary forms of moral reflection.

NOTES

INTRODUCTION

1. Michael Walzer, *The Company of Critics: Social Criticism and Political Commitment in the Twentieth Century* (New York: Basic, 1988), 230.

2. William Carlos Williams, "The Virtue of History," in Williams, *In the American Grain* (1925; Middlesex, Eng.: Penguin, 1971), 198.

3. I have borrowed this imagery of "yeasting" from the South African poet Breyten Breytenbach, who wrote, "I'm trying to yeast Afrikaner sensibilities from within and therefore I start with the bread we break together, even if only via the basic complicity of a common mumbo-jumbo, I mean language, I mean *taal*. How else could I have a say so? Ah, but how do I avoid the twisting and the bending, the kneeling and the back-stabbing, the compromises, the ethical corruption, in my attempts to 'hang in there'?" Breytenbach, *End Papers: Essays, Letters, Articles of Faith, Workbook Notes* (Boston: Faber, 1986), 205. For an illuminating discussion of Breytenbach's social criticim, see Michael Walzer, "Breyten Breytenbach: The Critic in Exile," in Walzer, *Company of Critics*, 210–24.

4. On the importance of speaking "in the first person plural," see Walzer, *Company of Critics*, 230.

5. I have borrowed the ideas and images in this paragraph—and learned much else—from Michael Walzer's wonderful book *The Company of Critics*.

6. Eugene Genovese, *The Southern Tradition: The Achievements and Limitations of an American Conservatism* (Cambridge: Harvard University Press, 1994), xiii.

7. Arthur M. Schlesinger Jr., *The Disuniting of America* (New York: Norton, 1992), 82.

8. In fact, though neither side likes to admit it, most of this argument had been thrashed out more than seventy years earlier, when the Progressive histori-

ans invented "the new history" in the 1880s. The Left's criticisms of traditional historical writing in the 1960s are remarkably similar to the Progressives' attack on established forms of historical writing at the end of the nineteenth century.

9. Gertrude Himmelfarb, "Postmodernist History," in Himmelfarb, *On Looking into the Abyss: Untimely Thoughts on Culture and Society* (New York: Knopf, 1994), 160. "Postmodernist History" originally appeared as "Telling It as You Like It," in the *Times Literary Supplement*, 16 October 1992.

10. For a description of the road from historicism to relativism, see Karl Popper's classic indictment, *The Poverty of Historicism* (London: Routledge and Kegan Paul, 1961).

11. See Peter Novick, *That Noble Dream: The "Objectivity Question" and the American Historical Profession* (Cambridge: Cambridge University Press, 1988), passim, but 598 in particular. The historian Alan Brinkley came to essentially the same conclusion: "I suspect that most historians, if pressed to discuss the issue, would concede that true objectivity is impossible to achieve, that all scholarship is coloured to some degree by the social or political inclinations of the writer. But most would admit that if objectivity is a myth, it is a useful one—something worth aspiring to if only because the aspiration serves as a check on a scholar's subjective impulses." Alan Brinkley, "Mythic but Useful," *Times Literary Supplement*, 10–16 November 1989, 1246.

12. Himmelfarb, "Postmodernist History," 161.

13. As the critic Robert Fuller put it, "Post-Modernism is outflanked by reactionaries on one side and novelty-seeking camp-followers on the other." Robert Fuller, "Building in the Past Tense," *Times Literary Supplement*, 24–30 March 1989, 296.

14. Kenneth Cmiel, "After Objectivity: What Comes Next in History?" *American Literary History* 2 (spring 1990): 170. See also Novick, *That Noble Dream.*

15. Jonathan D. Culler, *On Deconstruction: Theory and Criticism after Structuralism* (Ithaca: Cornell University Press, 1982), 90.

16. There is an interesting discussion of Holbein's painting in Julia Kristeva, *Black Sun: Depression and Melancholia* (New York: Columbia University Press, 1989), 105–38.

17. Herman Melville to Nathaniel Hawthorne, 17 (?) November 1851, in *The Letters of Herman Melville*, ed. Merrell R. Davis and William H. Gilman (New Haven: Yale University Press, 1960), 143. I am indebted to my daughter Anna for telling me about this letter.

18. See, for example, Derrida's essay "Ellipsis," in Jacques Derrida, *Writing and Difference* (Chicago: University of Chicago Press, 1978). For an interesting discussion, see Susan A. Handelman, *The Slayers of Moses: The Emergence of Rabbinic Interpretation in Modern Literary Theory* (Albany: State University of New York Press, 1982), 169ff.

19. David Hollinger, "The Return of the Prodigal: The Persistence of Historical Knowing," *American Historical Review* 94 (June 1989): 621.

20. Derrida as quoted by Handelman, *Slayers of Moses*, xiii.

21. Jacques Derrida, *Of Grammatology*, trans. Gayatri Chakravorty Spivak (Baltimore: Johns Hopkins University Press, 1976), 159.

22. Ibid., 141.

23. Thomas Hooker in Perry Miller and Thomas H. Johnson, eds., *The Puritans: A Sourcebook of Their Writings* (New York; Harper and Row, 1963), 293.

24. Derrida, *Of Grammatology*, 277.

25. Jacques Derrida, *Of Grammatology*, 233, as quoted by Michael Fischer, *Stanley Cavell and Literary Skepticism* (Chicago: University of Chicago Press, 1989), 56.

26. Henry Adams, *The Education of Henry Adams*, ed. Ernest Samuels (Boston: Houghton Mifflin, 1973), 91. Half a century later the novelist Wallace Stegner saw the same rupture between past and present. In his novel *Angle of Repose* (1971) the historian Lyman Ward remarks, "The elements have changed, there are whole new orders of magnitude and kind. This present of 1970 is no more an extension of my grandparents' world, this West is no more a development of the West they helped build, than the sea over Santorin is an extension of that once-island of rock and olives." Stegner, *Angle of Repose* (New York: Penguin, 1971), 17—18.

27. Adams, *Education of Henry Adams*, 472—73.

28. Gordon Wood, "America in the 1790s," *Atlantic Monthly*, December 1993, 134.

29. Gordon Wood, "Writing History: An Exchange," *New York Review of Books*, 16 December 1982, 59.

30. Joyce Appleby, Lynn Hunt, and Margaret Jacob, *Telling the Truth about History* (New York: Norton, 1994), 234, 254.

31. Gertrude Himmelfarb, "Supposing History Is a Woman—What Then?" *American Scholar* 53 (August 1984): 505.

32. Herman Melville, *Moby Dick* (New York: Bantam Classics, 1967), 156.

33. Ibid., 158.

34. Ludwig Wittgenstein, "Lecture on Ethics," *Philosophical Review* 74 (January 1965): 11—12.

35. Lionel Trilling, *The Liberal Imagination: Essays on Literature and Society* (New York: Viking, 1950), 19.

36. Jacques Derrida as quoted by Fischer, *Stanley Cavell and Literary Skepticism*, 20.

37. Wilhelm von Humboldt as quoted by Henry Louis Gates, *Figures in Black: Words, Signs, and the "Racial" Self* (New York: Oxford University Press, 1987), xxi.

38. Leszak Kolakowski, *Metaphysical Horror* (New York: Blackwell, 1988), 2.

39. The Historian's Prayer need not be long: Dear God, please spare us yet another treatise on pragmatism and objectivity.

40. Though he may not have known the latest techniques in historical research, Lionel Trilling knew the value of the past better than most contemporary historians. See Trilling, *Liberal Imagination*, 220.

41. Thus Lionel Trilling on Henry James: "It was 'the imagination of disaster' that cut James off from his contemporaries and it is what recommends him to us now." Trilling, *Liberal Imagination*, 60. But notice that Trilling does not claim he understands James better than his contemporaries understood him. After all, to claim that you learned something from the dead is not to claim

that you got them right. This is a subtle but crucial distinction. Here is Trilling's own explanation: "When we bring into conjunction with each other the certitude that great spiritual good is to be derived from the art of the past and the no less firmly held belief that an artistic style cannot be validly used in any age other than that in which it was invented, we confront what is surely one of the significant mysteries of man's life in culture." Lionel Trilling, "Why We Read Jane Austen," in Trilling, *The Last Decade: Essays and Reviews, 1965–1975*, ed. Diana Trilling (New York: Harcourt Brace Jovanovich, 1979), 218–19.

42. Wallace Stegner, "History, Myth and the Western Writer," in Stegner, *The Sound of Mountain Water* (Garden City, N.Y.: Doubleday, 1969), 201. I am indebted to my daughter Anna for this reference, as for so many other insights and references.

43. Ralph Waldo Emerson, *Self-Reliance and Other Essays* (New York: Dover, 1993), 89.

CHAPTER ONE

1. The classic description of language's return is Jacques Derrida's *Of Grammatology*. As Derrida says in the opening chapter, "Never as much as at present has [language] invaded, as such, the global horizon of the most diverse researches and the most heterogeneous discourses, diverse and heterogeneous in their intention, method, and ideology." Derrida, *Of Grammatology*, trans. Gayatri Chakravorty Spivak (Baltimore: Johns Hopkins University Press, 1976), 6. For a provocative discussion of literature's return specifically to history, see Linda Orr, "The Revenge of Literature: A History of History," *New Literary History* 18 (autumn 1986): 1–22.

2. Quentin Skinner, "Hermeneutics and the Role of History," *New Literary History* 7 (1975–76): 214.

3. Quentin Skinner, ed., *The Return of Grand Theory in the Human Sciences* (New York: Cambridge University Press, 1985), 1–20.

4. "There can be no doubt that the influence of the hermeneutic tradition has in general played a clarifying role in helping to propagate the idea of interpretation as essentially a matter of recovering and rendering the meaning of a text." Skinner, "Hermeneutics and History," 214.

5. Skinner regards "knowledge of such intentions" as "indispensable." Ibid., 211. This is what Martin Jay has referred to as "the illusion that texts are merely congealed intentionalities waiting to be reexperienced at a later date." Jay, "Should Intellectual History Take a Linguistic Turn? Reflections on the Habermas-Gadamer Debate," in *Modern European Intellectual History: Reappraisals and New Perspectives*, ed. Dominick LaCapra and Steven L. Kaplan (Ithaca: Cornell University Press, 1982), 106. This approach to texts first came under attack by the New Critics in the 1930s and 1940s. For a recent defense, see Steven Knapp and Walter Benn Michaels, "Against Theory," *Critical Inquiry* 8 (summer 1982): 723–42; the critical responses in ibid., 9 (June 1983) and 11 (March 1985); and Knapp and Michaels, "Against Theory 2: Hermeneutics and Deconstruction," ibid., 14 (autumn 1987): 49–68. Leo Strauss's followers, of course, have never given up the hope of recovering authorial intention. See

Gordon Wood's discussion of recent Straussian efforts to recover the "original intention" of the Founding Fathers in Woods, "The Fundamentalists and the Constitution," *New York Review* 25 (18 February 1988): 33—40.

6. Skinner, "Hermeneutics and History," 216.

7. Ibid., 213.

8. I do not mean to suggest that there are no significant differences between Derrida, Foucault, and de Man concerning the nature of textuality. For a discussion of the differences between Derrida and Foucault on this point, see Edward Said, "The Problem of Textuality: Two Exemplary Positions," *Critical Inquiry* 4 (1978): 673—714. Paul de Man was especially concerned to preserve something of language's referential capacity. See de Man, *Allegories of Reading: Figural Language in Rousseau, Nietzsche, Rilke, and Proust* (New Haven: Yale University Press, 1979), for his effort to identify the limits of deconstruction. The chapters on Rousseau are especially important in this regard.

9. See Roland Barthes, "The Death of the Author," in *Image-Music-Text: Roland Barthes*, ed. Stephen Heath (New York: Hill and Wang, 1977). "The names of authors or of doctrines have here no substantial value. They indicate neither identities nor causes. It would be frivolous to think that 'Descartes,' 'Leibniz,' 'Rousseau,' 'Hegel,' etc., are names of authors, of the authors of movements or displacements that we thus designate. The indicative value that I attribute to them is first the name of a problem." Derrida, *Of Grammatology*, 99.

10. And because it eclipses and transcends the discourse in which it was written. Derrida has argued that "the text constantly goes beyond this representation [i.e., the historian's representation of the text's 'proper' discourse] by the entire system of its resources and its own laws." Moreover, "the question of [the text's] genealogy exceeds by far the possibilities that are at present given for its elaboration." Derrida, *Of Grammatology*, 101.

11. As does Pocock. See J. G. A. Pocock, "An Appeal from the New to the Old Whigs? A Note on Joyce Appleby's 'Ideology and the History of Political Thought,'" *Intellectual History Newsletter* 3 (1981): 47. The classic works of speech act theory are J. L. Austin, *How to Do Things with Words* (New York: Oxford University Press, 1962), and John R. Searle, *Speech Acts: An Essay in the Philosophy of Language* (New York: Cambridge University Press, 1969).

12. Note, however, that it is precisely this "phonocentrism," this privileging of speech over writing, that Jacques Derrida has attacked so vociferously. Derrida wants to reduce speech to a form of writing, an "*archi-écriture.*" He wants to formulate "a new situation for speech," to enforce "its subordination within a structure of which it will no longer be the archon." Indeed, he even declares "the death of speech" (*Of Grammatology*, 8). His most explicit attack on Austin and speech act theory is in "Signature Event Context," *Glyph* 1 (1977): 172—97. But see John Searle's defense in "Reiterating the Differences," *Glyph* 1 (1977): 198—208, and Derrida's rejoinder, "Limited Inc abc," *Glyph* 2 (1977): 162—254. This debate has aroused great interest. Accounts can be found in Gayatri Chakravorty Spivak, "Revolutions That as Yet Have No Model," *Diacritics* 10 (1980): 29—49, and Christopher Norris, *Deconstruction: Theory and Practice* (London: Methuen, 1982), 108—15.

13. Paul Ricoeur, *Hermeneutics and the Human Sciences: Essays on Language, Action, and Interpretation* (New York: Cambridge University Press, 1981), 146. In Derrida's words, "writing is the name of these two absences." *Of Grammatology*, 40–41.

14. Jorge Luis Borges, "Pierre Menard, Author of *Don Quixote*," in Borges, *Fictions*, ed. Anthony Kerrigan (London: Calder and Boyars, 1974), 42–51.

15. Ibid., 46.

16. Ibid.

17. Ibid., 48.

18. Skinner, "Hermeneutics and History," 214.

19. Borges, *Fictions*, 46.

20. Hans-Georg Gadamer, *Truth and Method* (New York: Seabury, 1975), 245.

21. Gadamer recognizes that identifying "legitimate" prejudices is one of the "fundamental" problems of hermeneutics. Gadamer, "Prejudices as Conditions of Understanding," which constitutes part 2 of *Truth and Method*. See the first part of this section, "The Rehabilitation of Authority and Tradition," 245–53.

22. Gadamer refers to this process as "its constantly renewed reality of being experienced." Ibid., xix. Gadamer's position, as I have outlined it here, is in some ways an extension of Martin Heidegger's insistence on the historicity of the text, that is, his insistence that both our texts and our understandings of them are irremediably historical. See Richard Rorty's discussion of Heidegger in "Overcoming the Tradition: Heidegger and Dewey," in Rorty, *Consequences of Pragmatism* (London: Harvester Press, 1982), 37–59.

23. Gadamer, "Prejudices as Conditions of Understanding," xxi.

24. Ibid., 149. David Couzens Hoy has made the same point: meaning is not "a given, an in-itself, which only needs to be unfolded" but rather is "conditioned by its history of reception and influence." Hoy, *The Critical Circle: Literature, History, and Philosophical Hermeneutics* (Berkeley: University of California Press, 1978), 103, 93.

25. Skinner, *Return of Grand Theory*, 8.

26. Ibid., 1–20, passim. One hears historians voicing this sort of alarmist reaction more and more often these days. James Kloppenberg recently warned his colleagues that developments in literary criticism threaten to "bring all critical exchange to an end," that meaning itself—"all meanings"—will shortly "collapse into unintelligibility." Contemporary literary theory simply "makes writing history impossible." Kloppenberg, "Deconstruction and Hermeneutic Strategies for Intellectual History," *Intellectual History Newsletter* 9 (April 1987): 7, 10. Stanley Fish discusses such "theory fear" in "Consequences," *Critical Inquiry* 11 (1985): 439ff. For a suggestion that "theory fear" may be widespread among historians, see Dominick LaCapra, "On Grubbing in My Personal Archives: An Historiographical Exposé," *Boundary 2: A Journal of Postmodern Literature and Culture* 13 (winter–spring 1985): 43–68.

27. See, for example, J. G. A. Pocock, *Politics, Language, and Time: Essays on Political Thought and History* (New York: Atheneum, 1971); idem, *The Ancient Constitution and the Feudal Law: A Study of English Historical Thought in the*

Seventeenth Century (New York: Norton, 1957); and idem, *The Machiavellian Moment: Florentine Political Thought and the Atlantic Republic Tradition* (Princeton: Princeton University Press, 1975), his enormously influential book on early modern "civil humanism."

28. J. G. A. Pocock as quoted by Joyce Appleby, "Ideology and the History of Political Thought," *Intellectual History Group Newsletter* 2 (1980): 11.

29. Pocock as quoted by Appleby, ibid., 15.

30. J. G. A. Pocock, *Virtue, Commerce, and History: Essays on Political Thought and History, Chiefly in the Eighteenth Century* (New York: Cambridge University Press, 1985), 10.

31. Pocock, *Politics, Language and Time*, 3, 11. Pocock modestly concedes that he himself "seems to have been concerned in this transformation from an early stage" (3).

32. David Hollinger, "Historians and the Discourse of Intellectuals," in *New Directions in American Intellectual History*, ed. John Higham and Paul K. Conkin (Baltimore: Johns Hopkins University Press, 1979), 60 n. 2.

33. Appleby, "Ideology," 15.

34. Michel Foucault, "Human Nature: Justice vs. Power," in *Reflexive Water: The Basic Concerns of Mankind*, ed. Fons Elder (London: Souvenir, 1974), 133–97.

35. Michel Foucault, *The Archaeology of Knowledge and the Discourse of Language*, trans. A. M. Sheridan Smith (New York: Pantheon, 1972), 55. Foucault's perspective is hardly unique, of course; the dispersion of the subject has been a strong element of French intellectual life since the 1960s, most obviously in the work of Lévi-Strauss, Louis Althusser, and the *Annales* historians, among others.

36. As Foucault puts it, "Instead of referring back to the synthesis of *the* unifying function of a subject, the various enunciative modalities manifest his dispersion. To the various statuses, the various sites, the various positions that he can occupy or be given when making a discourse. To the discontinuity of the planes from which he speaks." Ibid., 54, 149.

37. Pocock, *Virtue, Commerce, and History*, 34.

38. Ibid., 1–2.

39. Ibid., 30; my emphasis.

40. Ibid., 7.

41. Ibid., 9.

42. Ibid., 23.

43. Ibid., 25.

44. Ibid.

45. But we did not have to wait for contemporary literary critics to tell us this; it was precisely the desire to find in the text some communion between writer and reader that Hawthorne warned us against in the preface to *The Scarlet Letter*: "When he casts his leaves forth upon the wind," Hawthorne wrote, the author imagines himself addressing "the few who will understand him, better than most of his schoolmates and lifemates . . . as if the printed book, thrown at large on the wide world, were certain to find out the divided segment of the writer's own nature, and complete his circle of existence by

bringing him into communion with it." Nathaniel Hawthorne, *The Scarlet Letter* (New York: American Penguin, 1973), 35.

46. Herman Melville, *Moby Dick* (New York: Bantam Classics, 1986), 156–57.

47. Pocock, *Virtue, Commerce, and History*, 8.

48. Ibid., 5.

49. Ibid., 25.

50. Hayden White has struggled with this same dilemma: on the one hand, an acute sensitivity to the ways language both constitutes and dissolves the subject; on the other hand, a deep commitment to liberal humanism, that is, to the human subject and his epistemological freedom. Hans Kellner has described White's dilemma with admirable deftness: "If language is irreducible, a 'sacred' beginning, then human freedom is sacrificed. If men are free to choose their linguistic protocols, then some deeper, prior, force must be posited. White asserts as an existential paradox that men are free, and that language is irreducible." Hans Kellner, "A Bedrock of Order: Hayden White's Linguistic Humanism," *History and Theory* 19, 4 (1980): 23.

51. Pocock, *Virtue, Commerce, and History*, 5.

52. Not all the discourse historians are so oblivious. Thomas Haskell, for example, has warned of a "profoundly deterministic" current in much of contemporary intellectual history, though this does not cause him to reconsider the call for a discourse-based history. See his "Deterministic Implications of Intellectual History," in Higham and Conkin, *New Directions*, 145.

53. John Dunn, *Political Obligation in Its Historical Context* (New York: Cambridge University Press, 1980), 15, as quoted by Richard Rorty in *Philosophy in History: Essays on the Historiography of Philosophy*, ed. Richard Rorty, J. B. Schneedwind, and Quentin Skinner (New York: Cambridge University Press, 1984).

54. Herbert Butterfield as quoted by George W. Stocking, "On the Limits of 'Presentism' and 'Historicism' in the Historiography of the Behavioral Sciences," in Stocking, *Race, Culture, and Evolution: Essays in the History of Anthropology* (New York: Free Press, 1968), 3.

55. Hollinger, "Historians and the Discourse of Intellectuals," 54.

56. In practice this has come to mean the various specialized discourses of intellectuals, a history of "the communities of discourse in which they function, and of the varying relations they manifest toward the larger culture." See Dominick LaCapra, "Rethinking Intellectual History and Reading Texts," in LaCapra and Kaplan, *Modern European Intellectual History*, 69. But see also the symposium on Intellectual History and the History of Discourses, *Intellectual History Newsletter* 1 (spring 1979), especially the pieces by Thomas Haskell, Bruce Kuklick, George Stocking, Quentin Skinner, David Hall, and William R. Taylor.

57. Both David Hollinger and Thomas Haskell use the term radical contextualism. See Hollinger, "T. S. Kuhn's Theory of Science and Its Implications for History," *American Historical Review* 78 (1973): 377, and Haskell, "Deterministic Implications," 138. The contextualists are well placed, well organized, and increasingly intolerant of alternative approaches. See LaCapra, "Grubbing

in My Personal Archives," and the discussion of Diggins's *The Bard of Savagery* below.

58. I have chosen not to deal here with a collateral problem: that the concept of a discourse implies the anterior concept of (and identification of) historical "periods." For an insightful discussion of this problem, see Fredric Jameson, *The Political Unconscious: Narrative as a Socially Symbolic Act* (London: Methuen, 1981), 28.

59. Thomas Haskell, "Veblen on Capitalism: Intellectual History in and out of Context," *Reviews in American History* 7 (1979): 559.

60. Hollinger, "Historians and the Discourse of Intellectuals," 55.

61. See Stocking, "On the Limits of 'Presentism' and 'Historicism,'" his essay in *Intellectual History Newsletter* (referred to in note 56 above), and the introduction to George W. Stocking Jr., *Victorian Anthropology* (New York: Free Press, 1987).

62. See the review by George Levine, *New York Times Book Review*, 1 March 1987.

63. Dominick LaCapra as paraphrased by Kloppenberg, "Deconstruction and Hermeneutic Strategies," 18.

64. As LaCapra has pointed out, "the context itself would have to be seen as a text of sorts. Its 'reading' and interpretation pose problems as difficult as those posed by the most intricate written text." Dominick LaCapra, *Rethinking Intellectual History: Texts, Contexts, Language* (Ithaca: Cornell University Press, 1983), 116–17.

65. "The age already in the past is in fact constituted in every respect as a text." Derrida, *Of Grammatology*, lxxxix; emphasis in the original. Fredric Jameson makes the same point: the context is not "immediately present as such, [is] not some common-sense external reality . . . but rather must itself always be reconstituted after the fact." Jameson, *Political Unconscious*, 81.

66. James as quoted by Richard Poirier, *The Renewal of Literature: Emersonian Reflections* (New York: Random House, 1987), 48; emphasis in the original.

67. As John Toews remarked after a discussion of the inevitable textualization of context, "One begins to wonder if it is possible to avoid the pitfalls of referential or representational theory at all without ceasing to 'do' history and restricting oneself to thinking about it." Toews, "Intellectual History after the Linguistic Turn: The Autonomy of Meaning and the Irreducibility of Experience," *American Historical Review* 92 (October 1987): 886. On the difficulty of identifying the "proper" context in advance, see Stefan Collini, "Interpretation Terminable and Interminable," in *Interpretation and Overinterpretation*, ed. Umberto Eco et al. (New York: Cambridge University Press, 1992), 13.

68. In addition to LaCapra's complaints, cited in note 71 below, see those of Norman Grabo and Patricia Caldwell in *The American Puritan Imagination: Essays in Revaluation*, comp. Sacvan Bercovitch (New York: Cambridge University Press, 1974), 26, 33, and 36.

69. Hollinger, "Historians and the Discourse of Intellectuals," 53.

70. "There is at present an excessive tendency to give priority to social and sociocultural approaches and to downgrade the importance of reading and interpreting *complex texts*." LaCapra, "Rethinking Intellectual History," 83. LaCapra

criticizes this tendency. Hollinger, on the other hand, wants us to go even further in that direction. He would have us approach complex texts in a thoroughly instrumental fashion, using them to illuminate the discourse of which they are but manifestations. See Hollinger, "Historians and the Discourse of Intellectuals," 43, 44.

71. LaCapra, "Rethinking Intellectual History," 83. See Hayden White, "The Context in the Text: Method and Ideology in Intellectual History," in White, *The Content of the Form: Narrative Discourse and Historical Representation* (Baltimore: Johns Hopkins University Press, 1987), 185–213, for an interesting discussion of this tendency. One of the ironies of contextualism is that in his attraction to, affinity for, and complicity with scientific rigor, the contextualist historian resembles no one so much as his archantagonist the deconstructionist critic. See Eugene Goodheart, *The Skeptic Disposition in Contemporary Criticism* (Princeton: Princeton University Press, 1984), 149–54, for an interesting discussion of deconstruction along these lines.

72. Northrop Frye as quoted by Jonathan Culler in his foreword to Tzvetan Todorov, *The Poetics of Prose* (Ithaca: Cornell University Press, 1977), 7.

73. Intertextuality is most closely associated with Roland Barthes (*From Work to Text*) and Julia Kristeva (*Desire in Language*), but the idea is hardly new with them. Jorge Borges, for example, has been playing with the notion for years. See his story "The Circular Ruins," in Borges, *Fictions* (1962), for a good example. For an attempt to save the autonomous text from the maw of intertextuality, see Stanley Fish, *Is There a Text in This Class: The Authority of Interpretive Communities* (Cambridge: Harvard University Press, 1980), and Geoffrey H. Hartman, *Saving the Text: Literature, Derrida, Philosophy* (Baltimore: Johns Hopkins University Press, 1981), esp. chapter 5, "Words and Wounds."

74. LaCapra makes the same point. See "Rethinking Intellectual History," 51. The problems and disagreements have less to do with identifying canonical works than with deciding how to interpret them. For an interesting discussion of (and response to) recent attacks on the canon in American literary history, see Werner Sollors, "A Critique of Pure Pluralism," in *Reconstructing American Literary History*. ed. Sacvan Bercovitch (Cambridge: Harvard University Press, 1986), 250–79.

75. Wolfgang Iser as quoted by Jerome Bruner, *Actual Minds, Possible Worlds* (Cambridge: Harvard University Press, 1986), 25. Iser believes this sort of reading is "unique to literature" (Iser, *The Act of Reading: A Theory of Aesthetic Response* [Baltimore: Johns Hopkins University Press, 1978], 109), but he nowhere explains why it cannot be applied to other narrative forms as well.

76. Roland Barthes, *The Pleasure of the Text*, trans. Richard Miller (New York: Hill and Wang, 1975), 6; emphasis in the original.

77. LaCapra, "Rethinking Intellectual History," 65. But see also Dominick LaCapra, *History and Criticism* (Ithaca: Cornell University Press, 1985), 18ff. and 38ff.

78. Frank Kermode, *Forms of Attention* (Chicago: University of Chicago Press, 1985).

79. Ibid., 75.

80. Iser, *Act of Reading,* 7. "Instead of being able to grasp meaning like an object, the critic is confronted by an empty space. And this emptiness cannot be filled by a single referential meaning, and any attempt to reduce it in this way leads to nonsense" (8).

81. Hayden White also draws a distinction between the comic books and the "classic texts." The difference "has to do with the extent to which the classic text reveals, indeed actively draws attention to, its own processes of meaning production and makes of these processes its own subject matter, its own 'content.' " *The Education of Henry Adams* is thus a classic text because of its "self-conscious and self-celebrating creativity." White, *Content of the Form,* 212.

82. In "The Limits of Historical Explanation," *Philosophy* 41 (1966): 199–215, for example, Skinner launched a devastating attack on "the influence model"—by which he meant the habit of treating earlier writers as if they were anticipating subsequent writers. Three years later he offered a greatly expanded version of that critique in "Meaning and Understanding in the History of Ideas," *History and Theory* 8 (1969): 3–53.

83. John G. Gunnell, *Political Theory: Tradition and Interpretation* (Cambridge, Mass.: Winthrop, 1979), 68. What is surprising is that this ideal construct should ever have been mistaken for a genuine historical tradition. Way back in 1919 T. S. Eliot explained that "the existing monuments form an *ideal* order among themselves, which is modified by the introduction of the new (the really new) work among them." "Tradition and the Individual Talent," in Eliot, *Selected Essays* (London: Faber and Faber, 1934), 15; my emphasis. Nevertheless, both contemporary history of philosophy and contemporary philosophy of history have been very largely shaped (or misshaped) by the "revelation" Gunnell describes. As David Hoy recently explained, "the really fundamental split in contemporary philosophy . . . is between those (like Dewey, Heidegger, Cavell, Kuhn, Feyerabend, and Habermas) who take Hegel and history seriously, and those who see 'recurring philosophical problems' being discussed by everybody." Hoy, "Taking History Seriously: Foucault, Gadamer, Habermas," *Union Seminary Quarterly Review,* winter 1979, 85.

84. Luther as quoted by Handelman, *Slayers of Moses,* 123.

85. See Brevard Childs's critical review of James Barr, *Holy Scripture: Canon, Authority, Criticism* (Philadelphia: Westminster, 1983), in *Interpretation* 38 (1984): 69–70.

86. Gadamer, *Truth and Method,* xix.

87. Eliot, "Tradition and the Individual Talent," 14.

88. J. G. A. Pocock as quoted by William Brock in "Questioning What American Stands For," *Times Literary Supplement,* 8–14 September 1989, 979.

89. I am indebted to Joyce Appleby for this insight. See Appleby, "One Good Turn Deserves Another: Moving beyond the Linguistic: A Response to David Harlan," *American Historical Review* 94 (December 1989): 1326–32.

90. F. R. Ankersmit, "Historiography and Postmodernism," *History and Theory* 28, 2 (1989): 150. See also the response to Ankersmit's article by Perez Zagorin, "Historiography and Postmodernism: Some Reconsiderations," *History and Theory* 29 (October 1990): 263–74, and Ankersmit's "Reply to Professor Zagorin," ibid., 275–96.

91. Gershom Scholem, *The Messianic Idea in Judaism and Other Essays on Jewish Spirituality* (New York: Schocken, 1971), 295.

92. Emmanuel Levinas as quoted by Handelman, *Slayers of Moses,* 172; emphasis in the original.

93. As quoted by Scholem, *Messianic Idea,* 289. Frank Kermode makes this notion of Torah the very definition of canonicity: "To be inside the canon is to be credited with indefinitely large numbers of possible internal relations and secrets, to be treated as a heterocosm, a miniature Torah." Kermode, *Forms of Attention,* 90.

94. Seder Nezikin, Tractate Baba Metzia, 58b—59b (10:351—52 of Baba Metzia in the Soncino translation).

95. E. P. Thompson, *The Making of the English Working Class* (1963; New York: Pantheon, 1964), 12—13; Richard Rorty, *Consequences of Pragmatism* (Minneapolis: University of Minnesota Press, 1982), 200ff., esp. 202.

96. For a celebration of one contemporary historian's determination to do just that (in this case to recover "the authentic, historical [William] James," to "confront James head-on, and to establish what his works said in the context in which he wrote them") see James T. Kloppenberg, "Deconstruction and Hermeneutic Strategies," 3—22, esp. 18—19. Kloppenberg contrasts Hollinger's traditional commitment to the historical subject with LaCapra's "self-defeating" deconstructive approach. Kloppenberg is afraid that LaCapra's method will "make writing history impossible" (7).

97. Anna Smith, "The Death of the Critic?" *Untold,* September 1987, 32—43.

98. The distinction between moral and epistemological privilege is Rorty's; see *Consequences,* 202.

99. Kermode, *Forms of Attention,* 75.

100. P. F. Strawson, *The Bounds of Sense: An Essay on Kant's "Critique of Pure Reason"* (London: Methuen, 1966). Rorty, in Rorty, Schneedwind, and Skinner, *Philosophy in History,* 49.

101. Rorty, Scheedwind, and Skinner, *Philosophy in History,* 52. This is precisely the practice Skinner condemned as "the Mythology of Coherence." See Skinner, "Meaning and Understanding," 16—20.

102. Pocock, for example, concedes that "restating the thought of ancients and predecessors in the language of one's own day" may be a "proper" and "legitimate" activity, but he insists that it is "obviously no part of the historian's business." Pocock, *Politics, Language, and Time,* 6, 8.

103. Toews, "Intellectual History," 891; Thomas Haskell, "Reply by Thomas Haskell," *Intellectual History Newsletter* 3 (1981): 29; Skinner, "Meaning and Understanding," 49. David Hollinger provides a good example of the position that has come to dominate intellectual history in America.

104. Historians are not the only ones to think so. In *The Aims of Interpretation* E. D. Hirsch distinguished "meaning" from "significance," the former being "the author's original meaning," the meaning she intended to convey, the latter referring to what later interpreters have found in the work (which Hirsch also calls "anachronistic meaning"). Hirsch insists that we cannot discuss a work's

"significance" until we have first determined its "meaning." Hirsch, *The Aims of Interpretation* (Chicago: University of Chicago Press, 1976), 79. Michael Ayers has drawn up a similar modus operandi for historians of philosophy. Ayers, "Analytical Philosophy and the History of Philosophy," in *Philosophy and Its Past*, ed. Jonathan Rée, Michael Ayers, and Adam Westoby (Hassocks, Eng.: Harvester, 1978). Quentin Skinner has gone even further, arguing that historians should avoid any discussion about the contemporary significance of the writers they study. Such discussion is "parasitic on the basic task of trying to recover how we think a given writer intended us to take his text." Skinner, "Hermeneutics and History," 219.

105. This is Rorty's description of the later work of Wittgenstein, Heidegger, and Dewey. See Rorty, *Philosophy and the Mirror of Nature* (Princeton: Princeton University Press, 1980), 5. Also, see Rorty's discussion of the difference between "systematic" and "edifying" philosophy in ibid., 365–72.

106. The phrase is Milton's, of course, by way of Harold Bloom, *The Breaking of the Vessels* (Chicago: University of Chicago Press, 1982), 3.

107. Kermode, *Forms of Attention*, 20.

108. As Roland Barthes put it, "A text's unity lies not in its origin but in its destination." Barthes, *Image, Music, Text* (New York: Hill and Wang, 1977), 148. Paul Rabinow and William Sullivan are even more emphatic about this: "Let us be clear. What we want to understand is not something behind the cultural object, the text, but rather something in front of it." Rabinow and Sullivan, eds., *Interpretive Social Science: A Reader* (Berkeley: University of California Press, 1979), 12. For an discussion of legal interpretation along the same lines, see Ronald Dworkin, "Law as Interpretation," *Critical Inquiry* 9 (September 1982): 193ff. Susan Sontag once complained that the historian or commentator too often "digs behind the text, to find a subtext [or 'discourse'] which is the true one. . . . The modern style of interpretation excavates, and as it excavates, destroys." Sontag, *Against Interpretation, and Other Essays* (New York: Anchor, 1966), 25.

109. Chomsky, *Language and Mind*, enl. ed. (New York: Harcourt Brace Jovanovich, 1972), 16.

110. For a stinging attack on Chomsky's "curious procedure in historical research and argument" see Hans Aarsleff, *From Locke to Saussure: Essays on the Study of Language and Intellectual History* (Minneapolis: University of Minnesota Press, 1982), 101–19. Aarsleff takes Chomsky to task for violating "the proper principles" of historical research, especially for failing to respect "the over-all coherence" of the period he studies (102). But as will be apparent below, Aarsleff has criticized Chomsky for failing to write a book he had no intention of writing.

111. Noam Chomsky, *Cartesian Linguistics: A Chapter in the History of Rationalist Thought* (New York: Harper and Row, 1966), 73.

112. Ibid., 2.

113. Noam Chomsky as quoted in Elders, *Reflexive Water*, 143.

114. Chomsky, *Cartesian Linguistics*, 3. In the introduction he says he wants to discover new ways to "exploit" Cartesian linguistics.

115. Chomsky, *Language and Mind*, 23.

116. Herbert Levine, "The Key to All Revolutions?" *Virginia Quarterly Review* 62 (summer 1986): 531.

117. Michael Walzer, *Exodus and Revolution* (New York: Basic, 1985), 8.

118. Ibid., 7.

119. For a recent expression of the belief that intellectual historians must address themselves to "the investigation of the contextually situated production and transmission of meaning," see Toews, "Intellectual History," 882. Toews believes intellectual historians "*must* address the issue of explanation, of why certain meanings arise, persist, and collapse at particular times and in specific sociocultural situations" (ibid.; my emphasis). Compare this formulation with the question Walzer thinks it important to ask: "Why is this story [Exodus] so endlessly reinvented? That is what I have tried to explain." Walzer, *Exodus and Revolution*, x. Toews's question moves us outside the text, away from the story it tells; Walzer's question can be answered only by moving *inside* the text, by asking, What is it about this particular text that has made it so generative for so many peoples at so many historical moments? Why is it that this particular story has made it possible for so many people to create so many stories of their own, each one germinated from the original text but each one new and uniquely empowering?

120. Walzer, *Exodus and Revolution*, 61, 7.

121. Ibid., 59, x; my emphasis.

122. John P. Diggins, *The Bard of Savagery: Thorstein Veblen and Modern Social Theory* (New York: Seabury, 1978), xi.

123. Haskell, "Veblen on Capitalism," 559.

124. Ibid., 559–60.

125. Dorothy Ross, review of Diggins, *The Bard of Savagery*, *American Historical Review* 84 (1979): 1179.

126. Note, however, that this interrogation will necessarily be mediated by the defamiliarization of the *present* produced by our encounter with the past. See Gadamer's discussion of the "fusion of horizons" (Gadamer, *Truth and Method*, 273ff., 337, 358) and Anthony Giddens's discussion of this "double hermeneutic" in Giddens, *New Rules of Sociological Method: A Positive Critique of Interpretive Sociologies* (New York: Basic, 1976), 158.

127. By using the word our I do not mean to imply a consensus concerning either questions *or* needs; I mean our *various and usually conflicting* questions, needs, and discourses. For an illuminating debate on this point, see Richard Bernstein, "One Step Forward, Two Steps Backward: Richard Rorty on Liberal Democracy and Philosophy," paper delivered at the Yale Law School Legal Theory Workshop, 5 November 1987 (mimeograph), 22, 24, and Rorty's response at the same workshop, "Thugs and Theorists: A Reply to Bernstein."

128. Rorty, in Rorty, Scheedwind, and Skinner, *Philosophy in History*, 6–7.

129. The conventional becomes "undoable," of course, only if one questions the epistemological assumptions on which the conventional has been built. But as Frank Kermode has pointed out, one need not ask such questions: "As long as we do things as they have generally been done—as long, that is, as the institution which guarantees our studies upholds the fictions which give them

value—we shall continue to write historical narrative as if it were an altogether different matter from making fictions, or *a fortiori,* from telling lies." Kermode, *The Genesis of Secrecy: On the Interpretation of Narrative* (Cambridge: Harvard University Press, 1979), 109. One leading American historian who thinks historians ought not to ask such questions is James Kloppenberg. He advises his colleagues to ignore the more virulent forms of contemporary criticism and get back to work. Like Roosevelt telling the nation it has nothing to fear but fear itself, Kloppenberg wants to reassure his colleagues that they can ride out the current wave of epistemological skepticism by simply maintaining "the courage of their conventions" (Kloppenberg, "Deconstruction and Hermeneutic Strategies," 8). Gordon Wood has also cautioned his colleagues against speculating about the "traditional" set of assumptions underlying and authorizing intellectual history. "Historians who cut loose from this faith," he warns, "do so at the peril of their discipline." Gordon Wood, "Writing History: An Exchange," *New York Review of Books,* 16 December 1982, 59.

130. Rorty, of course, has said much the same thing about philosophy. See *Consequences of Pragmatism,* 211–30, esp. 225–27. The most insistent call for such a paradigm for historical studies has come from David Hollinger. Hollinger believes that if an intellectual community expects to play an effective role in the larger culture it must organize itself around a set of shared commitments— commitments defined with enough rigor to "delimit problems, direct research, and establish criteria of judgment." See Hollinger, *In the American Province: Studies in the History and Historiography of Ideas* (Bloomington: University of Indiana Press, 1985), 177–81. Rabinow and Sullivan have characterized the enduring hope for such a paradigm as "the cargo-cult view of the 'about to arrive' science. . . . The time seems ripe, even overdue, to announce that there is not going to be an age of paradigm in the social sciences." Rabinow and Sullivan, *Interpretive Social Science,* 4. Derrida has also criticized the attempt "to reconstitute a system of essential predicates" that might govern the writing of history. "There is not one single history . . . but rather histories *different* as to their kind, their rhythm, their mode of inscription, unbalanced, differentiated histories, etc."—which is why he uses the word history "with quotation marks and precautions." Derrida, Interview with J.-L Houdebine and Guy Scarpetta, *Diacritics* 2 (winter 1972): 42, 43. Nevertheless, John Toews thinks we may even now be witnessing the emergence of just such a "consensual community." See Toews, "Intellectual History," 881ff. But see also John Higham, *History: Professional Scholarship in America* (Baltimore: Johns Hopkins University Press, 1983), 241.

CHAPTER TWO

1. Hebrews 13.
2. The literature on Perry Miller is voluminous. But see Francis T. Butts, "The Myth of Perry Miller," *American Historical Review* 87 (June 1982): 665–94; Ann Douglas, "The Mind of Perry Miller," *New Republic,* 3 February 1982, 26–30; David Hollinger, "Perry Miller and Philosophical History," *History and Theory* 7, 2 (1968): 189–202; James Hoopes, "Art as History: Perry Miller's *New England Mind*," *American Quarterly* 34 (spring 1982): 5–25; Robert M. Cal-

hoon, "Perry Miller," in *Dictionary of Literary Biography: Twentieth-Century American Historians* (Detroit: Gale, 1983), 272–85. See also the second issue of *Harvard Review*, which is entirely devoted to Miller's work and contains the following important articles: Donald Fleming, "Perry Miller and Esoteric History," *Harvard Review* 2 (1964): 25–29; Alan Heimert, "Perry Miller: An Appreciation," ibid., 30–48; Reinhold Niebuhr, "Perry Miller and Our Embarrassment," ibid., 49–51; and Edmund S. Morgan, "Perry Miller and the Historians," ibid., 52–59.

3. William Carlos Williams, "To Elsie," in *Selected Poems* (New York: New Directions, 1985), 55.

4. Contrast the situation among literary and intellectual historians of early America with Cornel West's description of "the contemporary intellectual scene in North America" generally: "After an obsession with European theories and philosophies, we are discovering some of what is needed in the American heritage. This intellectual turn to our heritage . . . is a symptom of just how blinded we often are to certain riches in the American intellectual and political past." West, *The American Evasion of Philosophy: A Genealogy of Pragmatism* (Madison: University of Wisconsin Press, 1989), 4.

5. One suspects that William Spengemann, the historian of early American literature, struck close to home when he wrote that "like the Plymouth pilgrims themselves, we chose this stony soil not for its riches but because no one else wanted it." Spengemann, "Discovering the Literature of British America," *Early American Literature* 18 (spring 1983): 3.

6. For a contrary and crucial discussion of Puritanism (or Calvinism) and its traditional place in American political culture, see John Patrick Diggins, *The Lost Soul of American Politics: Virtue, Self-Interest, and the Foundations of Liberalism* (New York: Basic, 1984). Diggins demonstrates that Calvinism and liberalism have been the dominant traditions in American thought and writing, with Calvinism serving as "the conscience of American liberalism." That liberalism in this country has its roots in Calvinist theology has meant that it possessed a particular moral vision, that it carried within it "the seeds of its own condemnation, particularly in its fostering of capitalism" (7).

7. See Edmund S. Morgan, "The Chosen People," *New York Review of Books*, 19 July 1979, 33. See also Norman Fiering's remark that "Sacvan Bercovitch in *The Puritan Origins of the American Self* (1975) has educed brilliantly the *Magnalia's* significance as the founding document of the American sense of destiny, 'the supreme colonial expression of what we have come to term the myth of America.'" Fiering, "The First American: Cotton Mather," *Reviews in American History* 12 (December 1984): 479. Nina Baym says that although Bercovitch writes in Miller's "shadow," "he is clearly the leading candidate to succeed Perry Miller as authority on the Puritans." Baym, review of *The American Jeremiad* and *The Puritan Origins of the American Self*, *Nineteenth Century Fiction* 34 (December 1979): 350. Leo Marx contends that Bercovitch "can be said to have filled in one motif in the grand design of New England intellectual history that Perry Miller had projected but left unfinished at his death in 1963." Marx, review of *The Puritan Origins of the American Self* by Sacvan Bercovitch, *New York Times Book Review*, 1 February 1976, 21. See also Alan Trachtenberg,

"The Writer as America," *Partisan Review* 44, 3 (1977): 468; Cushing Strout, "Paradoxical Puritans," *American Scholar* 45 (autumn 1976): 602; and David Hall, "On Common Ground," *William and Mary Quarterly* 44 (April 1987): 197–98. Like others, Marx suggests that, while modifying some specifics of Miller's argument, Bercovitch is essentially extending his vision. Robert Berkhofer, on the other hand, has recently suggested that Bercovitch's work may constitute not an extension of Miller's vision but an entirely new methodological paradigm for American studies. See Robert Berkhofer Jr., "A New Context for a New American Studies?" *American Quarterly* 41 (December 1989): 603. For a critique of Bercovitch's work from the left, see Donald Pease, "New Americanists: Revisionist Interventions into the Canon," *Boundary 2* 17 (spring 1990): 1–37, esp. 19–23. Among scholars of early American history, Bercovitch's citations in the *Social Science Citation Index* are second only to those of Miller himself.

8. Far from merely extending Miller's interpretation, Bercovitch, along with Emory Elliott, Larzer Ziff, Ursula Brumm, and some others, brought about what David Hall has called a "veritable revolution in our understanding of the Puritan 'imagination.'" See Hall, "On Common Ground," 195. The founding of *Early American Literature* in 1966 is the first and clearest indication that a new point of view was about to challenge Miller's authority.

9. Sacvan Bercovitch, *The American Jeremiad* (Madison: University of Wisconsin Press, 1978), xv.

10. "We know no time when we were not as now; / Know none before us, self-begot, self-rais'd / By our own quick'ning power" (Milton, *Paradise Lost*, book 5, lines 859–61).

11. "Giant cryptogram" is Edmund Morgan's phrase. See Morgan, "Perry Miller and the Historians," 57.

12. The most important of these early pieces are Sacvan Bercovitch, "New England Epic: Cotton Mather's *Magnalia Christi Americana*," *English Literary History* 33 (September 1966): 337–50; idem, "Typology in Puritan New England: The Williams-Cotton Controversy Reassessed," *American Quarterly* 19 (summer 1967): 166–91; idem, "The Historiography of Johnson's *Wonder-Working Providence*," *Essex Institute Historical Collections* 104 (April 1968): 138–61; idem, "Horologicals to Chronometricals: The Rhetoric of the Jeremiad," *Literary Monographs* 3 (1970): 1–124, 187–215; idem, "'Delightful Examples of Surprising Prosperity': Cotton Mather and the American Success Story," *English Studies* (the Netherlands) 51 (February 1970): 40–43; idem, "Puritan New England Rhetoric and the Jewish Problem," *Early American Literature* 5 (fall 1970): 63–71; and idem, "Cotton Mather," in *Major Writers of Early American Literature*, ed. Everett Emerson (Madison: University of Wisconsin Press, 1972), 93–149.

13. Bercovitch, "Typology in Puritan New England," 166–91.

14. Vernon Parrington, *Main Currents in American Thought: An Interpretation of American Literature from the Beginnings to 1920*, 3 vols. (New York: Harcourt, Brace, 1927–30), 1:62–75.

15. Perry Miller, *Roger Williams: His Contribution to the American Tradition* (Boston: Beacon, 1953); Perry Miller, "Roger Williams: An Essay in Interpreta-

tion," in *Complete Writings of Roger Williams*, rev. ed., ed. Perry Miller (New York: Russell and Russell, 1963), 7:5–25.

16. And like Foucault's notion of episteme (and his later notions of "archive"), rhetoric also works on the principles of association and exclusion, extension and repression. For Foucault on the idea of episteme, see Michel Foucault, *The Order of Things: An Archaeology of the Human Sciences* (New York: Pantheon, 1971); for Foucault on "archive," see Foucault, *The Archaeology of Knowledge* (New York: Pantheon, 1972).

17. See Sacvan Bercovitch, *The American Puritan Imagination: Essays in Revaluation* (New York: Cambridge University Press, 1974), esp. "The American Puritan Imagination: An Introduction," 1–16.

18. Bercovitch, "Typology in Puritan New England," 167. As Donald Fleming described it, typology is "the art of reading the Old Testament as a gigantic treasury of symbolic adumbrations of the New—Jonah swallowed and spewed out again by the whale as a 'type' of the future death and resurrection of Christ." Fleming, "Perry Miller and Esoteric History," 28. Karen Rowe contends, like Bercovitch, that there were two typological traditions, one historical, typified in the thought of John Cotton, the other Christ-centered, vehemently antihistorical, and best expressed in Roger Williams's essays and Edward Taylor's poems. Rowe, *Saint and Singer: Edward Taylor's Typology and the Poetics of Meditation* (New York: Cambridge University Press, 1986). On the other hand, Philip Gura contends that Puritan radicals were not typologists at all. See Gura, *A Glimpse of Sion's Glory: Puritan Radicalism in New England, 1620–1660* (Middletown, Conn.: Wesleyan University Press, 1984).

19. Though he admitted that Cotton had experimented with typology, Miller thought Cotton was exceptional in this. "Almost to a man the New England theologians, especially such vigorous leaders as Thomas Hooker and Peter Bulkeley, were so content with the consistency of their covenant or 'federal' version of the Bible that they saw in typology only a fantastic creation of the imagination which had no place in sound scholarship or in orthodox society." Miller, *Roger Williams*, 37. For an interesting critical discussion of what he calls "Miller's blindness to typology," see Everett Emerson, "Perry Miller and the Puritans: A Literary Scholar's Assessment," *History Teacher* 14 (August 1981): 459–67, esp. 463–67. Emerson believes Miller "failed to recognize the importance of typology in New England Puritanism" and, more generally, that he "denigrated the Puritan imagination" (466). See also Ursula Brumm, *American Thought and Religious Typology*, trans. John Hoaglund (New Brunswick, N.J.: Rutgers University Press, 1970), and Sacvan Bercovitch, ed., *Typology and Early American Literature* (Amherst: University of Massachusetts Press, 1972). For the argument that typology influenced not only the Puritans but virtually all of later American intellectual and literary history through the eighteenth and nineteenth centuries, see Mason I. Lowance, *The Language of Canaan* (New York: Cambridge University Press, 1980).

20. Bercovitch, "Typology in Puritan New England," 167.

21. Bercovitch thinks typology was "especially pronounced" in Puritan New England. Ibid., 180.

22. Ibid., 189.

23. Ibid., 169.

24. Though this will not become fully evident until "Horologicals to Chronometricals" appears in 1970, three years after "Typology in Puritan New England." See Bercovitch, "Horologicals to Chronometricals, 1–124, 187–215. As we shall see, this becomes the central argument of *The American Jeremiad.*

25. He will make this explicit in *The American Jeremiad:* "In America, the foundations of that system were laid in 17th century New England. . . . Within the first half century [the Puritans] had established the central tenets of what was to become (in Raymond Williams's phrase) our 'dominant culture.' " Bercovitch, *American Jeremiad,* xiii.

26. Ibid., 176.

27. This is very much like Terry Eagleton's notion of a "general ideology." See Eagleton, *Criticism and Ideology: A Study in Marxist Literary Theory* (London: NLB, 1976), 54–60. For another example of American history written in this mode, see Walter Benn Michaels, *The Gold Standard and the Logic of Naturalism: American Literature at the Turn of the Century* (Berkeley: University of California Press, 1987).

28. Bercovitch, "Typology in Puritan New England," 189.

29. Both Trachtenberg and Strout use this phrase in their reviews, but neither gives a reference.

30. "As my scope is wide, I have chosen a narrow focus." Sacvan Bercovitch, *The Puritan Origins of the American Self* (New Haven: Yale University Press, 1975), ix. Bercovitch has reprinted Mather's "Life of Winthrop" as an appendix to *Puritan Origins.*

31. Ibid., ix.

32. Ibid., 145.

33. Ibid., 1.

34. Ibid., 136.

35. Ibid., 143. "In retrospect, it seems clear that the Puritan myth prepared for the re-vision of God's country from the 'New England of the type' into the United States of America."

36. Ibid., 136.

37. Ibid., 184.

38. Ibid., 183, 173, 136, ix; Trachtenberg, "Writer as America," 469.

39. Bercovitch, *Puritan Origins,* 180, 169, 179.

40. See, for example, Nina Baym, review of *The American Jeremiad* and *Puritan Origins of the American Self* by Bercovitch, 348.

41. Bercovitch, *American Jeremiad,* 142.

42. Ibid., xii.

43. Ibid., xiii–xiv.

44. Ibid., 13, 115, 141. The idea of Puritan rhetoric as an instrument of social control had been broached in *Puritan Origins.* On page 134 Bercovitch wrote that the Puritans "had devised their rhetoric, after all, as a means of social control." But this was the only mention of "social control" in the whole book. On the jeremiad as a prisonhouse of the mind, Bercovitch's argument is essentially an inversion of the argument Louis Hartz first presented in *The Liberal Tradition in America: An Interpretation of American Political Thought since the*

Revolution (New York: Harcourt, Brace, 1955), with Puritanism serving the function Hartz had attributed to liberalism. As Bercovitch puts it, "The future [Americans] appealed to was necessarily limited, by the very prophecies they vaunted, to the ideals of the past." Bercovitch, *American Jeremiad,* 179.

45. Bercovitch, "New England's Errand Reappraised," in *New Directions in American Intellectual History,* ed. John Higham and Paul Conkin (Baltimore: Johns Hopkins University Press, 1979), 85.

46. Perry Miller, "Errand into the Wilderness," in Miller, *Errand into the Wilderness* (Cambridge: Harvard University Press, 1956), 2.

47. Bercovitch, "New England's Errand Reappraised," 87; Bercovitch, *American Jeremiad,* 6, 7.

48. "The exhortation to a reformation which never materializes serves as a token payment upon the obligation, and so liberates the debtors. . . . Under the guise of this mounting wail of sinfulness, this incessant and never successful cry for repentance, the Puritans launched themselves upon the process of Americanization." Miller, "Errand into the Wilderness," 9. Francis Butts has argued that Bercovitch "seriously misconstrued Miller and then offered as an alternative an interpretation that is in fact quite similar to Miller's. . . . Miller's portrait of the 'classic' jeremiad does indeed stress its ambivalence." Butts, "Myth of Perry Miller," 686-87. But Bercovitch's attitude toward Miller's interpretation is more complicated than this suggests. See, for example, his comments in *New Directions in American Intellectual History,* 85ff.

49. Bercovitch, *American Jeremiad,* 5–6, 10–11. "I am suggesting that 'the process of Americanization' began in Massachusetts not with the decline of Puritanism but with the Great Migration." This is "a fundamental truth about our culture." Bercovitch, "New England's Errand Reappraised," 92. For an insightful discussion of Bercovitch's and Miller's contrasting interpretations of the jeremiad, see Butts, "Myth of Perry Miller," 686–88.

50. Perry Miller, *The New England Mind: The Seventeenth Century* (1939; Boston: Beacon, 1961), xii. In 1959 Miller wrote, "I had commenced my work within an emotional universe dominated by H. L. Mencken. My contemporaries and I came of age in a time when the word 'Puritan' served as a comprehensive sneer against every tendency in American civilization which we held reprehensible—sexual diffidence, censorship, prohibition, theological fundamentalism, political hypocrisy, and all the social antics which Sinclair Lewis, among others, was stridently ridiculing." Perry Miller, *Orthodoxy in Massachusetts, 1630–1650* (Boston: Beacon, 1959), xviii. And see Miller's earlier recounting of the same episode in *Errand into the Wilderness,* in which his teachers told him that Puritanism as a field of study "was exhausted, all that wheat had long since been winnowed, there was nothing but chaff remaining." Miller, *Errand into the Wilderness,* viii.

51. On the solitary nature of Miller the historian, see Perry Miller, "The Plight of the Lone Wolf," in Miller, *The Responsibility of Mind in a Civilization of Machines,* ed. John Crowell and Stanford J. Searl Jr. (Amherst: University of Massachusetts Press, 1979), 8–14. The past ten years have produced several notable reassessments of Miller's work. Among the most interesting and instructive are Butts, "Myth of Perry Miller"; James Hoopes, "Art as History"; Emer-

son, "Perry Miller and the Puritans"; and Stanford Searl, "Perry Miller as Artist: Piety and Imagination in *The New England Mind: The Seventeenth Century,*" *Early American Literature* 12 (1977–78): 221–33.

52. See Randolph Bourne, "The Old Tyrannies," in Bourne, *The Radical Will: Selected Writings, 1911–1918* (New York: Urizen, 1977), 169–73.

53. As Andrew Delbanco recently remarked, "The historiographical revolution effected in the 1930s" by Morison, Murdock, and Miller "is proving to be insecure. We seem to be returning to an older, hostile view of the Puritans, as expressed in the 1920s by William Carlos Williams and recently summarized with sympathy by a sitting president of the Modern Language Association: the Puritans were the people, *tout court,* 'who massacred the Indians and established the self-righteous religion and politics that determined American ideology.'" Andrew Delbanco, *The Puritan Ordeal* (Cambridge: Harvard University Press, 1989), 7. For Miller on Puritanism as the original source of what he considered our finest values, see Perry Miller, "Individualism and the New England Tradition," in Miller, *Responsibility of Mind,* 26–44. For Bercovitch's counterview of Puritanism as the fountainhead of "possessive individualism" and "the laissez-faire state" in America, see Bercovitch, *American Jeremiad,* 107. For his identification of Puritanism and emergent capitalism, see Bercovitch, "New England's Errand Reappraised," 92. The following is typical of Bercovitch's perspective: "All of [John] Cotton's examples, from nature and the Bible, are geared toward sanctifying an errand of entrepreneurs whose aim is religion, or *mutatis mutandis* legalizing an errand of saints whose aim is entrepreneurial." Bercovitch, "New England's Errand Reappraised," 94. By way of contrast, Miller described himself as "one who reveres his ancestors." Miller as quoted by Donald Weber, review of *The Responsibility of Mind in a Civilization of Machines* by Perry Miller, *New England Quarterly* 53 (June 1980): 255.

54. Miller, *Responsibility of Mind,* 1.

55. Ibid.

56. Miller continually portrayed himself as an Adams-like figure, out of step with the twentieth-century world in which he found himself. For a typical example, see *Responsibility of Mind,* 8. The fin-de-siècle modernists and post–World War I writers also prepared Miller for Reinhold Niebuhr and the resurgence of neoorthodoxy in the 1920s and 1930s.

57. Miller as quoted by Donald Weber, review of *The Responsibility of Mind in a Civilization of Machines,* 255. On Miller's sense of alienation and personal isolation, see his autobiographcial essay "Plight of the Lone Wolf."

58. Miller, "Plight of the Lone Wolf," 3. Mann as quoted in Frank Lentricchia, *After the New Criticism* (Chicago: University of Chicago Press, 1980), 330.

59. Miller, *Responsibility of Mind,* 34, 32, 36, 15; Miller, *Errand into the Wilderness,* viii. Note, however, that Miller's estrangement never drove him as far as the position of Lionel Trilling, who at one point in 1930 wrote, "There is only one way to accept America and that is in hate; one must be close to one's land, passionately close in some way or other, and the only way to be close to America is to hate it." Trilling as quoted by Mark Krupnick, *Lionel Trilling and the Fate of Cultural Criticism* (Evanston, Ill.: Northwestern University Press, 1986), 40–41.

60. Miller, *Responsibility of Mind*, 10.

61. Ibid., 30.

62. "At the heart of Perry Miller's sense of Puritan decline was his feeling that the rise of materialistic capitalism betrayed Puritanism. Consequently Miller could use the Puritans as a stick to beat the Americans of his own day; by comparison with the Puritans, he implied, his contemporaries were decadent, self-indulgent, and unintellectual. Daniel Walker Howe, "Descendants of Perry Miller," *American Quarterly* 34 (1982): 91.

63. Miller, *Responsibility of Mind*, 36.

64. Ibid., 36.

65. Ibid., 35.

66. Ibid., 211. "An overall examination of American history from about 1815 gives no support to any contention that the religious solution is workable for more than a few votaries of particular persuasions" (203).

67. Michel Foucault, "The Subject and Power," in *Michel Foucault: Beyond Structuralism and Hermeneutics*, by Hubert L. Dreyfus and Paul Rabinow (Chicago: University of Chicago Press, 1982), 216; my emphasis.

68. Miller, *Responsibility of Mind*, 44.

69. Thomas Pynchon, *The Crying of Lot 49* (Philadelphia: Lippincott, 1966), 181.

70. Bercovitch, "New England's Errand Reappraised," 87.

71. Butts, "Myth of Perry Miller," 694.

72. For "The American ideology" see Sacvan Bercovitch, "Afterword," in *Ideology and Classic American Literature*, ed. Sacvan Bercovitch and Myra Jehlen (New York: Cambridge University Press, 1986), 428. For "the American way" see 432. For "the repressive force of the dominant culture" see 425. For "the American consensus" see Bercovitch, "The Ideological Context of the American Renaissance," in *Forms and Functions of History in American Literature: Essays in Honor of Ursula Brumm*, ed. Winfried Fluck, Jürgen Peper, and Willi Paul Adams (Berlin: Schmidt, 1981). "What I mean by the American consensus is neither a myth nor a statistic, but an ideology" (1). What Bercovitch means by "ideology" is best explained by Frederick Crews: it is "an attempt . . . to bind us to 'standards' that look eternally valid but merely reflect the liberal reluctance to embrace a non-hierarchical idea of culture." Crews, "Whose American Renaissance?" *New York Review of Books*, 27 October 1988, 80. See also Myra Jehlen's discussion of ideology—one to which Bercovitch would probably subscribe—in Jehlen, "Beyond Transcendence," in Bercovitch and Jehlen, *Ideology and Classic American Literature*, 1–18. For Bercovitch's own understanding of "ideology," see Sacvan Bercovitch, "The Problem of Ideology in American Literary History," *Critical Inquiry* 12 (summer 1986): 631–53.

73. See, for example, Howe, "Descendants of Perry Miller," 92; and Delbanco, *Puritan Ordeal*, 6.

74. See, for example, Bercovitch, "New England's Errand Reappraised," 92–93, 101 n. 8.

75. Hartz, *Liberal Tradition in America*, 6, 12, 9.

76. Bercovitch, *American Jeremiad*, 179; Hartz, *Liberal Tradition in America*, 11, 285.

77. Hartz, *Liberal Tradition in America*, 309.

78. Ibid., 12.

79. Ibid., 13; my emphasis.

80. Ibid., 287.

81. Ibid., 308. John P. Diggins has argued that "Hartz's ultimate aim or hope was not to establish the depths of the liberal tradition but somehow to find a way out of it." Diggins, "Knowledge and Sorrow: Louis Hartz's Quarrel with American History," *Political Theory* 16 (August 1988): 372. For a suggestion that Hartz did, in his later work, find "a way out," see Patrick Riley, "Louis Hartz: The Final Years, the Unknown Work," *Political Theory* 16 (August 1988): 377–99. I am indebted to Diggins for alerting me to Riley's article. For a more critical assessment of Hartz's argument, see Dorothy Ross, "The Liberal Tradition Revisited and the Republican Tradition Addressed," in Higham and Conkin, *New Directions*, 116–31. Ross believes that Hartz "narrowed and simplified the American mind" (116).

82. See Bercovitch, *American Jeremiad*, xiiin.

83. Sacvan Bercovitch, "The A-Politics of Ambiguity in *The Scarlet Letter*," *New Literary History* 19 (spring 1988): 651.

84. As both Frederick Crews and Gerald Graff have pointed out, this interpretation of American culture as monolithic and hegemonic had been anticipated by the counterculture of the 1960s. In Crews's words, it amounts to little more than "Marcuse's once modish notion of repressive tolerance retrofitted to the antebellum world." See Crews, "Whose American Renaissance?" 75; Gerald Graf, "Co-optation," in *The New Historicism*, ed. H. Aram Veeser (New York: Routledge, 1989), 169.

85. "To varying degrees, this strategy of fusion through fragmentation informs the entire course of American literary criticism." Bercovitch, "Afterword," 420. Stephen Greenblatt has warned against precisely this tendency: "[When] literature is viewed exclusively as the expression of social rules and instructions, it risks being absorbed entirely into an ideological superstructure. Marx himself vigorously resisted this function absorption of art." Greenblatt, *Renaissance Self-Fashioning: From More to Shakespeare* (Chicago: University of Chicago Press, 1980), 4.

86. Bercovitch, *American Jeremiad*, 28. It is, moreover, an astonishing rhetoric "that the rhetoric itself reflected and shaped."

87. Bercovitch and Jehlen, *Ideology and Classic American Literature*, xiii.

88. Note how this understanding inverts Gramsci's original meaning. Whereas Bercovitch portrays hegemony as a "historically organic formation," Gramsci had conceived of it as "a deliberate artifice rather than a natural phenomenon." And for Gramsci it was the "organic intellectuals" who possessed the "contradictory consciousness" necessary to undermine that hegemony. Bercovitch means to show us that intellectuals have always been ineffectual; Gramsci meant to show us that they have "a role, indeed the decisive role, in history's rendevous with reality." See John Patrick Diggins, "Gramsci and the Intellectuals," *Raritan* 9 (fall 1989): 132.

89. Bercovitch, "Problem of Ideology in American Literary History," 645.

90. Ibid.

91. Bercovitch, introduction to *American Puritan Imagination*, 5, 8, 7.

92. On the concept of cultural hegemony and its recent vicissitudes, see Diggins, "Gramsci and the Intellectuals"; T. Jackson Lears, "The Concept of Cultural Hegemony: Problems and Possibilities," *American Historical Review* 90 (June 1985): 567–93; Leon Fink, "The New Labor History and the Politics of Historical Pessimism: Consensus, Hegemony, and the Case of the Knights of Labor," *Journal of American History* 75 (June 1988): 115–36. See also the comments on Fink's piece, especially Lears, "Power, Culture and Memory," ibid., 137–40, and John Patrick Diggins, "The Misuses of Gramsci," ibid., 141–45.

93. Contrast this with M. M. Bakhtin's insistence that we approach every text as "a site whereon many discourses and genres meet, are subjected to parodistic defamiliarization, brought into communication or conflict with one another." See Hayden White, "The Authoritative Lie," *Partisan Review* 50 (1983): 308. Bercovitch insists that every book written in seventeenth-, eighteenth-, or nineteenth-century America must be read as the expression of a single overwhelming zeitgeist, what he calls "the American jeremiad" (not the Puritan jeremiad).

94. On the relation between Bercovitch's earlier and later work, see Philip F. Gura, "The Study of Colonial American Literature, 1966–87: A Vade Mecum," *William and Mary Quarterly* 45 (April 1988): 310.

95. Bercovitch, "Typology in Puritan New England," 171.

96. Bercovitch and Jehlen, *Ideology and Classic American Literature*, 420, 419.

97. Loren Baritz as quoted by Bercovitch, *American Jeremiad*, 194.

98. Ibid.

99. Bercovitch, "New England's Errand Reappraised," 99.

100. Bercovitch, *American Jeremiad*, 191.

101. Ibid., 190.

102. Ibid.

103. Ibid.

104. Ibid., 195.

105. Ibid., 196.

106. Ibid., 190.

107. Ibid., 180; emphasis in the original. Bercovitch and Jehlen, *Ideology and Classic American Literature*, 433.

108. Bercovitch, *American Jeremiad*, 193. Perhaps the most remarkable example of this logic is Walter Benn Michaels's insistence that even Bartleby's laconic "I prefer not" should be read as an affirmation of the capitalistic order. After all, "what could count as a more powerful exercise of the right to freedom of contract than Bartleby's successful refusal to enter into any contracts?" Bartleby thus "embodies . . . the purest of commitments to laissez-faire." Michaels, *Gold Standard and the Logic of Naturalism*, 19.

109. See Stephen Stein's criticism of Bercovitch's notion of the "anti-jeremiad" in Stein, review of *The American Jeremiad* by Sacvan Bercovitch, *American Historical Review* 84 (October 1979): 1142.

110. Bercovitch and Jehlen, *Ideology and Classic American Literature*, 433.

111. Bercovitch, *Puritan Origins*, 134.

112. Trachtenberg, "Writer as America," 472. In Bercovitch's *Wingspread* article, written in 1977, two years after *Puritan Origins*, he announced that "the concept of errand was a means of social control." But again, the idea was dropped into the text without elaboration or discussion. Bercovitch, "New England's Errand Reappraised," 100.

113. For example, here he is describing "the need to preclude alternatives": "We might say that the American ideology was made to fill that need. It undertakes, *above all, as a condition of its nurture* to absorb the spirit of protest for social ends. . . . It has accomplished this most effectively through its rhetoric of dissent. . . . Our classic texts re-present the strategies of a triumphant middle-class hegemony. Far from subverting the status quo," they "attest to the capacities of the dominant culture to co-opt alternative forms. . . . Having adopted the culture's *controlling* metaphor [emphasis in the original]—'America' as synonym for human possibility . . . they redefined radicalism itself as an affirmation of cultural values." Bercovitch, "Problem of Ideology in American Literary History," 645; my emphasis except where noted.

114. Bercovitch, *American Jeremiad*, 132, 134.

115. Ibid., 348.

116. Ibid., 141.

117. Ibid., esp. chap. 5, "The Ritual of Consensus." For Bercovitch's treatment of feminism, see 156–60. Bercovitch thinks the modernist sensibility or aesthetic serves only to reconfirm the very order it once promised to subvert. In this he would agree with Fredric Jameson: "The most influential formal impulses of canonical modernism have been strategies of inwardness, which set out to reappropriate an alienated universe by transforming it into personal styles and private languages: such wills to style have seemed in retrospect to reconfirm the very privatization and fragmentation of social life against which they were meant to protest. So it is that the initial, passionately subversive force of the modernist symbolic act is ever fainter and more distant for the contemporary reader." Jameson, *Fables of Aggression: Wyndham Lewis, the Modernist as Fascist* (Berkeley: University of California Press, 1979), 2.

118. Bercovitch and Jehlen, *Ideology and Classic American Literature*, 424, 428, 418.

119. Ibid., 433, 419–20, 432–33. As Donald Pease recently suggested, Bercovitch "uses his prior description of the American Jeremiad to subsume and co-opt the differences among his contributors." Pease, "New Americanists," 23.

120. Bercovitch and Jehlen, *Ideology and Classic American Literature*, 433. The book appeared in 1986; even a cursory glance at Bercovitch's subsequent work reveals him tilting at the same old monolith. For example, in "The A Politics of Ambiguity in *The Scarlet Letter*" (1988) we learn that Hawthorne's masterpiece "reflects the strategies of what we have come to term the American ideology. . . . *The Scarlet Letter* is not only a representation of ideologically mediated reality; it is a reenactment of the strategies by which liberalism established its dominance in antebellum America" (630, 652).

121. Lincoln as quoted by Diggins, *Lost Soul of American Politics*, 332.

122. Robert Daly, *God's Altar: The World and the Flesh in Puritan Poetry*

240 Notes to Pages 51–52

(Berkeley: University of California Press, 1978); Delbanco, *Puritan Ordeal;*
Charles Cohen, *God's Caress: The Psychology of Puritan Religious Experience*
(New York: Oxford University Press, 1986). Patricia Caldwell has recently ex-
plained why so many Puritan books give expression to what she calls "the more
sorrowful aspects of the Jewish experience." Caldwell, *The Puritan Conversion
Narrative: The Beginnings of American Expression* (New York: Cambridge Uni-
versity Press, 1983), 172. John Owen King has described something very much
like the psychological depth and redemptive potential that Miller saw in New
England Puritanism. Compare Miller's "The Augustinian Strain of Piety," in
Miller, *New England Mind,* 3–34, with the first chapter of King, *The Iron
of Melancholy: Structures of Spiritual Conversion in America from the Puritan
Conscience to Victorian Neurosis* (Middletown, Conn.: Wesleyan University
Press, 1983). In *The Lost Soul of American Politics* John P. Diggins explains
how the Puritan tradition became the conscience of American liberalism. See
also David R. Williams, "New Directions in Puritan Studies," *American Quarterly* 37 (spring 1985): 157: "Calvinist theology called for introspective self-
doubt and self-annihilation, not joy or acceptance."

123. See Diggins, *Lost Soul of American Politics,* 332.

124. Miller, *New England Mind,* 6.

125. Jean-Paul Sartre once said that "had my father lived, he would have
lain on me at full length and would have crushed me." See Robert Jay Lifton,
"Protean Man," *Partisan Review* 35 (1968): 19.

126. Bercovitch is hardly alone in this. As Diggins has pointed out, "the
social and economic implications of the liberal tradition have been examined
almost to the exclusion of its moral content and even its psychological depth."
But "once we see the Calvinist foundations of liberalism . . . we are in a better
position to see why in American intellectual history liberalism could carry the
seeds of its own condemnation." See Diggins, *Lost Soul of American Politics,* 7.

127. Breyten Breytenbach, *End Papers: Essays, Letters, Articles of Faith,
Workbook Notes* (Boston: Faber, 1986), 74.

128. Richard Rorty, "The Historiography of Philosophy: Four Genres," in
Philosophy in History: Essays on the Historiography of Philosophy, ed. Richard
Rorty, J. B. Schneedwind, and Quentin Skinner (New York: Cambridge University Press, 1984), 49; Michael Walzer, *The Company of Critics: Social Criticism
and Political Commitment in the Twentieth Century* (New York: Basic, 1988),
231.

129. Allan David Bloom, *The Closing of the American Mind: How Higher
Education Has Failed Democracy and Impoverished the Souls of Today's Students*
(New York: Simon and Schuster, 1987), 239. I take Harold Bloom to be saying
something like this when he insists that "strong poems strengthen us by teaching us how *how to talk to ourselves.*" Bloom as quoted by Lorna Sage, "Fear Is
the Spur," *Times Literary Supplement,* 14–20 April 1989, 389.

130. Richard Rorty contends that what unites us with others is "not a common language but just our susceptibility to pain and in particular to humiliation." Rorty, *Contingency, Irony, and Solidarity* (New York: Cambridge University Press, 1989), 92. I have learned much from Martha C. Nussbaum's exquisite

book *The Fragility of Goodness: Luck and Ethics in Greek Tragedy and Philosophy* (New York: Cambridge University Press, 1986).

CHAPTER THREE

1. In 1989 the critic Robert Fuller described postmodernism as "outflanked by reactionaries on one side and novelty-seeking camp-followers on the other." Fuller, "Building in the Past Tense," *Times Literary Supplement*, 24–30 March 1989, 296. And by 1996 Richard Rorty was calling postmodernism "increasingly obsolescent." Richard Rorty, "Something to Steer By," *London Review of Books*, 20 June 1996, 7.

2. Himmelfarb, "Supposing History Is a Woman—What Then?" *American Scholar* 53 (autumn 1984): 494–505.

3. George Steiner, *Real Presences* (Chicago: University of Chicago Press, 1990), 63.

4. Mark Edmundson once said something like this about Harold Bloom. See Edmundson, "Bloom's Giant Forms," *London Review of Books*, 1 June 1989, 13.

5. "By incessantly recontextualizing whatever memory brings back, both [Derrida] and Proust have extended the bounds of possibility." Richard Rorty, *Contingency, Irony, Solidarity* (New York: Cambridge University Press, 1989), 137.

6. See, for example, Fuller, "Building in the Past Tense," 296.

7. Rorty, *Contingency, Irony, and Solidarity*, 75.

8. Kant's position as described by Hayden White, *Metahistory: The Historical Imagination in Nineteenth-Century Europe* (Baltimore: Johns Hopkins University Press, 1973), 57.

9. Frank Lentricchia has called Showalter, along with Sandra Gilbert and Susan Gubar, "the best known and most influential of American literary feminists." Lentricchia, *Ariel and the Police: Michel Foucault, William James, Wallace Stevens* (Madison: University of Wisconsin Press, 1988), 159.

10. Elaine Showalter, *A Literature of Their Own: British Women Novelists from Brontë to Lessing* (Princeton: Princeton University Press, 1977), 7, 4.

11. Elaine Showalter, *Sister's Choice: Tradition and Change in American Women's Writing* (New York: Oxford University Press, 1991), 4, 175.

12. See Elaine Showalter, "Feminism and Literature," in *Literary Theory Today*, ed. Peter Collier and Helga Geyer-Ryan (Ithaca: Cornell University Press, 1990), 191.

13. Mill as quoted by Showalter, *Literature of Their Own*, 3.

14. Showalter, *Literature of Their Own*, 4, 15.

15. Ibid.

16. Ibid., 29.

17. Ibid., 33–34.

18. Ibid., 297.

19. Ibid., 304.

20. Showalter, "Introduction: The Feminist Critical Revolution," in *The New Feminist Criticism: Essays on Women, Literature, and Theory*, ed. Elaine Showalter (New York: Pantheon, 1985), 6. With characteristic modesty, Sho-

walter mentions the books by Spacks and Moers but fails to mention *A Literature of Their Own*, though it was in many ways the most influential of the
three. See Patricia Meyer Spacks, *The Female Imagination* (New York: Knopf,
1975), and Ellen Moers, *Literary Women* (Garden City, N.Y.: Doubleday, 1976).
Showalter herself introduced the term gynocriticism in "Toward a Feminist
Poetics," in Showalter, *New Feminist Criticism*.

21. Janet Todd, *Feminist Literary History* (New York: Routledge, 1988), 41;
Showalter, "Introduction," 12.

22. Showalter, *Sister's Choice*, 7.

23. Showalter, *Literature of Their Own*, 36.

24. Ibid., 10. Showalter describes *Sister's Choice* in remarkably similar terms.
Like *A Literature of Their Own*, it is literary history written "from the bottom
up," an attempt to recover the voices of the "disparaged and suppressed." Sho
walter, *Sister's Choice*, 159. Just as *A Literature of Their Own* tried to demonstrate that novels written by British women constituted a significant literary
tradition, so *Sister's Choice* tries to demonstrate that novels written by American
women constitute "a common, pluralistic heritage of races, genders and cultures." See Hermione Lee, "Separate Spheres and Common Threads," *Times
Literary Supplement*, 15 November 1991, 8.

25. Showalter, *Literature of Their Own*, 9, 5, 4.

26. Ibid., 5, 11; Showalter, *Sister's Choice*, 103.

27. Showalter, *Sister's Choice*, 4.

28. Ibid., 21.

29. Showalter, "Introduction," 12; Showalter, "Toward a Feminist Poetics,"
140.

30. Showalter, "Toward a Feminist Poetics," 140.

31. Ibid., 127.

32. Ibid., 139. She did, however, argue that "these defensive responses may
be rationalizations of the psychic barriers to women's participation in theoretical
discourse." Ibid., 128.

33. Ibid.

34. "The most consistent assumption of feminist reading has been the belief
that women's special experience would assume and determine distinctive forms
in art." Ibid., 135, 141, 127.

35. Elaine Showalter, "Feminist Criticism in the Wilderness" (1981) in Showalter, *New Feminist Criticism*, 244.

36. Showalter, "Toward a Feminist Poetics," 141.

37. Showalter, "Feminist Criticism in the Wilderness," 14.

38. Ibid., 248; my emphasis.

39. Ibid., 252.

40. Elaine Showalter, "A Criticism of Our Own: Autonomy and Assimilation
in Afro-American and Feminist Literary Theory," in *The Future of Literary
Theory*, ed. Ralph Cohen (New York: Routledge, 1989), 363; Showalter, "Feminist Criticism in the Wilderness," 263.

41. Showalter, "Feminist Criticism in the Wilderness," 263, 264; emphasis
in the original; Showalter, "Criticism of Our Own," 363.

42. Showalter, "Feminist Criticism in the Wilderness," 264.

43. Showalter, *Sister's Choice*, 150.

44. Houston Baker and Charlotte Baker, "Patches, Quilts and Community in Alice Walker's 'Everyday Use,'" *Southern Review* 21 (July 1985): 718, as quoted by Showalter, *Sister's Choice*, 163.

45. Elaine Showalter, "Introduction: The Feminist Critical Revolution" (1985), in Showalter, *New Feminist Criticism*.

46. Showalter, "Criticism of Our Own," 361–62.

47. Carolyn Heilbrun as quoted by Showalter, "Criticism of Our Own," 360.

48. Joyce Carol Oates as quoted in ibid., 360.

49. Ibid., 367.

50. Showalter, "Feminism and Literature," 179.

51. Ibid., 190.

52. Ibid., 188. She did nod in the direction of gender theory at the very beginning of the article, but virtually everything else in it suggested she was moving in precisely the opposite direction.

53. Ibid., 181; my emphasis.

54. Showalter, *Sister's Choice*, 7.

55. Ibid., 102.

56. Ibid., 4.

57. Ibid., 4, 5.

58. Ibid., 4.

59. Ibid., 7.

60. Ibid., 162.

61. In *A Literature of Their Own*, 18, Showalter admitted that she could find little or no influence linking one major writer to another.

62. Showalter, *Sister's Choice*, 18.

63. Stanley Cavell, *In Quest of the Ordinary: Lines of Skepticism and Romanticism* (Chicago: University of Chicago Press, 1988), 105, 27. In the same book he describes "my philosophical journey to locate an inheritance in Wittgenstein and Heidegger, and of Emerson and Thoreau before them" (105).

64. Ibid., 149, 150.

65. Denise Riley, *"Am I That Name?" Feminism and the Category of "Women" in History* (Minneapolis: University of Minnesota Press, 1988), 1–2.

66. See Scott's "Introduction" to *Feminism and History*, ed. Joan W. Scott (New York: Oxford University Press, 1996), esp. 5.

67. Joan Wallach Scott, *Gender and the Politics of History* (New York: Columbia University Press, 1988), 69. "Thompson did not present himself as an analyst outside the historically situated discourse; he spoke from within it, as an advocate." For politically active students like Scott (who was already working with Students for a Democratic Society), *The Making of the English Working Class* provided "inspiration and confirmation for advocates of grass-roots organizing." Scott, *Gender and the Politics of History*, 71.

68. E. P. Thompson, *Making of the English Working Class* (1963; New York: Pantheon, 1964), 12.

69. "I do not see class as a 'structure,' nor even as a 'category,' but as something which in fact happens (and can be shown to have happened) in human relationships." Ibid., 9.

70. Ibid., 11.

71. "My motive [in writing *Gender and the Politics of History*] was and is one I share with other feminists and it is avowedly political: to point out and change inequalities between women and men." Scott, *Gender and the Politics of History*, 3. Two years later: "If we are to formulate new kinds of political strategies, we need to understand how, in all their complexity, collective and individual differences are constructed, how, that is, hierarchies and inequalities are produced." Scott, "Response to Linda Gordon," 859.

72. Thus she explains that she wrote her newest book, *Only Paradoxes to Offer*, in the hope that "if we can understand the French feminists' struggles . . . we can also, perhaps, better understand, and so better address, the conflicts, dilemmas, and paradoxes of our own time." Joan W. Scott, *Only Paradoxes to Offer: French Feminists and the Rights of Man* (Cambridge: Harvard University Press, 1996), xi.

73. Joan Scott as quoted by Katherine Hinds, "Joan Wallach Scott: Breaking New Ground for Women," *Change* 17 (July–August 1985): 51.

74. Joan Scott, "Women in *The Making of the English Working Class*," in Scott, *Gender and the Politics of History*, 68–90.

75. Scott, *Gender and the Politics of History*, 1.

76. "After I joined the faculty at Brown (in 1980), I met feminists in literary studies, many of them working with French poststructuralist theory, and I began to reconsider my earlier frameworks. At Brown I was introduced to a way of thinking that explained things I hadn't been able to deal with before, for example, the persistence of gender inequalities, despite massive social change. As I argued with people about issues of interpretation, the value of history, the meanings of gender, I decided that I ought to be reading things I had never read, like Foucault and Derrida. Through this exposure to new ways of thinking I found I could make sense and think better about 'gender' that I had been able to think before." Joan Scott, "Interview with Joan Scott," *Radical History Review* 45 (fall 1989): 47.

77. Scott, "Women in *The Making of the English Working Class*," 68–90. This article should be read together with "On Language, Gender and Working-Class History," also in *Gender and the Politics of History*, which is a critique of Gareth Stedman Jones's *Languages of Class: Studies in English Working Class History, 1832-1982* (Cambridge: Cambridge University Press, 1983).

78. Scott, *Gender and the Politics of History*, 72.

79. Ibid., 85.

80. Ibid., 84.

81. "Gender: A Useful Category of Historical Analysis" is most conveniently found in Scott, *Gender and the Politics of History*, 28–50. It has been reprinted in (among other places) Scott, *Feminism and History*, 152–80. It was originally published in the *American Historical Review* 91 (December 1986): 1053–75.

82. William Sewell, review of *Gender and the Politics of History*, *History and Theory* 29, 1 (1990): 71.

83. Scott, *Gender and the Politics of History*, 28, 29.

84. Scott, "Introduction," 8.

85. "We need to replace the notion that social power is unified, coherent, and

centralized with something like Michel Foucault's concept of power as dispersed constellations of unequal relationships, discursively constituted in social "fields of force." Scott, *Gender and the Politics of History*, 42.

86. Ibid., 2.

87. Ibid., 42.

88. Scott, "Introduction," 8. Scott thinks this is what deconstruction amounts to. Thus in "Gender: A Useful Category of Historical Analysis" (41) she argues that "Derrida's definition of deconstruction . . . means analyzing in context the way any binary opposition operates, reversing and displacing its hierarchical construction, rather than accepting it as real or self-evident or in the nature of things."

89. Scott, *Gender and the Politics of History*, 4, 3. "I found it imperative to pursue theoretical questions in order to do feminist history."

90. Wai Chee Dimock, *Residues of Justice: Literature, Law, Philosophy* (Berkeley: University of California Press, 1996), 85.

91. Scott, *Gender and the Politics of History*, 6, 5.

92. Ibid., 30−31.

93. Scott discusses both responses in ibid., 30−31.

94. Ibid., 3−4.

95. Scott, "Deconstructing Equality-versus-Difference; or The Uses of Post-structuralist Theory for Feminism," *Feminist Studies* 14 (spring 1988): 35.

96. Scott, "Deconstructing Equality-versus-Difference," 35.

97. Scott, "Introduction," 8.

98. Scott, *Gender and the Politics of History*, 30.

99. Scott, "Comment" on Gayatri Chakravorty Spivak's "Feminism in Decolonization," *Differences: A Journal of Feminist Cultural Studies* 3, 3 (1991): 173.

100. Scott, *Gender and the Politics of History*, 39−40.

CHAPTER FOUR

1. Hollinger had written on the scientific ideal in American culture, Haskell on the emergence of the social sciences, and Kloppenberg on the relation between pragmatism and liberalism in the United States, Great Britain, France, and Germany between 1870 and 1920.

2. James Kloppenberg, "Objectivity and Historicism: A Century of American Historical Writing," *American Historical Review* 94 (October 1990): 1018.

3. Peter Novick, *That Noble Dream: The "Objectivity Question" and the American Historical Profession* (Cambridge: Cambridge University Press, 1988), 628; Kloppenberg, "Objectivity and Historicism," 1028, 1026−27.

4. Haskell, "Objectivity Is Not Neutrality," *History and Theory* 29, 2 (1990): 130, 144.

5. Thomas Haskell, "The Curious Persistence of Rights Talk in the 'Age of Interpretation,'" *Journal of American History* 74 (December 1987): 999.

6. Novick, *That Noble Dream*, 1.

7. Ibid.

8. Ibid., 625−26.

9. Haskell, "Objectivity Is Not Neutrality," 130.

10. Novick, *That Noble Dream*, 626; Hollinger, "T. S. Kuhn's Theory of Sci-

ence and Its Implications for History," *American Historical Review* 78 (1973): 370–93.

11. J. G. A. Pocock, "Languages and Their Implications: The Transformation of the Study of Political Thought," in Pocock, *Politics, Language, and Time: Essays on Political Thought and History* (New York: Atheneum, 1971), 13.

12. Pocock, "Languages and Their Implications," 13.

13. Ibid., 14 n. 6.

14. Hollinger, "T. S. Kuhn's Theory of Science," 381.

15. Pocock, "Languages and Their Implications," 14.

16. Hollinger, "T. S. Kuhn's Theory of Science," 381.

17. Ibid.

18. Kloppenberg thinks poststructuralism (and deconstruction in particular) "makes writing history impossible." He thinks historians can ride out the more virulent forms of epistemological skepticism by turning to the early pragmatists, particularly Peirce and Dewey. See James T. Kloppenberg, "Deconstruction and Hermeneutic Strategies for Intellectual History: The Recent Work of Dominick LaCapra and David Hollinger," *Intellectual History Newsletter*, April 1987, 8, 11.

19. Novick, *That Noble Dream*, 625–26.

20. Ibid., 626.

21. Thomas Haskell, "Deterministic Implications of Intellectual History," in *New Directions in American Intellectual History*, ed. John Higham and Paul K. Conkin (Baltimore: Johns Hopkins University Press, 1979), 136, 140.

22. Haskell, "Deterministic Implications," 142–43. As he points out, Haskell found this insight in R. G. Collingwood's *Essay on Metaphysics* (Oxford: Clarendon Press, 1940).

23. "The possibility of accounting either for Kuhn's paradigm shifts or Collingwood's changes in absolute presuppositions mainly by reference to 'reasons' rather than 'causes' seems quite remote." Haskell, "Deterministic Implications," 145.

24. Ibid., 140–41.

25. Ibid., 132–33.

26. Haskell, "Professionalism *versus* Capitalism: R. H. Tawney, Emile Durkheim, and C. S. Peirce on the Disinterestedness of Professional Communities," in *The Authority of Experts: Studies in History and Theory*, ed. Thomas L. Haskell (Bloomington: Indiana University Press, 1984), 207.

27. Haskell, "Professionalism *versus* Capitalism," 207.

28. Haskell, *Authority of Experts*, xxviii.

29. Ibid.

30. Haskell, "Professionalism *versus* Capitalism," 207; my emphasis.

31. This is one of the central themes that Peter Novick develops in *That Noble Dream*. Novick argues that what ultimately brought down the ideal of objectivity was the social and cultural diversification of the profession.

32. These are Theodore Hamerow's words, as quoted by Joan Wallach Scott, "History in Crisis? The Others' Side of the Story," *American Historical Review* 94 (June 1989): 686.

33. Scott, "History in Crisis?" 689.

34. Joan Scott, "The Evidence of Experience," *Critical Inquiry* 17 (summer 1991): 776.

35. Cmiel, "After Objectivity," 171.

36. Joan Scott, "Interview with Joan Scott," *Radical History Review* 45 (fall 1989): 55.

37. Scott, "Evidence of Experience," 780.

38. Megill, "Fragmentation and the Future of Historiography," 697. "With contingency comes the alleged threat of fragmentation. The sophisticated response to the alleged threat is the pragmatic, Peircean appeal to 'communities of the competent' . . . The response is most closely associated with Thomas Haskell," but "essentially the same position is to be found in the writings of a number of other historians who likewise appeal to a disciplinary consensus that would overcome conflicting positions." He then cites Hollinger and Kloppenberg and ends, "But this will not do." Ibid., 695 n. 7.

39. Novick, *That Noble Dream*, 518, 627.

40. Kloppenberg also had trouble grasping this point. Ten years later, in 1989, to the surprise of almost everyone, he trotted out the very same argument. See Kloppenberg, "Objectivity and Historicism," 1011–30. And as late as 1994 Hollinger was still arguing that "truth" emerges "from a consensus of practitioners." See David Hollinger, "Truth by Consensus," *New York Times Book Review*, 27 March 1994, 16.

41. Richard Rorty, "On Ethnocentrism: A Reply to Clifford Geertz," in Rorty, *Philosophical Papers* (New York: Cambridge University Press, 1991), 1: 209ff.

42. See Rorty, *Philosophical Papers*, 1:26.

43. Haskell, "Curious Persistence of Rights Talk," 991.

44. Haskell, "Deterministic Implications," 145.

45. Haskell, "Curious Persistence of Rights Talk," 991.

46. Thomas Nagel, *The View from Nowhere* (New York: Oxford University Press, 1986).

47. Haskell, "Curious Persistence of Rights Talk," 984, 1008.

48. Novick, *That Noble Dream*, 627.

49. Haskell, "Curious Persistence of Rights Talk," 991, 986.

50. Ibid., 993, 991.

51. Ibid., 990.

52. Ibid., 986.

53. Ibid., 1004.

54. Ibid., 984.

55. See David Bromwich, *A Choice of Inheritance: Self and Community from Edmund Burke to Robert Frost* (Cambridge: Harvard University Press, 1989), 45.

56. Haskell, "Curious Persistence of Rights Talk," 1002.

57. "By saying that rights are fictions we need not mean anything more than that they are human creations, *conventions*." Ibid., 1001.

58. Ibid., 1002.

59. William James, "Does Consciousness Exist?" In *Essays in Radical Empiricism* (Cambridge: Harvard University Press, 1976), 3–19.

60. Actually, several different scholars, writing from a variety of disciplines, have pointed out the necessity of *attributing* authors to texts. See, for example, the psychologist Jerome Bruner, *Actual Minds, Possible Worlds* (Cambridge: Harvard University Press, 1986), esp. 17–19; the philosopher Daniel Dennett, *Brainstorms: Philosophical Essays on Mind and Psychology* (Cambridge: MIT Press, 1978), esp. "Intentional Systems," 3–22, and Dennett, *The Intentional Stance* (Cambridge: MIT Press, 1989), passim; the literary historians Steven Knapp and Walter Benn Michaels, "Against Theory," *Critical Inquiry* 8 (summer 1982): 723–42, and idem, "Against Theory 2: Hermeneutics and Deconstruction," *Critical Inquiry* 14 (autumn 1987): 49–68.

61. Haskell, "Curious Persistence of Rights Talk," 1004–5; my emphasis.

62. Ibid., 1004 n. 37.

63. Ibid., 997, 1007.

64. Ibid., 990, 989, 1008; my emphasis.

65. Charles Jencks, *What Is Post-modernism?* (New York: Academy Editions/St. Martin's Press, 1989), 57.

66. Haskell, "Curious Persistence of Rights Talk," 1001.

67. Geoffrey O'Brien, "Killing Time," *New York Review of Books,* 5 March 1992, 39.

68. Jencks, *What Is Post-modernism?*

69. Haskell, "Objectivity Is Not Neutrality," 137.

70. Alan Brinkley, "Mythic but Useful," *Times Literary Supplement,* 10–16 November 1989, 1246.

71. Haskell, "Objectivity Is Not Neutrality," 143, 142. Thomas Nagel similarly describes them as "close to home" virtues. See Nagel, *View from Nowhere,* 171.

72. Stuart Hampshire and Ronald Dworkin have, individually, made very similar arguments. Hampshire contends that "it is the characteristic of men's [and women's] thought that it is reflexive and that the activity of thinking entails a process of stepping back, in order to attain greater objectivity, by making corrections for point of view. Active conscious thought in men [and women] *naturally* turns into self-consciousness, into thought about thought." See Stuart Hampshire, *Morality and Conflict* (Oxford: Blackwell, 1983), 51. Similarly Dworkin: "The practice of worrying about what justice really is" is "the single most important social practice we have." See Ronald Dworkin, "To Each His Own," *New York Review of Books,* 14 April 1983, 6.

73. He is quick to warn us, however, that "detachment does not promise access to any transcendental realm and always remains, as Thomas Nagel says, 'under the shadow' of skepticism." Haskell, "Objectivity Is Not Neutrality," 132.

74. Ibid.

75. Ibid., 138. In fact Becker was very much aware of the need for—and presence of—"constraints upon the will" of individual historians: "In thus creating his own history, there are, nevertheless, limits which Mr. Everyman may not overstep without incurring penalties. The limits are set by his fellows." See Carl Becker, "Everyman His Own Historian," in Becker, *Everyman His Own Historian: Essays on History and Politics* (New York: Appleton-Century-Crofts, 1935), 243.

76. Haskell, "Objectivity Is Not Neutrality," 151.

77. These are Haskell's own terms. See ibid., 134, 136.

78. Ibid., 136; emphasis in the original.

79. Ibid., 142; emphasis in the original.

80. "To struggle to formulate a superior, more inclusive, less self-centered alternative [view] is to strive for detachment and aim at objectivity." Ibid., 132. Haskell is following Thomas Nagel on this point. In *The View from Nowhere* Nagel argued that "ethics . . . requires a detachment from particular perspectives and transcendence of one's time and place" (186–87).

81. Haskell, "Objectivity Is Not Neutrality," 132; my emphasis.

82. Ibid., 134.

83. Ibid., 146, 136, 156 n. 36.

84. Ibid., 145.

85. Ibid.

86. Ibid., 146.

87. Ibid., 146, 146 n. 19.

88. Haskell, "Curious Persistence of Rights Talk," 986. Kloppenberg described the choice in similar terms. It is, he wrote, a choice "between the absolute authority of facts and the anarchy of idiosyncratic interpretations." Kloppenberg, "Objectivity and Historicism," 1029.

89. Haskell, "Objectivity Is Not Neutrality," 138 n. 15.

90. Haskell, "Curious Persistence of Rights Talk," 984.

91. Stanley Fish, *Doing What Comes Naturally: Change, Rhetoric, and the Practice of Theory in Literary and Legal Studies* (Durham: Duke University Press, 1989), 2. See chap. 1, "Going down the Anti-formalist Road," passim.

92. See Hayden White, "What Is an Historical System?" in *Biology, History, and Natural Philosophy*, ed. Allen D. Breck and Wolfgang Yourgrau (New York: Plenum, 1972), 239; Hayden White, *Metahistory: The Historical Imagination in Nineteenth-Century Europe* (Baltimore: Johns Hopkins University Press, 1973), 57; and Hans Kellner, "A Bedrock of Order: Hayden White's Linguistic Humanism," *History and Theory* 19 (1980): 27.

93. Rorty, *Contingency, Irony, Solidarity*, 55.

94. I take Robert Scholes to be saying essentially the same thing in his *Protocols of Reading:* "We are always outside any particular text we may attempt to read. This is why interpretation is a problem for us. But we are never outside the whole web of textuality in which we hold our cultural being and in which every text awakens echoes and harmonies. Every text that comes to us comes from before our moment in time, but each text can be read only by connecting it to the unfinished work of textuality. To read is to face the past, to accept what has happened as, in the words of L. P. Hartley, happening in 'another country,' where 'they do things differently.' Much as we might wish it, we cannot go *there*. To write, however, is to see world and text as unfinished." Scholes, *Protocols of Reading* (New Haven: Yale University Press, 1989), 6.

95. Ralph Waldo Emerson, "The American Scholar," in *The American Mind: Selections from the Literature of the United States*, ed. Harry R. Warfel, Ralph H. Gabriel, and Stanley T. Williams (New York: American Book Company, [1947]), 1:554.

250 *Notes to Pages 93–97*

96. See Adam Morton, "Relating Our Values to Theirs," *Times Literary Supplement*, 15 March 1991, 24, for an interesting discussion of this point.

97. See White, *Metahistory*, 433.

98. This is what Murray Krieger would call "a suspect rhetoric sponsored by bad faith." See Krieger, *Ekphrasis: The Illusion of the Natural Sign* (Baltimore: Johns Hopkins University Press, 1992), 28, 234.

99. Richard Rorty, *Philosophical Papers*, 1:67, 79.

100. Rorty makes this argument in ibid., 1:66.

101. Rorty has stated this with his usual succinctness: "You need to reformulate the principles to fit the cases, and to develop a *sense* [not a rule, but a *sense*] for when to forget about principles and just rely on know-how." Ibid., 1:68; my emphasis.

102. See Geoffrey Galt Harpham, "The Ethical Backlash," *Times Literary Supplement*, 28 August 1992, 19, and Harpham, *Getting It Right: Language, Literature, and Ethics* (Chicago: University of Chicago Press, 1992), especially that part of chapter 1, "Language and the Decay of Value."

Similarly, the historian Jean Howard has warned of the ethical backlash emerging among partisans of the new historicism: "There is a real danger that the emerging interest in history will be appropriated by those wishing to suppress or erase the theoretical revolution that has gone on in the last several decades. Ironically, the 'new history' may well turn out to be a backlash phenomenon: a flight from theory." This backlash may not involve an explicit rejection of such advances, of course; more likely historians will simply "ignore the problematics of their undertaking. And that no one will challenge them." Jean Howard, "The New Historicism in Renaissance Studies," in *Renaissance Historicism*, ed. Arthur Kinney and Dan Collins (Amherst: University of Massachusetts Press, 1987), 9.

103. Haskell, "Curious Persistence of Rights Talk," 992. But as Haskell admits, he has not actually read Derrida: "Only people with angelic patience and much time on their hands read Jacques Derrida, *Of Grammatology*. The rest of us read Jonathan Culler, *On Deconstruction*." Ibid., 992 n. 15.

104. Michael Sandel as quoted by Richard Bernstein, "Rorty's Liberal Utopia," *Social Research* 57 (spring 1990): 46–47.

105. Joseph Schumpeter as quoted by Bernstein, "Rorty's Liberal Utopia," 46–47.

106. Haskell, "Objectivity Is Not Neutrality," 134. Rorty says something very much like this in *Philosophical Papers*, 1:79.

107. "The only grounds for preferring one [way of prefiguring the historical field] over another are moral or aesthetic ones." White, *Metahistory*, 433.

108. F. Scott Fitzgerald, *The Great Gatsby* (New York: Scribner's 1986), 177.

109. Joyce Appleby, Lynn Hunt, and Margaret Jacob, *Telling the Truth about History* (New York: Norton, 1994), 8, 11.

110. Appleby, Hunt, and Jacob, *Telling the Truth*, 1–2.

111. "In this book we embrace a healthy skepticism, and we applaud the research that has laid the foundations for a multicultural approach to human history. But we reject the cynicism and nihilism that accompany contemporary relativism." Ibid., 4.

112. Ibid., 6.

113. Ibid., 7, 192; my emphasis.

114. Ibid., 206, 7.

115. Ibid., 243.

116. Ibid., 247 n. 6. Hilary Putnam, *Reason, Truth, and History* (Cambridge: Cambridge University Press, 1981).

117. Oddly enough, most of the reviewers seem to have missed this discrepancy. See the following for examples: Gordon Wood, *New Republic* 211 (7 November 1994): 46ff.; David Hollinger, *New York Times Book Review*, 27 March 1994, 16; and Raymond Martin, *History and Theory* 34, 4 (1995): 320.

118. Hilary Putnam, *Renewing Philosophy* (Cambridge: Harvard University Press, 1992), x–xi.

119. See Putnam, *Renewing Philosophy*, passim, but especially the luminous section "Wittgenstein and Religious Belief," 134–57.

120. Appleby, Hunt, and Jacob, *Telling the Truth*, 12.

121. Ibid., 248–49, 280.

122. Ibid., 171, 250.

123. Ibid., 241–42.

124. Ibid., 56.

125. Ibid., 10.

126. Ibid., 261, 255.

127. Ibid., 268.

128. "The system of peer review, open refereeing, public disputation, replicated experiences, and documented research—all aided by international communication and the extended freedom from censorship—makes objectivity possible. Research programs must be established and findings constantly tested." Ibid., 281. The plain implication, of course (though Appleby, Hunt, and Jacob shrink from stating it so baldly), is that historians who perversely continue to work outside this system cannot produce objective or reliable history.

129. "In this cultural milieu the practitioners of history are constrained by a complex set of rules" that make the appearance of "idiosyncrasies" highly unlikely. Ibid., 255, 261.

130. Perry Miller, "The Plight of the Lone Wolf" (talk given 1940, printed 1956), in Miller, *The Responsibility of Mind in a Civilization of Machines*, ed. John Crowell and Stanford J. Searl Jr. (Amherst: University of Massachusetts Press, 1979), 9–10.

131. Miller, "Plight of the Lone Wolf," 10.

132. Ralph Waldo Emerson, "The American Scholar," in *Selected Writings of Ralph Waldo Emerson*, ed. William H. Gilman (New York: Signet Classics, 1965), 224.

133. Appleby, Hunt, and Jacob, *Telling the Truth*, 295.

134. Ibid., 294.

135. Ibid., 301.

136. Ibid., 158.

137. Ibid., 159.

138. See, for example, F. R. Ankersmit, "Historiography and Postmodernism," *History and Theory* 28, 2 (1989), passim but particularly 137–38.

139. Appleby, Hunt, and Jacob, *Telling the Truth,* 159.
140. Novick, *That Noble Dream,* 577.
141. Appleby, Hunt, and Jacob, *Telling the Truth,* 291.
142. Ibid., 291, 156.
143. Ibid.

CHAPTER FIVE

1. Hayden White, "Historical Emplotment and the Problem of Truth," in *Probing the Limits of Representation: Nazism and the "Final Solution,"* ed. Saul Friedlander (Cambridge: Harvard University Press, 1992), 37–53.

2. Hayden White, "Introduction," in White, *Tropics of Discourse: Essays in Cultural Criticism* (Baltimore: Johns Hopkins University Press, 1978), 23; Ralph Cohen, ed., *The Future of Literary Theory* (New York: Routledge, 1989), xvii.

3. Hayden White, "The Burden of History," *History and Theory* 5, 2 (1966); reprinted in White, *Tropics of Discourse.*

4. Karl Marx as quoted by John Patrick Diggins, *The Promise of Pragmatism* (Chicago: University of Chicago Press, 1994), 471. Hayden White, *The Content of the Form: Narrative Discourse and Historical Representation* (Baltimore: Johns Hopkins University Press, 1987), 168.

5. White, *Content of the Form,* 82.

6. White, *Tropics of Discourse,* 35. See also Hayden White, *Metahistory: The Historical Imagination in Nineteenth-Century Europe* (Baltimore: Johns Hopkins University Press, 1973) 1–2.

7. Above all, this meant the failure of Carl Hempel's attempt to reconstruct historical studies on the solid foundation of "Covering Laws."

8. White, *Tropics of Discourse,* 40.

9. Ibid., 40–41; emphasis in the original.

10. Ibid., 47.

11. Richard Rorty, of course, has said much the same thing about philosophy. See Rorty, *Consequences of Pragmatism* (Minneapolis: University of Minnesota Press, 1982), 211–30, esp. 225–27.

12. White, *Tropics of Discourse,* 43.

13. Ibid., 44; my emphasis. On the other hand, White had no taste for the "manifestly reactionary . . . political posture" of Burckhardt's history. It was, White explained, "part of the effort mounted by social conservatives to meet the threat presented to them by Neo-Positivism in philosophy and by Marxism in politics." See Hayden White, "The Tasks of Intellectual History," *Monist* 54 (October 1969): 611, 612.

14. Many years later White would refer to this as "the idea that any given body of facts is infinitely variously interpretable and that one aim of historical discourse is to *multiply* the number of interpretations we have of any given set of events rather than to work toward the production of a 'best' interpretation." White, "Historical Emplotment and the Problem of Truth," 340 n. 3.

15. White, *Tropics of Discourse,* 41. Richard Rorty, J. B. Schneedwind, and Quentin Skinner offer an interesting defense of such historical presentism: "*Some* concern must dictate the questions we ask and the criteria of relevancy we use, and contemporary concerns at least make for interesting history.

Avoiding them will merely substitute the concerns of some previous generation. This can of course be done, but unless they are also our concerns there is no particular reason to do it." Rorty, Schneedwind, and Skinner, "Introduction," in *Philosophy in History: Essays on the Historiography of Philosophy*, ed. Rorty, Schneedwind, and Skinner (New York: Cambridge University Press, 1984), 11.

16. E. P. Thompson, *The Making of the English Working Class* (1963; New York: Pantheon, 1964), 12–13.

17. Frank Kermode, *Forms of Attention* (Chicago: University of Chicago Press, 1985), 75.

18. Hayden White, "What Is an Historical System?" in *Biology, History, and Natural Philosophy*, ed. Allen D. Breck and Wolfgang Yourgrau (New York: Plenum, 1972), 239.

19. Ibid., 239; emphasis in the original.

20. Ibid., 240, 238–39; emphasis in the original.

21. Ibid., 238. White made this point again, ten years later, in "Getting out of History: Jameson's Redemption of Narrative," *Diacritics* 12 (fall 1982): 2–13: "Human beings can will backward as well as forward in time; willing backward occurs when we rearrange accounts of events in the past that have been emplotted in a given way, in order to endow them with a different meaning or to draw from the new emplotment reasons for acting differently in the future from the way we have become accustomed to acting in our present. Something like this occurs in religious conversion of the sort described by Augustine, who threw off a cultural ancestry pagan in nature and adopted one Christian in nature. It happens in political conversions as well. . . . In the process of revolutionary political change, a whole society may decide to rewrite its history, so that events formerly regarded as unimportant are now redescribed as anticipations or prefigurations of the new society to be created by revolutionary action." Reprinted in White, *Content of the Form*, 150.

22. White, "What Is an Historical System?" 242.

23. Ibid., 240.

24. Ibid., 242.

25. Ibid., 240.

26. White, *Tropics of Discourse*, 55; emphasis in the original.

27. White cited Lévi-Strauss's *The Savage Mind* as his primary example. See *Tropics of Discourse*, 55ff.

28. Ibid., 56.

29. Ibid., 55, 56, 57. In "The Absurdist Moment in Contemporary Criticism" White wrote of "the grandiose, anticivilizational project of Lévi-Strauss," by which he meant "tak[ing] the side of nature against culture." Ibid., 269.

30. Ibid., 46.

31. Roger Scruton, "Making up for the Broken Word," *Times Literary Supplement*, 19-25 May 1989, 533.

32. At other places Frye calls them "informing patterns" and "pregeneric archetypes."

33. White, *Tropics of Discourse*, 58.

34. Ibid., 59.

35. Ibid., 58.

36. Ibid., 59.

37. In "The Historical Text as Literary Artifact," first published in 1974, just one year after *Metahistory*, White strengthened his adoption of Frye and Collingwood with new insights drawn from Charles S. Peirce, Claude Lévi-Strauss, and the literary critic Geoffrey Hartman.

38. White, *Tropics of Discourse*, 60; emphasis in the original.

39. Ibid., 84, 60; my emphasis.

40. Ibid., 60–61.

41. Ibid., 63.

42. White, "Historical Emplotment," 340 n. 1.

43. White, *Tropics of Discourse*, 66–67.

44. Ibid., 67.

45. Ibid., 71.

46. Ibid.

47. Ibid., 72.

48. Ibid.

49. Ibid., 2–4.

50. White, *Metahistory*, 34.

51. Oscar Handlin, *The Uprooted* (1951; New York: Little, Brown, 1973), 3.

52. Ibid., xi. This is true, White says, of "any field of study not yet reduced (or elevated) to the status of a genuine science."

53. White, *Tropics of Discourse*, 74. White reiterated this assertion two years later, in "The Historical Text as Literary Artifact": "The different kinds of historical interpretations that we have of the same set of events . . . are little more than projections of the linguistic protocols that these historians used to pre-figure that set of events prior to writing their narratives of it." Ibid., 95. See also White, "Foucault Decoded: Notes from Underground," in *Tropics of Discourse*, 254, where White discusses "the projective or generational aspect of language."

54. White, *Metahistory*, 430.

55. White, *Tropics of Discourse*, 72; my emphasis.

56. Ibid., 5–6, 7.

57. Ibid., 6.

58. Ibid.

59. Ibid., 15.

60. Ibid., 12.

61. Ibid., 5.

62. Ibid., 15. The tropes constitute "the cycles through which consciousness passes in its efforts to know a world which always surpasses our capacities to know it fully" (254). White contends that "a similar kind of tropological reduction underlies and sustains Foucault's analysis of the course of the human sciences from the sixteenth to the twentieth-century" (255). Note, however, that not all readers have seen it this way. Hans Kellner, White's most astute critic, thinks White is ambivalent "on the question of whether the tropes offer a set of 'stages' of mind knowing itself through time . . . or a spatial 'grid' of linguistic possibilities always already inherent in natural languages." See Kellner, "A Bed-

rock of Order: Hayden White's Linguistic Humanism," *History and Theory* 19 (1980): 20.

63. White, *Metahistory*, 38.

64. Ibid., 432, 433.

65. Ibid., 145. White is here describing Jules Michelet's attitude toward irony, but it reflects his own with equal force.

66. Ibid., 434.

67. White, *Tropics of Discourse*, 44.

68. As Frank Lentricchia remarked, "Once the Kantian turn from realism is made there is no way to disguise our 'inventions' with the mask of 'discovery.' " Lentricchia, *After the New Criticism* (Chicago: University of Chicago Press, 1980), 59.

69. Friedrich Wilhelm Nietzsche, *Thus Spoke Zarathustra*, trans. R. J. Hollingdale (Harmondsworth, Eng.: Penguin, 1961), 156, as quoted by Willson Havelock Coates and Hayden V. White, *The Ordeal of Liberal Humanism: An Intellectual HIstory of Western Europe* (New York: McGraw-Hill, 1970), 205.

70. "Any prose description of any phenomenon can be shown on analysis to contain at least one move or transition in the sequence of descriptive utterances that violates a canon of logical consistency. How could it be otherwise, when even the model of the syllogism itself displays clear evidence of troping. The move from the major premise (All men are mortal) to the choice of the datum to serve as the minor (Socrates is a man) is itself a tropological move, a 'swerve' from the universe to the particular which logic cannot preside over, since it is logic itself that is being served by this move." White, *Tropics of Discourse*, 3.

71. Ibid., 3–4.

72. Ibid., 4.

73. Ibid., 3.

74. Ibid., 23.

75. White, *Metahistory*, 434.

76. Ibid., 433.

77. Hans Kellner—perhaps the most sympathetic and perceptive of White's critics—has described the essential contradiction this way: "If language [rhetoric] is irreducible, a 'sacred' beginning, then human freedom is sacrificed. If men are free to choose their linguistic protocols, then some deeper, prior, force must be posited. White asserts as an existential paradox that men *are* free, and that language *is* irreducible." Kellner, "Bedrock of Order," 23.

78. On the idea of narrative form as the "deep structure"—as opposed to the "surface manifestation"—of a text, see Seymour Chatman, *Story and Discourse: Narrative Structure in Fiction and Film* (Ithaca: Cornell University Press, 1978).

79. White, *Content of the Form*, 1.

80. Ibid., 14. "Narrativizing discourse serves the purpose of moralizing judgments" (24).

81. Ibid., 4; my emphasis.

82. Louis Mink makes this point in "Critical Response: Everyman His or Her Own Annalist," *Critical Inquiry* 7 (summer 1981): 783. Hans Kellner made

the same point in a special symposium issue of *History and Theory* 19, 4 (1980): 16, and again on 29: "It is this willed Nietzschean forgetting that gives *Metahistory* its power."

83. White, *Content of the Form,* 31, 87; my emphasis. White is here following Gadamer and Ricoeur. For the latter, see A. J. Greimas and Paul Ricoeur, "On Narrativity," *New Literary History* 20, 3 (1989): 551–62, and Paul Ricoeur, "Narrative Time," *Critical Inquiry* 7, 1 (1980): 169–90.

84. Richard T. Vann is typical in his condemnation of "the full-fledged relativism which Hayden White had so unabashedly endorsed." See Vann, "Louis Mink's Linguistic Turn," *History and Theory* 26 (1987): 14.

85. In other words, it is not unlike Noam Chomsky's notion of a "generative grammar," the clearest exposition of which can be found in Chomsky, *Language and Mind,* enl. ed. (New York: Harcourt Brace Jovanovich, 1972).

86. Barbara Herrnstein Smith, "Narrative Versions, Narrative Theories," in *On Narrative.* ed. W. J. T. Mitchell (Chicago: University of Chicago Press, 1981), 209–32, esp. 212.

87. White, *Content of the Form,* 184.

88. Hans Kellner, " 'Never Again' Is Now," *History and Theory* 33 (May 1994): 7 of my downloaded copy.

89. Friedlander, *Probing the Limits of Representation,* 9.

90. Berel Lang, "Is It Possible to Misrepresent the Holocaust?" *History and Theory* 34 (February 1995): 3 of my downloaded version.

91. Martin Jay, "Of Plots, Witnesses, and Judgments," in Friedlander, *Probing the Limits of Representation,* 102.

92. White, "Historical Emplotment," 37–38.

93. Ibid., 40–41; my emphasis.

94. Ibid., 42, 41.

95. Ibid., 42. See Andreas Hillgruber, *Zweierlei Untergang: Die Zerschlagung des deutschen Reiches und das Ende des europäischen Judentums* (Berlin: W. J. Siedler, 1986).

96. White, "Historical Emplotment," 43.

97. Ibid., 42.

98. Ibid., 47, 48.

CHAPTER SIX

1. Hayden White, "What Is an Historical System?" in *Biology, History, and Natural Philosophy,* ed. Allen D. Breck and Wolfgang Yourgrau (New York: Plenum, 1972), 241; emphasis in the original.

2. White, *Tropics of Discourse: Essays in Cultural Criticism* (Baltimore: Johns Hopkins University Press, 1978), 264.

3. Hayden White, *The Content of the Form: Narrative Discourse and Historical Representation* (Baltimore: Johns Hopkins University Press, 1987), 75.

4. Richard Rorty, *Contingency, Irony, Solidarity* (New York: Cambridge University Press, 1989), 43.

5. Ibid., 74.

6. Richard Rorty, *Consequences of Pragmatism* (Minneapolis: University of Minnesota Press, 1982), 131.

7. Rorty, *Contingency, Irony, Solidarity*, 73.

8. See Daniel Bell, "The Mood of Three Generations" in Bell, *The End of Ideology: On the Exhaustion of Political Ideas in the Fifties* (New York: Free Press, 1960). The classic account of this intellectual and cultural sea change is, of course, John Patrick Diggins, *Up from Communism: Conservative Odysseys in American Intellectual History* (New York: Harper and Row, 1975). But see also Diggins, *The Rise and Fall of the American Left* (New York: Norton, 1992), esp. 145–217.

9. Bell, *End of Ideology*.

10. Richard Rorty, "Wild Orchids and Trotsky," in *Wild Orchids and Trotsky*, ed. Mark Edmundson (New York: Viking Penguin, 1993), 34. In 1939 the New International grouped James Rorty—Richard Rorty's father—with Max Eastman, Sidney Hook, Edmund Wilson, James T. Farrell, Louis Hacker, and others as leaders of a movement it described as "Intellectuals in Retreat." See Diggins, *Up from Communism*, 177-78.

11. Rorty, "Wild Orchids and Trotsky," 47.

12. Richard Rorty, "For a Moral Banal Politics," *Harpers Magazine* 284 (May 1992): 16.

13. Rorty, "Wild Orchids and Trotsky," 47.

14. James as quoted by Rorty, "Wild Orchids and Trotsky," 44, 46.

15. Ibid., 48, 46. Rorty wants us to hold fast to what he sees as "a certain contingent historical phenomenon—the gradual spread of the sense that the pain of others matters, regardless of whether they are of the same family, tribe, religion, nation, or intelligence as oneself." Ibid., 43.

16. Ibid., 47. You can get a sense of exactly how cautious Rorty's hopefulness is in the following passage: "I see the culture of the liberal democracies as still providing a lot of opportunities for self-criticism and reform. . . . This is not to say that there are particular reasons for optimism about America, or the rich North Atlantic democracies generally, in the year in which I write (1990). Several of these democracies, including the United States, are presently under the control of an increasingly greedy and selfish middle class—a class which continually elect cynical demagogues willing to deprive the weak of hope in order to promise tax cuts to their constituents. If this process goes on for another generation, the countries in which it happens will be barbarized." Richard Rorty, *Philosophical Papers* (New York: Cambridge University Press, 1991), 1:15 n. 29. Contrast this with Rorty's view in 1980: "On my view, we should be more willing than we are to celebrate bourgeois capitalist society as the best policy actualized so far, while regretting that it is irrelevant to most of the problems of most of the population of the planet." Rorty, *Consequences of Pragmatism*, 210 n. 16.

17. Rorty, *Consequences of Pragmatism*, 69.

18. Ibid., xx–xxi.

19. Milan Kundera, *The Unbearable Lightness of Being* (London: Faber and Faber, 1985), 35.

20. "In landlessness alone resides the highest truth, shoreless, indefinite as God." Herman Melville, *Moby Dick* (New York: Bantam, 1986), 105.

21. Rorty, *Contingency, Irony, Solidarity*, 22; emphasis in the original.

22. Rorty admits that even as late as 1990 "there is still an air of provincial-

ism about pragmatism." Richard Rorty, "Pragmatism as Anti-representational-ism," in *Pragmatism, from Peirce to Davidson*, ed. John P. Murphy (Boulder, Colo.: Westview, 1990), 1.

23. Sidney Hook, *John Dewey* (New York: John Day, 1939), 34–35, as quoted by Rorty, *Consequences of Pragmatism*, 74.

24. William James, "What Pragmatism Means" (1907), in *The American Intellectual Tradition*, ed. David Hollinger and Charles Capper (New York: Oxford University Press, 1989), 2:104. As Rorty explains, "The pragmatists identified truth with 'what we will believe if we keep inquiring by our present lights,' or 'what it is better for us to believe,' or 'warranted assertability.'" Richard Rorty, *Philosophy and the Mirror of Nature* (Princeton: Princeton University Press, 1980), 308.

25. On Sidney Hook's intellectual odyssey from Marxism to pragmatism, see Diggins, *Rise and Fall of the American Left*, 59–64.

26. Rorty, *Philosophical Papers*, 1:77. Rorty has been very frank about his differences with Dewey and Hook on what Dewey used to call "the scientific method." See, for example, Rorty's introduction to *John Dewey: The Later Works*, vol. 8, ed. Jo Ann Boydston (Carbondale: Southern Illinois University Press, 1986), ix–xviii, and Rorty, *Philosophical Papers*, 1:16–17, 64–72, esp. 74–77.

27. Rorty, *Philosophical Papers*, 1:216.

28. Rorty, *Consequences of Pragmatism*, 63.

29. Ibid. Rorty is clearly nostalgic about this "Deweyan experimentalism." In another place he calls it "the dominant intellectual movement of a more hopeful time." Rorty, *Philosophical Papers*, 1:77. For an interesting description of Rorty's early relationship with Hook, see ibid., 1:17n.

30. Rorty, "Professionalized Philosophy and Transcendentalist Culture," *Georgia Review* 30 (1976): 757-69, which reappeared as chapter 4 of Rorty, *Consequences of Pragmatism*.

31. Rorty, *Consequences of Pragmatism*, 64.

32. Ibid., xviii; see also 76, 203–8.

33. Rorty, *Philosophical Papers*, 1:77.

34. Rorty, *Philosophy and the Mirror of Nature*, xiii.

35. As Rorty puts it, he quickly learned that "a 'philosophical problem' was a product of the unconscious adoption of assumptions built into the vocabulary in which the problem was stated." Ibid., xiii.

36. J. G. A. Pocock, "Languages and Their Implications: The Transformation of the Study of Political Thought," in *Politics, Language, and Time: Essays on Political Thought and History* (New York: Atheneum, 1971), 25–26; my emphasis.

37. J. G. A. Pocock, as quoted by Joyce Appleby, "Ideology and the History of Political Thought," *Intellectual History Group Newsletter* 2 (1980), 15.

38. As Pocock explained, she had to reconstruct "the changing function, context and application of conceptual languages . . . found in particular societies at particular times." J. G. A. Pocock as quoted by Appleby, ibid., 11.

39. Joyce Appleby, "One Good Turn Deserves Another: Moving beyond the

Linguistic; a Response to David Harlan," *American Historical Review* 94 (December 1989): 1327.

40. Pocock, "Languages and Their Implications," 24.

41. Ibid., 25.

42. J. G. A. Pocock, *Virtue, Commerce, and History: Essays on Political Thought and History, Chiefly in the Eighteenth Century* (New York: Cambridge University Press, 1985), 5, 8.

43. See Quentin Skinner, "Hermeneutics and the Role of History," *New Literary History* 7 (1975-76): 211.

44. Richard Rorty, "Method, Social Science and Social Hope," in Rorty, *Consequences of Pragmatism*, 203. This essay was written for a conference at the University of California at Berkeley in 1980.

45. Louis Althusser as quoted by Houston A. Baker Jr., *Blues, Ideology, and Afro-American Literature: A Vernacular Theory* (Chicago: University of Chicago Press, 1984), 16.

46. William James, "The Will to Believe" (1897), in *Pragmatism: The Classic Writings*, ed. H. S. Thayer (New York: New American Library, 1970), 207.

47. Rorty, *Contingency, Irony, Solidarity*, 16.

48. See Stuart Hampshire, *Morality and Conflict* (Oxford: Blackwell, 1983), 51.

49. Alan Brinkley, "Mythic but Useful," *Times Literary Supplement*, 10–16 November 1989, 1246. Peter Novick makes essentially the same claim in *That Noble Dream: The "Objectivity Question" and the American Historical Profession* (Cambridge: Cambridge University Press, 1988), 598: "Working historians . . . pay less and less lip service to the ideal."

50. Charles Beard, "Written History as an Act of Faith," *American Historical Review* 39 (1934): 219.

51. "The human self is created by the use of a vocabulary rather than being adequately or inadequately expressed in a vocabulary." Rorty, *Contingency, Irony, Solidarity*, 7.

52. White, "What Is an Historical System?" 239; some emphasis added.

53. Rorty, *Contingency, Irony, Solidarity*, 6; emphasis in the original.

54. Richard Rorty, "Freud and Moral Reflection," in *Pragmatism's Freud: The Moral Disposition of Psychoanalysis*, ed. Joseph H. Smith and William Kerrigan (Baltimore: Johns Hopkins University Press, 1986), 2.

55. "There is no human nature which was once, or still is, in chains. Rather, our species has—ever since it developed language—been making up a nature for itself. This nature has been developed through ever larger, richer, more muddled, and more painful syntheses of opposing values." Rorty, *Philosophical Papers*, 1:213.

56. Rorty, *Contingency, Irony, Solidarity*, xiii.

57. René Descartes, *The Philosophical Works of Descartes*, trans. Elizabeth S. Haldane and G. R. T. Ross (Cambridge: Cambridge University Press, 1934), 1:101.

58. There is only "a tissue of contingent relations, a web which stretches backward and forward through past and future time, for a formed, unified,

present, self-contained substance [one's self], something capable of being seen steadily and whole." Ibid., 41.

59. Van Wyck Brooks, *The Wine of the Puritans: A Study of Present-Day America* (1908; London: Sisley's, 1969), 138.

60. Rorty, *Contingency, Irony, Solidarity,* 27; Rorty, "Freud and Moral Reflection," 20.

61. Rorty, *Contingency, Irony, Solidarity,* 29.

62. Ibid.

63. Ibid., 36.

64. Ibid., 42.

65. Rorty, "Freud and Moral Reflection," 12.

66. Sigmund Freud, *Civilization and Its Discontents* (1929; New York: Norton, 1961), 92, 93. In this Freud was simply echoing the thoughts of innumerable earlier thinkers. John Locke, for example, had insisted that men were driven to work by what he called their "fantastical uneasiness." Even the amiable Benjamin Franklin insisted that men worked less to find pleasure than to avoid pain. For an interesting and enlightening discussion along these lines see John P. Diggins, *The Lost Soul of American Politics: Virtue, Self-Interest, and the Foundations of Liberalism* (New York: Basic, 1984), 7ff.

67. Rorty, *Contingency, Irony, Solidarity,* 75; my emphasis.

68. Ibid., 41.

69. See, for example, Cornel West, *The American Evasion of Philosophy: A Genealogy of Pragmatism* (Madison: University of Wisconsin Press, 1989), 19−20.

70. Bell Hooks as quoted by Giles Gunn, *Thinking across the American Grain: Ideology, Intellect, and the New Pragmatism* (Chicago: University of Chicago Press, 1992), 10.

71. "The redescribing ironist, by threatening one's final vocabulary, and thus one's ability to make sense of oneself in one's own terms rather than hers, suggests that one's self and one's world are futile, obsolete, *powerless.* Redescription often humiliates." Rorty, *Contingency, Irony, Solidarity,* 90.

72. Ibid., 95, 144.

73. Jacques Derrida as quoted by Michael Fischer, *Stanley Cavell and Literary Skepticism* (Chicago: University of Chicago Press, 1989), 56, from Derrida, *Of Grammatology,* trans. Gayatri Chakravorty Spivak (Baltimore: Johns Hopkins University Press, 1976), 233. Thomas Wolfe, *Look Homeward, Angel* (1929; New York: Scribner's, 1957), 35.

74. Rainer Rilke as quoted by Charles Taylor, *Sources of the Self: The Making of the Modern Identity* (Cambridge: Harvard University Press, 1989), 346, from Rilke, *The Selected Poetry of Rainer Maria Rilke,* trans. Stephen Mitchell (New York: Vintage, 1984), 161.

75. Montaigne as quoted by Charles Taylor, *Sources of the Self,* 179, from Michel de Montaigne, *The Essays of Montaigne,* trans. John Florio (New York: Modern Library, 1933), 24.

76. Rorty, "Wild Orchids and Trotsky," 43, 41.

77. Harold Bloom as quoted in *Contemporary Literary Criticism,* ed. Sharon R. Gunton (Detroit: Gale, 1983), 24:70.

78. Harold Bloom, *The Anxiety of Influence: A Theory of Poetry* (London: Oxford University Press, 1973), 6. But see also Bloom, *Agon: Towards a Theory of Revisionism* (New York: Oxford University Press, 1982), in which he seems to regret (and indeed revises) his earlier Oedipal interpretation of poetic influence.

79. James H. Cone, *Martin and Malcolm and America: A Dream or a Nightmare* (Maryknoll, N.Y.: Orbis, 1991), 32.

80. Alice Walker, *In Search of Our Mothers' Gardens* (New York: Harcourt, Brace, Jovanovich, 1983), 89–91. Like Richard Rorty, Alice Walker tends to feel her way along by searching for predecessors she can adopt. In *In Search of Our Mothers' Gardens* she talks about the indebtedness she feels not only to Hurston but also to Flannery O'Connor, Jean Toomer, Colette, Anaïs Nin, Tillie Olson, and Virginia Woolf.

81. Ibid., 102; emphasis in the original.

82. Rorty, *Consequences of Pragmatism*, 65.

83. Rorty, "The Historiography of Philosophy: Four Genres," in *Philosophy in History: Essays on the Historiography of Philosophy*, ed. Richard Rorty, J. B. Schneedwind, and Quentin Skinner (New York: Cambridge University Press, 1984), 51; Rorty, *Consequences of Pragmatism*, 65. For another example, see Frank Lentricchia, "My Kinsman, T. S. Eliot," in Edmundson, *Wild Orchids and Trotsky*, 51–76. Mark Edmundson, one of Rorty's colleagues at the University of Virginia, recently remarked, "I am inclined to look for a productive angle of vision, not 'the whole truth and nothing but.'" Edmundson, "The Academy Writes Back," in Edmundson, *Wild Orchids and Trotsky*, 10.

84. Alexander Nehamas, *Nietzsche: Life as Literature* (Cambridge: Harvard University Press, 1985), 234.

85. Rorty, *Contingency, Irony, Solidarity*, 79–80; my emphasis.

86. Rorty, "Historiography of Philosophy," 6, 52. This is precisely the practice Skinner condemned as "the Mythology of Coherence." See Quentin Skinner, "Meaning and Understanding in the History of Ideas," *History and Theory* 8 (1969): 16–20. According to Peter Brooks, Malcolm Bowie does the same thing with Jacques Lacan: "Bowie regularly takes his reader back to the Freudian sources of Lacan's arguments, to show how they are reworked into what Freud might have said had he been trained in twentieth-century Saussurian linguistics rather than nineteenth-century thermodynamics and biology." Brooks, "The Proffered Word," *Times Literary Supplement*, 8 November 1991, 12.

87. Andrew Delbanco, "Talking Texts," *New Republic*, 9 January 1989, 31.

88. Henry Louis Gates, "The Weaning of America," *New Yorker*, 19 April 1993, 114; Rorty, *Philosophical Papers*, 1:95 n. 1. It is also what the historian Peter Burke calls "the strategy of the surprising juxtaposition."

89. Rorty, *Contingency, Irony, Solidarity*, 137.

90. Ibid., 134.

91. Rorty, *Philosophical Papers*, 2:2.

92. This is essentially what John G. Gunnell, the historian of political thought, has called a "retrospective analytical tradition." See Gunnell, *Political Theory: Tradition and Interpretation* (Cambridge, Mass.: Winthrop, 1979), 70.

93. Rorty, "Historiography of Philosophy," 51.

94. Alan Trachtenberg, foreword to Casey Nelson Blake, *Beloved Commu-*

nity: The Cultural Criticism of Randolph Bourne, Van Wyck Brooks, Waldo Frank, and Lewis Mumford (Chapel Hill: University of North Carolina Press, 1990), xii−xiii; my emphasis.

95. Rorty, *Contingency, Irony, Solidarity*, 22.

96. Rorty, *Philosophical Papers*, 2:2.

97. Rorty, *Consequences of Pragmatism*, xviii.

98. Rorty, *Philosophy and the Mirror of Nature*, 10.

99. Rorty, *Philosophical Papers*, 1:1. Rorty described in more detail how he goes about this in "Historiography of Philosophy."

100. Rorty, "Historiography of Philosophy," 54. This is what John Gunnell calls a "retrospective analytical tradition" and Rorty himself calls "rational reconstruction." For Rorty, see ibid.; for Gunnell, see Gunnell, *Political Theory*, 70.

101. James, "Will to Believe," 92−93.

102. Joan Didion, "On Morality," in *Slouching towards Bethlehem* (New York: Dell, 1968), 159−61.

103. Daniel T. Rodgers, "Before Postmodernism," *Reviews in American History* 18, 1 (1990): 77.

104. For two recent discussions see Martha Nussbaum, " 'Finely Aware and Richly Responsible': Moral Attention and the Moral Task of Literature," *Journal of Philosophy* 82 (1985): 516−29; and William E. Cain, "The Ethics of Criticism: Does Literature Do Any Good?" *College English* 53 (April 1991): 467−76.

105. See Lorna Sage, "Fear Is the Spur," *Times Literary Supplement*, 14− 20 April 1989, 389; Mark Edmundson, "Bloom's Giant Forms," *London Review of Books*, 1 June 1989, 13. Not everyone agrees that this approach is such a good thing, however; Stanley Cavell, for one, thinks this is precisely what is wrong with American intellectual life: "The effort of the American intellectual is not to relate himself to the world but to interrogate and discover himself." Cavell, "An Apology for Skepticism," in *The American Philosopher: Conversations with Quine, Davidson, Putnam, Nozick, Danto, Rorty, Cavell, MacIntyre, and Kuhn*, ed. Giovanna Borradori (Chicago: University of Chicago Press, 1994), 121.

106. Emily Dickinson, poem no. 1695.

107. I take this notion of a patterning of thought and desire from Martha C. Nussbaum's wonderful book, *Love's Knowledge: Essays on Philosophy and Literature* (New York: Oxford University Press, 1990).

108. Interestingly enough, this is pretty much what Rorty says about psychoanalysis: that it gives us a vocabulary we can use for striking up a conversation with our various unconscious selves—selves we might otherwise ignore. See Richard Rorty, "Freud and Moral Reflection," passim but esp. 5−7.

109. I have borrowed this idea from Wayne C. Booth, *The Company We Keep: An Ethics of Fiction* (Berkeley: University of California Press, 1988).

110. As John Patrick Diggins once put it, literature "opens the heart and educates the soul." Diggins, *Lost Soul of American Politics*, 332.

111. Melville, *Moby Dick*, 171.

112. Arthur Schlesinger, "The American Creed: From Dilemma to Decomposition," *New Perspectives Quarterly* 8 (summer 1991): 20. See also Schlesinger's more extended discussion of "the desperate necessity of national cohesion

within the frame of shared national ideals" in Schlesinger, *The Disuniting of America* (Knoxville, Tenn.: Whittle Direct Books, 1991), 14 and passim.

113. Schlesinger thinks that "the mechanism for translating diversity into unity has been the American Creed, the civic culture." Schlesinger, *Disuniting of America,* 79.

114. Henry Louis Gates, "Whose Culture Is It, Anyway?" *New York Times,* national ed., 4 May 1991, 15.

115. Randolph Bourne, "Trans-national America," in Hollinger and Capper, *American Intellectual Tradition,* 2:157. For a discussion of conservative opposition to just this sort of "multiculturalism" within the academy, see Jennifer Wong, "Conservative Scholars See 'Multiculturalism' as a Plague," *Chronicle of Higher Education,* 19 September 1990, A41.

116. Arthur Schlesinger, "A Dissent on Multicultural Education," *Partisan Review* 58 (fall 1991): 632.

117. Diggins, *Lost Soul of American Politics,* 8–9. In "The Virtues of Liberalism: Christianity, Republicanism, and Ethics in Early American Political Discourse," *Journal of American History* 74 (June 1987); 9–33, James Kloppenberg does something similar, arguing that Americans have traditionally checked their commitment to Lockean liberalism with the countertradition of eighteenth-century republicanism.

118. Abraham Lincoln, "Second Inaugural Address," in *Lincoln: Speeches and Writings* (New York: Library of America, 1989), 2:687. For Lincoln's reference to "the sacred rights of property," see ibid., 413.

119. Gordon Wood, "America in the 1790s," *Atlantic Monthly,* December 1993, 134.

CHAPTER SEVEN

1. "History," Adams concluded, "is only a value of relation." Henry Adams, *The Education of Henry Adams,* ed. Ernest Samuels (Boston: Houghton Mifflin, 1973), 405, 488.

2. Ibid., 302.

3. Wahneema Lubiano, "Henry Louis Gates and African-American Literary Discourse," *New England Quarterly* 62 (December 1989): 561.

4. Perhaps the most explicit example comes from the antebellum American South, where "there was only a pure-white category and its negation." Werner Sollors, *Beyond Ethnicity: Consent and Descent in American Culture* (New York: Oxford University Press, 1986), 37. For a discussion of how "the trope of blackness in Western discourse has signified absence at least since Plato," see Henry Louis Gates, *Figures in Black: Words, Signs, and the "Racial" Self* (New York: Oxford University Press, 1987), 235–76, esp. 274.

5. Jones as quoted by Werner Sollors, "Of Mules and Mares in a Land of Difference; or, Quadrupeds All?" *American Quarterly* 42 (June 1990): 181–82. The Senegalese poet Leopold Sedar Senghor once argued, in a similar vein, that "Emotion is Negro, as reason is Hellenic." See Roger Shattuck and Samba Ka, "Born Again African," *New York Review of Books* 37 (20 December 1990): 20. Sympathetic whites have sometimes offered the same sort of essentialist argument. In a well-known review of *The Autobiography of Malcolm X,* Richard

Gilman argued that the book "is not the potential possession—even by imaginative appropriation—of us all; hard, local, instransigent, alien, it remains in some sense unassimilable for those of us who aren't black." Gilman quoted in Sollors, "Of Mules and Mares in a Land of Difference," 184.

6. Larry Neal as quoted by Houston Baker, "Generational Shifts and the Recent Criticism of African-American Literature," *Black American Literature Forum* 15 (spring 1981): 5, 6; Henry Louis Gates, "Tell Me, Sir, . . . What *Is* 'Black' Literature?" *PMLA* 105 (January 1990): 14. Gates himself once described the Black Arts movement as "the cultural reflection of the epiphenomenal Black Power movement." Gates, "Charles T. Davis and the Critical Imperative in African-American Literature," in *Black Is the Color of the Cosmos: Essays on African-American Literature and Culture, 1942-1981*, by Charles T. Davis, ed. Henry Louis Gates (New York: Garland, 1982), xix.

7. Baker, "Generational Shifts," 4.

8. "'Black Power,' as a motivating philosophy for the Black Aesthetic, was deemed an ideological failure by the mid-seventies." Baker, "Generational Shifts," 11.

9. "From an assumed 'structural peculiarity' of African-American expressive culture, the emergence generation of intellectuals [the Black Arts Movement intellectuals] proceeded to assert a *sui generis* tradition of African-American art and a unique 'standard of criticism' suitable for its elucidation." Baker, "Generational Shifts," 6.

10. Gates earned his M.A. from Cambridge University in 1974.

11. Elaine Showalter, "A Criticism of Our Own: Autonomy and Assimilation in African-American and Feminist Literary Theory," in *The Future of Literary Theory*, ed. Ralph Cohen (New York: Routledge, 1989), 353. Baker has also described how, in the late 1960s "a generation of young blackmale poststructuralist critics (following the lead of white counterparts) became influential in the academy. These blackmale literary critics had moved decisively to nonhistorial, theoretical modes of inquiry by the mid-seventies." Houston A. Baker Jr., *Workings of the Spirit: The Poetics of Afro-American Women's Writing* (Chicago: University of Chicago Press, 1991), 16.

12. Baker, "Generational Shifts," 11.

13. Gates, "Tell Me, Sir," 14.

14. "What was identified as European or Western essentialism—masked under the rubric of 'universality'—was attacked by asserting an oppositional black or 'neo-African' essentialism." Ibid., 20.

15. The best treatment of these questions is still Sollors, *Beyond Ethnicity*. But see also Werner Sollors, ed., *The Invention of Ethnicity* (New York: Oxford University Press, 1989); and Sollors, "Of Mules and Mares in a Land of Difference," 167–90. For an interesting discussing of Sollors's argument by a leading black philosopher, see Anthony Appiah, "Are We Ethnic? The Theory and Practice of American Pluralism," *Black American Literature Forum* 20 (spring–summer 1986): 209–24.

16. Gates, *Figures in Black*, 53.

17. Ibid., 53.

18. Ibid., xxviii; Henry Louis Gates, "Preface to Blackness: Text and Pre-

text," in *Afro-American Literature: The Reconstruction of Instruction*, ed. Dexter Fisher and Robert B. Stepto (New York: Modern Language Association, 1978).

19. John Patrick Diggins, "The Problem of Contextualism in Intellectual History," *Intellectual History Newsletter* 3 (1981): 20. See also Hayden White, "The Context in the Text: Method and Ideology in Intellectual History," in White, *The Content of the Form: Narrative Discourse and Historical Representation* (Baltimore: Johns Hopkins University Press, 1987), 185–213, for an interesting discussion of contextualism.

20. See, for example, Dominick LaCapra, "Rethinking Intellectual History and Reading Texts," in *Modern European Intellectual History: Reappraisals and New Perspectives*, ed. Dominick LaCapra and Steven L. Kaplan (Ithaca: Cornell University Press, 1982), 83.

21. Gates, "Preface to Blackness," 44–45.

22. Ibid., 46. See also Henry Louis Gates, "What's Love Got to Do with It?" *New Literary History* 18 (winter 1987): 347–48. Interestingly enough, Thomas Jefferson was one of the few reviewers who interpreted Wheatley's book as evidence that Africans did *not*, in fact, possess the intellectual potential of Englishmen. "Religion," he wrote, "indeed has produced a Phillis Whately [*sic*] but it could not produce a poet." Jefferson as quoted in ibid., 46.

23. Gates, "Preface to Blackness," 52.

24. Ibid., 53.

25. William Dean Howells as quoted by Gates, ibid., 53–54.

26. Ibid., 54.

27. Ibid., 57.

28. Henderson as quoted by Gates, ibid., 59.

29. Gates, *Figures in Black*, 62.

30. Addison Gayle as quoted by Gates, "Preface to Blackness," 65.

31. Gates, *Figures in Black*, 53.

32. Ibid., 55.

33. Ibid., 56.

34. For a contrary—and more critical—view of Gates's position, see Baker, "Generational Shifts," 3–21, esp. 15–19. Baker charges that "despite his disclaimer, Gates feels that literature is unrelated to culture."

35. Gates, *Figures in Black*, 64.

36. Ibid., 56–57.

37. Gates, "Preface to Blackness," 67.

38. Gates later explained that he had wanted to shift attention to "that which I have identified as the most repressed element of African-American criticism: the language of the text." Gates, *Figures in Black*, xxviii.

39. Gates, "What's Love Got to Do with It?" 352; my emphasis.

40. On "experience" as a constituted category rather than a self-evident reality, see Joan W. Scott, "The Evidence of Experience," *Critical Inquiry* 17 (summer 1991): 773–97.

41. As Gates wrote in the final paragraph of "Preface to Blackness," "the tendency of black criticism toward an ideological absolutism, with its attendant Inquisition, must come to an end" (68).

42. Stephen Henderson as quoted by Gates, ibid., 60.

43. Ibid., 61.

44. Ibid., 60.

45. Ibid., 61, 60.

46. "My work arose as a direct response to the theories of the Black Arts Movement." Gates, "What's Love Got to Do with It?" 359.

47. Gates, *Figures in Black,* xxi.

48. Gates, "Tell Me, Sir," 21.

49. Gates, "Preface to Blackness," 67; my emphasis. Gates has been roundly criticized for this statement. See, for example, Baker, "Generational Shifts," 15; Joyce A. Joyce, "The Black Canon: Reconstructing Black American Literary Criticism," *New Literary History* 18 (winter 1987): 337.

50. Barbara Smith made just this argument in 1977. See Smith, "Toward a Black Feminist Criticism," in *All the Women Are White, All the Blacks Are Men, but Some of Us Are Brave,* ed. Gloria T. Hull, Patricia Bell Scott, and Barbara Smith (Old Westbury, N.Y.: Feminist Press, 1982), 157–75. For the term "whitemale intellectualdom," see Baker, *Workings of the Spirit,* 12.

51. Gates, "Criticism in the Jungle," in *Black Literature and Literary Theory,* ed. Henry Louis Gates (New York: Methuen, 1984), 3, 8; Gates, "What's Love Got to Do with It?" 349.

52. Gates, "Criticism in the Jungle," 3, 7–8.

53. Gates, "What's Love Got to Do with It?" 349.

54. Gates, *Figures in Black,* 43. Others were beginning to voice the same criticism, though somewhat less decorously. Wade Nobles, for example, warned African American critics and historians, "When we adopt other people's theories, we are like Frankenstein doing other people's wills. It's like someone drinking some good stuff, vomiting it, and then we have to catch the vomit and drink it ourselves. . . . Don't become the vomit-drinkers!" Nobles as quoted by Schlesinger, *Disuniting of America,* 47.

55. Gates, "Criticism in the Jungle," 4, 9.

56. Ibid., 9–10; emphasis in the original.

57. Ibid., 8.

58. T. S. Eliot, *Selected Essays* (London: Faber and Faber, 1934), 14.

59. Gates, "Criticism in the Jungle," 4.

60. Philip Rieff, *Freud: The Mind of the Moralist,* 3d ed. (Chicago: University of Chicago Press, 1979), 137.

61. Gates, "Criticism in the Jungle," 6; emphasis in the original.

62. Ibid., 9–10; my emphasis.

63. Ibid., 20.

64. Ibid., 3.

65. Henry Louis Gates, Interview, *Art in America* 78 (September 1990): 82.

66. Gates, *Figures in Black,* 235. Gates, "The Blackness of Blackness: A Critique on the Sign and the Signifying Monkey," was originally published in *Critical Inquiry* 9 (June 1983): 685–723, then was reprinted in Gates, *Black Literature and Literary Theory,* 285–321, and again in Gates, *Figures in Black,* 235–76. "The Blackness of Blackness" was widely circulated in manuscript for five or six years before Gates finally published it in 1983. See Lubiano, "Henry Louis Gates."

67. It is, as Gates puts it, "indigenously black"; a "uniquely black rhetorical concept." Gates, *Figures in Black*, 48, 49, 235.

68. As early as 1980, Michel Laguerre had traced the African American conjure tradition back to the Yoruba people of West Africa. See Laguerre, *Voodoo Heritage* (Beverly Hills, Calif.: Sage, 1980).

69. Gates, *Figures in Black*, 237.

70. Houston A. Baker Jr., *Blues, Ideology, and Afro-American Literature: A Vernacular Theory* (Chicago: University of Chicago Press, 1984), x.

71. Gates, *Figures in Black*, 239.

72. Gates, "Criticism in the Jungle," 6.

73. Gates, *Figures in Black*, 261.

74. On "thinking up some new metaphors," see Richard Rorty, *Contingency, Irony, and Solidarity* (New York: Cambridge University Press, 1989), 27, and Rorty, "Unfamiliar Noises: Hesse and Davidson on Metaphor," in Rorty, *Philosophical Papers* (New York: Cambridge University Press, 1991), 1:162–72.

75. Ellison as quoted by Gates, *Figures in Black*, 243.

76. Henry Louis Gates, *The Signifying Monkey: A Theory of Afro-American Literary Criticism* (New York: Oxford University Press, 1988), xix. As Gates explains elsewhere, "Critical parody, or repetition and inversion, is what I define to be critical signification, or formal signifying, and is my metaphor for literary history." Gates, *Figures in Black*, 247.

77. Gates, *Figures in Black*, 236.

78. Gates, "What's Love Got to Do with It?" 358–59.

79. Ishmael Reed, *Mumbo Jumbo* (New York: Avon, 1972), 224.

80. "The vast and terrible text of blackness [is] produced in a dynamic process and manifested in discrete forms, as in black music and black speech acts." Gates, *Figures in Black*, 272.

81. Henry Louis Gates Jr., "The Master's Pieces: On Canon Formation and the African-American Tradition," *South Atlantic Quarterly* 89 (winter 1990): 108; reprinted in *The Bounds of Race: Perspectives on Hegemony and Resistance*, ed. Dominick LaCapra (Ithaca: Cornell University Press, 1991), 17–38.

82. Gates, *Figures in Black*, 242.

83. For one example among many, see ibid., 242.

84. Ibid.; my emphasis.

85. Henry Louis Gates, ed., *Bearing Witness: Selections from African-American Autobiography in the Twentieth Century* (New York: Pantheon, 1991), 8.

86. Françoise Lionnet, "Autoethnography: The An-archic Style of *Dust Tracks on a Road*," in *Writing Black, Writing Feminist: A Critical Anthology*, ed. Henry Louis Gates (New York: Penguin, 1990), 382–414.

87. Françoise Lionnet as quoted by Gates, *Writing Black, Writing Feminist*, 15. In her own study, *Autobiographical Voices* (Ithaca: Cornell University Press, 1989), Lionnet draws on the autobiographies of four black women (two African Americans, one Franco-Algerian, one from the Caribbean, and one from Mauritius) to show how black women autobiographers, in the very act of self-fashioning, have rewritten (and thereby transvalued) the notion of the "feminine" that had prevailed in each of their cultures.

88. Houston Baker makes a similar argument in *Workings of the Spirit*, 38–

39. He contends that the severity of white oppression led blacks to emphasize "autobiographical inscription."

89. Gates, *Bearing Witness*, 3, 4.

90. Ibid., 8.

91. As Sacvan Bercovitch might have put it. See Bercovitch, *The Puritan Origins of the American Self* (New Haven: Yale University Press, 1975), 179–80.

92. As the *New York Times* noted, "Gates's views have been attacked by a broad spectrum of critics, from black separatists intent on promoting 'Afrocentricity' to self-styled defenders of Western culture who decry the spread of 'victim studies.'" Adam Begley, "Henry Louis Gates, Jr.: Black Studies' New Star," *New York Times Magazine*, 1 April 1990, 48.

93. Baker, *Workings of the Spirit*, 12, 45.

94. Joyce A. Joyce, "Black Woman Scholar, Critic, and Teacher. The Inextricable Relationship between Race, Sex, and Class," *New Literary History* 22 (summer 1991): 557.

95. Joyce, "Black Woman Scholar, Critic, and Teacher," 552; emphasis in the original.

96. See Norman Harris, "'Who's Zooming Who': The New Black Formalism," *Journal of the Midwest Modern Language Association* 20 (spring 1987): 37–44.

97. Joe Weixlmann and Houston Baker Jr., "Introduction," in *Studies in Black American Literature*, vol. 3, *Black Feminist Criticism and Critical Theory*, ed. Weixlmann and Baker (Greenwood, Fla.: Penkevill, 1988), i–ii; Gates, *Signifying Monkey*, 42. As one African American critic put it, "To be sure, Gates indicates that his 'theory of interpretation' is 'arrived at from within the black cultural matrix,' but when he practices that theory the results send me flying back to the question, 'Who's zoomin' who?'" Norman Harris, "'Who's Zooming Who,'" 41.

98. Joyce, "Black Woman Scholar, Critic, and Teacher," 550.

99. As one influential black critic complained, Gates is trying "to move away from African-American literary criticism that can be construed as political or social." Harris, "'Who's Zooming Who,'" 37.

100. See Harris, "'Who's Zooming Who,'" 39.

101. Baker, "Generational Shifts," 4. Baker's oblique criticism is typical: "Like their immediate forerunners, the 'reconstructionists' were interested in establishing a sound theoretical framework for the future study of African-American literature. In their attempts to achieve this goal, however, some spokesmen for the new generation (whose work I shall discuss shortly) were hampered by a literary-critical 'professionalism' that was a function of their emergence class interests." Ibid., 11. Gates is the most prominent of the "spokesmen" Baker discusses later in his essay.

102. Joyce A. Joyce, "'Who the Cap Fit': Unconsciousness and Unconscionableness in the Criticism of Houston Baker and Henry Louis Gates," *New Literary History* 18 (winter 1987): 376; Lance Jeffers as quoted by Joyce, "Black Woman Scholar, Critic, and Teacher," 554.

103. For example, Houston Baker habitually extols "a right reading," of

texts; he insists that they be "properly understood." See *Workings of the Spirit*, 153, for one illustration.

104. Gates, *Figures in Black*, xxviii.

105. Gates, "Preface," in Davis, *Black Is the Color of the Cosmos*, xi.

106. Wright as quoted by Houston A. Baker Jr., *Long Black Song: Essays in Black American Literature and Culture* (Charlottesville: University Press of Virginia, 1972), 20.

107. See Anthony Appiah, "Strictures on Structures: The Prospects for a Structuralist Poetics of African Fiction," in Gates, *Black Literature and Literary Theory*, 127–50. William Raspberry has made the same argument less formally. See Raspberry, "Euro, Afro and Other Eccentric 'Centrics,' " *Washington Post*, 10 September 1990. For an example of the contrary argument—that there is only one "African Cultural System," see Molefi Kete Asante, *Afrocentricity* (Trenton, N.J.: Africa World Press, 1988).

Anthony Appiah is a close friend of Gates. He has written extensively on "black," "African," and "race" as culturally constructed categories. See, for example, Appiah, "The Uncompleted Argument: W. E. B. DuBois and the Illusion of Race," in *"Race," Writing, and Difference*, ed. Henry Louis Gates (Chicago: University of Chicago Press, 1986); Appiah, "The Conservation of 'Race,' " *Black American Literature Forum* 23 (spring 1989): 37-60; and Appiah, "Alexander Crummell and the Invention of Africa," *Massachusetts Review*, 31 (autumn 1990): 385–406.

108. Joyce, " 'Who the Cap Fit,' " 373.

109. Ibid., 380.

110. Baker, *Workings of the Spirit*, 22; Baker, *Long Black Song*, 144.

111. Joyce, " 'Who the Cap Fit,' " 372. Not everyone on the African American left thinks poststructuralism is reactionary, of course. Houston Baker, for one, insists that the work of "poststructuralist thinkers such as Derrida, Althusser, Lacan, and Baudrillard," far from being reactionary, is inherently subversive, that its politics are "in clear harmony with, say, the freedom cries of millions of blacks in South Africa bent on a new and revolutionary existence." Baker, "In Dubious Battle," *New Literary History* 18 (winter 1987): 369. For Baker and for some other African Americans on the left, poststructuralism is "the political and academic heralding note of a new and liberating future." Ibid., 369.

112. Richard Rorty talking about the terms human being and woman. Rorty, "Feminism and Pragmatism," *Michigan Quarterly Review* 30 (spring 1991): 238. I have borrowed many of the ideas for these next two paragraphs from "Feminism and Pragmatism."

113. What Catharine Stimpson once said about the category "female"—that it is an empty category—applies with equal force to the category "black": "The commonality of the female becomes nothing more, nothing less, than an accident of birth, a chromosomal draw." Catharine Stimpson, "Woolf's Room, Our Project: The Building of Feminist Criticism," in Cohen, *Future of Literary Theory*, 143.

114. "Finding metaphors . . . from within the African-American tradition, and combining these with that which is useful in contemporary literary theory,

is the challenge of African-American literary history." Gates, *Figures in Black*, 47–48.

115. Robert B. Reich, *The Work of Nations: Preparing Ourselves for Twenty-first Century Capitalism* (New York: Knopf, 1991). Robert B. Reich, "Secession of the Successful," *New York Times*, 20 January, 1991.

116. This is the question that animates Reich, *Work of Nations*, part 4, "The Meaning of Nation," and especially chapter 25, "Who Is 'Us'?"

117. Schlesinger, *Disuniting of America*, 81.

118. Rorty, *Philosophical Papers*, 1:203.

119. Henry Louis Gates, "Multicultural Madness," *Tikkun* 6 (November–December 1991); 56.

120. "Being an African-American or an Italian-American is a particular mode of being an American and not a way of being African or Italian. Descent, here, is the pretext, not the cause, of a certain kind of consent." Appiah, "Are We Ethnic?" 223. Appiah is paraphrasing the argument Werner Sollors presented in *Beyond Ethnicity*.

121. What is most distinctive about American culture, from this point of view, is that it "unifies and harmonizes an extraordinarily diverse group of races and nations." Editorial, *National Review*, 27 May 1991, 18.

122. Donald Kagan, "Western Values Are Central," *New York Times*, national ed., 4 May 1991, 15.

123. Ibid. Notice, however, that Kagan is not decrying racial diversity so much as cultural fragmentation, as he himself makes clear: "Happily, student bodies have grown vastly more diverse. Less happily, students see themselves increasingly as parts of groups, distinct from other groups."

124. Carl Degler, "In Search of the Un-hyphenated American," *New Perspectives Quarterly* 8 (September 1991): 51.

125. Arthur Schlesinger, "A Dissent on Multicultural Education," *Partisan Review* 58 (fall 1991): 630.

126. Schlesinger, *Disuniting of America*, 8. The term actually comes from Gunnar Myrdal, as Schlesinger explains.

127. Ibid., 67.

128. Arthur Schlesinger, "The American Creed: From Dilemma to Decomposition," *New Perspectives Quarterly* 8 (summer 1991): 21.

129. Schlesinger, "American Creed," 21; Schlesinger, *Disuniting of America*, 71.

130. Schlesinger, *Disuniting of America*, 76.

131. Schlesinger, "Dissent on Multicultural Education," 634. Richard Rorty had made the same argument. See Rorty, "The Opening of the American Mind," *Harpers Magazine*, July 1989, xx.

132. Henry Louis Gates, "Whose Culture Is It, Anyway?" *New York Times*, 4 May 1991, national ed., 15. This has become the position among moderate advocates of multiculturalism. See Peter Erickson, "Rather Than Reject a Common Culture, Multiculturalism Advocates a More Complicated Route by Which to Achieve It," *Chronicle of Higher Education* 37 (26 June 1991): B1–4.

133. Gates, "Whose Culture Is It, Anyway?" 15.

134. Henry Louis Gates as quoted by Karen J. Winkler, "Proponents of 'Multicultural' Humanities Research Call for a Critical Look at Its Achievements," *Chronicle of Higher Education* 37 (28 November 1990): A5.

135. Gates, Interview, 82.

136. Gates, *Figures in Black*, 50–51.

137. Gates, *Signifying Monkey*, xxiii, xxv.

138. Gates, "Master's Pieces," 108.

139. Gates, Interview, 82.

140. Ibid., 82.

141. Ibid.

142. Ibid.; my emphasis.

143. Gates, "Whose Culture Is It, Anyway?" 15.

144. Ibid.

145. Andrew Delbanco, "Talking Texts," *New Republic*, 9 January 1989, 33.

146. Diane Ravitch, "Multiculturalism: E Pluribus Plures," *American Scholar* 59 (summer 1991): 341; my emphasis.

147. Gates, "Master's Pieces," 92–93.

148. Ibid.

149. Gates, *Signifying Monkey*, xi–xii.

150. Gates, "Master's Pieces," 111.

151. George Steiner, *Real Presences* (Chicago: University of Chicago Press, 1990), 63.

152. Gates, "What's Love Got to Do with It?" 347.

153. Steiner, *Real Presences*, 64.

154. Gates, *Figures in Black*, xxi–xxii.

155. Gates, "What's Love Got to Do with It?" 352; Gates, *Figures in Black*, xxi–xxii. George Steiner has made this same responsibility argument in *Real Presences:* "The relationship between word and world, inner and outer, has been held 'in trust.' This is to say that it has been conceived of and existentially enacted as a relation of responsibility. As noted before, this noun houses a primary notion of 'response,' of answerability. . . . Responsible response, answering answerability make of the process of understanding a moral act" (90).

156. Gates, "Master's Pieces," 105. Houston Baker has made the same argument: "The first impulse of the black men and women who came in from the cold with the new left to serve as drivers and students of [the new] Black Studies [programs] was to discover and expound *historical bases* for their right to subjecthood and subject status in university curricula. But . . . an influential cadre of the whitemale academy turn to quite *nonhistorial* modes of theory and analysis. My analogy for the state of affairs represented by this disjunctivenesss (of not suplicity or hypocrisy vis-à-vis Black Studies) is the turn-of-the-century training of blacks for vocational/technical jobs that they could not possibly hope profitably to occupy in a segregated economy." Baker, *Workings of the Spirit*, 16.

157. Gates, "Tell Me, Sir," 21.

158. Gates, "Master's Pieces," 105.

159. Ibid., 106.

CHAPTER EIGHT

1. There is simply no end to the dangers to interpretive purity perceived by academic historians inclined to sniff out such threats. Dominick LaCapra worries that without institutional constraints his colleagues will begin treating their texts as if they were "ideological trampolines." See Dominick LaCapra, *Rethinking Intellectual History: Texts, Contexts, Language* (Ithaca: Cornell University Press, 1983), 62–63. Similarly, David Hollinger worries that the historical profession is being infiltrated by "scholars who think of themselves as 'intellectual historians' but who are, in fact, potential volunteers for the new International Brigades, with battalions no doubt named for Saussure and Peirce." David Hollinger, *In the American Province: Studies in the History and Historiography of Ideas* (Bloomington: Indiana University Press, 1985), 188.

2. Richard Rorty, "The Pragmatist's Progress," in *Interpretation and Overinterpretation*, ed. Umberto Eco et al. (New York: Cambridge University Press, 1992), 97.

3. Jonathan Edwards, "A Treatise concerning Religious Affections" (1746), in Edwards, *Basic Writings*, ed. Ola Elizabeth Winslow (New York: New American Library, 1966), 200.

4. See Nussbaum, *Love's Knowledge: Essays on Philosophy and Literature* (New York: Oxford University Press, 1990), esp. 3–53 and 148–67.

5. Edwards, "Treatise concerning Religious Affections," 185.

6. Norman Fiering, *Moral Philosophy at Seventeenth Century Harvard: A Discipline in Transition* (Chapel Hill: University of North Carolina Press, 1981), 135.

7. I have learned much along these lines from Bernard Harrison's insightful book *Inconvenient Fictions: Literature and the Limits of Theory* (New Haven: Yale University Press, 1991).

8. Stanley Cavell, "An Apology for Skepticism," in *The American Philosopher: Conversations with Quine, Davidson, Putnam, Nozick, Danto, Rorty, Cavell, MacIntyre, and Kuhn*, ed. Giovanna Borradori (Chicago: University of Chicago Press, 1994), 128.

9. Cavell, "Apology for Skepticism," 130.

10. Richard Wright, *Black Boy: A Record of Childhood and Youth* (1937; New York: Harper and Row, 1966), 272–73.

11. It may be that we are simply "unable to avoid making the linguistic mistake of responding to a necessity of language as if it had ontological force and authority." J. Hillis Miller, *The Ethics of Reading* (New York: Columbia University Press, 1987), 127.

12. Perry Miller as quoted by Ann Douglas, "The Mind of Perry Miller," *New Republic*, 3 February 1983, 28. For all the recent criticism of Cornel West, it is worth noting that while Edward Said, Barbara Ehrenreich, and some others on the academic left have called for the return to a universal humanistic interpretive perspective, Cornel West and Richard Rorty have stood virtually alone in insisting that the only thing we have in common—the only basis on which such a comprehensive perspective could be imagined—is our susceptibility to suffering. For Rorty, see chapter 6 above; for West, see Paul Berman, ed.,

Debating P.C.: The Controversy over Political Correctness on College Campuses (New York: Laurel, 1992), 330–31.

13. See William Kerrigan: "We believers in the individual . . . have our delight in the luxurious figurations of the old poets; we feel gratitude, which like its result, fame, always aims at individuals, for having inherited the inexhaustible gift of great literature." Kerrigan, "Individualism, Historicism, and New Styles of Overreaching," *Philosophy and Literature* 13 (April 1989): 122.

14. Mill as quoted by David Bromwich, *Politics by Other Means: Higher Education and Group Thinking* (New Haven: Yale University Press, 1992), 244 n. 2.

15. Charles Taylor, *Sources of the Self: The Making of the Modern Identity* (Cambridge: Harvard University Press, 1989), 184.

16. James Kloppenberg, "The Virtues of Liberalism: Christianity, Republicanism, and Ethics in Early American Political Discourse," *Journal of American History* 74 (June 1987): 11.

17. Allan David Bloom, *The Closing of the American Mind: How Higher Education Has Failed Democracy and Impoverished the Souls of Today's Students* (New York: Simon and Schuster, 1987), 239. This is what Harold Bloom had in mind when he said that "strong poems strengthen us by teaching us how *how to talk to ourselves*." Bloom as quoted by Lorna Sage, "Fear Is the Spur," *Times Literary Supplement*, 14-20 April 1989, 389.

18. Perry Miller, *Roger Williams: His Contribution to the American Tradition* (Boston: Beacon, 1953), 27.

19. See Richard Rorty, *Contingency, Irony, Solidarity* (New York: Cambridge University Press, 1989), particularly chapter 2, "The Contingency of Selfhood." Rorty asks us to "think of any human life as the always incomplete, yet sometimes heroic, reweaving of such a web." But he also wants us to believe "that human beings are something more than centerless webs of beliefs and desires" (43, 88).

20. This is what the literary critic Robert Scholes calls "centripetal" reading. For an explanation of why he considers it a "reactionary" form, see Scholes, *Protocols of Reading* (New Haven: Yale University Press, 1989), 7–8, 79, 88, 151, 152.

21. "Comparison is the expedient of those who cannot reach the heart of the things compared." George Santayana as quoted by John P. Diggins, *The Bard of Savagery: Thorstein Veblen and Modern Social Theory* (New York: Seabury, 1978), x.

22. As Michel Foucault puts it, "Continuous history is the indispensable correlative of the founding function of the subject." Foucault as quoted by Mark Poster, "Foucault and History," *Social Research* 49 (spring 1982): 120.

23. For three particularly insightful examples of contemporary phenomenological accounts, see Richard Wollheim in *The Thread of Life* (Cambridge: Harvard University Press, 1984); David Carr, *Time, Narrative, and History* (Bloomington: Indiana University Press, 1986); and Genevieve Lloyd, *Being in Time: Selves and Narrators in Philosophy and Literature* (London: Routledge, 1993).

24. See Augustine's *Confessions,* especially book 11.

25. Paul Ricoeur comes to much the same conclusion. See Ricoeur's discussion of Augustine in Ricoeur, *Time and Narrative* (Chicago: University of Chicago Press, 1988), 3:12–22. See also Lloyd, *Being in Time,* 14–42, esp. 22–26.

26. It is not necessary to take sides in the argument between Hayden White and Louis Mink on the one side, who insist that we must be the authors of our autobiographies, and Alastair MacIntyre and Wilhelm Schapp on the other, who argue that this is an impossible ideal, that all we can do is choose among the story elements our particular culture provides. It is enough to say that whether I create or choose, it is I who must accept the responsibility.

27. See Hayden White, "The Value of Narrativity in the Representation of Reality," in White, *The Content of the Form: Narrative Discourse and Historical Representation* (Baltimore: Johns Hopkins University Press), 1987. For criticisms of White's position, see Marilyn Waldman, " 'The Otherwise Unnoteworthy Yr 711,' " and Louis Mink, "Everyman His or Her own Annalist," both in *Critical Inquiry* 7 (summer 1981): 777–92.

28. Fredric Jameson thinks the breakdown of narrative, the inability to unify past, present, and future, inaugurates a descent into a "cultural schizophrenia" (not to be confused with the narrower clinical understanding of that term). See Jameson, "Post-modernism or the Logic of Late Capitalism," *New Left Review* 146 (July–August 1984): 53–93. For a very different view, see Anthony Giddens, *Modernity and Self-Identity: Self and Society in the Late Modern Age* (Stanford: Stanford University Press, 1991), 65. Giddens thinks that "shame" "is essentially anxiety about the adequacy of the narrative by means of which the individual sustains a coherent biography."

29. Nathanael West, *Day of the Locust* (New York: New Classics, 1939).

30. James Baldwin, *Notes of a Native Son* (1955; Boston: Beacon Press, 1990), 6–7; my emphasis. On Baldwin's recognition of how little he has in common with the Africans in Paris, see 121–22.

31. Baldwin, *Notes of a Native Son,* xxxii. Richard Wright describes something like this in *Black Boy* (1937), the first volume of his autobiography: "Whenever I thought of the essential bleakness of black life in America, I knew that Negroes had never been allowed to catch the full spirit of Western civilization, that they lived somehow in it but not of it. And when I brooded upon the cultural barrenness of black life, I wondered if clean, positive tenderness, love, honor, loyalty, and the capacity to remember were native with man. I asked myself if these human qualities were not fostered, won, struggled and suffered for, preserved in ritual from one generation to another" (45).

32. Ralph Ellison, *Shadow and Act* (1953; New York: Random House, 1964), 93.

33. Ibid., xvii.

34. Ibid., xvi.

35. See, for a good example, Houston Baker, "Generational Shifts and the Recent Criticism of Afro-American Literature," *Black American Literature Forum* 15 (spring 1981): 6, 4, 7.

36. Richard Rodriguez, "The Birth Pangs of a New L.A.," *Harpers Magazine,* July 1993, 20.

37. Hayden White, "What Is an Historical System?" in *Biology, History, and Natural Philosophy,* ed. Allen D. Breck and Wolfgang Yourgrau (New York: Plenum, 1972), 239; emphasis in the original.

38. Abraham Lincoln, *Speeches and Writings* (New York: Library of America, 1989), 1:456.

39. Margaret Mead as quoted by Werner Sollors, *Beyond Ethnicity: Consent and Descent in American Culture* (New York: Oxford University Press, 1986), 208. Sollors gives no reference, though there are a number of index entries under Mead's name, and one book and one article by Mead are listed in his bibliography. I suspect the quotation comes from the article.

40. Mary Antin as quoted by Sollors, *Beyond Ethnicity,* 208. Sollors again gives no reference, though there are a number of index entries under Antin's name, and two books by her are listed in his bibliography.

41. Nathan Glazer, "In Defense of Multiculturalism," *New Republic,* 21 September 1991, 19; my emphasis. What unites such otherwise disparate minds as Nathan Glazer, Irving Howe, and John Searle is their common conviction that they and their generation acquired from their Western Civilization courses a set of progressive and even subversive beliefs and ideals. Howe asks, "Is there a more penetrating historian of selfhood than Wordsworth? A more scathing critic of society than the late Dickens?" Howe in Berman, *Debating P.C.,* 161. Searle and Howe contend that the contemporary "cultural left" has not acquired this sort of an inheritance because it has insisted that the culture of the United States has been deeply sexist, racist, imperialist, and so on. See the essays by Searle and Howe in ibid., esp. 158–59. But this is not generally true of the work being done by historians on the left today. See, for example, the essays gathered in the section on historical studies in *Rethinking Popular Culture: Contemporary Perspectives in Cultural Studies,* ed. Chandra Mukerji and Michael Schudson (Berkeley: University of California Press, 1991), or Donald E. Pease's *Visionary Compacts: American Renaissance Writings in Cultural Context* (Madison: University of Wisconsin Press, 1987). Pease and others offer a convincing demonstration that the nineteenth-century working class had its own distinctive traditions, and that it has continually turned the culture of the elite to its own purposes—that is, it has continually "troped," or "signified on," that culture.

42. Henry Louis Gates, "Discussion and Dad: Dialect and Descent," in *Afro-American Literature: The Reconstruction of Instruction,* ed. Dexter Fischer and Robert B. Stepto (New York: Modern Language Association of America, 1979), 92.

43. Alice Walker, *In Search of Our Mothers' Gardens* (New York: Harcourt Brace Jovanovich, 1983), 13–14.

44. Henry Louis Gates Jr., "The Master's Pieces: On Canon Formation and the African-American Tradition," *South Atlantic Quarterly* 89 (winter 1990): 92–93; reprinted in *Hegemony and Resistance,* ed. Dominick LaCapra (Ithaca: Cornell University Press, 1991).

45. Harold Bloom, *The Anxiety of Influence: A Theory of Poetry* (London: Oxford University Press, 1973), 6.

46. Richard Hofstadter, *The Progressive Historians: Turner, Beard, Parrington* (1968; Chicago: University of Chicago Press, 1979), xiii–xiv.

47. Charles Taylor, "Rorty in the Epistemological Tradition," in *Reading Rorty: Critical Responses to "Philosophy and the Mirror of Nature" (and Beyond)*, ed. Alan R. Malachowski and Jo Burrows (Cambridge, Mass.: Blackwell, 1990), 257.

48. See lectures 6 and 7 but especially the conclusion of William James, *The Varieties of Religious Experience* (New York: Longmans, Green, 1925).

49. Vincent van Gogh as quoted by Walker, *In Search of Our Mothers' Gardens*, 4.

50. "The story tries to mold me into its limited shape, giving me practice, as it were, in wanting and fearing certain minimal qualities and ignoring all others. I am to become, if I enter that world, *that kind of desirer*, with precisely the kinds of strengths and weaknesses that the author has built into his structure." Wayne C. Booth, *The Company We Keep: An Ethics of Fiction* (Berkeley: University of California Press, 1988), 204. For a very similar argument, see Nussbaum, *Love's Knowledge*, 234–35.

51. Not everyone agrees, of course. Gordon Wood insists that "we seriously err in canonizing and making symbols of authentic historical figures who cannot and should not be ripped out of their own time and place." Wood, "Jefferson at Home," *New York Review of Books*, 13 May 1993, 9.

52. Stanley Cavell, *In Quest of the Ordinary: Lines of Skepticism and Romanticism* (Chicago: University of Chicago Press, 1988), 105, 27.

53. Cavell, *In Quest of the Ordinary*, 149, 150

54. Thomas Hooker as quoted in Perry Miller and Thomas H. Johnson, eds., *The Puritans: A Sourcebook of Their Writings* (New York: Harper and Row, 1963), 305.

55. Thomas Hooker as quoted in *The Puritans in America: A Narrative Anthology*, ed. Alan Heimert and Andrew Delbanco (Cambridge: Harvard University Press, 1985, 177–78, 24.

56. John Cotton as quoted in Miller and Johnson, *Puritans*, 323.

57. Thomas Hooker as quoted in Miller and Johnson, *Puritans*, 301.

58. Cavell, *In Quest of the Ordinary*, 33.

59. Joe David Bellamy, "The Dark Lady of American Letters: An Interview with Joyce Carol Oates," *Atlantic Monthly* 22 (February 1972): 65.

60. Elaine Showalter, *Sister's Choice: Tradition and Change in American Women's Writing* (New York: Oxford University Press, 1991) 166. Sir Thomas More condemned Tyndale's translation of the New Testament as "poisoned bread." Stephen Greenblatt, *Renaissance Self-Fashioning: From More to Shakespeare* (Chicago: University of Chicago Press, 1980), 95.

61. Showalter, *Sister's Choice*, 29–33.

62. William Carlos Williams, *In the American Grain* (1925), as quoted by Quentin Anderson, "The Emergence of Modernism," in *Columbia Literary History of the United States*, ed. Emory Elliott (New York: Columbia University Press, 1988), 709.

63. Rorty, *Contingency, Irony, Solidarity*, 75.

64. Eliot thought these "existing monuments form an ideal order among themselves, which is modified by the introduction of the new (the really new) work among them." T. S. Eliot, "Tradition and the Individual Talent," in Eliot,

Selected Essays (London: Faber and Faber, 1934), 15. See also Edward Said's comments in Berman, *Debating P.C.*, 182.

65. Michael J. Oakeshott, *The Voice of Poetry in the Conversation of Mankind: An Essay* (London: Bowes and Bowes, 1959), 11.

66. "Each voice is at once a manner of speaking and a determinate utterance." Ibid., 13.

67. David Hollinger, "Banality and Enigma," *Journal of American History* 81 (December 1994): 1152—56.

68. Oakeshott, *Voice of Poetry*, 10.

69. Louis Menand, "Being an American: How the United States Is Becoming Less, Not More, Diverse," *Times Literary Supplement*, 30 October 1992, 3—4.

70. Richard Rodriguez, "The Fear of Losing a Culture," *Time* 132 (11 July 1988): 84.

EPILOGUE

1. Hayden White, "The Burden of History" (1966), in White, *Tropics of Discourse: Essays in Cultural Criticism* (Baltimore: Johns Hopkins University Press, 1978), 29, 40—41.

2. Clifford Geertz, "Blurred Genres: The Refiguration of Social Thought," *American Scholar* 49 (1980): 166; Geertz, *Local Knowledge: Further Essays in Interpretive Anthropology* (New York: Basic, 1983), 8, 11.

3. As he does, for example, in Clifford Geertz, "Found in Translation: On the Social History of the Moral Imagination," in Geertz, *Local Knowledge*.

4. Peter Novick, "My Correct Views on Everything," *American Historical Review* 93 (June 1991): 702, 699—700.

5. What else but a love of certain books could have drawn us into this perpetually jobless field?

6. David S. Reynolds, *Walt Whitman's America: A Cultural Biography* (New York: Knopf, 1995).

7. Gertrude Himmelfarb, *On Looking into the Abyss: Untimely Thoughts on Culture and Society* (New York: Vintage, 1994), 31.

8. "Anything imaginational grows in our minds, is transformed, socially transformed, from something we merely know to exist or have existed, somewhere or other, to something which is properly ours, a working force in our common consciousness. It is not a matter (not for us at least) of the past recaptured, but of the strange construed. . . . The passage is from the immediacies of one form of life to the metaphors of another." Geertz, *Local Knowledge*, 47—48.

INDEX

.

Jl